Future of Business and Finance

The Future of Business and Finance book series features professional works aimed at defining, describing and charting the future trends in these fields. The focus is mainly on strategic directions, technological advances, challenges and solutions which may affect the way we do business tomorrow, including the future of sustainability and governance practices. Mainly written by practitioners, consultants and academic thinkers, the books are intended to spark and inform further discussions and developments.

More information about this series at http://www.springer.com/series/16360

Mariusz Soltanifar · Mathew Hughes ·
Lutz Göcke

Editors

Digital Entrepreneurship

Impact on Business and Society

 Springer

Editors
Mariusz Soltanifar
Hanze University of Applied Sciences
International Business School
Groningen, The Netherlands

Open University
Faculty of Management
Heerlen, The Netherlands

Lutz Göcke
Nordhausen University of Applied Sciences
Chair of Digital Management
Nordhausen, Germany

Mathew Hughes
Loughborough University
School of Business and Economics
Loughborough, Leicestershire, UK

*To all the digital entrepreneurs out there,
who are driven to put a dent in the universe!*

Foreword

In the digital age, entrepreneurship is now more in demand than ever before. However, digital entrepreneurship is not limited to holding online meetings, paperless office or communication on social media. Rather, it must be seen as a holistic approach to thinking that encompasses all processes of an organisation, including communication and service provision. If we succeed in "thinking digitally", such as integrating digital process support at all levels, we can experience long-term success and keep uprising competitors at bay.

Data, information and knowledge are the new factors of success that lead to new market opportunities and business models through their intelligent combination and networking with operational performance and service provision. This ranges from platform economics to support systems, as well as the use of new technologies to make processes more effective and elegant. It is precisely the exploration of promising opportunities and the creation of unique ideas that offer digital entrepreneurs the potential to successfully develop their business. The design of business models, the planning of the architecture of software and hardware components, as well as the storage of individual data, information and knowledge components, form the core of the new digital entrepreneurial approach.

There has been much discussion of agility, disruptive processes and the constantly increasing speed of market developments. Therefore, the digital entrepreneurial personality must maintain the following competencies:

- Creativity, organisational skills and a feel for market opportunities
- Strong knowledge of the technical requirements and the competitive environment
- Courage to apply the process of creative destruction to their own business or its processes at any time.

In doing so, new ideas and their implementation must be kept in view, as well as one's own service offerings, and the way they are created. In particular, the demands on quality, efficiency and speed of the processes force entrepreneurship when updating and revising internal processes.

At the University of Applied Sciences, Nordhausen, we have initiated two major developments on our path to an entrepreneurial university and to qualify our students as digital entrepreneurs. We have developed a Bachelor of Arts in Digital

Product Management to enable students to identify market opportunities for digital products and realise these products together with software engineers. In addition, we created an incubation program to boost early stage start-up founders at our university with financial and consultative support.

This book aims to provide an overview of the main factors influencing digital entrepreneurship and will be of value for any digital entrepreneur. The authors have considered the determining factors for digital business, aspects of corporate entrepreneurship and legal framework conditions. A characteristic feature of these observations is that the digital entrepreneur is consistently placed at the centre of attention. We will leverage the created content in our courses of studies as well as our entrepreneurial programs to create entrepreneurial personalities.

Prof. Dr. Jörg Wagner
President of the University of
Applied Sciences Nordhausen
Nordhausen, Germany

Acknowledgements

We would like to acknowledge each author who has contributed to this book. We recognise the hard work you do to support digital entrepreneurship in your roles at universities and companies, and we thank you for the time and effort spent on writing your respective chapters.

Thanks to Jörg Wagner of the University of Applied Sciences, Nordhausen, and the Thuringian state government in Germany for the generous funding to enable the open access publishing of this book. The developed thoughts are of open access to all entrepreneurs and their teams globally.

We would like to express our gratitude to our participating companies for the cases discussed in this book. Many have provided great insights and opened their resources to develop the cases.

We also thank everyone who has trusted us in the quality of our work by writing an endorsement for this book.

We also thank Stefan Hertanu, Suzan Snijder, Siyuan Sun, and Ivaylo Tenev, the International Business School students of the Hanze University of Applied Sciences in Groningen, The Netherlands for assisting in the dissemination process of the book and communicating its value to our readers.

Introduction

Digital entrepreneurship is reshaping business and communication with cloud services, augmented and virtual reality, artificial intelligence and blockchains as some of the technologies that comprise our increasingly digitised world. This book examines these and other digital developments for their impact on entrepreneurship. In our understanding, digital entrepreneurship focuses on leveraging digital technologies or digital business models to explore and exploit entrepreneurial opportunities. Our quest in this book is to shed new light on digital entrepreneurship, understand the critical factors in successful digital entrepreneurship and understand the context sensitivity of digital entrepreneurship efforts, including, but not restricted to, the individual, the firm and the international business contexts. To achieve these elements, this book contains contributions from scholars from all over the world, consistent with how digital entrepreneurship brings global challenges to entrepreneurs, firms, public institutions and governments.

A cornerstone of our book is the effort to bridge the theory–practice divide. Each of the chapters provides two contributions: First, each chapter is embedded in theory and literature on the phenomenon of interest; second, each chapter contains digital entrepreneurship vignettes as insightful cases into digital entrepreneurship practice. Each chapter strives to connect research and practice with cases, insights and tools.

A key component of digital entrepreneurship is how digital technologies and the process of digitisation transform how entrepreneurs can create new sources of value and wealth. However, digitalisation is also transforming what it means to be entrepreneurial and the skills and capabilities required. Our further objective with this publication is to shed light on the entrepreneurial process and its content in various digital contexts.

The entire entrepreneurial process can focus on a digital venture as the content of an entrepreneurial journey. Some of the authors in this book investigate the impact of technologies, such as artificial intelligence, distributed ledger technologies or the industrial Internet of things, on new or established business models. Others discuss the influence of digital technologies on the entrepreneurial process of generating an idea or leveraging digital options to finance the entrepreneurial journey. Throughout the entrepreneurial process, we believe that a deep understanding of digital creativity can help an entrepreneur create the right ideas at the right time.

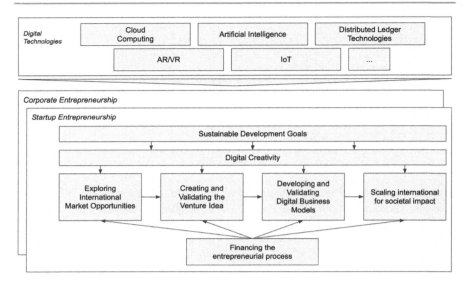

Fig. 1 Overview of subjects discussed in this book

Digital entrepreneurship holds potential not just for the wealth of entrepreneurs and organisations but society as well through its close connection to sustainable development goals. Figure 1 aims to illustrate the connections among the subjects that are covered within this book.

Chapter "Developing a Digital Entrepreneurial Mindset for Data-Driven, Cloud-Enabled, and Platform-Centric Business Activities: Practical Implications and the Impact on Society", written by Mariusz Soltanifar and Edin Smailhodžić, discusses the need for adopting a digital entrepreneurial mindset that is impacted by five trends shaping the digital future: (1) mobile computing, (2) cloud computing, (3) social media, (4) the Internet of things and (5) big data. The success stories of Domino's, Tesco and Tate Art Galleries and their data-driven, cloud-enabled, platform-centric business activities are analysed through the lens of these trends. This chapter also provides a guide for entrepreneurs on how to encourage a digital entrepreneurial mindset throughout their ventures. Finally, the practical implications of adopting digital entrepreneurial mindset and its impact on society are presented. An exploration of how the digital age challenges the assumptions about the nature of creativity is offered.

Digital creativity and audiences have had an enormous impact on the meaning, expression and reach of creativity. The traditional techniques of stimulating creativity have been replaced and aided by technology-driven innovations, such as artificial intelligence (AI), virtual reality (VR) and the Internet of things (IoT). Chapter "Unleashing the Creativity of Entrepreneurs with Digital Technologies" is written by Robert Hisrich and Mariusz Soltanifar and offers three case studies on how technology is currently used to support creativity through encouraging entrepreneurs and their teams to make connections, develop ideas, derive meaning, collaborate and communicate.

What if when asking "Alexa, what can I do tonight?", travellers no longer receive the answer "I don't know?". Moreover, could start-ups use all tourist data freely and without restrictions to develop innovative applications for travellers at any time (German National Tourist Board, n.d.)? These similar questions are currently being asked by those responsible for tourism marketing and product development, such as destination management organisations (DMOs) in Germany (German National Tourist Board), and are addressed in the Chapter "Digital Entrepreneurship and Agile Methods—A Hackathon Case Study", which is authored by Nancy Richter and Djanina Dragoeva. In particular, regarding the travel destination of Thuringia, "We were looking for a way to make the data of Thuringian tourism up-to-date, findable and freely usable and thus provided the path for open innovation and new technologies" (Detlef Klinge, Thüringer Tourismus GmbH, retrieved from the German National Tourist Board, n.d.). To meet these challenges, the DMO relies on the processing of open data in a tourist content architecture and on entrepreneurial management methods, such as the hackathon. This chapter answers the question of how these technologies and management methods must be implemented in destination management organisations so that they generate sustainable competitive advantages and customer benefits for the respective travel destination.

A vast majority of digital start-ups leverage the lean start-up approach to validate the attractiveness of their venture, reduce investing into scarce resources and structure the venturing process. Chapter "Business Model Development and Validation in Digital Entrepreneurship", authored by Lutz Göcke and Robin Weninger, proposes a structured approach, or the venture pyramid, to (in)validate digital business models in the face of high uncertainty. Furthermore, different types of digital business models with patterns of minimum viable products are mapped, and two case studies of German start-ups that applied a process of rigorous iteration and learning to their venture process are presented. A robust discussion is offered of the specific challenges that digital entrepreneurs face when validating their platform business model concept. In nearly every industry, platform business models evolve by optimising costs or by leveraging a significant increase in innovativeness.

Many entrepreneurs choose this business model to create and capture value, but while platform business models have demonstrably immense growth potential, they also present unique challenges for early stage start-ups. Chapter "Development and Validation of Platform Businesses in Digital Entrepreneurship", written by Lutz Göcke and Philip Meier, offers a processual model based on the venture pyramid to validate the critical assumptions of platform business models. Case studies of early stage start-ups shed light on the dynamics of testing platform business models and discuss different approaches to develop a minimally viable platform.

Chapter "Blockchain as an Approach for Secure Data Storage on Digital Consulting Platforms", written by Sebastian Gerth and Lars Heim, examines data security in a society increasingly shaped by digital technologies. Notably, data security and privacy in health-related services are considered since highly sensitive data are stored and processed during health-related online consultations. This chapter uses a case example to examine how blockchain technology provides a valuable opportunity to create trust in digital platforms.

The role of AI applications on the strategic level and its influence on business models is explored through case studies in the chapter "AI-Enhanced Business Models for Digital Entrepreneurship", written by Wolfgang Pfau and Philipp Rimpp. The role of AI in a company's business model, both for new market participants in the form of start-ups and incumbents, such as tech giants, is examined to produce a classification scheme of the influence of AI on business models.

Chapter "The Role of an Entrepreneurial Mindset in Digital Transformation-Case Study of the Estonian Business School", written by Mari Kooskora, discusses the entrepreneurial mindset in digital transformation through a detailed overview of digitalising in the higher education sector. A case study about leading the digital transformation in an Estonian private business school is presented. The study reveals how the ongoing digital process has changed the organisation itself and how students are taught to deal with changes in the digital world.

Three case studies are presented in the chapter "Digital Creativity: Upgrading Creativity in Digital Business", authored by Edin Smailhodžić and Denis Berberović, to illustrate how implementing small but fruitful adjustments to the work environment and the overall management of the workforce can unleash powerful creative energy that offers new services to the market, new approaches to solving existing problems, or, in one case, may bring in a completely new business model based on creative solutions and innovative approaches.

Industrial firms are also under severe pressure to innovate by leveraging the industrial Internet of things (IIoT) and emerging digital technologies. Digital entrepreneurship for existing organisations (corporate digital entrepreneurship) is a critical differentiating factor in a highly competitive and disruptive environment. Through three case studies presented in the chapter "Corporate Digital Entrepreneurship: Leveraging Industrial Internet of Things and Emerging Technologies", authored by Swapan Ghosh, Mat Hughes, Paul Hughes and Ian Hodgkinson, the importance of emerging digital technologies for digital entrepreneurship is discussed, and a conceptual framework of corporate digital entrepreneurship is presented highlighting three elements: business model transformation, operating model transformation and cultural transformation.

Near ubiquitous access to the Internet, platformisation, advances in cloud computing, machine learning and artificial intelligence and blockchain are changing the sources, basis and quantum of funding in ways that were unimaginable at the turn of the century. The key sources and characteristics of alternative sources of finance available to entrepreneurs, including start-ups, are presented in the chapter "New Sources of Entrepreneurial Finance", authored by Theo Lynn and Pierangelo Rosati. Two online alternative finance sources, crowdfunding and token offerings, are discussed in greater detail and illustrated with case studies.

Digitalisation has opened new possibilities for intrapreneurship. However, there is limited attention to the role of digital intrapreneurs within existing organisations. Through an examination of three case studies, a unique definition of digital intrapreneurship and its position in the digital landscape is presented in the chapter "Digital Intrapreneurship: The Corporate Solution to a Rapid Digitalisation", written by Gifford Pinchot III and Mariusz Soltanifar, along with numerous ways to foster digital intrapreneurship, including a set of practical ways for managers to identify, surface and empower digital intrapreneurs.

Digitalisation has tremendously challenged how international opportunities are created and captured. A comprehensive framework towards the impact of digital technologies on opportunity pursuit in foreign markets is offered in the chapter "Pursuing International Opportunities in a Digitally Enabled World" by Di Song and Aiqi Wu through identifying two perspectives of digital technologies, that is, digital technologies as a "driving force" and digital technologies as a "disrupting force". By bridging these two perspectives with the notion of market-specific knowledge and general knowledge within internationalisation process theory, some arguments regarding what specific influences DTs play on international opportunity pursuit are further introduced.

The obstacles and opportunities that digital entrepreneurs encounter when they operate in developing countries are analysed in the chapter "Challenges and Opportunities for Digital Entrepreneurship in Developing Countries", written by Georges Samara and Jessica Terzian. Three interviews, two of digital entrepreneurs and one of a consultants, offer insight into the challenges and opportunities for digital entrepreneurs operating in a developing context. Weak institutional infrastructure and an environment characterised by corruption result in inaccessibility to start-up funds and a lack of policies and regulations that protect and support e-commerce, as well as a deficiency in digitally competent and experienced labour capital. However, the use of family wealth as a source of start-up financial capital, the use of personal connections as a source of social and human capital and the rising education on digital entrepreneurship have their unique benefits. Suggestions on improving the current institutional infrastructure for digital entrepreneurs in developing countries are offered.

In 2020, the United Nations launched the Decade of Action to achieve the Sustainable Development Goals (SDGs) by the year 2030. As the SDGs are interdependent and interdisciplinary, so must be their solutions. Entrepreneurship is arguably the best way to identify, develop and scale solutions of such quality by building on the principles of open innovation, cutting-edge technologies and social business.

The 2020 COVID-19 pandemic serves as a stark reminder of the interdependent and interdisciplinary nature of the SDGs, as well as the challenges we face in achieving them. The third SDG (SDG-3), Good Health and Well-Being, is discussed with this theme in mind. The potential for digital entrepreneurship to foster the rise of new forms of (digital) health care and to accelerate the digitalisation of the healthcare sector is explored. Three case studies are provided in the chapter "Digital Entrepreneurship for the 'Decade of Action'", authored by Manouchehr Shamsrizi, Adalbert Pakura, Jens Wiechers, Stefanie Pakura and Dominique V. Dauster, as examples of digital entrepreneurship that utilise in whole or in part a combination of open innovation, future and emerging technologies, and or social business, thereby supporting our argument. The emergence of the COVID-19 pandemic has threatened to roll back progress, particularly for SDG-3. At this time, innovations in digital entrepreneurship in the healthcare sector are particularly vital to maintaining growth in this SDG.

Bridging Theory and Practice. A Set of Practical Tools on Digital Entrepreneurship for Entrepreneurs and Scholars

Our book offers a set of practical tools on how to put digital entrepreneurship into action, as listed in Table 1, to inspire digital entrepreneurs and scholars alike.

Table 1 Overview of practical tools on digital entrepreneurship

Chapter	Putting digital entrepreneurship into action
1	Understand the necessity and learn how to develop a digital entrepreneurial mindset throughout ventures among entrepreneurs and their teams
2	Explore how to support creativity through the use of artificial intelligence, virtual reality and the Internet of things, thereby encouraging entrepreneurs and their teams to make connections, develop ideas, create meaning, collaborate and communicate
3	Understand how technologies and management methods must be implemented in destination management organisations so that they generate sustainable competitive advantages and customer benefits
4	Get to know a structured approach to test the venture idea and see examples of different minimum viable products to inspire the testing process
5	Learn how to test the specific dynamics of platform business models and how to develop a minimum viable platform through different approaches
6	Explore how to use blockchain to provide security during online consulting
7	Learn how to apply artificial intelligence-enhanced business models in digital entrepreneurship
8	Explore how to implement digital transformation content through the entire organisation
9	Delve into how to incorporate creativity in the fabric of digital enterprise processes to promote greater innovation
10	Test the conceptual framework of corporate digital entrepreneurship highlighting three elements: business model transformation, operating model transformation and cultural transformation
11	Investigate how to engage new sources of entrepreneurial financings, such as crowdfunding and token offerings
12	Apply ten criteria for intrapreneurs proposals for digital innovation and learn how to create and nurture the culture supporting digital entrepreneurship
13	Use a roadmap to the interaction of digitalisation and international opportunity
14	Examine how to improve the current institutional infrastructure for digital entrepreneurs
15	Understand the necessity and potential for digital entrepreneurship on the Sustainable Development Goals in the Decade of Action and learn how to develop the venture accordingly

This book contains contributions by a group of scholars, university professors, researchers, entrepreneurs and managers whose expertise in their given areas offers valuable insights into the theme of digital entrepreneurship. In addition to the editorial work provided by the editors and authors, multiple cases have been consulted, redeveloped or written alongside the companies' representatives. Each chapter follows a general structure, introducing the significance and importance of its theme to scholars and practitioners, followed by an explanation of the content grounded in scholarly research. From there, the chapters present a conceptual framework that can be used as a tool by practitioners, followed by a series of case studies illustrating their application. Each chapter then draws conclusions with insights for practitioners. We trust you will find new knowledge, ideas and inspirations about digital entrepreneurship through the course of this book.

Contents

Editors and Contributors

About the Editors

Mariusz Soltanifar is a lecturer and coach in marketing and entrepreneurship at the International Business School at Hanze University of Applied Sciences in Groningen, Netherlands. He obtained a master's degree in International Marketing and Business from the University of Łódź (Lodz) in Poland while writing his thesis at the Fraunhofer Institute for Systems and Innovation Research ISI, located in Karlsruhe, Germany, and at the Helsinki University of Technology in Finland. He is currently finalising his Ph.D. research at the Open University of the Netherlands at the Faculty of Management in the Strategy and General Management Department on exploring the behaviour of non-managerial employees in the corporate entrepreneurship process. For many years, he has been a guest lecturer among others at universities in South Korea, Lebanon, Malaysia, Indonesia, Switzerland and Germany.

He has contributed his marketing and entrepreneurship expertise to several academic textbooks published by McGraw-Hill, Pearson and Springer. His research has also been cited in publications on multinational management. From 2012 to 2018, he served as the CEO of the largest networking platform connecting Polish professionals abroad. In 2016, he received the Golden Owl Award in Vienna for his achievements. In addition to his accomplishments in academic institutions and texts, he has made practical contributions to innovative marketing projects across the globe.

Most importantly, he is a husband and a father, and in his free time, he enjoys long-distance running, cooking Persian dishes and serving local church communities.

Dr. Mathew Hughes is a professor and chair in Entrepreneurship and Innovation at the Loughborough University School of Business and Economics. Before this appointment, he was a reader in Entrepreneurial Management at the Durham University Business School and served as the director of their Ph.D. program. Earlier in his career, he served as an assistant professor and an associate professor of Entrepreneurship and Innovation and was the director of the M.Sc. Entrepreneurship and the deputy director of the Doctoral Program at Nottingham

University Business School. He holds a Ph.D. in Strategic Management and Entrepreneurship from the University of Wales, Aberystwyth.

He has received several awards both for his teaching and his research. In 2016, he received the Durham University Business School Innovation in Teaching and Learning Award and the Dean's Award for Teaching Excellence. In 2015, he was awarded by the Durham University Excellence for a Doctoral Supervision Award. In 2017, for his research, he was nominated for the Best Paper at the Family Business track, Best Conference Paper at the ISBE annual conference and received the Highly Commended Paper Award. In 2015, he was the recipient of the Emerald Citation of Excellence Award for the most highly cited and influential paper published in 2012 in Business Management: "Drivers of innovation ambidexterity in small-to-medium-sized firms", published in the *European Management Journal*, 30(1), 1–17. In 2020, he was the joint winner of the Best Reviewer Award for the *British Journal of Management*.

His work has been published in a variety of journals, including the *Strategic Entrepreneurship Journal*, the *Journal of Product Innovation Management*, the *Journal of World Business*, the *British Journal of Management* and the *Journal of Small Business Management*. He has served as a keynote speaker at international conferences and is a member of the Strategic Management Society and the Academy of Management. His research interests and specialisations include entrepreneurial orientation, innovation and ambidexterity, social capital, absorptive capacity, corporate entrepreneurship and strategy, family firms, internationalisation and business acceleration. In addition, he sits on the editorial review boards of several journals, including the *Journal of Management Studies*, the *Journal of Business Venturing*, the *British Journal of Management* and the *New England Journal of Entrepreneurship*. He is also an editor of the *Entrepreneurship Research Journal* and Associate Editor of the *Journal of Family Business Strategy*.

Outside academia, he is a husband and father and enjoys playing basketball with his son, listening to music, watching documentaries and walking.

Dr. Lutz Göcke is a professor in Digital Business and Entrepreneurship at the University of Applied Sciences in Nordhausen, Germany. He holds a doctorate in Strategic Management and Economics from the Technical University Clausthal. His research focuses on Business Model Innovation and Corporate Entrepreneurship. He is the initiator and the director of the Bachelor Program Digital Product Management, as well as the head of the academic incubation programme HIKE at the University of Applied Sciences, Nordhausen.

Early in his career, he worked as a digital product manager and intrapreneur in the Volkswagen Group on various digital projects, such as the Open Innovation Platform, Carsharing, Connected Car and Digital Ecosystem Volkswagen WE. After leaving Volkswagen, he founded SWAN ventures. Still Without a Name, or SWAN, illustrates his fascination for the lean start-up approach in building businesses. The company focuses on management consulting in the corporate entrepreneurship domain. He is a lecturer at the Technical University Clausthal and

University of Applied Sciences for Engineering and Economics, Berlin. Furthermore, he advises start-ups in their development process.

More importantly, he is a father of two awesome boys and a beloved husband. He enjoys playing tennis and hiking.

Contributors

Denis Berberović University of Sarajevo, Sarajevo, Bosnia and Herzegovina

Dominique V. Dauster Yunus + You - the YY Foundation, Wiesbaden, Germany

Djanina Dragoeva Bauhaus University, Weimar, Germany

Sebastian Gerth University of Erfurt, Thuringian Competence Center Economy 4.0, Erfurt, Germany

Swapan Ghosh Menlo College, Atherton, California, USA

Lutz Göcke Chair of Digital Management, Nordhausen University of Applied Sciences, Nordhausen, Germany

Lars Heim Clausthal University of Technology, Clausthal-Zellerfeld, Germany

Robert D. Hisrich Kent State University, Ohio, USA

Ian Hodgkinson Loughborough University, Loughborough, UK

Mathew Hughes Loughborough University, Loughborough, UK

Paul Hughes De Montfort University Leicester, Leicester, UK

Mari Kooskora Estonian Business School, Tallinn, Estonia

Theo Lynn Irish Institute of Digital Business, DCU Business School, Dublin, Ireland

Philip Meier Alexander Von Humboldt Institute of Internet and Society, Berlin, Germany

Adalbert Pakura RetroBrain R&D GmbH, Hamburg, Germany

Stefanie Pakura Chair of Management & Digital Markets, University of Hamburg, Hamburg, Germany

Wolfgang Pfau Clausthal University of Technology, Clausthal-Zellerfeld, Germany

Gifford Pinchot, III Seattle, USA

Nancy Richter University of Applied Sciences, Schmalkalden, Germany

Philipp Rimpp Clausthal University of Technology, Clausthal-Zellerfeld, Germany

Pierangelo Rosati Irish Institute of Digital Business, DCU Business School, Dublin, Ireland

Georges Samara University of Sharjah, College of Business Administration, Sharjah, UAE;
American University of Beirut, Olayan School of Business, Beirut, Lebanon

Manouchehr Shamsrizi gamelab.berlin of Humboldt-Universität and RetroBrain R&D GmbH, Hamburg, Germany

Edin Smailhodžić University of Groningen, Faculty of Economics and Business, Groningen, The Netherlands

Mariusz Soltanifar Hanze University of Applied Sciences, International Business School, Groningen, The Netherlands;
The Open University, Faculty of Management, Heerlen, The Netherlands

Di Song Zhejiang University, Hangzhou, China

Jessica Terzian American University of Beirut, Olayan School of Business, Beirut, Lebanon

Robin Weninger Global Institute of Leadership and Technology (GILT), Eschborn, Germany

Jens Wiechers Mensa International, Riskful Thinking Ventures LLC, Cologne, Germany

Aiqi Wu Zhejiang University, Hangzhou, China

Characteristics of Digital Entrepreneurs

Developing a Digital Entrepreneurial Mindset for Data-Driven, Cloud-Enabled, and Platform-Centric Business Activities: Practical Implications and the Impact on Society

Mariusz Soltanifar and Edin Smailhodžić

Abstract

The term 'digital' concerns not only technology but also people. This chapter emphasises the necessity of adopting a digital entrepreneurial mindset when operating in a digitised world. The chapter proposes a definition of a digital entrepreneurial mindset that is rooted in cognitive psychology, organisation theory and entrepreneurship literature. We also focus on the five trends that are shaping the digital future: mobile computing, cloud computing, social media, the Internet of Things and Big Data. The chapter discusses the challenges and opportunities that pervasive digitalisation offers for designing new digital business models and changing interactions with customers. Discussing the success stories of Domino's Tesco and Tate Art Galleries helps to examine data-driven, cloud-enabled, platform-centric business activities, for which developing a digital entrepreneurial mindset is the first step towards success in the digital age. Collectively, the aforementioned cases suggest that businesses that rely on a digital entrepreneurial mindset enjoy better financial performance. Both managers and employees in these companies have shown the inclination and ability to discover, evaluate and exploit opportunities emerging from digital technologies. This chapter also provides a practical guide for entrepreneurs on the steps they can take to encourage a digital entrepreneurial mindset throughout their entire organisations. Finally, we elaborate on the practical implications of adopting a digital entrepreneurial mindset and its impact on society.

M. Soltanifar (✉)
Hanze University of Applied Sciences, Groningen, The Netherlands
e-mail: m.soltanifar@pl.hanze.nl

M. Soltanifar
Open University, Heerlen, The Netherlands

E. Smailhodžić
University of Groningen, Groningen, The Netherlands

© The Author(s) 2021
M. Soltanifar et al. (eds.), *Digital Entrepreneurship*, Future of Business and Finance,
https://doi.org/10.1007/978-3-030-53914-6_1

1   Introduction

To be successful in the modern era, businesses need to consider online reservations, online reviews, online discount coupons, automation of order processing and many other technology-related aspects. Going digital is important for success, not only for the restaurant trade but for many other industries. For instance, transport companies have to gain and retain passengers by positioning their services high in search results and by providing a smooth booking process. The emergence of digital technologies has transformed how businesses and entrepreneurship work (Nambisan et al. 2019). Distant communication, content overload and big data are just a few of the many consequences of digitalisation with which entrepreneurs need to cope today. Today, entrepreneurs need to be aware that they can be disrupted not only by competitors but quite possibly by consumer interaction with other similar digital products and services. Such constantly evolving integration has led to the creation of new digital and responsive business models. The manner in which businesses operate has been disrupted. Reacting promptly to the demands of continuous product innovation, providing added-value services, improving the customer service experience and moving towards successful omnichannel marketing have become the new standards for doing business in the digital age.

Businesses must navigate five significant trends that are shaping the digital future: mobile computing, cloud computing, social media, the Internet of Things (IIoT) and Big Data (Valacich and Schneider 2018). These trends are transforming individuals, organisations and society for several reasons. There has already been a significant shift towards the use of mobile technologies for all transactions, from searching for product information and comparing alternatives all the way through to completing the purchase. The number of mobile device users worldwide is expected to reach 7.26 billion by 2023 (O'Dea 2019). Social media use has developed beyond enabling family and friends to connect by allowing businesses to operate or advertise products through their own social media pages. The proliferation of social media platforms has enabled entrepreneurs to better connect with their customers and to engage them in the development of new products and product launches. For example, Aral and Dellarocas (2013) and Roberts et al. (2017) have indicated this fact. The IoT is often used to sell products, automate workflows and engage with consumers (Valacich and Schneider 2018). Cloud computing and applications, such as data storage, servers, databases, networks and software, are widely utilised by modern entrepreneurs and often lead to cost savings, increased productivity, greater efficiency, higher financial performance and better security. It is notable that insight from big data analytics tends to influence companies' strategic decisions to introduce new products and services (Arnason 2017).

Overall, data-driven, cloud-enabled, platform-centric business activities deliver crucial insights for improving financial performance (Caldwell 2018). However, this pervasive digitalisation is not only opening new windows of opportunities; it also brings new challenges. These range from changing methods of communication to shifting business models to an entirely digital environment. Adopting a digital mindset and analytic capabilities may be a crucial means of dealing with these challenges as an enabler of data processing. Entrepreneurs wishing to remain competitive in a digitised business environment need to overcome the challenges and grasp the opportunities of the changing digital market.

This chapter discusses how companies can adopt a digital entrepreneurial mindset for data-driven, cloud-enabled, platform-centric business activities.

2 Conceptualising a Digital Entrepreneurial Mindset

There are many definitions of 'entrepreneur'. Many of these explain the term in the context of an individual who displays entrepreneurial behaviour. An entrepreneur is usually seen as someone who engages in the process of discovering, evaluating and exploiting opportunities that lead to value creation (Shane and Venkataraman 2000).

2.1 What Does It Mean to Be Entrepreneurial?

The concept of being entrepreneurial evolved simultaneously with the development of the concepts of being an entrepreneur. However, the question remains as to what it means to be entrepreneurial. Entrepreneurship literature emphasises proactiveness, innovativeness and risk-taking as three standard dimensions of entrepreneurial behaviour. As entrepreneurship is the discovery, evaluation and exploitation of opportunities, individuals vary in the extent to which they exhibit these behaviours. Being entrepreneurial is relevant to more than just start-ups; it is crucial for all organisations and businesses looking to progress, regardless of their existing size or intended development. Even though there are many types (and sizes) of entrepreneurial opportunities, this chapter argues that being entrepreneurial requires the creation of value and involves embracing the uncertainty that lies at the heart of discovery, evaluation and exploitation of opportunities (Soltanifar 2016). Being entrepreneurial is the defining characteristic of an entrepreneur whose dreams are greater than their resources (Pinchot 1985). Undoubtedly digitised environments open new possibilities and access to borderless resources. Consequently, following such a path requires a mindset shift and the creation of a digital strategy.

2.2 How Is an Entrepreneurial Mindset Defined?

Before presenting a definition of the digital entrepreneurial mindset, it is important to focus first on defining the entrepreneurial mindset itself. We start by examining the definition of a mindset of an individual and then explain entrepreneurial digital mindsets.

The concept of a mindset comes from the fields of cognitive psychology and organisation theory. According to cognitive psychology literature, a mindset represents the cognitive processes activated in response to a given task (French 2016). As such, a mindset represents the sum of one's knowledge, including one's beliefs about the world. Through our mindsets, we determine how we receive and react to information. Thus, a mindset is a filter for information we obtain. In organisation theory literature, a mindset is quite often discussed in tandem with organisational change, which is an ongoing process in businesses. In line with Gleeson (2019), one of the most critical drivers of organisational change is the mindset of change. Through its effects on behaviour, a mindset also creates the culture of an organisation.

Overall, the mindset of an entrepreneur is a product of histories, and it evolves through an interactive process. An individual's current mindset guides them in collecting and interpreting new information. If the new information is consistent with the current mindset, it reinforces that mindset. From time to time, however, new data appears that is genuinely novel and inconsistent with the existing mindset. When this happens, entrepreneurs either reject the latest information or change their mindset. The likelihood that an entrepreneur's mindset will change depends largely on how explicitly self-conscious they are of their current mindsets; when an individual's cognitive filters are more hidden and subconscious, they are less likely to adapt their mindset.

People's mindsets are commonly categorised into two major types, namely fixed and growth. The mindset refers to the assumptions, notions and methods of a person. While a fixed mindset assumes that talents and abilities are set, the growth mindset believes that skills and abilities can be developed. For example, individuals with a fixed mindset believe that their intelligence is a static trait that can only be present rather than developed further. Meanwhile, people with a growth mindset believe they could change through hard work. Nevertheless, it is essential to point out that a mindset can change (Dweck and Yeager 2019). This typically occurs when an individual develops a greater awareness of their current mindset and takes steps to purposefully start thinking and reacting in new ways. Changing your mindset towards a growth mindset is crucial as it leads to better relationships and interactions with others and happiness (Van Tongeren and Burnette 2018). The shift to a digital business landscape also requires changes in the entrepreneurial mindset. One such example would be if a manufacturing company moves away from the traditional linear model of supply, manufacture and distribution towards a networked and connected model in which all data is stored in clouds and is accessible to the entire value chain at all times. In this scenario, it is not only entrepreneurs but also individual employees who are enabled to observe and influence the whole supply chain process in real time. Such opportunities redefine the decision-making processes of entrepreneurs and making sense of the high volume of available data that has grown exponentially across supply chain. Thus, it is vital that entrepreneurs also embrace a growth mindset and embrace the possibility of changing their approach.

2.3 Putting It All Together: The Digital Entrepreneurial Mindset

Based on the review of entrepreneurship and digitalisation literature, it is possible to define a digital entrepreneurial mindset (DEM) as the inclination and ability to discover, evaluate and exploit opportunities while adopting digital technologies more quickly than a regular entrepreneur.

The process of discovering new digital opportunities involves careful consideration of current products and services in the target market and the role of digital technologies in their provision. This should be considered from the customer's perspective; thus, considering customers' needs and identifying how digitising current products and services may improve a company's ability to meet customers' needs. In particular, this involves understanding current business models that serve the public and generate value as well as considering new configurations of business models that will add more value for customers. In the case of Turo, an American peer-to-peer car-sharing company, customers are looking for ways to solve their transport needs. Trough the app customers can borrow a car rather than lend their own Turo understood this need and designed its business model to offer short-term rentals of vehicles, which can be rented for a period of just a few minutes up to a few hours by using only an app (Growjo 2018).

Evaluation concerns careful consideration of a digital opportunity. Particular attention should be paid to the (potential) market size for a digital opportunity. Before exploiting the opportunity, it should be clear that there will be demand for the product or service. Furthermore, entrepreneurs should evaluate whether or not they can deliver the necessary value of this product based on their resources. In this respect, entrepreneurs should also consider factors such as their management skills and their passion and persistence for developing the product. Digital opportunity evaluation may also include the application of the stage-gate process, in which you pursue an opportunity only if it passes all 'gates', including factors such as risk objectives, financial resources and other criteria. Airbnb started when its founders were struggling to pay their rent and started renting their home to strangers. However, before proceeding with their business, the founders evaluated the potential market for their idea.

Once you prioritise digital solutions or technologies, you can exploit the entrepreneurial opportunity. This final step of opportunity exploitation represents an essential step to making a digital business successful. This last step includes activities and investments that an entrepreneur conducts to receive returns from the new digital opportunity by constructing an efficient business system (Fig. 1).

Pervasive digitalisation leads not only to spotting emerging opportunities in the digital environment, but also, more importantly, to prioritising them over other possible products. Implementing a digital mindset should result in a business recognising and exploiting opportunities arising from phenomena such as:

1. Technological developments and advances in infrastructure
2. Artificial intelligence used to enhance the quality of decisions

Fig. 1 Number of guests staying with an Airbnb Host during the summer. *Source* Myler (2017)

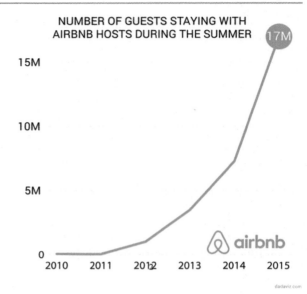

3. Augmented reality used to broaden entrepreneurs' horizons
4. Cloud services
5. Borderless connections in exploiting emerging opportunities
6. The sale of digital products or services across electronic networks

Fundamentally, many digital technologies provide possibilities for efficiency gains and customer intimacy. However, if people lack the right mindset to implement change and the current organisational practices are flawed, digital transformation will simply magnify the existing flaws.

The following questions are applicable to entrepreneurs involved in any kind of data-driven, cloud-enabled, platform-centric business:

1. How does the transformation affect the structure and borders of the sector?
2. How are the value chain and its associated competitive activities influenced?
3. What new strategic decisions do companies have to make to secure a competitive advantage?
4. What organisational effects does the new product type have and what challenges are associated with the product? Rödl & Partner (n.d.)

To illustrate the application of such questions in a real-life business scenario, it is useful to consider Airbnb again. Airbnb recognised the right time to expand into other markets outside the USA. Accordingly, it acquired a German competitor, Acceleo, to successfully exploit an opportunity in Europe, which resulted in Airbnb opening its first European office in Hamburg in 2011.

Overall, it can be argued that a DEM relates to more than just the ability to incorporate technology into daily operations and extract value from the technology. Also, a DEM is about much more than harnessing new technologies. It is a collection of attitudes and actions that enable an entrepreneur to foresee possibilities and exploit opportunities accordingly. A DEM is a way of thinking about business and operating in a new networked and connected business environment. A DEM is based on customers and employees. It is not only about the ability to augment entrepreneurial capabilities, but also the capabilities of employees.

Digitalisation means the integration of digital technologies into everyday life and all its activities. From an entrepreneurial mindset perspective, it is about turning interactions, communication, business functions and models into a digital form in order to grasp emerging opportunities. Another aspect of digitalisation is the entrepreneurial environment or area where it takes place, such as a digital workplace or recruiting employees from a digital pool of talent. At its most basic, digitalisation can relate to businesses' efforts to become paperless. However, many other facets occur at the basis for digital transformation to which an entrepreneur is exposed.

Communication is an excellent example of a workplace system that can easily be transformed and improved. Meetings can take place online and files can be transferred much more quickly using online sharing facilities instead of relying on traditional postal methods. Digital transformation is a process through which entrepreneurs seek to improve themselves by making significant changes to their business process through the use of a combination of information, computing, communication and connectivity technologies in their daily operations (Vial 2019).

As discussed previously, digital transformation provides entrepreneurs with the use of a combination of data and mobile technologies that allow faster problem-solving and smarter, more informed decision-making processes. Such decision-making processes empower entrepreneurs and employees to engage more fully with business operations.

As 'digital' becomes a new norm for businesses, entrepreneurs need to develop a strategy to prioritise opportunities emerging from digital technologies and address the impact such technologies have on their businesses and their financial performance. A DEM in business is not only about technology. A company can introduce digital technology in its strategic plans, but that does not mean that it has taken on a digital mindset. Therefore, entrepreneurs, directors and individual employees need to share a strategy to develop an organisation-wide DEM. For example, an open line of communication between an organisation's leadership and its employees, which embraces a growth mindset, a culture of freedom to choose and innovate or a shared vision and purpose, might undoubtedly facilitate an organisation-wide DEM. The implementation of digital squads, virtual meeting rooms and agile methodology is undoubtedly helpful in the process of digital transformation. Through the adoption of these tools, a DEM is more likely to be adopted throughout an entire organisation. The following section focuses on how businesses can shift towards becoming more data-driven, cloud-enabled and platform-centric.

2.3.1 Digital Entrepreneurial Mindsets for Data-Driven Business Activities

A DEM is necessary to better understand whether a company is data-driven. Being data-driven helps companies to prioritise opportunities emerging from digital technologies (Marr 2016). The following questions can be used to assess whether a company is data-driven and makes use of the opportunities arising from considerable amounts of data:

1. Are the CEO and executives ready for change in the company, with the right creative and passionate mindset for data generation?
2. Is the data accessible and democratised for all employees?
3. Are the employees ready for the change and can they decrypt and understand the data?
4. How will the data be managed and how can you avoid a data overload?
5. Does every level of the organisation share the opinion of the top management about adopting a data-driven culture?

These five areas are considered to be five standard features of data-driven companies (Peregud 2018). As such, entrepreneurs running data-driven companies should be able to automate their company's operations to distil data-driven insights and to incorporate those insights into business processes. Such processes certainly help entrepreneurs to discover, evaluate and exploit opportunities emerging from digital technologies, which is the very purpose of a DEM. According to Dykes (2019), being ready to accumulate a variety of data systems and tools and being aware of proper data management, shifting the mindset is crucial for a business to foster a data-driven culture. Turning an entrepreneurial mindset into a digital one requires diligence and patience as managers have to attempt to steer their team in a new direction relying on digital technologies. Although there are some limitations associated with being a data-driven company, such as losing sight of the work beyond the data and becoming driven by the data in a way that does not drive markets and innovation, there is not room in this chapter to elaborate further on such issues.

2.3.2 Digital Entrepreneurial Mindset for Cloud-Enabled Business Activities

Cloud-enabled solutions are seen as the catalyst for digitalisation of all business activities and are designed to store all of a business' information. Clouds enhance the flexibility and efficiency of all kinds of business activities (Rishi et al. 2017), especially those rising from persuasive digitalisation and which are crucial to a DEM. This helps digital businesses to evaluate and exploit emerging opportunities more quickly, as employees, customers and third parties are able to work together and collaborate on projects without slower, unnecessary offline communication (Nulaw 2020). Moreover, systems can interoperate with other systems through the cloud, which simplifies the process of upscaling and downscaling a business (Dynamic Quest 2019). For cloud computing, as an entrepreneur, you only need to contact the host server of a cloud. Operating in clouds also reduces overall costs because there is no need to rely on big data centres or other kinds of storage (Castillo 2019).

The following five questions help assess a company's readiness for cloud-enabled business activities:

1. Does the business require an increase in the agility of business applications such as reducing IT costs via the use of data centres, tools, operating systems or platform consolidation? (cloud-enabled agility)
2. What tangible benefits (both business and IT) are associated with cloud-based infrastructure, for instance, balancing between customer experience and IT costs? (cloud-enabled infrastructure)
3. What data security and data disaster recovery processes does the business operate currently? (cloud-enabled solutions management)
4. What department leads the cloud transformation? For instance, does the business have its own Cloud Centre of Excellence? (cloud-enabled implementation)
5. What training is necessary for the business and its employees to be up to date with cloud techniques? (cloud-enabled resources)

Procter and Gamble is one of the biggest consumer goods corporations in the world (Norton 2019). The company discovered an opportunity to revolutionise the basic desktop of its employees, evaluated this opportunity and decided to exploit it. The company began to implement a strategy to fully digitise its processes from 2011 (Chui and Flemming 2011). The Business Sphere and Decision Cockpits software enabled the company to implement this solution. Through this program, the company has made analytical solutions available to 38,000 users since the product was launched in 2010. However, Procter and Gamble failed in its goal to become the most digitalised company in the market, leading the CEO to resign (Morgan 2019). The Business Sphere tool was developed with the help of other companies. The purpose of this program was to offer executives predictions about market share and other performance indicators extending as far as up to 12 months into the future. The company has also solved the issues of gathering lots of data from meetings by enabling employees to have data in front of them. For this purpose, the company developed Decision Cockpits, which allows all 58,000 employees to have the same dashboards in front of them, which are linked to current data (Davenport 2013). The Decision Cockpits use a series of analytic models that identify what is happening in a business at that time, why it is happening and what actions the company can take. Further integration of technology, visualisation and information enabled the leaders to drill-down into the data to get answers in real-time ('Harvard Business School 2018). Therefore, entrepreneurs need to integrate clouds into their daily operations and use their benefits in decision-making processes. Doing so can lead to greater efficiency, which speeds up the process of discovering, evaluating and exploiting opportunities. This would enable businesses to be set apart from regular entrepreneurs. Brynjolfsson et al. (2011) state that companies that embrace data-driven decision-making have output and productivity that is 5–6% higher than regular companies.

2.3.3 Digital Entrepreneurial Mindset for Platform-Centric Business Activities

More and more companies that were originally product-focused are becoming platform-centric. Pursuing platform-centric activities achieves better results in both long-term revenue and growth, due to the greater prioritisation of digital opportunities through the reliance on a DEM. This is evident in businesses such as Uber, which is now one of the most valuable and influential businesses in the world (Rahman and Thelen 2019). Whereas big companies previously focused solely on products, today's world is increasingly being dominated by platforms such as Amazon, Google and Facebook (Cusumano et al. 2019). Such platforms have established new ways to create and capture value. Uber is connecting parties that either demand or supply a service, while Amazon connects sellers and customers. Thanks to their data and algorithms, today's platforms exercise profound control (Rahman and Thelen 2019). Therefore, entrepreneurs need to consider developing and adopting a DEM that recognises these profound changes in our society. The key digital platform trends that an entrepreneur with a DEM need to spot are agility and flexibility offered by microservice architectures (software as a service), the containerised environment (platform-centric programs and applications), serverless computing (using third parties to manage databases, servers and other core business activities) and digital ecosystems encapsulating digital trends (digital partnerships).

According to Srinivasan and Venkatraman (2018), digital platforms and their constant development give companies more operational agility and provide entrepreneurs with a vision for long-term growth and value creation. The departure from short-term value creation to long-term value creation has started with big companies, like Facebook, focusing on customer retention and acquisition over short-term profits. Entrepreneurs with DEMs need to transform most of their business processes into digital platforms, data and new technologies, leading to new digital business models, new digital business strategies and the digitalisation of customer interactions, business operations and workforce processes (Raia 2017).

When paired with digital platforms, all five types of digital trends listed previously will improve over time. The first stage of this process is for businesses to link their services to dominant platforms, which allows them access to a broader market immediately. Such an advantage is not available to a regular entrepreneur. Another advantage is that these platform dominant companies can invest in these entrepreneurs' businesses to help them through the start-up period. The second stage is about making choices and maintaining early success. Businesses must rapidly scale up their operations in order to maintain growth. Keeping up with technological changes and being able to realign knowledge with this technological trajectory is of utmost importance for such businesses. Following the study of entrepreneurship in digital platforms, it is essential to focus on the strategic aspect. Entrepreneurs have to develop and adapt their strategies and business models when providing their products and services across digital platforms.

One of the best examples of a platform-centric business is Uber. Uber has adopted new ways of structuring a firm and expanding industry boundaries. It has shifted business away from selling products towards the facilitation of economic exchanges between two or more user groups (Täuscher and Laudien 2018). As such, Uber is different from traditional manufacturing businesses that focus on work with a network of suppliers. Instead, Uber mediates interactions between parties and can conduct business at a lower cost, which has affected traditional taxi businesses. As a highly successful platform-centric business, Uber now has 103 million active users, 3.9 million drivers worldwide and more than 20,000 employees (Smith 2020). It operates in more than 700 cities across 65 countries and completes 17 million trips every day (Smith 2020). The platform that Uber has created has had a significant impact on jobs. Twenty thousand jobs are created every month through Uber, and thousands of entrepreneurs are using it to build their small businesses (Kasselman 2014). This shows how well Uber discovered, evaluated and exploited the opportunities.

2.4 Practical Guide for Adopting the Digital Entrepreneurial Mindset

The developments in the area of data-driven, cloud-enabled, and platform-centric activities give rise to the question of how businesses can become digital. Table 1 provides a list of steps that entrepreneurs can use to develop a DEM for their business. It clarifies which sections of a company are key to any such transformation and describes the necessary actions to achieve this. It also offers examples of companies that have been through the process of digital transformation and have adopted a DEM.

By executing the suggested steps, entrepreneurs and all employees are likely to be better prepared for exploiting the opportunities arising from digital transformation and to be more able to adopt a digital culture where DEMs can flourish.

Table 1 Practical guide for adopting a digital entrepreneurial mindset

Dimension	Action/steps	Practicalities/example
Harnessing technology	Make use of mobile technologies to make data and insights accessible to employees to help them make the right decisions	Procter and Gamble's Decision Cockpits provide a real-time screen enabling all employees to check the current state of its business and relevant trends. As a result, its employees are well informed and can take part in the decision-making process at any time
Interconnectedness	Adapt to the scale of output and accelerate every form of interaction and action. Grasp the impact of interconnectedness	Boeing created an Intranet that enables employees to be easily connected and to receive company news quickly. In this way, employees are more flexible and can easily share their work remotely with colleagues around the globe, thus improving collaboration

(continued)

Table 1 (continued)

Dimension	Action/steps	Practicalities/example
Data use	Make use of data from the organisation or other available data	ASOS found a way to use customer data and their online searches to provide more personalised offers and offer more straightforward website navigation. Thus, its customers are able to find products on the website quickly
Cloud space	Move your data to the cloud and start benefiting from the scale and low-cost infrastructure this offers	Netflix is an excellent example of how a company can move to a cloud space. Netflix understood that its traditional centres for data storage were not large enough. As a result, it decided to turn to the cloud. This decision offered better scalability as it prepared the company for spikes in demand and customers' activity
Learning culture	Facilitate a culture of continuous learning in which all staff are empowered to experiment and shape new technology solutions	Google encourages its employees to spend 20% of their work time on thinking and experimenting with new ideas that will improve the products and services, thus enabling their creativity and innovation. Making the shift from a traditional way of doing business towards digital thinking and acting is easier said than done. Google also uses annual internal surveys to monitor its culture, innovation, autonomy, forward-thinking and teamwork
Customer-centric	Be customer-centric, not cost-driven. Ask, 'how can we use new technologies to enhance customer experiences?' This move will deliver more significant business growth	The US online clothing retailer Everlane is using technology to enable its customers to see and understand the work of the factories and partners that work for it. In this way, the company is taking a customer-centric approach offering high transparency to customers by allowing them to understand how the products are created and priced
Augmented workforce	Consider how you can use automated tools to enable your people, increasing their productivity, skills and value	Pizza Hut is trying to relieve its staff from some basic and routine tasks such as taking orders. Therefore, it uses chatbots to enable its customers to order pizzas, respond to queries and provide offers

3 Digital Maturity Model

A DEM can be adopted in many ways and is determined by various factors. Although this chapter focuses mostly on the DEMs of individual entrepreneurs or start-up businesses, it is also useful to consider them in terms of entire organisations. Each entrepreneur or employee is within certain organisational boundaries; therefore, it is useful to consider a model that potentially accommodates DEMs within existing companies or organisations.

In 2019, Deloitte and MIT Sloan Management Review developed a Digital Maturity Model. Based on a multi-annual survey of more than 3500 executives and managers, the Digital Maturity Model was proposed as a tool to enable digital transformation. Digital maturity refers to the state of being ready for digital transformation. The Digital Maturity Model represents a tool that can enable a digital transformation and represents the first industry standard for assessing digital maturity. There are five business dimensions that are used to evaluate the digital capability of a business: *customers*, *strategy*, *technology*, *operations* and *organisation and culture*.

In this respect, the *customers* dimension accounts for activities such as customer engagement and customer experience. Businesses should strive to achieve a situation in which their customers will see them as their digital partner. The dimension of *strategy* focuses on the management of the brand, ecosystems, stakeholders, innovation and aspects of strategic management. It aims to increase businesses' competitive advantage through digital initiatives that become part of an overall strategy. Another critical dimension is the *technology* itself. This dimension is the crucial foundation of the digital strategy as it facilitates the storage and secure processing of data to meet customers' demands. In this dimension, businesses need to evaluate aspects such as the network, security and applications. The *operations* dimension refers to issues such as agile change management and real-time analytics. As such, it relates to the fostering and execution of tasks and processes using digital technologies to improve the efficiency and effectiveness of the business. The final dimension to consider is *organisation and culture*. Businesses should aim to develop an organisational culture that supports the achievement of digital transformation and flexibility to achieve that goal. The essential aspects of this dimension are leadership and governance. Assessing the Digital Maturity Model according to these dimensions facilitates the assessment of current digital capabilities, decision-making in terms of prioritising skills based on the business' goals and, eventually, measurement of the impact of digital initiatives. Depending on a company's ambitions, it may decide to invest more or less money into some aspects of the Digital Maturity Model. Figure 2 provides an overview of the Digital Maturity Model dimensions and related elements.

The Digital Maturity Model, with its core components of *customer*, *strategy*, *technology*, *operations* and *organisation and culture* spread across 179 digital criteria, is a suitable audit tool to assess the digital maturity of an organisation and to identify the key practices of companies that are developing into more mature

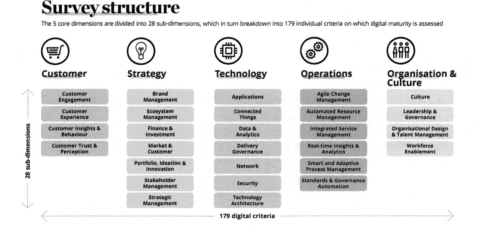

Survey structure

The 5 core dimensions are divided into 28 sub-dimensions, which in turn breakdown into 179 individual criteria on which digital maturity is assessed

Fig. 2 Dimensions of a Digital Maturity Model

digital organisations (Kane et al. 2017). The Digital Maturity Model provides a useful indication of how organisations should systematically prepare to continuously adapt to ongoing digital change.

4 Examples from Practice/Case Studies

4.1 Domino's: Embracing Digital Technology to Differentiate in a Highly Competitive Market

Domino's is an American multinational pizza takeaway chain. Domino's has a tremendous and proven track record of success. In 2018, its franchised and corporate stores generated $13.5 billion in global retail sales, which is an increase of $5.5 billion per annum from five years ago. Domino's operated 16,500 stores in 85 countries in 2018, having operated approximately 8500 in 2008 (Domino's 2018). Domino's is an excellent example of a business that has experienced explosive growth due to embracing a DEM and prioritising digital technology to differentiate itself in a highly competitive market. Over the last few years, the company has faced the challenges of standing out in a crowded market and appealing to the new breed of digital-age consumers. To cope with this challenge, Domino's decided to leverage technology to transform the pizza-ordering experience and to build a highly available, scalable and secure IT backbone to support digital transformation.

In 2012, the company decided to design a new strategy to strive for hyper-convenient pizza ordering. The new mindset was to become the most accessible pizza delivery service and, thus, stand out from the overcrowded market. By using a digital entrepreneurial approach, the company was able to connect

14,000 stores to a common platform and collect data relating to customers' pizza-purchasing habits. As a result, the company can predict customer behaviour by developing a 360° view of the customer that offers to:

- Bring the best value and experience to the customer;
- Use a Snapchat channel for offering discount codes; and
- Offer American customers the possibility of ordering by sending a pizza emoji to @Domino's on Twitter.

Adopting a DEM and using the advantages of technology innovations has helped Domino's to drive a 2000% increase in stock price over the past 10 years. Additionally, digital ordering, data insights and better in-store experience have driven more sales. Domino's has seen double-digit growth for several consecutive quarters. By harnessing technology and a DEM, Domino's has embedded itself into the lives of its customers by delivering a better experience. The firm also took all the steps that we have described in this chapter, from being data-driven to being platform-centric and cloud-enabled.

4.2 Tesco: Building the Virtual Store for Non-ordinary Customers

Tesco, a British multinational company that sells groceries and general merchandise, is the third biggest UK retailer in terms of gross revenue. It currently operates 6800 stores worldwide across several sectors. Tesco operates supermarkets, hypermarkets, superstores and convenience stores. The company earned a net income of £1674 million (Tesco 2019) and has 450,000 employees worldwide. Tesco wanted to infiltrate the South Korean market, a market where consumers have no time to do traditional grocery shopping. This meant that Tesco had to come up with new ideas and techniques to make its business profitable in the new market. Fortunately, digitalisation had opened a window of opportunity of which a grocer with a DEM could take advantage.

Tesco discovered that South Koreans generally use a large amount of technology as part of their daily routine, have long working hours and have a longer commute than most Europeans. Therefore, Tesco created a 'virtual store' called HomePlus, demonstrating its inclination and ability to discover, evaluate and exploit opportunities emerging from digital technologies. HomePlus stores are set up in public spaces like subways and bus stops. Consumers download the HomePlus app on their smartphones. They use their smartphones to scan the codes at the virtual stores and purchase their orders online. The products can be stored in a virtual shopping basket and paid for online as well. Customers can also schedule a home delivery. This means a busy person can buy their groceries in a more convenient manner. The virtual store has been a considerable success in South Korea. The app has already been downloaded 900,000 times, and online sales have risen by 130% since its introduction. There are several HomePlus virtual stores across South Korea, and the brand is the country's top retailer, making the HomePlus app the most popular shopping app in South Korea.

4.3 Tate: Organising Digital Events with Live Streaming of Art Performances

Tate runs a collection of four major art galleries in the UK, including the Tate Modern. The Tate Modern gallery was visited by almost 5.9 million people in 2018. Tate was also the first online art gallery with a website that offered basic functionalities. Later, Tate created extensive online databases so that people could search for all the objects in its collection. However, to further its online presence, Tate began creating an online gallery that would operate as Tate's fifth gallery. Tate wanted to enable everything from viewing the gallery online to being able to participate in fundraising and public programmes.

Tate launched its new website in 2012. Tate wanted to create a rich experience for its customers and to offer new content. It also wanted to create a platform that would allow user participation by allowing users to comment on posts and join online communities. As a part of these efforts, Tate created digital events in which it enabled a live stream of art performances. To further streamline the experiences of visitors, Tate moved from traditional audio guides to interactive guides, which allowed visitors more flexibility. This new site was focused on being customer-centric, which is one of the steps in the practical guide to digital entrepreneurship in Sect. 2.5 (Table 1).

John Stack, Head of Tate Online, was a key person in the process of creating Tate's new online presence and building its web strategy. By conducting this process, John Stack exhibited an excellent DEM by harnessing technology, interconnectedness, data usage, learning culture and a customer-centric focus. He managed to turn Tate's online presence into a virtual world with exciting and engaging activities and content. Another important factor in the success of this shift was the support provided by the company's management. They provided Stack and his department with the resources and freedom necessary to carry out the digital initiatives (Avery 2017). This exhibit of a DEM by Stack and his team achieved positive results including a better connection to customers, increased ticket sales and higher revenues.

5 Conclusion and Implications

Mobile technologies, social media, IoT, cloud computing and big data have disrupted and continue to disrupt the business world today, permeating every aspect of business and life, including the lives of customers. 'Digital' is becoming all-pervasive. Everything now needs to be plugged in and the lines separating the physical from the digital are becoming blurred. This has begun to influence the way in which entrepreneurs think and act. Sharing economies are on the rise and embed businesses in a rapidly changing landscape of exponentially exploding data, information and algorithms. At the same time, the existence of a networked society necessitates a significant shift in organisational strategies, structures, leadership, processes and policies as disruptions become a new way of living and acting as an entrepreneur. Thus, adopting a DEM is no longer a choice but a necessity. A DEM is required to reimagine an existing business model and convert it into a digital one. By applying a DEM, an entrepreneur may reconsider the infrastructure they use, the type of insurance they require or the marketing activities they plan.

Data-driven, cloud-enabled, platform-centric business activities dominate the business world today. By presenting the three success stories of Domino's, Tesco and Tate, in which developing a DEM was the first step to succeeding in the digital age, this chapter has demonstrated the value of responding to opportunities created by digitisation. Both managers and employees in these companies have shown the inclination and ability to discover, evaluate and exploit opportunities arising from digital technologies and convert them into concrete actions that have led to better financial performance. Digital transformation, to which every business is exposed today, has replaced the cost-focused operating model of the past and looks set to develop into a fully networked digital business model in the future. Thus, entrepreneurs need to adhere to the new reality where adopting a digital entrepreneurial mindset is the key. This chapter has provided some tools and examples of how entrepreneurs have prepared their businesses to cope with new digital challenges and turn them into opportunities. However, it is important to emphasise that the presence of DEMs in these companies has not led to changes in decision-making processes but has had a tremendous impact on the society around us.

Acknowledgements We acknowledge, with much appreciation, the many constructive insights that Lars Meijburg has provided for this chapter. Thank you for your input, commitment and passion, which have increased the quality of this work. We are looking forward to seeing your digital entrepreneurial mindset in action.

References

Annual Report and Financial Statements 2019, *Tesco*. (2019). https://www.tescoplc.com/media/476422/tesco_ara2019_full_report_web.pdf.

Aral, S., Dellarocas, C., & Godes, D. (2013). Introduction to the special issue—social media and business transformation: A framework for research. *Information Systems Research, 24*(1), 3–13.

Arnason, G. (2017). 2016 FICO decision management innovation award goes to Southwest Airlines. *Financial News.* https://financial-news.co.uk/2016-fico-decision-management-innovation-award-goes-to/.

Avery, J. (2017). *The Tate's digital transformation.* HBS No. 314122-PDF-ENG. Boston, MA: Harvard Business School Publishing.

Brynjolfsson, E., Hitt, L. M., & Kim, H. H. (2011). Strength in numbers: how does data-driven decision-making affect firm performance? *SSRN Electronic Journal.* SSRN: https://ssrn.com/abstract=1819486 or http://dx.doi.org/10.2139/ssrn.1819486.

Caldwell, L. (2018). how digitisation is driving new business models for manufacturers. https://www.forbes.com/sites/lisacaldwell/2018/11/27/how-digitisation-is-driving-new-business-models-for-manufacturers/#1160d3946aa6.

Castillo, A. (2019). Where is the real cost savings in cloud computing? https:// cloudcomputingtechnologies.com/where-is-the-real-cost-savings-in-cloud-computing/.

Chui, M., & Flemming, T. (2011). Inside P&G's digital revolution. *McKinsey Quarterly*. https:// www.mckinsey.com/industries/consumer-packaged-goods/our-insights/inside-p-and-ampgs-digital-revolution.

Cusumano, M. A., Gawer, A., & Yoffie, D. B. (2019). *The business of platforms*. Harper Business.

Davenport, T. H. (2013). How P&G presents data to decision-makers. *Harvard Business Review*. https://hbr.org/2013/04/how-p-and-g-presents-data.

'Domino's annual report', *Domino's*. (2018). http://www.annualreports.com/HostedData/ AnnualReports/PDF/NYSE_DPZ_2018.pdf.

Dweck, C. S., & Yeager, D. S. (2019). Mindsets: a view from two eras. *Perspectives on Psychological Science, 14*(3), 481–496.

Dykes, B. (2019). The four key pillars to fostering a data-driven culture. *Forbes*. https://www. forbes.com/sites/brentdykes/2019/03/28/the-four-key-pillars-to-fostering-a-data-driven-culture/ #1cdb529f7d90.

Dynamic Quest. (2019). *Creating a scalable enterprise with cloud*. https://dynamicquest.com/ creating-a-scalable-enterprise-with-cloud/.

French, R. P. (2016). The fuzziness of mindsets: Divergent conceptualizations and characterizations of mindset theory and praxis. *International Journal of Organisational Analysis, 24*(4), 673–691.

Gleeson, B. (2019). Five key ingredients for successful organisational change. *Forbes*. https:// www.forbes.com/sites/brentgleeson/2018/12/27/5-key-ingredients-for-successful-organisational-change/#4b4225f476dd.

Growjo. (2018). Turo revenue, number of employees, annual growth and funding. https://growjo. com/company/Turo.

Harvard Business School. (2018). *P&G: bringing CPG into the digital age*. https://digital.hbs.edu/ platform-rctom/submission/pg-bringing-cpg-into-the-digital-age/.

Kane, G. C., Palmer, D., Phillips, A. N., Kiron, D., Buckley, N. (2017). *Achieving Digital Maturity*. MIT Sloan Management Review and Deloitte University Press.

Kasselman, L. (2014). An Uber impact: 20,000 jobs created on the Uber platform every month. Uber transportation network now covers 43 percent of the U.S. population. *Business Wire*. https://www.businesswire.com/news/home/20140527005594/en/Uber-Impact-20000-Jobs-Created-Uber-Platform.

Marr, B. (2016). Data-driven decision-making: 10 simple steps for any business. , *Forbes*. https:// www.forbes.com/sites/bernardmarr/2016/06/14/data-driven-decision-making-10-simple-steps-for-any-business/.

Morgan, B. (2019). Companies that failed at digital transformation and what we can learn from them. *Forbes*. https://www.forbes.com/sites/blakemorgan/2019/09/30/companies-that-failed-at-digital-transformation-and-what-we-can-learn-from-them/.

Myler, L. (2017). Some Airbnb hosts producing job-quitting cash with this emerging business model. *Forbes*. https://www.forbes.com/sites/larrymyler/2017/09/07/some-airbnb-hosts-producing-job-quitting-cash-with-this-emerging-business-model/#1a25439121ef.

Nambisan, S., Wright, M., & Feldman, M. (2019). 'The digital transformation of innovation and entrepreneurship: progress, challenges and key themes. *Research Policy, 48*(8). https://doi.org/ 10.1016/j.respol.2019.03.018.

Norton, S. (2019). Procter & Gamble. *Forbes*. https://www.forbes.com/companies/procter-gamble/.

Nulaw. (2020). *4 communication strategies to reduce unnecessary communication*. https://nulaw. co/2020/01/20/4-communication-strategies-to-reduce-unnecessary-communication/.

O'Dea, S. (2019). Forecast number of mobile users worldwide from 2019 to 2023 (in billions). *Statista*. https://www.statista.com/statistics/218984/number-of-global-mobile-users-since-2010/.

Peregud, I. (2018). Five characteristics of a data-driven company. *TDWI*. https://tdwi.org/Articles/ 2018/09/26/PPM-ALL-Five-Characteristics-Data-Driven-Company.aspx?Page=1.

Pinchot. (1985). *Intrapreneuring: why you don't have to leave the corporation to become an entrepreneur.* New York, Harper & Row.

Rahman, K. S., & Thelen, K. (2019). The rise of the platform business model and the transformation of twenty-first-century capitalism. *Politics & Society, 47*(2), 177–204.

Raia, M. R. (2017). Business process automation and digital transformation. *Integrify.* https://www.integrify.com/blog/posts/business-process-automation-digital-transformation/.

Rishi, S., Karpovich, B., & Kesterson-Townes, L. (2017). Beyond agility how cloud is driving enterprise innovations. *IBM Institute for Business Value.* https://www.ibm.com/thought-leadership/institute-business-value/report/beyondagility.

Roberts, D., Candi, M., & Hughes, M. (2017). Leveraging social network users for new product launch'. *Industrial Management & Data Systems, 117*(10), 2400–2416.

Rödl & Partner. (n.d.). Digitalisation: opportunities and challenges for entrepreneurs. https://www.roedl.com/insights/digitalisation/opportunities-challenges-entrepreneurs.

Shane, S., & Venkataraman, S. (2000). The promise of entrepreneurship as a field of research. *The Academy of Management Review, 25*(1), 217–226.

Smith, C. (2020). 110 amazing Uber statistics, demographics and facts (2020). *DMR.* https://expandedramblings.com/index.php/uber-statistics/.

Soltanifar, M. (2016). Corporate entrepreneurship and triple helix. In R. Segers (Ed.), *Multinational management* (pp. 275–299). Cham: Springer.

Srinivasan, A., & Venkatraman, N. (2018). Entrepreneurship in digital platforms: a network-centric view. *Strategic Entrepreneurship Journal, 12*(1), 54–71.

Täuscher, K., & Laudien, S. M. (2018). Understanding platform business models: a mixed methods study of marketplaces. *European Management Journal, 36*(3), 319–329.

Valacich, J. S., & Schneider, C. (2018) *Information systems today: managing in the digital world (Subscription),* 8th edn. Pearson.

Van Tongeren, D. R., & Burnette, J. L. (2018). Do you believe happiness can change? An investigation of the relationship between happiness mindsets, well-being and satisfaction. *The Journal of Positive Psychology, 13*(2), 101–109.

Vial, G. (2019). Understanding digital transformation: a review and a research agenda. *The Journal of Strategic Information Systems, 28*(2), 118–144.

Unleashing the Creativity of Entrepreneurs with Digital Technologies

Robert D. Hisrich and Mariusz Soltanifar

Abstract

For decades, creativity has been used to generate ideas among entrepreneurs and their teams. Although extensive research has been conducted on creativity, the majority of studies have focused on traditional ways of stimulating creativity, such as focus groups, the collective notebook method, brainstorming, brainwriting, reverse brainstorming and problem inventory analysis. However, the digital age appears to challenge much of this existing work on the nature of creativity. It is clear that online creativity and audiences are affecting the meaning, expression and impact of creativity. The traditional techniques of stimulating creativity have been replaced and aided by technology-driven innovations, such as artificial intelligence (AI), virtual reality (VR) and the Internet of things (IoT). This chapter explores ways to activate the creativity of entrepreneurs and their teams through the use of digital technologies. We believe that this chapter provides a rich source of examples on how technology is currently being used to support creativity by encouraging entrepreneurs and their teams to make connections, develop ideas, create meaning, collaborate and communicate. We present, in detail, three case studies and discuss practical implications for the future.

R. D. Hisrich (✉)
Kent State University, Ohio, USA
e-mail: rhisrich1@kent.edu

M. Soltanifar
Hanze University of Applied Sciences, Groningen, The Netherlands

M. Soltanifar
Open University, Heerlen, The Netherlands

© The Author(s) 2021
M. Soltanifar et al. (eds.), *Digital Entrepreneurship*, Future of Business and Finance,
https://doi.org/10.1007/978-3-030-53914-6_2

1   Introduction

One could argue that what ultimately distinguishes humans from other species on this planet is our creativity. It has given us the unique ability to shape our own destiny, whether for good or bad. Creativity has enabled us to shape the present, recreate what came before us and build the future that we envision for ourselves. As a species, we can visualise things that do not exist, allowing us to bring them to life, changing the world. For example, for some time, various creativity techniques, such as free association, forced relationships and attribute listing, and parameter analysis, have been used as ways to generate ideas among entrepreneurs and their teams. Today's organisations operate in an increasingly competitive and globalised environment, making creativity a crucial part of organisations (Amabile and Khaire 2008; Landry 2017). In addition, this competitive and globalised environment has now become digitised.

Pervasive digitisation is not only opening a new window of opportunity but also changes the way in which ideas are generated and how creative tools are applied. Creativity fuels big ideas and opens the door for new opportunities while challenging employees to think creatively by tapping into their creative outputs. Through accommodating the creative ideas of employees, the company can continually innovate its products and services to sustain a competitive advantage (Soltanifar 2016). The importance of creativity has grown throughout the years, with companies focusing on it more each year. For instance, based on IBM's survey of more than 1500 chief executive officers, creativity has been ranked as the number one factor for future business success (Landry 2017). A 2018 Deloitte survey of 500 companies—each with revenues somewhere between $100 million USD and over $1 billion annually—found that approximately 57% of companies of this size plan on spending even more on tech in the years ahead than they have in the past (Deloitte 2018).

Although creativity has been present in research and practice for many years (Gabora 2013), resulting in extensive research on creativity (British Council 2020; Said-Metwaly et al. 2017; Banaji 2010), the majority of studies still focus on the traditional ways of stimulating creativity, as mentioned above. Creativity, as such, has not changed much, though its surrounding landscape has changed dramatically through the increasingly digitised business environment (Johnson 2016). Traditional techniques of stimulating creativity have been replaced and enhanced by technology-driven tools, such as virtual rooms, decision cockpits, various communication tools and interactive dashboards. In particular, the Internet of things (IoT), artificial intelligence (AI) and virtual reality (VR) have an impact on the creativity of entrepreneurs and their teams, which is the focus of this chapter. These tools can enhance creative processes. For example, AI can be used to uncover certain statistics and help determine marketing opportunities, which can be more efficient and diverse compared with traditional practices. Furthermore, the use of the IoT has now made it possible for ideas to be sourced from virtually anywhere, going beyond the capabilities of manpower. This impact is seen in the hiring of more creative-minded individuals, the incorporation of design thinking, particularly in the area of new products and services, the design of new packages that are not only recyclable but also can be used for other purposes, more expressive and meaningful social media messaging, and incorporating a thinking-outside-the-box mentality when addressing various marketing problems.

The sourcing of ideas is now more than ever being influenced by larger changes in interactions between people, communities, creative processes, knowledge domains and wider social contexts. As there is a sizeable research gap in linking the digital environment to creativity, the aim of this chapter is to understand how entrepreneurs and their teams can use digital technologies to support creativity. Based on this, our research question for this chapter is: *How can we support the creativity of entrepreneurs and their teams using digital technologies, and in particular, how can we do this through artificial intelligence, virtual reality and the Internet of things?*

By reviewing recent literature on creativity and discussing three practical cases, we link creativity to digital business and highlight the importance of creativity for digital businesses. More specifically, we position creativity as a way of stimulating entrepreneurial behaviour, using creativity as a basis for innovation and creating a working environment where ideas can flourish. We also investigate how entrepreneurs and their teams can utilise digital technologies to support creativity. In this chapter, we examine how entrepreneurs can harness digital technologies to ignite creativity, power human enterprise and support creativity among themselves and their teams. We contribute to the literature on creativity and entrepreneurship in three major ways. First, this paper expands our understanding of creativity by adding a new dimension of creativity stimulated by digital technology. Second, we emphasise the need for positioning companies into a digital business environment landscape that encourages the application of digital tools to support creativity. Third, we shed light on managerial practices and deliver practical implications to corporate executives and managers and individual entrepreneurs and their teams.

2 Conceptualising Creativity in Digital Business

Artistic expression, co-creation and the dissemination of business ideas are now more common than ever before, being transformed through rapidly evolving digital technologies (Gardner and Weinstein 2018). In the field of artistic expression, lines are also being blurred with the advent of these digital technologies, as audience engagement takes on a whole new meaning in which communication with the audience and performance intertwine and, occasionally, become one. For instance, the affinity groups are a great example of co-creation, as they allow individuals with similar interests to mentor and support each other in the development of their creative skills. Sites such as Behance, DevianArt and Dribble allow professional artists and designers to share their work and receive constructive feedback and inspiration. Both feedback and inspiration may lead to business ideas and improvements. Social networking services (SNSs) have also had a major impact on creativity and the creation thereof. It has become especially apparent how large their impact has been and will continue to be when looking at the unprecedented and seemingly endless number of interactions taking place on these networks.

With digital technologies, the possibilities for individuals to express themselves in exactly the way that they see fit have become nearly infinite. Individuals can now express themselves and showcase their talents without bounds and may connect with audiences that have similar interests. This phenomenon becomes very evident on platforms such as Medium, Instagram and YouTube. All three platforms allow for future professionals, artists and amateurs to post content on these platforms and test the market for future business endeavours. An interesting perspective to consider is that when millions of photos are taken and uploaded to Instagram, there are bound to be great creative shots as a result. The same could be assumed for the 500 million tweets posted daily. The probability for great content and creativeness rises with frequency (Chamorro-Premuzic 2015).

Before we present various ways to foster creativity by making use of digital technologies, we will define creativity and elaborate on the importance of creativity for digital businesses.

2.1 Defining Creativity

Over the years, the process of defining creativity has led to the development of various perspectives. The areas of cognition, personality and the stimulation of creativity in people were the main focus of defining creativity in the 1950s to 1970s (Mehta and Dahl 2019). Later, in the 1980s and 1990s, that focus shifted to the influence of environments and the social context of the creativity of individuals. In 2005, Cropley reviewed numerous attempts to classify creativity. One of the more notable attempts was of Joy Paul Guilford, American psychologist, stressing the importance of 'divergent' thinking in human psychology, noting the role of creativity in successful technological and economic ventures. Guilford settled on three elements of the variety of discussions about creativity: novelty, effectiveness and ethicality, and focused on people that demonstrated these characteristics and interacted with others while in a 'creativity-friendly' environment (Loveless 2002).

Several reviews exist that help to define and theorise the nature of creativity. Dust's (1999) review provides recommendations for achieving the goals of exploration, exploitation and explanation to achieve the main objective: the promotion of talent, innovativeness and creativity in the fields of science, technology and art. However, it is important to note that much of the work cited in various literature has been undertaken in the USA, UK and Europe, meaning we must acknowledge the possibility of 'cultural saturation' in Western concepts of creativity, as it might lead to limitations in understanding the creativity of other cultures. A key point in defining creativity is whether to focus on unique and one-of-a-kind creative individuals, such as Albert Einstein or Charlie Parker, who possess paradigm-shifting abilities in society's way of knowing, or to focus on any and all individuals and the normal person's ability and potential for self-actualisation. For our paper, the focus is broad, as we aim to find ways to stimulate creativity in employees/intrapreneurs.

Creativity can be defined in different ways, and truthfully, everyone has their own understanding of the concept. Creativity in business can be defined as an act that generates or makes use of a new idea and requires a different approach to the problem. This is the sole definition that can be projected onto any person who is labelled 'creative'. This definition is, however, quite broad, and it might help to investigate some definitions which dive below the surface. According to Naiman, the founder of Creativity Work and a mentor in creative output, creativity can be summed up as the ability to tap into our 'inner' pool of resources—knowledge, insight, information, inspiration and all the fragments populating our minds. Thus, it is not only the forming of ideas but also our ability to access them and put them to use. While these two definitions are different, they both place creativity into one category, which can be summarised as a complex process of the creation of ideas and the further development of these ideas. Whether it is an artist writing a song, or an employee at a company meeting during a brainstorming session, these individuals attain an idea and try to make it into something tangible. Creativity can be regarded as not only a quality found in exceptional individuals but also as an essential life skill through which any employee can develop their potential to use their imagination to express themselves and make original and valued choices in their lives. This is enhanced through an evergreen termed 'the artist way', which assists individuals in entrepreneurship and digital marketing to become more creative.

In this chapter, we refer to creativity as the ability of an individual, or a small group of individuals, to generate novel and useful ideas to take advantage of the new opportunities offered by digital technologies. Creativity, a process that can result in incremental improvements, is the core of innovation and necessary for the development of new business concepts. While there are numerous perspectives (psychological, social, individual, economic and organisational), creativity is the application of an individuals' ability to identify and develop new ideas, processes or concepts in novel ways. These new ideas, processes or concepts must be useful and have value or meaning. For instance, Netflix is a creative company that recognised an opportunity and capitalised on the success of the DVD and Internet streaming services. Netflix overcame a series of hurdles to launch and become a $9 billion company. Creativity leads to perseverance, passion and commitment, which can be seen from companies such as Apple, Amazon, Facebook, Google, Salesforce.com, Samsung, Twitter, Virgin Atlantic and 3M. Digital technology implies a broad range of information and communications technologies (including new digital media) that can be used for different purposes by entrepreneurs in many situations. Next, we elaborate on the importance of creativity for stimulating entrepreneurial behaviour, using creativity as a basis for innovation, and creating a working environment where ideas can flourish.

2.2 The Importance of Creativity for Digital Entrepreneurship

Creativity brings numerous benefits to entrepreneurs and their teams. One of the major benefits of creativity is to stimulate entrepreneurial behaviour, and in particular, innovativeness, proactiveness and risk-taking (Kuratko and Morris 2018). Therefore, it is worthwhile to explore the effects of digital technologies on creativity in an entrepreneurial context. There are many attributes that fall under entrepreneurial behaviour, but perhaps one of the most important ones is the need and want for change, or in other words, innovation. Innovation is an inevitable aspect of the business world, as without it there would be no progress. Creativity and innovation are two terms that go hand in hand from an entrepreneurial perspective. Judging by the creativity types explained above, you may find that creativity is not just a state of mind but also the work, training and the will to create something of worth for yourself and others. Entrepreneurs are drivers of change and are persistent in perfecting the techniques and skills in their given field.

'A composer must use the piano to test a song he is creating, but, if he does not know the piano execution techniques well, his mind will be absorbed by choice of the correct notes, and it will distract him from his composition' (Kamel et al. 2017, p. 5).

In thinking about the above quote, we may gather that entrepreneurs work on perfecting their techniques to pave the way for new ideas they want to implement.

A good example of an entrepreneur taking their knowledge of the industry and creating a new, digitally creative business idea is Chinese entrepreneur Jenny Zhiya Qian, who co-founded Luckin Coffee in October 2017. Knowing the Chinese market and their habits, the company stepped away from traditional coffee shop tactics and has opted for selling their products through a delivery service rather than at a brick-and-mortar location. Through creative digital innovation, Luckin Coffee has become one of the fastest-growing start-ups, with the average total items sold that increased 470.1% from 7.8 million in the third quarter of 2018 to 44.2 million during the recent quarter. Revenue was strong, with total net revenue of $215.7 million USD (Cardwell 2020). Without creativity, there are no innovative solutions/ideas. Creativity, in its most basic form, is about idea generation, innovation and the implementation of ideas (Gilson and Litchfield 2017). Digital technologies play a crucial role in facilitating meaningful, collaborative activity. Such collaborative activity refers to any project that involves building something together through a process of co-creation. The need for creativity and the use of digital technologies may be more valuable in digital entrepreneurship compared with traditional business since it is driven by ideas and innovations. Digital businesses require a degree of individual and collective creativity to be able to stand out and develop an online/digital presence. As this chapter indicates, creativity and digitalisation are important as companies must innovate faster than ever to keep pace and stay alive in today's hypercompetitive market. This is perhaps even more important in a digital business than a traditional one due to (1) the increasingly growing number of digital businesses, (2) the increase in innovation in the Internet and global devices, (3) the development of a new consumer who is more technically sophisticated and globally interconnected, (4) the advent of new industries and (5) the rapid increase in emerging markets.

2.3 Digital Technologies Supporting Creativity

The digital age presents a different challenge to the existing view on the nature of creativity. Online creativity and audiences are affecting the meaning, expression and impact of creativity. Although many studies have been conducted on creativity, the majority of studies still focus on traditional ways of stimulating creativity. This opens up a discussion about the different roles that these technologies play in regard to creativity and the potential for personal and collaborative creativity. In addition, there is a need for research that does not just embrace technology but also critically examines the relationship towards Information and Communications Technology (ICT) and digitalisation (Pedersen et al. 2019). Existing research has highlighted the importance of effectiveness and novelty as two fundamental criteria for creativity. In digital or social advertising agencies, most practitioners regard interactivity as the most important criterion for creativity. Therefore, the degree of interaction of digital technologies should be considered when exploring the relationship with creativity (Chen et al. 2019).

While selecting the digital technologies that support creativity for further detailed examination in this paper, we analysed the general trends and predictions with regard to digital technologies that transform the way we live, from everyday tasks to complex, large-scale projects. The usage of such technologies helps with the decoupling of location, meaning creativity can be exploited from anywhere, whether in transit, at home or anywhere with access to a phone/computer. For further examination, we chose the following arguments for AI, the IoT and VR, which will shape the future of machine learning and automated systems (see Table 1).

Digital technologies, such as AI, VR and the IoT, are reshaping the way in which people live, learn, work and generate ideas and have increasingly become a fascination for individuals, society and companies (Bruno and Canina 2019a, b). Digital technologies are reducing the cost of iteration and experimentation in creative work, which opens up new possibilities for both individuals and businesses (Austin 2016). A global study done by Adobe found that businesses that invest in creativity experienced increased employee productivity (78%), satisfied customers (80%), produced a better customer experience (78%), fostered innovation (83%) and were financially successful (73%) (Adobe 2016).

Next, we introduce each technology and elaborate on its role in supporting the creativity of entrepreneurs and their teams.

Table 1 Characteristics of artificial intelligence (AI), the Internet of things (IoT) and virtual reality (VR) impacting businesses

Digital technology	Characteristics
Artificial intelligence (AI)	• The global AI software market is expected to reach 126 billion USD in 2025 and is forecasted to experience massive growth in the coming years (Liu 2020) • Artificial intelligence will account for almost 70% of the global economic impact by 2030 (Rao and Verweij 2017) • Thirty-seven per cent of organisations have implemented some form of AI, which is a 270% increase over the last four years (Stamford 2019) • It is estimated that in 2020, 9.6 billion US dollars will be spent on intelligent process automation. In this context, AI is autonomous decision-making through a system or systems designed to simulate human thought processes (Liu 2020) • 51% of marketers are already using AI, while 27% of them are planning to incorporate it within their digital marketing strategy (Leftronic 2019)
Virtual reality (VR)	• The global VR market is expected to reach 56.25 billion USD by 2025 (Globenewswire 2020) • It is estimated that in 2025, 87.97 billion USD will be spent on VR (Mordorintelligence 2020) • Globally, there are over 171 million users of VR in 2019 (Petrov 2019) • Globally, 18 million standalone VR devices will be sold in 2022 (Petrov 2019) • Global standalone VR devices will grow 16 times between 2018 and 2022 (Petrov 2019)
The Internet of things (IoT)	• Global spending on the IoT is expected to reach 1.1 trillion USD by 2023 (Liu 2020) • The global industrial IoT market is expected to reach 14.2 trillion USD by 2030 (Weber 2019) • There are expected to be 21.4 billion IoT devices in the world by 2025 (Liu 2020) • Cellular IoT connections are expected to reach 3.5B in 2023, increasing at a CAGR of 30% (Columbus 2018) • Seventeen per cent of the global respondents identified the IoT as the top technology game-changer in driving business transformation (KPMG 2018)

2.4 Artificial Intelligence

Artificial intelligence is one of the most mysterious and fascinating technologies of our time. Many might know the term AI; however, the majority of people would not understand what exactly AI refers to. For a definition, we look towards Copeland (2020), who defined AI as 'the ability of a digital computer or computer-controlled robot to perform tasks commonly associated with intelligent beings'. Copeland (2020) further expands on this by elaborating on the components that make up intelligence, such as learning, reasoning, problem solving, perception and language (Copeland 2020). The definition of AI changes throughout the literature, and a specific definition has yet to take hold. In the latest Artificial Intelligence Special Report, published by The New York Times, it was suggested that we are currently witnessing a supervised-learning revolution in which computers are taught to see patterns and learn on their own (Smith 2020).

Moreover, also being relevant to the topic are the Gartner 2019 top Hype Cycle trends in AI, which are augmented intelligence, chatbots, machine learning and intelligent (enterprise) applications, among others (Goasduff 2019). Gartner predicted that in 2020, chatbots would be responsible for 85% of customer service (Milenkovic 2019). Accenture believes that AI will not only increase businesses financial gains, going as far as doubling economic growth by 2035, but also drastically change the way people work. Their research suggests that 40% of business leaders believe that AI will increase worker productivity in the future (Milenkovic 2019). This is great news for entrepreneurs and their teams, as AI will most likely assist in maximising their employees' output while maintaining a good work–life balance (Milenkovic 2019).

Considering how AI supports creativity, there have already been several exciting developments, one of which has taken place in one of the arguably most creative fields of human expression: art. Artificial intelligence has already begun creating music, painting and designing fashion (Magalhães 2019). Examples of this can be found in music studios, where AI is now helping in the mastering of songs. Expanding further into art, AI can now create original paintings and rework existing pieces of art, which would have simply not been possible a few decades ago (Marr 2020). There is now AI capable of sifting through enormous amounts of data and creating something new with a handful of the data that it had just analysed. A painting created by AI in 2018 sold for $432,500 USD at a Christie's auction. This might not be a very impressive sum to an art enthusiast; nevertheless, considering the fact that it was not created by a human makes it quite impressive (Magalhães 2019). Another example of creative use of AI in business is the world's first robot artist, who already held her first solo exhibition, equipped with facial recognition technology and a robotic arm system (Haynes 2019) or algorithms can read recipes and create images of what the final dish will look like, supporting the cooking process (Whyte 2019).

According to Nicola Morini Bianzino, EY Global Chief Client Technology Officer, AI can encourage human creativity in freeing up time for humans to focus on innovation, thereby offering opportunities to creatively combine technologies to create new ways of working and actively augmenting human decision-making by adding a layer of machine-driven data analysis to guide our creative choices (Bianzino 2020). However, AI is not meant to wander off and create art for the rest of its days. What constitutes the interesting element of AI when examining creativity is how it can enhance the creativity of creatives, such as artists, musicians or professionals. To create one of AI's components, machine learning (ML) might be the most interesting. Machine learning makes it possible for an artist to feed the AI piles of data that it can then analyse. The AI will then provide the artist with a range of options for starting points, rather than having to think of a starting point themselves. Artists would no longer be limited by the ideas they get but rather by their ability to translate the ideas of an AI into a work of art (Magalhães 2019).

Interestingly, Forbes speculated that AI would level the intellectual differences of individuals. Individual IQs will decrease in importance, as AI will aid those with lower IQs. Moreover, the conclusion is that creativity and imagination will become increasingly important in the years to come. Forbes reports that the World Economic Forum made a prediction in 2016 that creativity would be the third most important skill to employers in 2020. Creativity previously held the 10th place in 2015 (Fatemi 2018). Another important aspect of AI mentioned by Forbes is that AI alleviates people from the mundane, time-consuming and repetitive tasks that might take an employee days or weeks to complete. Relieving an employee of these tasks will greatly increase the time they have available for creative endeavours (Fatemi 2018). However, we must consider the limits of technologies such as AI at this time, since much is yet to be learned about its capabilities and uses. For example, the dangers of integrating AI into our daily lives must be explored, as it could bring risks that are not yet foreseeable.

In conclusion, AI can be seen as a catalyst to push human creativity. While machine and human collaboration can produce exciting results, novel approaches and combinations would not likely develop if either were working alone (Marr 2020). Moving beyond its simple existential purpose of analysing vast amounts of data, AI has the potential to become humanity's best tool for advancing itself creatively and does so by stimulating entrepreneurial minds to find entirely new ways to utilise data.

2.5 Virtual Reality

Constructs such as VR, augmented reality (AR) and AI are often regarded as similar and interchangeable, which can stop managers and entrepreneurs from exploring their potential and effectiveness. To avoid any confusion between AR and VR, we would like to clarify the difference (Marr 2018). Augmented reality is already widely used in business processes and departments that benefit from technological solutions. In business and management, it is often difficult to distinguish the differences between new available technologies. Understanding the differences between different virtual, physical and possible constructs is crucial for successful integration of such technologies in business processes. Hence, a clear definition of AR is provided before exploring its relation to creativity and overall benefits and risks. Moreover, AR is the integration of digital information in a real-world environment, such as virtual, statistical and auditory content. A layer of digital information is made accessible to people and is generated by computer software (Farshid et al. 2018). This technology can be provided for a wide range of uses and platforms. Most popularly used are applications on smartphones or other devices and wearables. The layers that are added to the actual world can be both sensory and data-based. Augmented reality technology can provide various solutions for both businesses and consumers. This technology is already a popular tool used by both start-ups and large corporations, offering utility for a wide range of purposes.

Unlike AR, VR represents a full digital representation of the actual world with virtual content and information. Virtual reality is a complete virtual replacement of the real world, whereas AR adds content to it (Farshid et al. 2018). This could be a three-dimensional (3D) digital environment generated by computers, which can be used for different purposes. A popular function is the ability to play videogames and view immersive video content through VR headsets. In a business context, however, VR technology can be used to make creative content. Businesses are looking for digital solutions for automation and productivity for their internal processes.

There are many success stories regarding the implementations of VR technology in which the technology has increased productivity and creativity in external and internal processes. Several VR-supported approaches have been tested to examine its effects on creativity. Alahuhta et al. (2014) identified eight affordances for the support of creativity by virtual environments. Characteristics of VR technology, such as immersion and rich visual information, were determined to be important aspects to support creativity. In experiments conducted by Lau and Lee (2012), a focus was put on learning creativity and the support of learning experiences. From experimenting with highly interactive virtual environments, it showed that entertaining and explorative factors were essential. Another VR-supported approach concerning creativity that primed virtual environments was tested by Bhagwatwar et al. (2013). Here, the idea-generation process of humans was investigated by exposing them to these virtual environments. Graessler et al. (2017) tested six generated virtual environments, consisting of different contents and grades of mobility and interaction. As a consequence, Graessler and Taplick (2018) tested the Sensory Stimulus Environment Technique with pre-developed virtual environments to investigate its efficiency. By comparing this technique with 'brainstorming' and the Sensory Picture Technique, they were able to improve the creativity technique supported by VR technology. These approaches have assisted in the exploration of the relationship between creativity and virtual environments. Moreover, a common example is the use of virtual tours of houses and other properties in the real estate industry. Real estate firms are now able to offer creative digital content in the form of VR tours that allow potential customers to get a realistic and immersive impression of the property. When integrated successfully, VR technology can replace harmful or complex situations in terms of training. Like AR, this technology can also provide solutions for remote access and communication, which can standardise certain operations and reduce the carbon footprint (Fade 2020).

Visual tools and technologies are effective ways to foster creativity in business model development processes and idea development. Augmented reality can help us visualise data and information in the real world to give a realistic perspective of an idea or concept. Digital technologies such as AR enable entrepreneurial activities and ease the process of bringing ideas to life or improving communication and other processes (Elia et al. 2020). One of the great purposes of augmented reality is the visual aid to support departments and customers. Many firms have explored the use of augmented reality to bridge the gap between working with customers remotely.

As an example, the global medical technology firm Becton Dickinson required an augmented reality software to aid the field engineers and medical firms that rely on their products. Becton Dickinson uses the software Help Lightning, which allows them to give remote assistance and support through an application on a tablet that shows data and visual content about their machines (York 2020). Moreover, the laboratory technician can see the hands of the experts while being guided through the process of inspection, maintenance or repair. Augmented reality enhances interaction and the visualisation of ideas, which allows for increased creativity. It shows great potential in adding value for external activities, such as customer support and marketing, as well as internal business activities like design, cooperation and efficiency (van Lopik et al. 2020). This technology not only benefits creative industries, such as arts, music, architecture or design, but can also be creatively utilised in any industry in various forms.

Additionally, AR is a creative learning method that is very effective for training employees. Training with integrated AR technologies is more immersive and interactive, which can make employees more effective and time-efficient (Hamdouna 2018). It allows trainees to use their imagination and give their input through digital content, which boosts overall creativity and collaboration. These benefits are further reinforced by the ability to simplify difficult processes and instructions. A potential risk is a reliance on such technologies in important processes, such as customer support. If the software does not work or is not understood by both parties, it can lose its value and may require personnel support. However, technological advancement in the future will provide many opportunities for AR technology, as it could be integrated into many different daily usages both commercially and privately. In a matter of years, this tool has grown from its early adoption stage to standardisation in various industries and will continue to have a great impact on creative processes.

2.6 Internet of Things

According to Ernst and Young Americas (2018), the introduction of connected technologies over the last decade has changed our lives. Across all manner of physical objects, sensors are being embedded that can track and share information, self-optimise and learn how to better perform—with or without human intervention, creating a truly connected world of the IoT (EY Americas 2018). The IoT not only impacts many aspects of daily life but also leads to new opportunities for businesses. This means that new needs and types of consumers will continue to emerge, and new innovations and ideas will emerge to meet those needs. Businesses that can fully adopt the IoT will be able to improve their bottom line by growing their overall productivity, lowering operating costs or entering new markets (Phaneuf 2020). The IoT allows for greater connectivity and the collection of data but will also have a significant effect on creative processes.

To explore the relationship between the IoT and creativity, the different purposes of using such technologies in creative processes should be considered. Additionally, the importance of combining data and creativity in today's digitalised society is emphasised. The creative use of collected data on customer behaviour and preferences will determine the success of new innovations and business models. For instance, in a marketing context, the IoT will have a significant impact on creativity in designing advertising campaigns. Marketers will be able to grasp every need of every individual customer that will share his or her preferences and information via IoT devices (Hu 2015). An example of this can be the use of programmatic ads that could be highly personalised and published in a timely manner. The IoT means that any object can be connected to the Internet and retrieve data. Like AI, this will allow for revolutionised ways of gaining customer insights and offering creative marketing content that is personalised to every individual's needs. However, the technology could be integrated into much simpler objects, such as an electric toothbrush. The connected toothbrush can collect data on usage patterns and ultimately make suggestions or offerings to the customers, such as changing the brush or scheduling a dentist appointment. Rather than simply pushing advertisements, the IoT can work as a tool to accordingly time the offering to add value to the right moments when customers need it. The timing of such moments will play a significant role in customer satisfaction.

No matter what role technology plays, it still comes down to the creative abilities of marketing departments and idea development. The effective and holistic adoption of the IoT in management is perhaps the greatest barrier to overcome. Many firms still struggle to apply such technologies, as well as to reshape their business model to become more meaningful and sustainable. To effectively connect both data and creativity, businesses must maintain a more holistic approach. This means that creative departments should be able to make use of such technologies and have access to data, whereas departments working with data should be empowered to think creatively (Balis 2018). Namely, data provides business with insights into customers to anticipate their needs, which can reduce clutter and refine advertising. Creative processes working with the IoT should be encouraged across all platforms and will become more machine-driven in order to generate ideas based on content from acquired data. Moreover, the IoT draws a blueprint that every device in our lives will eventually be connected to the Internet and function as a sensor for data collection, which is reinventing creativity with billions of IoT devices around the world.

2.7 Supporting Creativity Through Digital Technologies

The digital age appears to challenge much of the existing work on the nature of creativity. Digital technology and related ICT can be seen as a set of tools to be used when appropriate in the creative process. Information and Communications Technologies provide new tools, media and environments for entrepreneurs and employees to be creative. Through ICT, imagination, expression, autonomy and collaboration can be heavily reinforced. Information and Communications Technologies, when fully taken advantage of, can give purpose and foster originality.

Table 2 Distinguished features of digital technologies, including artificial intelligence, virtual reality and the Internet of things, used to support creativity

Feature	Characteristics
Automatic functions	Selecting a variety of ideas or pre-screening processes
Capacity and range	Spacing the ways in which it affords access to vast amounts of information locally and globally in different time zones and geographical places
Evolvement	Greater processing capacities, leading to dramatic price-performance improvements and lower costs
Flexibility	Easiness to use or reconfigure the data
Interactivity	Involving users at a number of levels, from the playing of a game, which gives feedback on decisions made, to the monitoring of a space probe through immediate and dynamic feedback is provided
Provisionality	Enabling users to make changes, try alternatives and keep a 'trace' of the development of ideas
Speed	Allowing tasks of storing, transforming and displaying information to be carried out by the technologies, enabling users to read, observe, interrogate, interpret, analyse and synthesise information at higher levels
Unpredictability/generativity	Provoking changes in technologies' overall capacity, which are driven by large audiences that can disrupt industries

Information and Communications Technologies offer new opportunities to be creative in novel contexts and in ways that were previously inaccessible without the recent developments in technology. Admittedly, the term digital technologies is broader than ICT. Digital technologies exhibit numerous features that enable users to do things that could not be done as effectively, or at all, using other tools, and digital technologies provide features that can be further exploited by users to make a distinctive contribution to entrepreneurial activities (see Table 2).

Digital technologies exhibit numerous features, as presented in Table 2, which enable entrepreneurs, employees and users to do things that could not previously be done as effectively, or at all, using other less sophisticated tools.

Next, we will elaborate on a variety of ways in which digital technology can enhance innovation by facilitating the conditions necessary for the development of employees' creative ideas and the implementation of these ideas in organisations. We begin by arguing that three conditions are necessary for employees to generate creative ideas (1) access and exposure to new and diverse information, (2) full engagement in the work role and (3) the experience of socioemotional or instrumental support. We posit that the implementation of employees' creative ideas requires the mobilisation of support and sponsorship of the ideas from credible allies. As such, we discuss the possibility that digital technology shapes the degree of creativity of ideas generated by employees and the implementation of these ideas by influencing each of these conditions. Digital technologies with the above-described features have also been used to support the early stages of imaginative play, speculation and 'brainstorming', which all together help to unleash the creativity of entrepreneurs and their teams.

There is a great deal of evidence that suggests that technology enhances creativity (Kapoor 2019). Research has shown empirically how the Internet environment and the advent of new digital technology have altered the cognitive behaviours and structures involved in information processing, executive control and reward-processing (Bruno and Canina 2019a, b). Individual creativity and group creativity are both important to sustaining an innovative environment. The latter has been affected in many positive ways by the rise of digital platforms and the tools for better communication. Moreover, digitalisation has influenced idea creation and implementation in many ways. The digitalisation of information exchange and communication techniques have had a great impact on the exchange of ideas and decision-making processes. These technological developments have improved group work efficiency and communication, which can be beneficial to the successful realisation of new business ideas. Since creativity is at the heart of an organisation's innovative capabilities and its ability to grow, its importance must always be considered. Often, employers and employees may feel pressure to achieve their financial targets and goals within a given timeframe, which makes it difficult to prioritise creativity daily. Managers must offer teams sufficient time and space to let their creativity be involved in their daily work and problem solving (Brodherson et al. 2017). An organisation should also be open to allow technology to drive its business processes and foster a company culture. It is important for individuals of an innovative firm to be flexible and ready to adapt to continuous forms of change. Technological innovation occurs more often than breakthrough innovation and can be continuous. Firms should offer training to employees as soon as new technologies are integrated into the business processes. Furthermore, employees could also suggest the use of new technologies at the firm when possible. New applications and other forms of communicative platforms continue to change and improve, some being more beneficial than others.

Management should be open to creative ideas from their employees on new digitalisation opportunities. As mentioned above, new technologies may improve communication in terms of efficiency and allow peers to give their creative input. The encouragement of creativity can also be applied through the use of stimulating environments or practices. For example, inspiration for new ideas can be fostered through activities that do not directly relate to daily tasks. Innovations and ideas tend to originate through the creation of environments in which ideas of individuals are able to connect and feed each other. This may give rise to different perspectives and insights on the problem. Firms that are able to form a team with different perspectives allow these individuals to challenge and support one another. Such an environment can directly quicken the process of innovation and may be a very important factor in today's world of constant change. This can be achieved by allowing individuals to experiment and to step out of their comfort zones (EY Global 2018). Another way in which digitalisation within companies is encouraged is the pressure from competitors. Many industries have been disrupted by the introduction of digitalised and innovative business ideas. One example is the success of Uber, which has disrupted many taxi industries worldwide. The market is now being redefined, largely as a result of technological factors. Uber has also given rise to many similar ride-sharing services, such as Lyft. These services connect drivers and customers through an online platform and mobile application, which is very different from traditional taxi services (Cramer and Krueger 2016).

In conclusion, we would like to discuss some possible risks of digital technology use. Artificial intelligence, among others, brings great risks to our way of living once it is fully developed, as there is a fear of being replaced by intelligent machines (Frey and Osborne 2017). Many argue that continuous innovation and the integration of technologies could mean that we will one day be replaced by intelligent machines. Sharing creativity and posting is not always positively received. It can be argued that digital technology creates higher levels of distraction. For example, SNS users often create posts for short-term amusement, causing alarm or eliciting controversy. Moreover, SNS memes go viral and are shared across huge networks. These memes and jokes are expressive, but they are forgotten as quickly as they are generated (Gardner and Weinstein 2018). The remixing and rapid dissemination of these personal works in NDM have diminished the importance of traditional notions of appropriateness and authorship of media (Gardner and Weinstein 2018). More seriously, designers of technology, executives and researchers have all recently expressed their concern about the implications of an attention-based economy being the basis for business models focused on digital tools. The goal of maximising users' time online can result in the malicious hijacking of the mind, via the monetisation of thoughts, emotions and actions with potentially serious consequences for mental health, relationships and democracy.

Digital technologies can and do exploit human vulnerability and reduce autonomy through addiction by design, which might have significant implications for the creativity of entrepreneurs and their teams. Hence, the digital realm offers new arenas and opportunities for group engagement, from which creativity can emerge, but also new dilemmas about the value and purpose of creative work and how to distribute it respectfully.

2.8   Digital Creativity Model

Given the many definitions of creativity, it is difficult to imagine that an accepted definition of digital creativity will emerge, and it is even more difficult for digital creativity to emerge in entrepreneurship, particularly since terms have different descriptions and meanings across disciplines.

One model of digital creativity is proposed in Fig. 1, showing the key dimensions (participating, making, compose, code, edit, curate, perform, author and producer) and their relationships with each other.

The first line of the model, the activity which has the aspects of participating or making, indicates that there are different levels of intensity of engagement at different periods of time. An entrepreneur will typically be leading (making) the creative activity but will also be involved in creative digital activities initiated by

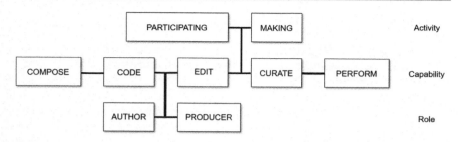

Fig. 1 Digital creativity model. *Source* Sefton-Green (2018)

members of his or her team and other employees throughout the organisation (participating). The more the entrepreneur can create an environment in his or her organisation that provides the atmosphere for more and more creativity to occur, the more the results will be creative projects that he or she can be involved in through participation.

The second line of the model, capability, involves various roles, such as compose, code, edit, curate and perform. Typically, this indicates that often, entrepreneurial digital creativity involves a complex team with different job specifications. While some creative activities in an entrepreneurial environment will not require all five roles to be present when developing a new product or service, each role is needed. Some individual(s) in the entrepreneurial organisation must generate a new idea or a new way of doing things (compose), develop the idea into something actionable (code), refine the idea through test marketing and evaluations at various stages of the product development process (edit), accumulate the various parts, equipment and procedures to make the idea into a marketable product or service (curate), and then ensure the customer is satisfied with the results (perform).

The third line of the model is the entrepreneurship role that involves the position of the entrepreneur and creates the team. Is the role more of being the creator of the idea (author) or being able to develop and market the new idea for a product or service (role). It will be interesting to view the models that develop as a result of the use of digital technologies in areas of marketing, such as consumer purchasing process, product planning and development, pricing, distribution systems and promotion.

It is important to realise that all three components of this model are interdependent and must be balanced in order for the potential of digital creativity to be unlocked. The level of engagement must match the capabilities of entrepreneurs and their teams, who in turn, must take on a role that can effectively convert the first two components into creative output. This will ensure that the resources used to attain said output are appropriate and that such resources are available and not wasted. If an entrepreneur, for example, were to not put themselves in the right role and then create an environment that is poorly chosen for creativity maximisation, no team, no matter how well-chosen and complex, will be able to provide the entrepreneur with the creative output they desire.

3   Examples from Practice/Case Studies

3.1   Brandmark: Developing a Logo and Brand Using Artificial Intelligence Software with Brandmark

Brandmark.io is a smart logo-generating tool based on AI technology. It is a tool that shows the technical possibilities of AI and its impact on creative processes. This case illustrates how the design of visual elements can be creatively developed with the use of digital technologies. The firm was founded in Vancouver, Canada, by electrical systems engineer and web developer Jack Qiao, who has developed a series of AI-powered design tools (Loper 2018).

The Brandmark website offers various AI tools for making a creative logo. One AI-powered tool on the Brandmark web application is called the AI Colour Wheel. The AI Colour Wheel automatically colourises logos, illustrations, wireframes and other graphic art (Brandmark 2020). Brandmark uses deep learning tools to generate logos composed of an icon, typography, colour scheme and specifications made by the user. The specific technologies used are ConvNets, word embeddings and GAN. The technology uses machine learning to generate logo idea presets that consider the specification and preferences made by the user. Brandmark's neural net approach can group highly similar icons, and its derived legibility score and uniqueness score are able to find legible and less-common shapes. Another system driven by AI is the logo rank tool. It is programmed on over one million images to give the user tips, inspiration and ideas. In addition, it can be used to check if your designer took inspiration from stock icons. The third AI tool is called the logo crunch tool, which uses computer vision to make high-resolution logos legible at lower resolutions. This tool is useful in making icons and logos that work on both high and low resolutions and different scales. Overall, it makes the process of creating separate logos for each size much easier than other online-based logo generators, since these mostly use the naïve scaling method. The font generator is another smart tool offered on the Brandmark website. It produces unique font pairings from Google fonts. All of these smart AI tools significantly simplify the logo creation process and deliver high visual quality.

The use of quality and original visuals is very important in brand development. Uniqueness and legibility are crucial elements of logos to be brandable. They should stand out and be recognisable. Small business owners looking to re-brand are the main target audience for Brandmark. It is a cost-effective way to create visuals for a new brand since it does not require human labour. However, the premium 'Enterprise' bundle gives the buyer up to 10 original concepts created by Brandmark's in-house design team. Moreover, the AI logo design process is very time-efficient, as it produces professional design ideas in a matter of minutes. This process only requires three simple steps in which certain preferences, such as keywords, business name and tagline, and colour styles, are taken into consideration. Then, the given presets can be further edited to the user's preferences, such as the logo, font and colour. The logo-making process is free, and payment is only required when the user wishes to download it.

Despite Brandmark being one of the most capable and innovative logo-makers available to date, it still maintains its limitations and risks. The effect of AI technologies on an individual's creativity is still subject to further research. Technologies, such as Brandmark, use smart AI tools to make the design process easier and faster. However, the level of creativity remains subjective. It comes down to human judgement, which is currently still beyond the capabilities of AI technology (Ghoshal 2017). Nevertheless, AI can help to pick and gather many different ideas that can lead to creative innovations. It can help to ingest, store and access unprecedented numbers of ideas to aid human creativity and input (Uzzi 2019). Another benefit of AI is that it is not prone to certain biases and gathers ideas in systematic ways. Artificial intelligence technologies have been proven to be effective tools for thinking outside the box and collect ideas based on algorithms in ways that human minds are not able to. Therefore, AI technologies, such as Brandmark, have the potential to assist human creativity and contribute to breakthrough ideas and innovations. Many people would suggest that logos created on the Brandmark website or similar services are too generic. Its biggest constraint is the ability to find logo ideas and icons that are not commonly used. It raises the question of whether AI technology is yet capable of replacing the creative input of humans, or whether it is a possibility in the near future. For now, Brandmark functions as a helpful tool to create design ideas.

3.2 HOK: Empowering Creativity Through the Powerful Use of Virtual Reality as a Creative Tool for Architects and Designers

Founded in 1955, HOK is a global design, architecture, engineering and planning firm. Across the USA, EMEA and APAC, the 1800 employees of HOK, based in 24 different offices worldwide, use design to help clients succeed and create places that enrich people's lives (HOK 2020). HOK has won multiple awards, including NCSEA Awards Firms for Structural Engineering Excellence 2019 Category 6 (Long 2019) and CRE Awards 2019: Best Tenant Improvement Project (Los Angeles Business Journal, 2019 and Fast Company's Most Innovative Companies list in 2019). HOK has some famous projects under its belt, including the LaGuardia Airport New Terminal B in New York, Mercedes-Benz Stadium in Atlanta, Georgia and the King Abdullah University of Science and Technology in Thuwal, Saudi Arabia, that all stood out for their creativity.

Virtual reality is used at HOK in many different ways to improve clients' understanding, interaction and relations, but also to make more detailed and enhanced prototypes (Howarth 2018). As an architecture firm, the relationship between the client and project leaders is very important. It can be difficult for architects to help clients understand technical plans since clients do not always have the same knowledge and visual imagination that architects and engineers have

(Howarth 2018). Virtual reality also creates new opportunities for client feedback in the design process. Below, we have listed ways that VR is leveraged as a creative resource at firms like HOK.

First, VR enables architects and engineers to articulate concepts to their clients through a more experiential medium. Using advanced technology, architects can help clients better understand complex architectural plans, sections and design concepts.

Second, architects receive better feedback from clients when the client can visualise design concepts. Virtual reality encourages participation in the creative process, allowing the client to share more accurate and candid feedback with the architects.

Third, visualisation tools can contribute to an architect's creativity, as they are able to explore the space they have designed. Furthermore, VR can allow the architect to better spot possible errors or flaws in their designs.

As VR technology evolves, it plays an increasingly important role in the design process. HOK has even developed its own VR app, available to anyone in the industry or general public for free, which aims to better facilitate leveraging the technology for the design process. The app allows for increased collaboration, as multiple clients can view spaces simultaneously and provide real-time feedback. From allowing architects to create more detailed fvisualisations involving clients in the creative process, the technology can impact project outcomes, verify adjacencies and desired workflows within spaces and benefit client relationships.

The above case has been prepared in cooperation with HOK. We would like to thank Annie Merrill and the team for their useful insights.

3.3   Scandit: Offering Computer Vision for the Modern Enterprise by the Internet of Things

Established in 2009, Scandit is a Swiss company that develops software for mobile enterprise apps with high-quality barcode scanning, text and object recognition as well as augmented reality solutions (Scandit 2020). Serving customers and partners across the USA, EMEA and APAC, Scandit provides billions of scans per year, making it a trusted market leader (Scandit 2020). With a vision to bring the IoT to everyday objects, the company wants to converge the physical and digital worlds by creating machines that can identify everyday objects that are not connected to the Internet. At Scandit, the 200+ employees produce an estimated 32 million USD in revenue (Owler 2020), covering organisations present in over 80 countries (Science Business 2013).

Scandit is using the IoT to connect objects through smart device technology. The company has developed data capture software, which turns smart devices equipped with a camera into universal sensors. These sensors can identify barcodes, creating opportunities for companies and consumers who can, in turn, improve their productivity and drastically improve their quality of life (Scandit 2019). The technology of Scandit enables companies and consumers to get creative by connecting the physical world to real-time data through smartphones, tablets, drones and robots. It has been applied in industries like health care, manufacturing, retail, and transportation and logistics (Butcher 2017; Sawers 2018; Scandit 2019; Science Business 2013).

In terms of creative solutions, Scandit provides many opportunities for retail stores on how to upgrade their retail processes. In the past, before Scandit's solutions were offered, retail stores used various devices to scan barcodes that were unnecessary and costly being a bottleneck for the supply chain from warehouses to consumers. Due to the economies of scale, personal smart devices have faster innovation and better performance. First, these personal smart devices can be used instead of the barcode scanning devices. It allows the consumer to explore, buy and re-order products anywhere and at any time. Second, it allows the consumer to receive more in-store product information, have a virtual shopping bag and then pay with a click option. Finally, it will allow the consumer to receive personalised discounts.

The software offered by Scandit supports the work of in-store employees, as it allows them to scan barcodes as well as IDs without the need for limited and expensive hardware. Furthermore, it allows the employees to show stock, delivery dates and price verification with a short scan, thereby drastically reducing human error. In the warehouse, it assists employees in receiving detailed inventory management, shipping and receiving dates and the ability to verify stock in a matter of seconds (Scandit 2019).

For Scandit, the IoT software creates new opportunities and creativity, and four of these opportunities are mentioned below. First, through the IoT software, Scandit and its clients, like Coop, Switzerland's largest wholesale company with more than 2300 sales outlets in Switzerland (Coop 2020), can monitor the buying behaviour of consumers. This data can be useful for companies and create new opportunities. For instance, Scandit could monitor the buying behaviour of consumers and create personal discounts. Such data can be further used for designing creative marketing campaigns. These discounts will increase consumer satisfaction and most likely lead to higher client loyalty, thereby increasing sales. Seasonal discounts and combinational discounts could attract consumers to buy more products. Combinational discounts could, for example, allow the consumer to buy a meal that is on sale, instead of just one product. Furthermore, the IoT software could use the data from consumers to make their life easier while highlighting the creative side of the company. When a consumer scans a product, the software could produce many recipes that contain that product. This would allow the consumer to pick recipes within seconds that consist of products at that store. Second, the IoT software could allow the consumer to buy the product it needs for certain diets. For example, when a consumer has a specific medical diet restriction, the IoT could create a pop-up when that product is scanned. This is applicable for medical restrictions or allergies but also for food plans. If a consumer would prefer to live a healthy life, only eat vegan meals or prefer biological products, the IoT would supply the consumer with a creative list of meals and available products to order, either online or at the store. In addition, the IoT software could even know what the consumer has in the fridge and supply a list of meals that contain those products, thereby fighting food waste and providing an enriching shopping experience. Third, for stores, the IoT software would drastically increase efficiency. If the IoT is used for inventory management, many new opportunities will arise. For example, through marketing and advertising, the store managers could guide the sale of certain products. This could be useful when certain stock is piling up in the warehouses or when stock is approaching its expiration date. In addition, since it can closely monitor the sales per product, it could improve just-in-time (JIT) management. The IoT software provided by Scandit collects a large amount of data, which, in turn, can forecast the sales of products, making it undoubtedly supportive in managing the demand for the product. Fourth, the IoT would allow a store to easily follow a certain strategy. Today, an increasing number of stores are prioritising their strategy of being cheap, fair-trade or biological. With the IoT software from Scandit, stores are able to filter products from their suppliers based on those characteristics, allowing them to select the desired product instead of searching them manually.

The IoT has an enormous impact on companies and their creative processes, not only in terms of retail and supply chain but also in its ability to be used for other purposes. Concerning Scandit, the opportunities spurned from its IoT barcode software are endless. Scandit has proven that the IoT can be used to boost creativity processes, which ultimately help grow and optimise company processes and relationships with customers.

4   Conclusion and Implications

This chapter explores the use of digital technologies by entrepreneurs to support their own as well as that of their teams and other members of their company. Creativity is the ability of an individual or small group of individuals to generate novel, useful ideas and take advantage of new opportunities offered by digital technologies. While there is no doubt about the importance and need for creativity in entrepreneurs and their organisations, the role of digital technologies such as artificial intelligence, virtual reality and the Internet of things in this process is just starting to take shape. The digital technologies being used to date in areas, such as brainstorming, imaginative play, innovation and visual learning exhibit features of provisionality, interactivity, capacity, range, speed and automatic functions. Entrepreneurs, no matter the size and industry of their company, must be open to creative ideas resulting from digitalisation opportunities. While there are risks involved, digital technologies offer new arenas and opportunities for creativity along with new dilemmas concerning the value and purpose of creativity and how the results should be distributed.

As with the beginning of any new era and in the realm of creativity, the era of digital technologies used by entrepreneurs offers many new research activities. The present chapter described the ways digital technologies can impact creativity in an entrepreneurial company, regardless of its size and industry. The case studies present the output of this in practice. This chapter provides the foundation for not only the use of digital technologies but also specific examples of its use and results. By focusing on the role of specific digital technologies (artificial intelligence, virtual reality and the Internet of things), the chapter furthers the understanding of the impact of digital technologies on entrepreneurship in general and specifically on the creativity required for the successful start, operation and growth of a new venture. This chapter discusses and illustrates the importance of creativity in digital business as a result of the numerous changes occurring at an increasing rate. Digital businesses will find it difficult to not only compete for sales but also for talented employees. Future research must further refine its use by entrepreneurs, examine various uses across size and industry of the entrepreneurs and their organisations, and develop specific models, rather than the general model proposed in this research, in areas such as the customer purchasing process, innovation, distribution systems and channels, and various promotion activities. Indeed, future research in the area of digital technologies unleashing the creativity of entrepreneurs is promising.

We are all moving towards digital enhancement, and companies should be able to train with, collaborate and interact with digital technologies to generate novel and useful ideas. As the world of digital technologies and human creativity continues expanding, it is time to stop worrying about whether digital technologies can foster creativity and focus on how the human and machine worlds can intersect for creative collaborations that have never been dreamt of. Rather than worry about the rise of AI, VR and the IoT, businesses should embrace the opportunity technology is bringing to unleash a new wave of human creativity and power human enterprise. Such technologies can free up time spent on innovating, provide new combinations of technologies to enable better ways of working and help guide us on the path towards even more effective creative ideas to be implemented in various stages of business. It is therefore fundamental to entrepreneurs and their teams to understand what is happening in the field of creativity, as it is tremendously impacted by digitisation.

Acknowledgements We acknowledge, with much appreciation, the many constructive insights of Daniel Steggerda, Thom van der Meer, Vincent Jochum, the International Business School students at the Hanze University of Applied Sciences.
Daniel, thank you for your great input, commitment and passion, which have altogether increased the quality of this work. We wish you all the best in your future, and we are looking forward to seeing your creativity supported by digital technologies in action.
Thom, thank you for your valuable input throughout this chapter, providing content and literature with great insight and commitment. With relevant research and writing, your input has been valuable in guiding the direction of the project and finalising this chapter. We wish you all the best and hope to see you utilise your knowledge on entrepreneurship and digital creativity in the future. Vincent, thank you for your contributions to finalise the chapter. Thank you for your useful insights in artificial intelligence and input throughout the chapter. We hope to see you put your entrepreneurial mindset to great use, and we wish you the best in your future.

References

Adobe. (2016). *State of create: 2016.* https://www.adobe.com/content/dam/acom/en/max/pdfs/AdobeStateofCreate_2016_Report_Final.pdf.

Alahuhta, P., Nordbäck, E., Sivunen, A., & Surakka, T. (2014). Fostering team creativity in virtual worlds. *Journal for Virtual Worlds Research, 7*(3).

Amabile, T., & Khaire, M. (2008). *Creativity and the role of the leader.* https://hbr.org/2008/10/creativity-and-the-role-of-the-leader.

Austin, R. (2016). *Unleashing creativity with digital technology.* https://sloanreview.mit.edu/article/unleashing-creativity-with-digital-technology/.

Balis, J. (2018). *Why tomorrow's media must combine creativity and data.* https://www.ey.com/en_gl/digital/why-tomorrow_s-media-must-combine-creativity-and-data.

Bhagwatwar, A., Massey, A. & Dennis, A. R. (2013). Creative virtual environments: Effect of supraliminal priming on team brainstorming. In *2013 46th Hawaii international conference on system sciences* (pp. 215–224). IEEE.

Bianzino, N. (2020). *Is AI the start of the truly creative human?* https://www.ey.com/en_eg/ai/is-ai-the-start-of-the-truly-creative-human.

Brandmark. (2020). *AI Color Wheel.* https://brandmark.io/color-wheel/.

Brodherson, M., Heller, J., Perrey, J. & Remley, D. (2017). *Creativity's bottom line: How winning companies turn creativity into business value and growth.* https://www.mckinsey.com/business-functions/mckinsey-digital/our-insights/creativitys-bottom-line-how-winning-companies-turn-creativity-into-business-value-and-growth.

British Council. (2020). *Defining Creativity: Literature review part 1.* https://www.britishcouncil.org/programmes/creative-play/defining-creativity-literature-review-part-1.

Butcher, M. (2017). *Scandit, which replaces barcode scanners with phones, closes $7.5 M from Atomico.* https://techcrunch.com/2017/01/10/scandit-which-replaces-barcode-scanners-with-phones-closes-7-5m-from-atomico/.

Bruno, C., & Canina, M. (2019). Creativity 4.0. Empowering creative process for digitally enhanced people. *The Design Journal, 22*(sup1), 2119–2131.

Bruno, C., & Canina, M. (2019). Creativity 4.0. Empowering creativity in the digital era. In *DS 95: Proceedings of the 21st International Conference on Engineering and Product Design Education (E&PDE 2019), University of Strathclyde, Glasgow*, September 12–13, 2019.

Cardwell, J. (2020). Luckin coffee sets the table for continued growth. *Nasdaq.* https://www.nasdaq.com/articles/luckin-coffee-sets-the-table-for-continued-growth-2020-01-19.

Chamorro-Premuzic, T. (2015). Is technology making us more creative? *The Guardian.* https://www.theguardian.com/media-network/2015/jun/18/technology-creative-creativity-web-content.

Chen, H., Wang, R., & Liang, X. (2019). Americanized or localized: a qualitative study on Chinese advertising practitioners' perceptions of creativity and strategy in the digital age. *Global Media and China, 4*(2), 233–253.

Columbus, L. (2018). *2018 roundup of Internet of things forecasts and market estimates.* https://www.forbes.com/sites/louiscolumbus/2018/12/13/2018-roundup-of-internet-of-things-forecasts-and-market-estimates/#3dcf3a0f7d83.

Copeland, B. J. (2020). *Artificial intelligence.* https://www.britannica.com/technology/artificial-intelligence/Reasoning.

Coop. (2020). *Who we are.* https://www.coop.ch/en/company/about-us/who-we-are/retail.html.

Cramer, J., & Krueger, A. B. (2016). Disruptive change in the taxi business: The case of Uber. *American Economic Review, 106*(5), 177–182.

Deloitte. (2018). *Technology in the mid-market: Embracing disruption.* https://www2.deloitte.com/content/dam/Deloitte/us/Documents/deloitte-private/us-private-tech-report-2018.pdf.

Dust, K. (1999). Culture, value and personality: Three flowering agents of creativity development process. *American Journal of Applied Psychology.* 2017, *5*(1), 1–6.

Elia, G., Margherita, A., & Passiante, G. (2020). Digital entrepreneurship ecosystem: How digital technologies and collective intelligence are reshaping the entrepreneurial process. *Technological Forecasting and Social Change, 150,* 119791.

Ernst and Young Americas. (2018). *How creativity can help the C-suite seize IoT opportunities.* https://www.ey.com/en_us/digital/how-creativity-can-help-the-c-suite-seize-iot-opportunities.

Fade, L. (2020). Council post: How virtual reality is impacting enterprise training. *Forbes.* https://www.forbes.com/sites/theyec/2020/03/10/how-virtual-reality-is-impacting-enterprise-training/#13a1c453704b.

Farshid, M., Paschen, J., Eriksson, T., & Kietzmann, J. (2018). Go boldly!: Explore augmented reality (AR), virtual reality (VR), and mixed reality (MR) for business. *Business Horizons, 61* (5), 657–663.

Fatemi, F. (2018). *How AI will augment human creativity.* https://www.forbes.com/sites/falonfatemi/2018/08/17/how-ai-will-augment-human-creativity/#48a6d66711b4.

Frey, C. B., & Osborne, M. A. (2017). The future of employment: How susceptible are jobs to computerisation? *Technological Forecasting and Social Change, 114,* 254–280. https://doi.org/10.1016/j.techfore.2016.08.019.

Gabora, L. (2013). Psychology of Creativity. In E. G. Carayannis (Ed.), *Encyclopedia of creativity, invention, innovation, and entrepreneurship* (pp. 1515–1520).

Gardner, H., & Weinstein, E. (2018). Creativity: The view from Big C and the introduction of tiny c. In R. Sternberg, J. Kaufman (Eds.), *The nature of human creativity* (pp. 94–109). New York, NY: Cambridge University Press.

Ghoshal, A. (2017). *This AI-powered logo design service shows how much we need human designers.* https://thenextweb.com/artificial-intelligence/2017/08/08/this-ai-powered-logo-design-service-shows-how-much-we-need-human-designers/.

Globenewswire. (2020). *Global VR market is expected to reach usd 56.25 billion by 2025: Fior markets.* https://www.globenewswire.com/news-release/2020/02/25/1989760/0/en/Global-VR-Market-is-Expected-to-Reach-USD-56-25-Billion-by-2025-Fior-Markets.html.

Gilson, L. L., & Litchfield, R. C. (2017). Idea collections: A link between creativity and innovation. *Innovation, 19*(1), 80–85.

Goasduff, L. (2019). *Top trends on the Gartner Hype cycle for artificial intelligence.* https://www.gartner.com/smarterwithgartner/top-trends-on-the-gartner-hype-cycle-for-artificial-intelligence-2019/.

Graessler, I., Taplick, P., & Pottebaum, J. (2017). Enhancing innovation processes by disruptive technologies. *SCIFI-IT, 2017,* 19–26.

Graessler, I., & Taplick, P. (2018). Virtual reality unterstützte Kreativitätstechnik: Vergleich mit klassischen Techniken. *Krause, D., Paetzold, K. and Wartzack, S. (Hrsg.) Design for X - Beiträge zum 29.* DfX-Symposium, S. 215–226.

Hamdouna, M. (2018). *Augmented reality in businesses: What will the future look like?* https://www.entrepreneur.com/article/324411.

Haynes, S. (2019). *This robot artist just became the first to stage a solo exhibition. What does that say about creativity?* https://time.com/5607191/robot-artist-ai-da-artificial-intelligence-creativity/.

HOK. (2020). *About.* https://www.hok.com/about/.

Howarth, D. (2018). *Architectural renderings are "troublesome and problematic" says Es Devlin.* https://www.dezeen.com/2018/05/10/architectural-renderings-troublesome-problematic-es-devlin-interview/.

Hu, L. (2015). *Creativity in the Internet of things era.* https://www.provokemedia.com/agency-playbook/sponsored/article/creativity-in-the-internet-of-things-era.

Johnson, C. (2016). *How digital media has changed creativity.* https://www.deseret.com/2016/11/23/20600988/how-digital-media-has-changed-creativity#corrina-harrington-3-of-eau-claire-wis-plays-with-air-blowers-in-the-forces-at-play-exhibit-at-the-minnesota-childrens-museum-in-st-paul-minn-on-tuesday-nov-22-2016.

Kamel, J. A. N., Martins, C. V., Pessanha, M. B., & de Andrade, M. W. (2017). Creativity and innovation for corporate happiness management. *Brazilian Journal of Science and Technology, 4*(1), 1.

Kapoor, P. (2019). *How to boost employee creativity with technology, and why you should.* https://thriveglobal.com/stories/boosting-employee-creativity-with-technology/.

KPMG. (2018). *The changing landscape of disruptive technologies.* https://assets.kpmg/content/dam/kpmg/pl/pdf/2018/06/pl-The-Changing-Landscape-of-Disruptive-Technologies-2018.pdf.

Kuratko, D. F., & Morris, M. H. (2018). Corporate entrepreneurship: A critical challenge for educators and researchers. *Entrepreneurship Education and Pedagogy, 1*(1), 42–60.

Landry, L. (2017). *The importance of creativity in business.* https://www.northeastern.edu/graduate/blog/creativity-importance-in-business/.

Lau, K. W., & Lee, P. Y. (2012). The use of virtual reality for creating unusual environmental stimulation to motivate students to explore creative ideas. *Interactive Learning Environments, 23*(1), 3–18.

Leftronic. (2019) *Artificial intelligence statistics.* https://leftronic.com/artificial-intelligence-statistics/.

Liu, S. (2020). *Internet of things.* https://www.statista.com/topics/2637/internet-of-things/.

Long, D. (2019). *NCSEA awards firms for structural engineering excellence.* http://www.ncsea.com/downloads/files//2019%20Summit/Press%20Releases/2019%20NCSEA%20Awards%20Press%20Release.pdf.

Loper, N. (2018). *Brandmark.* https://www.virtualassistantassistant.com/brandmark.

Loveless, A. (2002). Literature review in creativity, new technologies and learning. https://telearn.archives-ouvertes.fr/hal-00190439.

Magalhães, R. (2019). *Come together: Using AI to enhance creativity.* https://unbabel.com/blog/artificial-intelligence-creativity/.

Marr, B. (2018). *The key definitions of artificial intelligence (AI) that explain its importance.* https://www.forbes.com/sites/bernardmarr/2018/02/14/the-key-definitions-of-artificial-intelligence-ai-that-explain-its-importance/#203124ae4f5d.

Marr, B. (2020). *Can machines and artificial intelligence be creative?* https://www.forbes.com/sites/bernardmarr/2020/02/28/can-machines-and-artificial-intelligence-be-creative/#48ab79374580.

Mehta, R., & Dahl, D. W. (2019). Creativity: Past, present, and future. *Consumer Psychology Review, 2*(1), 30–49.

Milenkovic, J. (2019). *Astounding artificial intelligence statistics for 2020.* https://kommandotech.com/statistics/artificial-intelligence-statistics/.

Owler. (2020). *Scandit's competitors, revenue, number of employees, funding and acquisitions.* https://www.owler.com/company/scandit.

Pedersen, J. S., Slavich, B., & Khaire, M. (2019). Technology and creativity: Production, mediation and evaluation in the digital age. *Technology and Creativity,* 1–11.

Petrov, C. (2019). *35 virtual reality statistics that will rock the market in 2020.* https://techjury.net/stats-about/virtual-reality/#gref.

Phaneuf, A. (2020). *Top IoT business opportunities, benefits, and uses in 2020.* https://www.businessinsider.com/iot-business-opportunities-models?international=true&r=US&IR=T.

Rao, A. & Verweij, G. (2017). *Sizing the price.* https://www.pwc.com/gx/en/issues/analytics/assets/pwc-ai-analysis-sizing-the-prize-report.pdf.

Said-Metwaly, S., Van den Noortgate, W., & Kyndt, E. (2017). *Approaches to measuring creativity: A systematic literature review.* https://content.sciendo.com/view/journals/ctra/4/2/article-p238.xml?lang=en.

Sawers, P. (2018). *GV leads $30 million investment in Scandit to bring AR and computer vision to mobile barcode scanning.* https://venturebeat.com/2018/07/26/gv-leads-30-million-investment-in-mobile-barcode-scanning-company-scandit/.

Scandit. (2019). *Understanding the Internet of things.* https://www.scandit.com/blog/understanding-the-internet-of-things/.

Scandit. (2020). *About Scandit.* https://www.scandit.com/company/.

Science Business. (2013). *Scandit develops highly optimized glass-based scanning experience for Google glass applications.* https://sciencebusiness.net/news/76367/Scandit-Develops-Highly-Optimized-Glass-Based-Scanning-Experience-for-Google-Glass-Applications.

Sefton-Green, J. (2018). *Is there such a thing as digital creativity?* https://clalliance.org/blog/is-there-such-a-thing-as-digital-creativity/.

Smith, C. S. (2020). *Computers already learn from us. But can they teach themselves?* https://www.nytimes.com/2020/04/08/technology/ai-computers-learning-supervised-unsupervised.html.

Soltanifar, M. (2016). Corporate entrepreneurship and triple helix. In *Multinational Management* (pp. 275–299). Springer, Cham.

Stamford, C. (2019). *Gartner survey shows 37 percent of organizations have implemented AI in some form.* https://www.gartner.com/en/newsroom/press-releases/2019-01-21-gartner-survey-shows-37-percent-of-organizations-have.

Uzzi, B. (2019). *When mind meets machine: How AI can boost your creativity.* https://www.forbes.com/sites/brianuzzi/2019/06/26/when-mind-meets-machine-how-ai-can-boost-your-creativity/#4ddbb40c7629.

van Lopik, K., Sinclair, M., Sharpe, R., Conway, P. & West, A. (2020). Developing augmented reality capabilities for industry 4.0 small enterprises: Lessons learnt from a content authoring case study. *Computers in Industry, 117,* 103208.

York, G. (2020). *Help lightning strikes success by using Vonage Video API.* https://www.vonage.com/resources/customers/help-lightening/.

Weber, J. (2019). *Fascinating facts about the Internet of things.* https://www.sagiss.com/small_business_technology_blog/2019-edition-20-fascinating-facts-about-the-internet-of-things.

Whyte, C. (2019). *AI created images of food just by reading the recipes.* https://www.newscientist.com/article/2190259-ai-created-images-of-food-just-by-reading-the-recipes/#ixzz6K6GK35So.

Digital Entrepreneurship and Agile Methods—A Hackathon Case Study

Nancy Richter and Djanina Dragoeva

Abstract

"What if, when they ask 'Alexa, where can I do something here tonight?', travellers no longer receive the answer 'I don't know'? And, could start-ups use all tourist data freely and without restriction to develop innovative applications for travellers at any time?" ("German National Tourist Board", n.d.). These and similar questions are currently being asked by those responsible for tourism marketing and product development, such as destination management organisations (DMO: "Public or public–private entity whose aim is to foster, plan and coordinate the tourism development of a destination as a whole".) ("IGI Global", n.d.) in Germany. In particular, the travel destination Thuringia sees itself as a pioneer on topics such as AI, decentralised data structures and new types of interactions: "We were looking for a way to make the data of Thuringian tourism up-to-date, findable and freely usable and thus provide the path for open innovation and new technologies." (Detlef Klinge, Thüringer Tourismus GmbH retrieved from "German National Tourist Board", n.d.). To meet these challenges, the DMO relies on the processing of open data in a tourist content architecture and on entrepreneurial management methods such as the hackathon. This method, in turn, must be embedded in a holistic management approach; otherwise, creative results will be lost even before they come to the market. The question is how these technologies and management methods must be implemented in DMOs so that they generate sustainable competitive advantages and customer benefits for the respective travel destination.

N. Richter (✉)
University of Applied Sciences, Schmalkalden, Germany
e-mail: n.richter@hs-sm.de

D. Dragoeva
Bauhaus University, Weimar, Germany

M. Soltanifar et al. (eds.), *Digital Entrepreneurship*, Future of Business and Finance,
https://doi.org/10.1007/978-3-030-53914-6_3

1   Introduction: The Development of the Tourism Market

The travel market is saturated and has long since developed into a buyer's market. Marketing has therefore played an important role for tourism providers since the mid-1970s. At the turn of the millennium, the Internet began to turn the travel industry upside down. Travel portals have influenced travel decisions since the late 1990s. Especially, the launch of lastminute.com in 1998 was one of the defining inventions of online travel. The company still sells last minute package deals at short notice which is a great advantage over traditional agents. This was followed by digital content platforms for the display of photos and videos, social networks, digital travel portals, geo-targeting, the virtualisation of reality (VR) and the expansion of reality (AR) ("Tourismuszukunft", n.d.). These developments have an impact not only on travel decisions, but also on travel arrangements during a trip. Digital technologies have changed the entire customer journey.[1] But the development does not stop there. Artificial intelligence (AI), decentralised data structures and the associated evolution of customer interaction will transform customer journeys even more extensively. These developments offer numerous opportunities. At the same time, these processes are extremely challenging for the industry. Representatives of the industry are already using digitalisation options, but complain about the lack of financial resources, the lack of know-how, the lack of quality of content from the individual companies and the lack of broadband when implementing digital instruments (Statista 2019).

The tourism industry is characterised by small-scale provider structures and a high level of complexity of tourism service packaging (Freyer 2015). Many individual organisations are involved in the creation of a single tourist product. Packages could combine for example transport, accommodations, meals, attractions and entertainment. With the latest digital developments, the provision of tourism service packages becomes more personalised and multichannel (Keller et al. 2017). Travellers receive a more active role and co-create their travel experience in real time using different channels. Given these developments, DMOs need to consider a strategic realignment. In order to support digital innovation, they need to become digital platforms to improve the travel experience for their guests. The chapter will present a case study on how DMOs in Germany currently deal with developments related to artificial intelligence and decentralised data structures. Further, it will be asked if an open data hackathon is a suitable approach to help ensure the competitiveness of tourist destinations. These questions will be answered by analysing a hackathon case study.

How are the current developments around artificial intelligence and decentralised data structures changing tourism?

---

[1]Customer Journey: Customer journey refers to the path followed by a customer via so-called touchpoints before making a purchase decision (Yachin 2018).

Artificial Intelligence and Linked Open Data Create Smart Destinations

Machine-readable data in the form of linked open data (LOD) and artificial intelligence (AI) as a generic term for different automated computing methods and machine learning (ML) are directly related. But what do these terms have in common and what do they have to do with tourism? With the help of ML, patterns can be recognised in data to derive predictions (Horster and Kärle 2019a). Data is processed based on computing models or algorithms. The more data is processed, the better the algorithm becomes. The algorithm develops independently after several rounds, therefore one speaks of AI. A machine is particularly good at interpreting data that is structured in a uniform language or ontology, e.g. schema. org. The structuring and the provision of a large amount of data, such as POI, events, hotels and personal preferences of the guests, and their connection through AI algorithms, enable interesting basic applications for tourism (Samochowiec et al. 2019).

In the future, a smart assistant will be able to use the data to answer individual inquiries from guests or to give tips and will be available at any time when travelling. Automated access at events, cashless payment in event parks, navigation on ski slopes or real-time information on the smart watch at the holiday location are also conceivable (Horster and Foltin 2020). To enable this scenario, however, destination management organisations have to become digital platforms to connect the offers of the destination with the guest and his or her preferred devices like smartphones, laptop computers, tablets or smart watches.

Knowledge Graphs depict Tourism Reality

People and machines can intuitively capture data that is represented in a knowledge graph or a graph database as a network structure (Paulheim 2016). A knowledge graph describes real entities such as a hotel and a review about it, as well as the relationships of these entities to each other (Horster and Kärle 2019b). The knowledge graph is semantic because the data is given meaning. This means that a smart assistant such as Alexa becomes better at understanding what specific information is meant when a traveller asks for it. In this way, a digital image of the touristic reality is created piece by piece. The knowledge graph can be filled infinitely with data and their relevant context and is able to gradually recognise relationships between these data automatically. This is a great advantage over previous relational databases, the entries of which can later be changed or supplemented only with great difficulty and where the data has little relationship to one another (Horster and Kärle 2019b). With the help of knowledge graphs, data can be transformed into information, which can then be transformed into knowledge and lead to actions by the guest (Stichbury 2017). Initially, only individual data is available, for example for a hotel or bike path. This data can be aggregated and assigned to addresses, opening hours or special offers, and then all these entities can be related to each other. Data relationships between a hotel and a bike path then help a guest to decide in real time where to stay at night, or if there is something special near his or her location. Knowledge graphs thus have a real-time influence on the specific guest behaviour during the customer journey.

The Evolution of the Web 3.0

With the developments described above, the World Wide Web is changing into a semantic Web or Web 3.0 (Kinlan 2016; Horster and Kärle 2019c). The future development, especially in tourism, is that travellers will receive answers and recommendations in real time, depending on the provider, interest and output device. To realise this, machines have to be able to interpret data. For users, it is becoming increasingly irrelevant where the data comes from and via which channel (Sommer 2018). The classic web design takes a back seat, and DMOs have to focus on the data architecture instead of on their websites ("semantify", n.d.). Large players such as Google or Facebook are currently driving these developments. The Google Knowledge Graph, which now provides answers to questions without listing websites at the top of the results of a Google search, makes this all too clear. If you enter terms in the Google search engine, you increasingly get an overview at the top of the search results page. Voice assistants are going in a similar direction, providing answers instead of links. In this way, large platforms build "walled gardens", a web on the web that the user no longer has to leave to receive information. The advantages for the user or traveller are obvious, but the tourist actors and DMOs are increasingly invisible as senders of messages, unless they store their details in the designated virtual locations and an appropriate data format, for example, Google My Business. Destinations could make company data and further information such as events and information on hiking trails available in the same way on the entire web, to break up the power of the walled gardens and to create a web or a data basis that is open to anyone. On the other hand, the use or labelling of data in formats like schema.org also helps to increase the visibility of a DMO on large platforms, as they and their information are displayed more prominently (Hauer 2020).

1.1   How Do Tourism Destinations in Germany deal with AI, Decentralised Data Structures and New Types of Interactions in the Web 3.0?

Tourism is one of the most "affected" sectors when it comes to digitisation. It appears that the industry has lost control of the data. The big players Google and Facebook, or travel platforms such as TripAdvisor, are striving for information monopolies or already have them. Travellers are using these and other channels to obtain information about their trips and are not very interested in where the information comes from. This is also supported by the falling number of visitor clicks on the destination websites. The data flow is establishing itself as increasingly more important than the data channel (Sommer 2018, p. 4). Another challenge for tourism is the purely technical one: "There is a fragmented picture of different data formats with very varying levels of detail and often severely restricted possibilities for data use. Harmonisation is difficult, but would make it much easier" (Sommer 2018, p. 5).

Organisationally, however, a decision has to be made regarding who will take care of this "data infrastructure" and how it will be managed. This is the biggest challenge. The goal is to create and provide valuable and readily available data (Sommer 2018, p. 5). The formula is clear: the higher the quality, the greater the value of the data is. However, the rapid pace of this change requires a rapid change in management that not every single tourist information office or every single company or service provider can solve on its own. A central content architecture, managed by a DMO, can help to exploit and bundle the possibilities of digitisation. A technical embedding and linking of the content are necessary so that the resources and content can be connected. Due to the decentralised content management that still prevails in many destinations, problems often appear, such as duplication of content in different content silos or duplication of tasks and responsibilities, as well as deviations in content structures between organisations in the respective destination. To avoid this, the interface between the fields of action must be ensured in order to achieve optimal effects (Dwif-Consulting 2017, p. 44). The DMOs of the federal states in Germany deal with these developments in very different ways. A federal state which deals intensively with content architectures is Thuringia. This example is described below.

1.2 Open Data and Digital Content Architectures as an Opportunity in Tourism: The Example of the Destination Management Organisation Thüringer Tourismus GmbH (TTG)

In Thuringia, the destination management organisation is currently developing a central content architecture for tourism (ThüCAT), which should was completed this year and has been available as a beta version since summer 2019. The goal is to create a database for all tourism-related content in Thuringia. This content should be made available to all the stakeholders in Thuringia including tourist regions, locations, service providers such as hotels and restaurants (Honig 2019). An important goal is that the information can not only be obtained via the website of the respective institution, but it also reaches the customer on all other channels. This means that ThüCAT information flows to the traveller at all points and in all phases of the customer journey ("Tourismusnetzwerk Thüringen", n.d.). This is a project that can only work by collaborating with all the organisations involved in the creation of touristic offers. Technically, this is realised via a graph database, which then enables the presence of the data on different channels, which in turn means that the tourist can be accompanied as mentioned on all the stages of his or her tour. The semantic labelling and structuring of the data are carried out according to schema. org models, in a format that is universally understandable and machine-readable, which is a basic requirement for processing data by applications that are based on AI. A "knowledge graph" links a wide variety of information such as contact dates, opening times and guided tours in such a way that the guest can get a comprehensive and, if possible, target group-specific or even personalised answer to any of his questions ("Tourismusnetzwerk Thüringen", n.d.).

Since ThüCAT is filled with content such as images, videos, articles, description texts, geodata, tours and prices that should be available to all players, all the data must be open and accessible. Open data refers to data that is characterised as follows: it may be used, distributed and modified by anyone for any purpose. The only restrictions are to safeguard the origin and openness of this knowledge, for example by naming the author (von Lucke and Geiger 2010, p. 2). The approach of providing open data not only leads to greater transparency and democratic use for society as a whole, but it can also increase the overall economic added value. The decisive factor for this increase is whether the data is used as a strategic core component for social action or not (Sommer 2018, p. 1).

In addition, open data can help transform companies from the inside out by incorporating the digital world and carrying out a so-called digital transformation (Carrara et al. 2015, p. 5). The issues of openness, maturity and value creation are closely linked to open data. The destination management organisation must also deal with these aspects as part of ThüCAT. Based on the data spectrum of the Open Data Institute (ODI),[2] the ThüCAT data is available on open licence, the highest level at which everyone can freely use and access them. Furthermore, the data should have the highest level of maturity (https://5stardata.info/en/), based on the maturity model by Tim Berners-Lee (2010). In relation to ThüCAT, this means that the data that flows into the system is required in a format that enables automated processing or optimally supports it. The semantic labelling of the data gives the content a future-proof structure that also makes it suitable for the requirements of AI such as voice assistants.

With regard to the added value, the tourism players are aware that it is only the diverse options for subsequent use that make open data work. The management of the data itself has no added value, but only enables the creation of added value for everyone else in the subsequent steps (Dapp et al. 2016, p. 25). The aim should therefore be to ensure that the data is reused using suitable management methods so that applications are created for different costumer segments. The implementation of hackathons to reuse the available data through the integration of external creators seems to make sense. Especially since the tourism stakeholders often lack the corresponding digital know-how, the resources for hiring programmers are scarce. Hackathons and other open innovation methods could thus possibly compensate for the lack of digital know-how in the tourism industry and develop attractive applications for visitors.

---

[2]The Open Data Institute (ODI) was founded in 2012 by the British government. With its help, open data usage should increase, and the institute should be a support in the development of new business models for start-ups. Web inventor Sir Tim Berners-Lee is in charge (Ksoll et al. 2017, p. 10).

2 Management Methods for Improving the Performance of Destination Management Organisations via the Hackathon

A Short Definition

A hackathon is an event in which programmers and others involved in software development work intensively in order to create something new in a short or limited time to contribute to the development of a product (Briscoe and Mulligan 2014, p. 2). The term "hackathon" is a combination of the two words "hack" and "marathon". Hack here means researching software and lines of code. Marathon describes the concentrated and targeted effort to find a solution for the development of software or, in some cases, hardware.

Relevance and Application of Hackathons

The number of Hackathon events is growing faster and faster, and as a result, the hackathon phenomenon has established itself as an effective approach to promoting innovation with technologies in a variety of different areas (Briscoe and Mulligan 2014, p. 1 ff.). With the proliferation of hackathons, the participation of non-technical expertise such as that of marketing experts, business developers and designers has increased (Briscoe and Mulligan 2014, p. 4). Facebook is one of the first companies to decide to continuously integrate this phenomenon into its structure. Today, approximately every two months, many of Facebook's more than 700 engineers meet for a 24-h competition in the company's offices. Many of Facebook's trademarks, including the Like button, started as hackathon projects. The winners will receive posters in a limited edition, on which distinctive phrases such as "In Hack we trust" are shown (Leckart 2012).

The Hackathon Process

The hackathons often begin with presentations or discussions so that the participants can recognise and convey a common understanding of the problem. Then ideas and suggestions are collected and examined by teams. The team members have mixed backgrounds and skills and form their team autonomously in the process (Richter et al. 2018). A hackathon can usually last between one day and one week (Richter et al. 2018: 115; Briscoe and Mulligan 2014, p. 4; Yueh Perng et al. 2017, p. 2). Depending on the level of funding and organisational resources of the organisers, hackathons can take place in a single city, in several locations or simultaneously all over the world. At the end of the event, a jury will announce the winning prototypes based on how well they have tackled the proposed challenges and what potential they have to be launched as a marketable product. The winners are often rewarded with a cash prize and/or enrolment in incubator and accelerator programmes.[3] The enrolment comes with prestige, which provides access to broader corporate networks and investment opportunities for venture capitalists or

---

[3]The GroupMe app is a good example of this. It was created as part of a hackathon and raised $10.6 million in the first year. Barely one year later, the GroupMe app was sold to Skype for $85 million (Leckart 2012; Uffreduzzi 2017, p. 3).

multinational companies (Yueh Perng et al. 2017, p. 3). In the end, the hackathons turn out to be catalysts for new ideas. These events stimulate people intellectually and creatively. The hackathons also require personalities who know how to work quickly with new people in small teams under time pressure. Although not all participants are necessarily successful under such conditions, these events have proven to be successful (Briscoe and Mulligan 2014, p. 11 f.). The cost factor must not be forgotten either. In contrast to permanent jobs in product development, where the financial risk is quite high for the organisations, the cost of failures at hackathons is relatively low or zero (Uffreduzzi 2017, p. 6).

Advantages and Disadvantages of Hackathons

Advantages and disadvantages exist for both the participant and the company side. Advantages for the organisers clearly would be the fast development of ideas and the testing of prototypes, networking and community creation, recruitment and corporate branding (Uffreduzzi 2017, p. 31). In sum, they outweigh the disadvantages like the costs and time an organiser must invest. Hackathons also appear beneficial to the participants. Benefits would be the opportunity to learn and work with new technologies, networking with firms and other participants and the prize that is awarded at the end of the hackathon. Disadvantages would be that the organisers have the right on all ideas generated during the process (intellectual property rights) and that many ideas are not pursued by the organiser.

Hackathons as Part of an Open Innovation Strategy to Enhance Entrepreneurial Management Behaviours of Organisations

However, looking at a single management tool is not enough to develop sustainable solutions. Depending on the goal of a hackathon, this is part of an organisation's holistic innovation strategy. This can be carried out, for example, as part of open innovation, which involves the exchange of knowledge across company boundaries (Grichnik et al. 2017, p. 385ff). "Open Innovation is the use of purposive inflows and outflows of knowledge to accelerate internal innovation, and expand the markets for external use of innovation, respectively" (Grichnik et al. 2017, p. 385ff; Chesbrough et al. 2006). Open innovation can be carried out as an "inbound process", in which external knowledge is included in the innovation process, for example to carry out external technology sourcing or to integrate suppliers or customers. This also includes the hackathon. The other direction would be an "outbound process" in which knowledge is commercialised externally if it cannot be used in one's own company, for example licences, technologies, advice. In a "coupled process", the two are connected to independent organisations such as alliances or joint ventures.

For both open innovation as an innovation management method and individual initiatives such as the implementation of a hackathon to be successful for an organisation in the long term, a holistic approach is required that strengthens entrepreneurial action in the respective organisation. A basic orientation can be strategic entrepreneurship as a management approach. This approach implements innovation in the organisation to achieve strategic advantages over competitors (Grichnik et al. 2017, p. 385ff; Kuratko and Audretsch 2009). This can be done in at least five different ways: strategic realignment, continuous regeneration, new establishment of a business area (Grichnik et al. 2017, p. 385ff; Covin and Miles 1999) as well as organisational innovation and development of a new business model (Kuratko and Audretsch 2009). A strategic realignment means a fundamental repositioning on the market or against competitors. This can be triggered by new competitors in the market or new technologies. Ongoing regeneration consists of introducing new products or existing products into other markets. The new establishment of a business field means that a company proactively recognises a new product–market combination and acts here as a "first mover". When it comes to organisational renewal, processes and organisational structures are adjusted to achieve efficiency and effectiveness advantages. When developing and implementing a business model, it is a matter of completely breaking down the existing structures and restructuring them (see also Gassmann et al. 2017; Osterwalder and Pigneur 2010). While a hackathon is a unique event, the measures listed form the basis for a sustainable innovation strategy. An organisation needs to reconsider its future role and decide for a way, e.g. a strategic realignment to implement innovation in the overall organisation. An open innovation tool like the hackathon that is embedded in such an entrepreneurial strategy can then increase the innovative strength of an organisation in a "resource-saving" manner by incorporating external knowledge or developing internal knowledge together with partners (Grichnik et al. 2017, p. 385ff).

3 ThüCAThon: A Hackthon Case Study

The following section details the case study that was carried out as part of a hackathon. It also looks at how the DMO subsequently dealt with the results, which goals were pursued beforehand and which adjustments have been made in terms of strategic entrepreneurship. The ThüCAThon case study (Yin 2009) was accompanied by interviews with the participants and those responsible for the DMO, evaluations of the websites and pre-questionnaires as well as a 24-h ethnographic observation to see how the teams worked together. The ideas of the three winning teams will also be presented.

The hackathon was prepared and carried out by the Thuringian Ministry of Economic Affairs in cooperation with the DMO of Thuringia. The event took place from 22 to 23 June 2019 in Jena, Thuringia, under the title ThüCAThon. The spacious and modern rooms of the dotSource Company were used for this. Each team was given its own room, each with a large whiteboard. There was also sufficient food available around the clock.

Almost 30 people from different areas of tourism and other fields took part, creating six teams. Registration was free for the participants. They could apply as individuals or be posted on behalf of a company or community. Programmers from the fields of IT and software development, IT consulting, IT and e-commerce and DBS/CRM solutions took part in the event. Two of the programmers also had a background in tourism and astrophysics. The remaining participants came roughly equally from the creative industries including the areas of e-commerce, PR marketing, film and animation, consulting, SAP consulting and IT consulting. Students from Thuringian universities and participants from the tourism industry with specialisations in the museum and logistics sector also took part in the process.

The basic data was made available to the teams via the structure of ThüCAT. There were more than 4000 entities with linked data. So that a broader database could be created, a connection was made with other open data such as geography, weather and traffic data. The jury of experts consisted of representatives of the TMWWDG, the TTG and experienced experts from the fields of tourism, digitisation and open data. After all the teams had presented their pitch presentations of the prototypes created at the ThüCAThon, the jury after a long, drawn-out discussion decided which three ideas should be rewarded with prizes.

One of the main goals was to test the ThüCAT database during its development as a beta version and to develop first applications. This hackathon was a good opportunity to network actors at all levels and to see how quickly the incredibly large potential for innovation can be used through digitisation. The ThüCAThon should also serve as proof that the stages created up to that time can be implemented and used to promote digital tourism in Thuringia. Another goal of this hackathon was to attract potential cooperation partners who work in other areas, such as IT specialists, to enable an even more effective implementation of the database.

Process of the Hackathon

Because it is about a completely new database system that is still in its beta phase, the organisers held a community event the evening before the hackathon, in which there was an explanation of the technical requirements and their limits. On this evening, there was also the opportunity to ask questions, to get to know each other and to start with the team building of the participants. On the first full day after this evening event, the essential part of the work for the participants began and everything went like a "classic" hackathon. First, there was a greeting from the moderator and an introduction and explanation of the format and the procedure. Then the goals of digitisation in tourism were explained. The starting signal was given at 11 a.m. and the 24-h countdown began. First, everyone was allowed to briefly present their idea. All the ideas were collected on a chatboard and categorised by subject area. More than 20 ideas came up. After the BarCamp phase, each participant and each of the organisers were allowed to vote for their three favourites. As a result, six ideas were chosen and a corresponding team was set up with three to six people each. Then the teams had about an hour to develop the original idea and prepare a short pitch. The individual pitches were followed by feedback and questions that continued to lead to interesting discussions. For example, one team changed its entire concept because the other participants recognised the potential in a detail of the basic idea, which led to a significant change in the main approach. The organisers' mentors supported and accompanied the teams on site to better adapt the ideas and results to the existing strategy. Representatives of Join (the agency that was responsible for the technical implementation of ThüCAT) were available for technical questions or problems. Within the 24 h, all teams without exception managed to develop their ideas to the maximum, create first prototypes of apps and show their results not only theoretically but also practically. The presentations were public, and each team had approximately six or seven minutes to present their product and answer questions.

There were a total of three award winners as follows.

"First place: The winner of the hackathon was the "What a Day" app team. A personalised, target group-specific travel configurator accompanies the guest interactively along the entire customer journey and always takes current situations or needs into account. The team has managed to integrate all four customer segments listed in the regional tourism strategy and to offer them various organised day tours which guests can adapt as they wish with simple swiping and filter functions.

Second place went to the "Sesame Street" team, which developed an easy way to migrate data from the existing content management systems of tourists to ThüCAT. They also impressed with an entertaining and professional presentation.

Third place went to the team for the "B @ on" project, which proposes to install a so-called dash button for restaurants to signal "We are open" or "We are closed" with the simple click of a button. This smart button then transmits this information directly to ThüCAT, from where it is to be played in real time on all different channels. Restaurants avoid disappointment in front of closed bars; the visitor can always know reliably which nearby restaurants are open"[4] (Grinda 2019).

Analysis of the Case Study

The survey gave the following answers: for almost all participants, the ThüCAThon was the first hackathon ever. Only two of the participants had already attended such events, one of which was a cultural management hackathon in which the format was very different. The other experienced participant was already a hackathon "veteran" with five hackathons under their belt. All the respondents named different motivations for participation. For some, including students, the main motivation was to get to know new people and make contacts that might be helpful later for finding an employer. Others saw this as a way to gather more information about ThüCAT to better understand how it works. Another reason for participating was the challenge of quickly developing something new and learning something new. Others were sent by their company. And everyone also enjoyed working on community projects.

Regarding the question of the extent to which open innovation methods, and in particular the hackathon tool, are suitable for contributing to the development or problem-solving in tourism, the study concluded that the implementation is enormously valuable for tourism. It is the flexibility, the quick reaction to changes and the difficulty in predicting trends in people's travel behaviour that make tourism a branch of the economy that the nature of open and experimental methods is well suited to.

---

[4]Free translation from German by the author, (Grinda 2019).

An examination of the ThüCAThon leads to the following results:

- This hackathon led to many ideas within a short time. Some of these were followed up and completed with specific details during the 24 h. The ThüCA-Thon has proven to be a method that can be helpful for the rapid development of data-driven projects in tourism.
- Many different actors were integrated into the network, making the whole undertaking more productive. The involvement of many different organisations and people made the proposals very diverse and heterogeneous. The participants brought in their specific knowledge, and if they were lacking expertise in other areas, this was balanced by their motivation and creativity. This type of constructive event is more goal-oriented when various actors are integrated into such a network, because the mixture of different disciplines means that the confluence of the individual specialist qualities in the groups makes it much easier to solve complex questions. Especially due to the short stages and fast rounds of evaluation, both the work dynamics and the motivation remain consistently high over the entire development process. In general, it can be said that the hackathon format offers the opportunity to intensively connect large network structures within a short time and with manageable effort. The role of mentors in a hackathon should not be underestimated, because their presence at ThüCAThon has proven to be an important detail. They helped with any questions or decisions that arose within the groups, because they knew exactly which tourism strategy and which operational goals are pursued by ThüCAT. In this way, they made a decisive contribution to keeping the creative teams on course in all phase of their work, thus guiding the final results towards the goals of the organiser.
- The organisers saved costs thanks to the many ideas collected and prototypes created within 24 h. As already mentioned in the case study, more than 20 ideas were collected at ThüCAThon, mostly from people who did not get any money for it, apart from the three award winners at the end. Of course, money is spent on the organisation of such an event, but considerable results are achieved, from starting with the idea, continuing through the collaboration of IT, marketing and tourism experts to creating a prototype. All of these components would burden a company's budget significantly in conventional, i.e. closed processes, especially if they had to pay several teams at once. However, according to the participants, the prize money was not their main reason for participating in the ThüCAThon, instead, curiosity about this new construct and the opportunities for networking were the strongest motivations.
- The organisers very quickly received expert and constructive feedback for the beta version of ThüCAT from many different specialists at the current time. The hackathon is not only a good approach for collecting ideas. A completely new system, namely ThüCAT, was shown with its capabilities in the beta version. This enabled the participants to get to know ThüCAT and to make their comments or recommendations. The ThüCAT was supplied with the data, it was then checked to see whether it could work well, and finally the first product developments in the form of application prototypes were made available based on ThüCAT.

However, there are also learnings and traps that should be avoided: for future hackathons, a more generous prize for the winners could be considered in order to continue to attract even more capable and motivated people to such events. Another problem, already mentioned above, is that ideas have not been not pursued by the organiser. An interview with one of the managers responsible at the DMO half a year after the event showed that there is a need to follow up on the sustainability or recycling of ideas. So far, the ideas from the ThüCAThon have not been developed, but are in the drawer or only on the website (Grinda 2019). However, this is also due to the development process that is still in full swing. The interview partner described the future role of the DMO as follows: the hackathon was a first test balloon for such a format in Thuringian tourism, with thoroughly positive feedback from the participants. After the current project phase of the technical creation of ThüCAT with all its components, including graph database, website kit, search engine, editor for recording and interface connection, the collaboration phase begins. On the one hand, the goal is to find interested parties for the data: here among others the creative industries play a role, developing innovative technical solutions and formats and using tourist data from ThüCAT. It does not have to be a purely tourist product; sometimes only a small part of the tourism data is used. Here the development of ideas from the hackathon could be an approach to force concrete implementations. On the other hand, the goal is also to use the network to link with other open databases relevant to tourist use, for example weather data in conjunction with appropriate excursion tips. The role of the DMO will lie in checking the Thuringian data pool regarding topicality, completeness and data quality, as well as in the technical support of the system and the search for the most attractive multipliers such as ADAC[5] (Allgemeine Deutsche Automobil-Club e. V.), AirBnB, WWF or others for high-reach draws. As our interview partner from the DMO states: "In the course of product development, I see great opportunities to create useful use cases together with the tourism partners in Thuringia and to launch model projects. The TTG will act in an advisory and supportive manner in the sense of networking. We rarely, or not at all, commission our own innovative applications."[6]

4　Conclusion

In the beginning, we have posed the question of how new digital technologies and management methods must be implemented in destination management organisations so that they generate sustainable competitive advantages and customer benefits for the respective travel destination. We also intended to find out if an open data hackathon is a suitable approach to help ensure the competitiveness of tourist destinations. The answer is twofold: firstly, from our case study we can subsume that a hackathon can be very useful for producing many ideas within a short time. It

---

[5]The ADAC is an automobile association in Germany. It is the equivalent of RAC or AA in UK.
[6]Translation from an interview with the team leader of the development and implementation of the ThüCAT at TTG.

is also a good method to integrate different actors into a network in order to make the process more productive. Especially, the role of the mentors is important to align the ideas to the overall tourism strategy. Another aspect is the cost-saving opportunity when creating prototypes compared to developing them inhouse or with a service provider. Also the feedback for the beta version of the ThüCAT has been extremely useful for the DMO.

However, when looking at the overall goal of achieving customer benefits and ensuring the competitiveness of a tourist destination, a DMO must additionally guarantee a high quality of the results and the sustainability of the ideas produced during a hackathon. From our case study, we have learned that for ensuring a high quality of ideas produced, it would be recommendable to award more generous prizes for the winners in order to attract even more capable and motivated people especially programmers. Giving the aspect of sustainability, many ideas are not pursued by organisers of hackathons. This is also the case for the ThüCAThon. It must be shown how ideas deriving from hackathons are pursued, refined and applied, and their effects on the market must be measured. It is important to realise that with the new approaches to data provision and data processing, new holistic management methods are necessary. Making the best use of all technical innovations and meeting new customer demands can only be achieved through adaptations in organisational strategy and rethinking in management. A hackathon as an entrepreneurial management tool must therefore be embedded in an overall approach to strategic entrepreneurship (see Fig. 1).

However, from the case study, we have learned that the DMO in Thuringia is currently actively rethinking and developing its role in the renewal process (organisational innovation, see Fig. 1). For this purpose, the DMO has created a competence centre for the implementation of ThüCAT, which takes on the responsibility of guiding and distributing all content that comes from partners, tourism organisations at the regional and local level and from tourism service providers at the company level. This means that not every single company has to go digital, but the TTG develops concepts and solutions, implements them and involves all actors in Thuringia in them or passes the results on to them (Dwif-Consulting 2017: 45 ff.). In view of the statements made by those responsible, the DMO is pursuing an open innovation strategy in which active "inbound" processes are carried out by integrating creative people by using tools such as hackathons. Furthermore, the DMO follows "outbound" processes because it is looking for interested parties for the data available and sees itself as a platform that ensures the quality and up-to-datedness of the data and encourages approaches to its use. Following this approach, the DMO could also try to find partners who are willing to test and bring applications to the market (see Fig. 1, steps 7 & 8). It then follows an outbound process, following its new role as a smart data platform. Strategic entrepreneurship approaches can help to reclassify and define this role. When considering the DMO presented here, a strategic realignment (see Fig. 1) is already taking place in order to reposition itself against competitors in the digital economy such as Google or Facebook and powerful travel portals like booking.com or Expedia. This realignment was triggered by the technologies shown in this

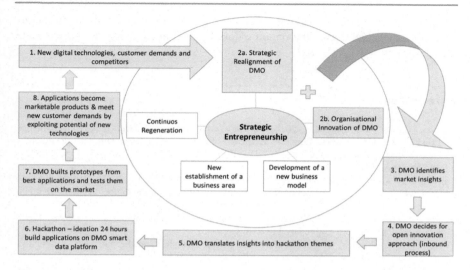

Fig. 1 Eight steps for implementing hackathons in DMO's. Learning's from the ThüCAThon case study

chapter. The ordinary channels such as the destination management website move into the background. The focus is on the content or data, which is structured by schema.org and made freely available in the sense of open data. This not only benefits the powerful platform providers like Google, but as the hackathon showed all participants in the market can use the data and, based on this, develop their own business ideas, including individual creatives and start-ups. Nevertheless, the DMO uses the power of Google and Facebook and their channels to bring their content to the guest. The visibility of the DMO increases compared to the current situation, and the DMO can influence the quality of the data.

The strategic realignment is radical and entails a change in the classic tasks of a DMO. The DMO itself becomes a smart data platform and must therefore also adapt its processes and structures in order to achieve efficiency and effectiveness advantages. Future research work can actively accompany these developments. Action research methods in which researchers and practitioners cooperate would be suitable. It would also be interesting to examine the effects on other market participants. Is a hackathon suitable to stimulate the formation of startup teams that use the available data for own business ideas, or to pursue projects in the company in the sense of intrapreneurship? Will DMOs develop their own applications in the future although they do not currently see their tasks in the area of customer applications? These and other questions need to be answered as part of the new opportunities and challenges. The potential of hackathons and other open innovative approaches in tourism is far from being exhausted, in fact it is only just beginning, and it can be expected that it will be used to an increasing extent in the future. The aspects of cost and time savings through open innovation with constant feedback, avoiding dead ends in development, quick error correction and enormous capacity for change during the ongoing development process are just too valuable to ignore.

References

Briscoe, G., & Mulligan, C. (2014). *Digital innovation: The Hackathon phenomenon.* London: Creative works London. Retrieved from https://pdfs.semanticscholar.org/cb8e/44ec1bcd6062e5fccafb6837030be334731d.pdf?_ga=2.252250953.1703906457.1587300572-1942274566.1587300572.

Carrara, W., Fischer, S., Oudkerk, F., van Steenbergen, E., & Tinholt, D. (2015). *Analytical report 1: Digital transformation.* Retrieved from https://www.europeandataportal.eu/sites/default/files/edp_analytical_report_n1_-_digital_transformation.pdf. Accessed 11 July 2019.

Chesbrough, H., Vanhaverbeke, W., & West, J. (Eds.). (2006). *Open innovation: Researching a new paradigm.* Oxford University Press on Demand.

Covin, J. G., & Miles, M. P. (1999). Corporate entrepreneurship and the pursuit of competitive advantage. *Entrepreneurship Theory and Practice, 23*(3), 47–63.

Dapp, M., Balta, D., Palmetshofer, W., Krcmar, H., & Kuzev, P. (Eds.). (2016). Open data. *The benefits. Das volkswirtschaftliche Potential für Deutschland.* Berlin: Konrad-Adenauer-Stiftung e.V., Sankt Augustin. Retrieved from https://www.kas.de/c/document_library/get_file?uuid=3fbb9ec5-096c-076e-1cc4-473cd84784df&groupId=252038. Accessed 11 July 2019.

Dwif Consulting. (2017). *Tourismusstrategie Thüringen 2025.* Berlin. Retrieved from https://wirtschaft.thueringen.de/fileadmin/user_upload/Publikationen/Pub-Tourismusstrategie-Thueringen-2025.pdf. Accessed 15 Mar 2020.

Freyer, W. (2015). *Tourismus: Einführung in die Fremdenverkehrsökonomie.* Berlin: De Gruyter Verlag.

Gassmann, O., Frankenberger, K., & Csik, M. (2017). *Geschäftsmodelle entwickeln: 55 innovative Konzepte mit dem St. Galler business model navigator.* Carl Hanser Verlag GmbH Co KG.

German National Tourist Board. (n.d.). *ThüCAT—Das Konzept eines digitalen Tourismus.* Retrieved from https://open-data-germany.org/thuecat-das-konzept-eines-digitalen-tourismus/. Accessed 15 Mar 2020.

Grichnik, D., Brettel, M., Koropp, C., & Mauer, R. (2017). *Entrepreneurship: unternehmerisches Denken.* Schäffer-Poeschel: Entscheiden und Handeln in innovativen und technologieorientierten Unternehmen.

Grinda, I. (2019). *Thüringens erster Hackathon im Tourismus.* Retrieved from https://thueringen.tourismusnetzwerk.info/2019/06/24/thueringens-erster-hackathon-im-tourismus/. Accessed 15 Mar 2020.

Hauer, L. (2020). *Strukturierte Daten: Mehr Aufmerksamkeit in den SERPs.* Retrieved from https://www.luna-park.de/blog/29207-strukturierte-daten/. Accessed 15 Mar 2020.

Honig, K. (2019). *Best practice—Open data in Thüringen.* Retrieved from https://open-data-germany.org/best-practice-open-data-in-thueringen/. Accessed 3 Apr 2020.

Horster, E., & Foltin, C. (2020). *Smart Destinations—Vernetzung von analoger und digitaler Welt.* Retrieved from https://www.neusta-ds.de/blog/author/prof-dr-eric-horster-und-constantin-foltin/. Accessed 15 Mar 2020.

Horster, E., & Kärle, E. (2019a). *Linked open data und Künstliche Intelligenz. The perfect Match?* Retrieved from https://open-data-germany.org/linked-open-data-und-kuenstliche-intelligenz/. Accessed 15 Mar 2020.

Horster, E., & Kärle, E. (2019b). *Knowledge Graphen. Ein Spiegel der (touristischen) Wirklichkeit.* Retrieved from https://open-data-germany.org/knowledge-graphen/. Accessed 15 Mar 2020.

Horster, E., & Kärle, E. (2019c). *Das Headless Web. Datenmanagement modular denken.* Retrieved from https://open-data-germany.org/headless-web/. Accessed 15 Mar 2020.

IGI Global. (n.d.). *Tourism knowledge.* Retrieved from https://www.igi-global.com/dictionary/tourism-knowledge-destination/34186. Accessed 3 Apr 2020.

Keller, B., Möhring, M., Toni, M., Di Pietro, L., & Schmidt, R. (2017). Data-centered platforms in tourism: Advantages and challenges for digital enterprise architecture. In W. Abramowicz, R. Alt, & B. Franczyk (Eds.), *Business information systems workshops. BIS 2016. Lecture notes in business information processing* (Vol. 263). Cham: Springer.

Kinlan, P. (2016). *The headless web.* Retrieved from https://paul.kinlan.me/the-headless-web/. Accessed 15 Mar 2020.

Ksoll, W., Schildhauer, T., & Beck, A. (2017). *Open data—Wertschöpfung im digitalen Zeitalter.* Retrieved from https://www.bertelsmann-stiftung.de/fileadmin/files/Projekte/Smart_Country/OpenData_2017_final.pdf. Accessed 20 July 2019.

Kuratko, D. F., & Audretsch, D. B. (2009). Strategic entrepreneurship: Exploring different perspectives of an emerging concept. *Entrepreneurship Theory and Practice, 33*(1), 1–17.

Leckart, S. (2012). *The Hackathon is on: Pitching and programming the next killer app.* Retrieved from https://www.wired.com/2012/02/ff_hackathons/. Accessed 21 June 2019.

Osterwalder, A., & Pigneur, Y. (2010). *Business model generation: A handbook for visionaries, game changers, and challengers.* New York: Wiley.

Paulheim, H. (2016). *Knowledge graph refinement: A survey of approaches and evaluation methods. semantic Web 0 (2016) 1–01.IOS.* Retrieved from: Press. http://www.semantic-web-journal.net/system/files/swj1167.pdf. Accessed 15 Mar 2020.

Richter, N., Schildhauer, T., & Jackson, P. (2018). *Meeting the innovation challenge: Agile Processes for established organizations.* In N. Richter, P. Jackson, & T. Schildhauer (Eds.), *Entrepreneurial innovation and leadership: Preparing for a digital future.* Cham: Palgrave Pivot.

Samochowiec, J., Kwiatkowski, M., & Breit, S. (2019). *Unterwegs mit smarten Assistenten. Ein Szenario zum Reisen der Zukunft.* Retrieved from: Studie. https://www.gdi.ch/de/publikationen/studien-buecher/unterwegs-mit-smarten-assistenten. Accessed 15 Mar 2020.

Semantify. (n.d.). https://semantify.it/. Accessed 15 Mar 2020.

Sommer, G. (2018). *Herausforderungen und Chancen einer offenen, digitalen Dateninfrastruktur im Tourismus. Ergebnisse des ersten Think Tanks zum Thema „Open Data im Tourismus" sowie aktuelle Entwicklungen.* Retrieved from https://okfn.de/files/blog/2018/08/ThinkTank2017_Whitepaper_formatiert_Final.pdf. Accessed 20 June 2019.

Statista. (2019). *Was sind aktuell die größten Hindernisse in der Implementierung digitaler Instrumente in Ihrer Destination?* Retrieved from https://de.statista.com/statistik/daten/studie/1079727/umfrage/hindernisse-in-der-implementierung-digitaler-instrumente-im-bereich-tourismus/. Accessed 15 Mar 2020.

Stichbury, J. (2017). *WTF is a knowledge graph? Unpicking a tangle of terminology to conclude it's semantic, smart and alive.* Retrieved from https://www.hackernoon.com/wtf-is-a-knowledge-graph-a16603a1a25f. Accessed 11 July 2019.

Tourismuszukunft. (n.d.). *Digitalisierung im Tourismus.* Retrieved from https://www.tourismuszukunft.de/wp-content/uploads/2020/03/0403-Tourismuszukunft-Infografik-2020.pdf. Accessed 15 Mar 2020.

Tourismusnetzwerk Thüringen. (n.d.). *Thüringer Content Architektur Tourismus.* ThüCAT. https://thueringen.tourismusnetzwerk.info/inhalte/digitales-content/thuecat/. Accessed 15 June 2019.

Uffreduzzi, M. (2017). *Hackathon as emerging innovation practice: Exploring opportunities and challenges through 8 in-depth case studies* (Master Thesis). Retrieved from https://www.politesi.polimi.it/bitstream/10589/137237/5/Hackathon%20as%20Emerging%20Innovation%20Practice.pdf. Accessed 15 June 2019.

Von Lucke, J., & Geiger, C.P. (2010). *Open government data. Frei verfügbare Daten des öffentlichen Sektors*. Zeppelin University, Friedrichshafen, Bodensee. Retrieved from https://www.zu.de/institute/togi/assets/pdf/TICC-101203-OpenGovernmentData-V1.pdf. Accessed 7 Sep 2019.

Yachin, J. M. (2018). The 'customer journey': Learning from customers in tourism experience encounters. *Tourism Management Perspectives, 28,* 201–210.

Yin, R. K. (2009). *Case study research. Design and methods*, 4th edn. Los Angeles: Sage (Applied social research methods series, 5).

Yueh Perng, S., Kitchin, R., & Mac Donncha, D. (2017). Hackathons, entrepreneurship and the passionate making of smart cities: The Programmable City Working Paper 28.

Perspectives on Digital Business Models

Business Model Development and Validation in Digital Entrepreneurship

Lutz Göcke and Robin Weninger

Abstract

Every venture is developed under high uncertainty and causal ambiguity. A large majority of digital startups leverage the lean startup approach to validate the attractiveness of their venture, to reduce avoidable investments of scarce resources, and to structure the venturing process. Digital entrepreneurs highlight that prioritization and the definition of MVPs are two challenges that entrepreneurs face when applying the lean startup approach. We provide support on these particular challenges through a structured approach—the venture pyramid—to (in)validate digital business models in the face of high uncertainty. Furthermore, we map different types of digital business models with patterns of minimum viable products to inspire digital entrepreneurs and scientists alike. To illustrate our thoughts, we have developed two case studies of German startups that applied a process of rigorous iteration and learning to their venturing processes.

1 Introduction

A recent study shows that 93% of digital startups use the lean startup approach to find product-market fit fast, to avoid unnecessary resource investment, or to structure the development process of the venture (Ghezzi 2019). The same study

L. Göcke (✉)
Chair of Digital Management, Nordhausen University of Applied Sciences, Nordhausen, Germany
e-mail: lutz.goecke@hs-nordhausen.de

R. Weninger
Global Institute of Leadership and Technology (GILT), Eschborn, Germany

M. Soltanifar et al. (eds.), *Digital Entrepreneurship*, Future of Business and Finance,
https://doi.org/10.1007/978-3-030-53914-6_4

Table 1 Advantages and disadvantages of applying the lean startup approach (Ghezzi 2019)

Advantages	1. Reducing time and cost for startup testing (74%)
	2. Aligning business idea to customer needs (68%)
	3. Verifying and pivoting all business model parameters (52%)
	4. Receiving rounds of financing (39%)
Disadvantages	1. Defining and designing MVPs (82%)
	2. Identifying and engaging early evangelists and trial users (69%)
	3. Defining testing priorities and designing tests (52%)
	4. Missing other market opportunities and threats (39%)
	5. Obtaining information about the startup sources of advantage (36%)

identifies the advantages and disadvantages that digital startups face in the application of the lean startup approach (Ghezzi 2019) (Table 1).

The prioritization, definition, and design of experiments (incl. MVPs) are some of the major challenges that digital entrepreneurs have in the application of the lean startup approach to their business. One founder in the study mentioned that "lean tells you to build an MVP but gives you no clear guidelines or indications whatsoever on how to do so" (Ghezzi 2019). In this article, we offer a structured approach to test digital business ideas and to identify minimum viable products that help a startup within this journey.

2   (Theoretical) Background

2.1   Digital Business Models

A business model can be understood as the core logic of a firm to create and deliver value for its customers and to capture value for itself (Zott et al. 2011; Göcke 2016). When we talk about business models, it is very important to stress out that a business model is not the same as a revenue model. Both terms are getting mixed up very frequently in practice and are often seen as the same, which is not the case (see also Ghaziani and Ventresca 2005). A business model is a holistic perspective on the overall setup of the business and includes every process along the value chain. Various conceptualizations of business models have been developed to guide researchers and practitioners alike to analyze or develop business models (e.g., Chesbrough and Rosenbloom 2002; Teece 2010; Gassmann et al. 2014; Schneider and Spieth 2013). The "Business Model Canvas" of Osterwalder and Pigneur (2011) and the "Lean Canvas" of Maurya (2012) are prominent conceptualizations that are widely spread in practice. Central to most of these conceptualizations are the components value proposition, value creation, and value capture (Clauss 2017). This includes the cost model and the revenue model. The revenue model is thus a component of every business model. Every company can run on multiple business models (think different products) and on multiple revenue streams. Also, a single business model can be run with multiple revenue models. Whenever we work on a business model, it is required to also work on the revenue model. However, if we work on a revenue model, it is not necessarily required to change the whole business model (Cavalcante et al. 2011). Every entrepreneur's task is to get the equation in a business model right. A company's value proposition needs to be valuable for a user and create a proper willingness to pay, which is able to compensate the costs of the value creation and captured with a proper revenue model. All components need to be coherently aligned to a business model fit.

Digital business models define how a firm creates and captures value through extensive use of digital artifacts. Digital artifacts as bits and bytes differ from physical artifacts as they can be characterized as editable, interactive, open/reprogrammable, and distributed (Kallinikos et al. 2013). They can thus be easily modified and scaled. Remane et al. (2017) distinguish pure digital and digital-enabled business models. Pure digital business models, like Google as a search engine or Airbnb as an online broker, create and capture the value and build their business model on digital artifacts only, without the use of physical assets in their value creation activities. Digital-enabled business models like sensor-as-a-service business models require both—physical assets and digital artifacts—for the creation of value. Pure digital and digital-enabled business models alike share the characteristics of digital artifacts. In this chapter, we will focus our thoughts on pure digital business models. In order to shed light on the differences in the development of minimum viable products, we follow the 4-C digital business model typology of Wirtz (2019). The author distinguishes four business model categories for B2C-businesses with different business model types (see the business model categories and types in Table 2).[1] These business model types are deviated based on the functional aspects of the value proposition of the business model (Wirtz 2019).

2.2 Development Processes of Digital Business Models

The development of an attractive, repeatable, and scalable business model is the objective of every firm and has received a lot of attention in research in the last ten years. Following Osterwalder et al. (2014), the identification of a replicable and scalable business model builds upon product-market fit and a business model fit. Fit can be understood as a situation where the product or the business model favorably matches the conditions in the environment of a firm (Miles and Snow 1984). This idea is consistent with the contingency theory in strategic management, where the fit of a company's activities with its environment is an essential prerequisite for a company to exist. Achieving a situation of fit requires a dynamic search process that aligns the business with its environments and deploys resources alike (Miles and Snow 1984; Blank 2010).

Entrepreneurs make their decisions in circumstances of high uncertainty and causal ambiguity (Furr and Ahlstrom 2011). Customer needs are unknown in the early stages, and proper solutions, technologies, or business models need to be

---

[1]In addition, Wirtz (2019) discusses four B2B-business model categories for digital businesses.

Table 2 Business model typologies (reference to Wirtz 2019)

Business model category	Business model types	Examples
Content compilation of content, depiction and provision of content on domestic platform	e-information	wsj.com, handelsblatt.com, Wikipedia
	e-entertainment	partypoker.com, Spotify, WoW
	e-education	udacity, udemy, coursera
	e-infotainment	nba.com, sport1.de
Commerce Initiation and/or settlement of business transactions	e-attraction	AdSense, Shopping.com
	e-bargaining/negotiation	eBay, Groupon
	e-transaction	Paypal, Klarna, Bitcoin
	e-tailing	Amazon, Expedia, book a tiger, zappos.com
Context Classification and systematization of information available on the Internet	Search engines	Google, Yahoo, Bing, DuckDuckGo, Indeed.com
	Web directories	Yahoo.com,
	Book-marking	Citeulike.org
Connection Creation of the possibility to exchange information in networks	Intraconnection (Community)	Facebook, Snapchat, Skype, Flickr, Yelp, Gmail, Dropbox
	Interconnection	earthlink.net, sonic.net, att.com, t-mobile.com

explored. Decision making under uncertainty and causal ambiguity is constrained by various types of cognitive biases—e.g., confirmation bias, overconfidence bias, or escalation of commitment (Zhang and Cueto 2015). This includes the development of a product without a validated customer problem or the scaling of activities without an attractive business model. Under the influence of cognitive biases in an uncertain context, entrepreneurs are ignorant to disconfirm information (confirmation bias), too optimistic about their success chances (overconfidence), and susceptible to continue investing in an unpromising business idea (escalation of commitment). These cognitive biases can lead to premature scaling of activities, which means the inappropriate scaling of activities. Premature scaling is thus one of the major drivers of startup failure (StartupGenomeReport 2011; CBInsights 2018). To improve decision making under high uncertainty, effective entrepreneurs run experiments to validate/invalidate critical business assumptions (Ries 2011; Blank and Dorf 2012; Gambardella et al. 2018). The process of experimenting to validate/invalidate critical assumptions can be understood as deliberate and dynamic search process to find an attractive, replicable, and scalable business model and is core to the lean startup approach (Blank 2010; Maurya 2012; Ries 2011; Frederiksen and Brem 2017). Ries (2011) suggests a build–measure–learn loop, where an entrepreneur identifies the most critical business assumptions, builds an experiment to test these assumptions, measures the user behavior, and creates learnings from the gathered data (Fig. 1).

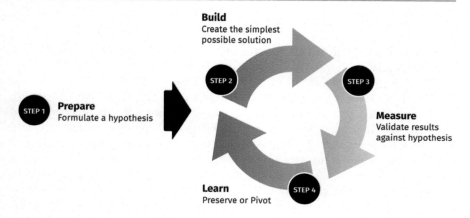

Fig. 1 Build–measure–learn loop (reference to Ries 2011)

These learnings include the information on the falsification or corroboration of the tested assumption and guide the entrepreneurs' decision making to either pivot to a new/adapted idea or to persevere on the current path (Ries 2011; Bajwa et al. 2017). The challenge with the build–measure–learn loop is that the infinite character of the loop gives entrepreneurs no guidance when to change the nature of experiments. It is not very practical nor useful to try to validate everything. But what is important is to validate the things that really matter to the business. It does not matter how many hypotheses an entrepreneur validates if none of them is critical for the success of the business. The ability to zoom out and clear the big picture is highly important to run successful iterations that matter. In practice, we see quite often entrepreneurs that use the iteration in an early stage to validate features—which is great in general—but forget to validate the value proposition first. This can be seen as premature scaling because an entrepreneur loses sight of the critical assumptions.

Another important cornerstone of the lean startup approach is the development of experiments that create targeted learning at a minimum investment of time and money. One instrument to create this fast learning is a minimum viable product (MVP), which is a specific experiment (Ries 2011). There has been a lot of confusion on the term minimum viable product. Some authors and practitioners equal the MVP with every potential form of a business experiment (e.g., a customer interview), others equal an MVP with a prototype, etc. (Duc and Abrahamson 2016). This missing clarity does not reduce complexity but adds complexity for entrepreneurs and does thus not help to structure the development process of a venture.

In the subsequent chapter, we aim to offer a structural approach to validate/invalidate the essential components of digital business models. In addition, we aim to identify the specifics that different business model types encounter when they are tested.

3   Conceptual Model/Empirical Insights

3.1   Venture Pyramid to Iteratively Develop Digital Business Models

Following the ideas of Ellis (2013), Osterwalder et al. (2014) and Göcke (2017b), we introduce the venture pyramid as a concept to structure the deliberate and dynamic search process to identify business model fit. The venture pyramid structures the most critical business assumptions. The most critical assumptions reside at the bottom of the pyramid as the foundation of the business and have the highest magnitude of impact in case they prove wrong. This includes required changes over a certain period of time. It is important to highlight that there is no "one-size-fits-all" approach to the venture pyramid and that, depending on the scenario, different foundations are possible to start from (e.g., founders' competence, a technology, or a market need). For the following, we are taking market attractiveness as the foundation of the venture pyramid to make the process tangible. However, starting with a different foundation (e.g., the problem-solution fit before dealing with the market) might sometimes be a better way to get started. As with everything, every step in an entrepreneurial venture needs careful decision making without falling into analysis-paralysis (Fig. 2).

At the bottom of the pyramid as the foundation of the business lays an attractive group of potential customers (market attractiveness: seize/growth of group). Building on top of an attractive group of potential customers, we see the existence of a pressing customer pain of this group of potential customers as the next fundamental layer of critical assumptions (customer-problem fit). At the level of problem-solution fit, we aim not only to clarify if the customer favors our solution but also if customers are willing to pay for the solution. We suggest to test the critical assumptions at problem-solution fit only by the communication of value proposition and price but without enabling customers to experience the value proposition (e.g., with a landing page smoke test). Without the customers' willingness to pay, the development of a product or the supply-side of a business would

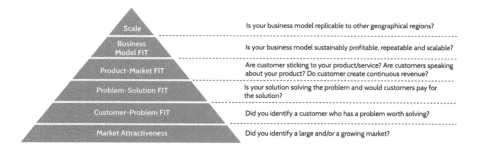

Fig. 2   Venture pyramid to structure the search process of a business model (reference to Göcke 2017a)

not be required at all. A CBInsights (2018) analysis of startup failures shows that a majority of startups fail because of a missing market need. Assuring that this market need exists is central to the first levels of the venture pyramid (e.g., customer segments, problems value proposition). Whenever we work with the build–measure–learn iteration, it is very important to understand the big picture and to be as precise as possible with the hypothesis because sometimes small changes in the details lead to a very different result. For example, if you want to validate a feature or attribute of your product or service, just changing the customer segment gives a completely different result. Think about developing a bike. If you change the customer segment from a 23-year-old male athlete to a 34-year-old mother of two children, the bike looks completely different. Sure, one could argue that this is common sense but as entrepreneurs, we do not want to work based on common sense but on validated knowledge. And exactly, this is the reason why the build–measure–learn iteration is so useful and appreciated by many entrepreneurs. After having identified the demand at a particular price point, startups can test the experience of their value proposition by offering a minimum viable product. At this level, the product is handed to customers, and startups can validate/invalidate whether the product gets traction through continuous revenue, retention, and referral (McClure 2007; Croll and Yoskovitz 2013), which we see as product-market fit (Dennehy et al. 2016). With achieving a business model fit, startups (in)validate the operations of a business model. Here, it is central to identify incremental profits for every new user (action). At the scaling level, startups need to validate/invalidate what elements of their business model require adaptation to local contexts and what elements can be standardized (Göcke 2016).

There are multiple options for an entrepreneur at every level of the venture pyramid to choose and to validate/invalidate. Many potential customer groups with a great variety of problems exist in the field. And there are multiple ways to solve a customer's problem. A startup's aim is to identify the solution that is not only a local maximum but a global maximum (Sommer et al. 2009), so the best possible solution for the customer group that generates the highest willingness to pay. The same is true for the product. A startup will choose to develop a minimum viable product out of a number of alternatives, again aiming to globally maximize the return identified alternative. We suggest illustrating the different levels of the venture pyramid with various circles that illustrate the possible alternatives at every level (Frederiksen and Brem 2017). The decisions are path-dependent and limited by a startup's capabilities (Frederiksen and Brem 2017) (Fig. 3).

With every new build–measure–learn loop at the different levels of the venture pyramid, a startup runs through the process of identifying and validating the most attractive alternative at a particular level. A frequently used approach to structure this creative process is the framework "Double Diamond" (Design Council 2019). The double diamond is originally split into a problem space/idea space (left diamond) and the solution space (right diamond). Both diamonds follow the same structure: one divergent thinking phase (the left side of each diamond) and one convergent thinking phase (the right side of the diamond). Divergent thinking requires a startup team to think about getting as many alternatives on paper as

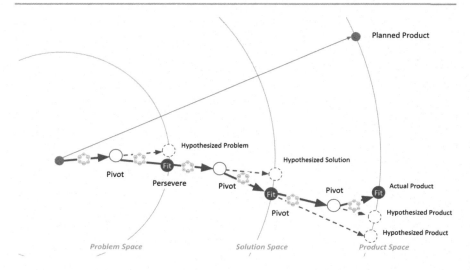

Fig. 3 Path of deliberate entrepreneurial experimentation with the venture pyramid (reference to Göcke 2017b)

possible to increase the probability of identifying the global maximum. At every level of the venture pyramid, there are different creativity techniques (e.g., analogies or patterns) that can be applied to support the process of divergent thinking. Convergent thinking takes an analytical approach to identify the best possible alternative. In our understanding here, the first diamond aims to identify the riskiest assumptions at the particular level of the venture pyramid. In short, through divergent thinking, a startup ideates a range of alternative assumptions, and the convergent thinking processes allow the startup to select the riskiest assumption. The end of the phase often marks the so-called How might we (HMW) question (Knapp et al. 2016), which opens the second diamond and asks how this assumption can be tested. The second diamond reflects the ideation (divergent thinking), selection (convergent thinking), and finally the conduction of an appropriate experiment at every level of the venture pyramid. To support the ideation of alternative experiments at the level of product-market fit, we match different digital business models with patterns of minimum viable products in the subsequent chapter.

3.2   Identifying Minimum Viable Products for Digital Business Models

There are multiple ways to test the most critical assumptions at every level of the venture pyramid. At the lowest level of the venture pyramid, startups can choose to use secondary market research or behavioral data (e.g., Google keyword searches) to identify if a certain topic catches attention. The level of customer-problem fit is best achieved with the help of intense customer discovery interviews. At the level of problem-solution fit, the core idea is to run a pre-sales test, where potential customers signal their willingness to buy the product at a particular price. We define experiments at this level of the venture pyramid as smoke tests. These smoke tests can be triggered by landing pages, an email, or a customer interview.

Following Ries (2011, 2016) and Duc and Abrahamson (2016), we distinguish four types of minimum viable products (MVP) that are able to create the targeted product experience at a low level of cost in order to validate product-market fit:

- The *single feature MVP* focuses on the development and implementation of the most important feature of a particular product. A very prominent example is Google's search engine. Google started with a performing search engine to find manually listed Web sites.
- Developing a *concierge MVP* means being in contact with the end-user. The founding team is personally involved in delivering value to the customer. Airbnb is an often-cited example of this experiment. The owners identified that design conference visitors in San Francisco were not able to book a hotel. As a consequence, the founders offered three airbeds and breakfast in their flat.
- The *Wizard-of-Oz MVP* tricks the user as the user experiences the product or service with full functions and as completely automated, but the startup mocks the process in the back. Zappos is one startup that had to validate that people were willing to buy shoes online. The front end illustrated a fully automated process, but in the back, everything was operated by humans.
- Groupon is one startup that used a *piecemeal MVP* to validate the continuous demand of users. A piecemeal MVP means that the initial version of a product is developed on standardized components.

Table 3 aims to provide examples of MVPs for the different digital business models to work as inspiration for startups to find a way to achieve a product-market fit and for researchers to initiate more intense research on MVP types. The use of the 4-C business model typology focuses on the functional aspects of digital business models. Different approaches to business model typologies (e.g., with a stronger focus on operations) might add additional value to the development of minimum viable products.

3.3 Case Studies

In order to illustrate our thoughts with some practical insights, we have created two different case studies with startups based in Germany (Siggelkow 2007). We conducted structured interviews that followed an interview guideline. The respective companies have been selected randomly.

Table 3 Matching of business models and MVP

	Single feature MVP	Piecemeal MVP	Concierge MVP	Wizard of Oz MVP
Content (Compilation of content, depiction and provision of content on domestic platform)	*Duolingo* initially offered programmes only for Spanish and German *Source* https://wwwquora.com/What-was-Duolingos-MVP-like	*Spotify* leveraged pirate Bay technology to build the first version of the service *Source* https://torrentfreak.com/how-the-pirate-bay-helped-spotify-become-a-success-180319/	*Twitch* initially started as Justin.TV where the founder Justin streamed his life and soon developed a platform for others to stream. *Source* https://earlyusergrowth.com/startups/	The early stage startup *winstate.io* automatically generates content for customer to become thought leaders in their domain. In its early days, the content was generated by hired bloggers *Source* Own interview
Commerce (Initiation and/or settlement of business transactions}	In its early days, *Amazon* listed only books as products to purchase *Source* https://www.revelx.co/blog/mvp-examples/	The startup *Kawaloo* launched their platform for storage capacity with existing components (e.g. WordPress) *Source* Own interview	*Amical.io/assistant* created a personalized career advice *Source* Own interview	*Zappos* initiated created its shoe shopping experience based on a manual process in the backend *Source* https://www.entrepreneur.com/article/329012
Context (Classification and systematization of information available on the Internet)	*Google* started with the single feature of searching the web. Websites needed to be added manually and there was no AdWords in place *Source* https://www.slideshare.net/smoblast/lean-startup-analytics-and-mvp-lecture-and-workshop-at-zeppelin-university	*Yahoo* initiated its development with a curated list of links *Source* https://mlsdev.com/blog/minimum-viable-product-examples	*Craigslist* was developed as Concierge MVP by its founder Craig Newmark. Most of the early postings were generated by the founder himself *Source* Hanson (2016), The Social Media Revolution	*Google Adword Express* seemed to be fully automated from the beginning, but was operated by a backend of students in the early days to create copy *Source* https://www.revelx.co/blog/mvp-examples/

(continued)

Table 3 (continued)

	Single feature MVP	Piecemeal MVP	Concierge MVP	Wizard of Oz MVP
Connection (Creation of the possibility to exchange information in networks)	*Snapchat* had initially only the feature to share a foto for a couple of seconds *Source* https://growthhackers.com/growth-studies/snapchat	*No example identified*	*Zapier* founder, Wade Foster, initially contacted users of various forums to get insights on potential integrations and started building these integrations after the personal connection *Source* https://earlyusergrowth.com/startups/?ref=producthunt#dropbox	*No example identified*

3.3.1   Electry: The Linkedin for Skilled Blue-Collar Workers

Julian Lindinger and Konrad Geiger started their ventures' journey as students of the WHU in 2018 with the objective to solve a big problem of HR departments—the attraction of talent for their company. In addition, the founders observed that they frequently recommended others for jobs, but that there were no financial benefits for them to do so. They were thus doing the job of headhunters without benefiting from the value they created. The idea of amical.io as UBER for head-hunting was born. The idea can be understood as an e-attraction business model, where job offers are aggregated and users are incentivized to recommend others for the jobs. With a high level of excitement and great support from family and friends, Julian and Konrad decided to build the platform and launched the service at the end of 2018. They intuitively chose to build a Wizard-of-Oz MVP, where they mocked the B2B-processes. After launching the service, they soon realized that the platform missed the required traction from the user side. This was in conflict with one of the riskiest assumptions they had at the time—great jobs will attract talent to our platform. The business did not show traction although it had very attractive vacancies, e.g., from Quora and Zeitgold, on their platform. Many companies were attracted by the solution, but it turned out that the potential employees and recommenders did not choose the platform. After several interviews with users, the amical.io founders identified that the most important component is to attract talent because jobs will come anyway. Thus, they decided to pivot to future employees and developed a concierge MVP for a digital career assistant—amical.io/assistant. Every time a talent signs up for career assistance and expresses the interest to take on a new opportunity, the amical team starts to search for potential jobs. They are thus reversing the recruitment process from a head-hunting to a job-hunting model. Simultaneous to testing the amical.io/assistant in general, the team tested attractive verticals in the recruitment markets, where specific job profiles are highly demanded. After experiencing the costly pivot from the recommendation platform, amical.io tested its critical business assumptions in a more lean and rigorous manner. Based on the rigid experimentation, the team developed "Electry—the Linkedin for skilled blue-collar workers". In 2020, Electry has been accepted for the YCombinator acclerator programme and is now receiveing seed funding.

3.3.2   Acomodeo: Serviced Appartments for Corporate Travelers

Acomodeo was founded by David Wohde and Eric-Jan Krausch and was named as one of Europe's Top 100 Proptech Startups in 2018. Today, Acomodeo is leading the market of long-stay apartment stays for business travelers and working with a good majority of German and international corporates. But that is not what Acomodeo started as. Acomodeo was born out of the market need for long-stay apartments for journalists during major sports events like the Olympics or the Soccer World Cup. Working in the travel industry, David first served this market need by searching, acquiring, and connecting apartments with journalists looking for a long-stay apartment. This was their first concierge MVP that existed before the company was actually founded. Following the described process of business model discovery, the first three pillars of the venture pyramid were already covered and validated in a very early stage. Building on these early successes and confident from the early market feedback, David and Eric started the business to work on a digital marketplace for long-stay apartment bookings. After finalizing the first version of the platform, Acomodeo had to learn that the market is much harder to acquire compared to the times of sporting events. Their first version of the platform was serving at individual business travelers to book long-stay apartments directly with them. However, business travelers in this category are bound to corporate business travel policies most of the time and could not just book their apartment with Acomodeo. In fact, their users of the product were business travelers. However, the buyer was the corporate travel manager that they had to serve first. This is a great lesson on product-market fit and the importance of understanding customer segments from a user and buyer perspective. Product-market fit is also a lot about understanding the buyer and the user (which is not always the same). Fast forward, David and Eric pivoted the platform to serve the needs of the corporate business travel manager and included the features they needed to approve Acomodeo as a platform for corporate travelers.

4 Practical Implications for Digital Entrepreneurs

In the previous thoughts, we have seen that many digital startups leverage the lean startup approach but have challenges in applying it to their own journey. Our presented thoughts on the venture pyramid and MVPs for digital business models are aiming at structuring the search process for an attractive business model. This approach is designed to reduce uncertainty (not to eliminate it) and to provide guidance on the challenging journey. The different types of MVPs shall inspire startups to identify a way of testing and validating their business idea in the search process to an attractive business model. We understand the startup process as two-fold. While a startup searches for a repeatable and scalable business model, it also needs to achieve operational excellence in team structuring, management, accounting, sales, and so on. Additionally, reality will always bring surprises along the way. We have seen great business models that work out extremely well, but then within weeks, one of the key partners goes bankrupt and nothing seems to work anymore. We have not covered this in this chapter, but it should be within the radius of awareness of every entrepreneur, and it stresses the urge to regularly work and update the business model.

We furthermore believe that every entrepreneurial discovery process is only as good as the willingness of the entrepreneurs to learn, adapt, and challenge their own thoughts and ideas. Or simply put, the success of a venture lies in the execution of the idea rather than in the methodology itself. Every entrepreneur needs to decide individually how they want to build their business and what tools to use at the right time. As a general take away, we recommend embracing iterative validation based on hypotheses, a mindset to test, and a divergent and convergent thinking processes.

References

Bajwa, S. S., Wang, X., Duc, A. N., & Abrahamsson, P. (2017). Failures to be celebrated. An analysis of major pivots of software startups. *Empirical Software Engineering, 22,* 2373–2408.

Blank, S. (2010). *What's a startup? First principles.* https://steveblank.com/2010/01/25/whats-a-startup-first-principles/. Retrieved October 09, 2019.

Blank, S., & Dorf, B. (2012). *The startup owners manual: The step-by-step guide for building a great company.* K&S Ranch.

Cavalcante, S. A., Kesting, P., & Ulhoi, J. P. (2011). Business model dynamics and innovation. (Re)establishing the missing linkages. *Management Decision, 8*(3), S. 1327–1342.

CBInsights. (2018). *The top 20 reasons startups fail.* Online: https://www.cbinsights.com/research/startup-failure-reasons-top/. Retrieved October 09, 2019.

Chesbrough, H., & Rosenbloom, R. (2002). The role of business model in capturing value from innovation. Evidence from XEROXCorporation's technology spin-off companies. *Industrial and Corporate Change, 11* (3), S. 529–555.

Clauss, T. (2017). Measuring business model innovation. Conceptualization, scale development and proof of performance. *R&D Management, 47*(3), 385–403.

Croll, A., & Yoskovitz, B. (2013). *Lean analytics. Use data to build a better startup faster.* O'Reilly and Associates.

Dennehy, D., Kasraian, L., O'Raghallaigh, P., & Conboy, K. (2016). Product market fit frameworks for lean product development. In *R&D Management Conference*, June 2016, Cambridge (UK).

Design Council (2019). The double diamond. https://www.designcouncil.org.uk/news-opinion/double-diamond-15-years. Retrieved July 16, 2020.

Duc, A. N., & Abrahamson, P. (2016). Minimum viable product or multiple facet product? The role of MVP in software startups. In *International Conference on Agile Software Development (XP 2016). Agile Processes in Software Engineering, and Extreme Programming* (pp 118–130).

Ellis, S. (2013). *The startup pyramid.* Online: https://www.startup-marketing.com/the-startup-pyramid/. Retrieved October 09, 2019.

Frederiksen, D. L., & Brem, A. (2017). How do entrepreneurs think they create value? A scientific reflection of Eric Ries' Lean Startup Approach. *International Entrepreneurship Management Journal, 13,* 169–189.

Furr, N. R., & Ahlstrom, P. (2011). *Nail it then scale it. The entrepreneur's guide to creating and managing breakthrough innovation.* NISI Institute.

Gambardella, A., Camuffo, A., Cordova, A., & Spina, C. (2018). *A scientific approach to entrepreneurial decision making: Evidence form a randomized control trial* (October 16, 2018). Forthcoming in Management Science.

Gassmann, O., Frankenberger, K., Csik, M. (2014). The business model navigator. 55 models that will revolutionise your business. *Financial Times Prent.*

Ghaziani, A., & Ventresca, M. J. (2005). Keywords and cultural change: Frame analysis of business model public talk, 1975–2000. *Sociological Forum, 20*(4), 523–559.

Ghezzi, A. (2019). Digital startups and the adoption and implementation of lean startup approaches: Effectuation, bricolage and opportunity creation in practice. *Technological Forecasting and Social Change, 146,* 945–960.

Göcke, L. (2016). *Geschäftsmodellentwicklung im Spannungsfeld multinationaler Unternehmen. Eine Fallstudie am Beispiel der Elektromobilität.* Wiesbaden: Springer.

Göcke, L. (2017a). *Why the Venture Pyramid changes how you think about innovation.* https://www.swan.ventures/blog/2017/8/22/venture-pyramid. Retrieved July 15, 2020.

Göcke, L. (2017b). *How to track progress in the Build-Measure-Learn Loop.* https://www.swan.ventures/blog/2017/8/31/howto-track-progress-in-the-build-measure-learn-loop. Retrieved July 15, 2020.

Kallinikos, J., Aaltonen, A., & Marton, A. (2013). The ambivalent ontology of digital artifacts. *MIS Quarterly, 37,* 357–370.

Knapp, J., Zeratsky, J., Kowitz, B. (2016). *Sprint. How to solve big problems and test new ideas in just five days.* Simon & Schuster.

Maurya, A. (2012). Running lean. Iterate from Plan A to a Plan that Works. O'Reilly and Associates.

McClure, D. (2007). *Product marketing for pirates: AARRR!* Online: https://500hats.typepad.com/500blogs/2007/06/internet-market.html. Retrieved October 08, 2019.

Miles, R. E., & Snow, C. C. (1984). Fit, failure and the hall of fame. *California Management Review, 26*(3), 10–28.

Osterwalder, A., Pigneur, Y. (2011). *Business model generation. Ein Handbuch für Visionäre, Spielveränderer und Herausforderer.* Frankfurt am Main: Campus.

Osterwalder, A., Pigneur, Y., Bernarda, G., & Smith, A. (2014). *Value proposition design. How to create products and services customers want.* New York: Wiley.

Remane, G., Hanelt, A., Tesch, J. F., & Kolbe, L. M. (2017). The business model pattern database. A tool for systematic business model innovation. *International Journal of Innovation Management, 21*(1), 1750004 (61 pages).

Ries, E. (2011). *The lean startup. How constant innovation creates radically successful businesses.* Penguin Random House.

Ries, E. (2016). *The leader's guide to adopting lean startup at scale.* Kickstarter.

Schneider, S., & Spieth, P. (2013). Business model innovation. Towards an integrated future research agenda. *International Journal of Innovation Management, 17*(1), S. 1340001-1–1340001-34.

Siggelkow, N. (2007). Persuasion with case studies. *Academy of Management Journal, 50*(1), 20–24.

Sommer, S. C., Loch, C. H., Dong, J. (2009). Managing complexity and unforeseeable uncertainty in startup companies. *An Empirical Study. Organization Science, 20* (1), 118–133.

StartupGenome. (2011). Startup genome report. A new framework for understanding why startups succeed. https://s3.amazonaws.com/startupcompass-public/StartupGenomeReport1_Why_Startups_Succeed_v2.pdf. Retrieved October 06, 2019.

Teece, D. (2010). Business models, business strategy and innovation. *Long Range Planning, 43,* 172–194.

Wirtz, B. W. (2019). *Digital business models. Concepts, models, and the alphabet case study.* Springer Nature Switzerland.

Zhang, S. X., & Cueto, J. (2015). The study of bias in entrepreneurship. Entrepreneurship theory and practice.

Zott, C., Amit, R., & Massa, L. (2011). The business model: Recent developments and future research. *Journal of Management, 37*(4), 1019–1042.

Development and Validation of Platform Businesses in Digital Entrepreneurship

Lutz Göcke and Philip Meier

Abstract

Platform business models grow in relevance in nearly every industry by an optimization of transaction costs or a significant increase in innovativeness. Many entrepreneurs choose platform business models to create and capture value. Although the benefits of platform business models demonstrably have immense growth potential, these business models are also accompanied by unique challenges for startups in their early stages of development. In this chapter, we aim to discuss the specific challenges that digital entrepreneurs face when validating their platform business model concept. We also develop a processual model, based on the venture pyramid (discussed in Chap. 4 of this book) to validate the critical assumptions of platform business models. Based on three case studies of early-stage startups, we shed light on the dynamics of testing platform business models and discuss different approaches to develop a minimum viable platform.

1 Introduction

In late 2018, six out of the ten most valuable companies based on market capitalization run one or several platform business models (Handelsblatt, 2018). Examples such as Amazon Marketplace or Apple AppStore illustrate the character

L. Göcke (✉)
Chair of Digital Management, Nordhausen University of Applied Sciences, Nordhausen, Germany
e-mail: lutz.goecke@hs-nordhausen.de

P. Meier
Alexander Von Humboldt Institute of Internet and Society, Berlin, Germany

M. Soltanifar et al. (eds.), *Digital Entrepreneurship*, Future of Business and Finance, https://doi.org/10.1007/978-3-030-53914-6_5

of this particular type of business model. By occupying a mediating role in a multi-sided market environment, the platforms mentioned reduce transaction costs for supply and demand, simplify the occurrence of direct interactions, and thus bind both market sides to their own infrastructure. The economic power of digital giants such as Amazon and Apple stands for platform success that drives practical interest in this model from different industries. But for startups and traditional companies (incumbents), setting up a platform business also seems desirable. According to Gründerszene (2018), five of the eleven fastest-growing startups in Germany operated a multi-sided platform business model in 2018. Although digital platforms hold high growth and earnings potential caused by its mediating character, the setup phase is particularly challenging. This is so because instead of one stakeholder group, with suppliers and buyers, two or more groups are to be addressed. However, this is not unusual for firms that have supplier networks or network-based value chains. The distinctive aspect of platform business models lies in the demand for an ecosystem of direct transactions between the actors involved, which grows through network effects, without taking on the steering role, e.g., of an original equipment manufacturer (OEM) in the automotive supply chain. How difficult it is to develop a viable business model even in advanced stages of business activity due to the mechanisms of the multi-sided market is shown, for example, by Uber's high loss statement of more than 2.5 billion dollars in 2019, 10 years after the company was founded. Operating in the on-demand mobility market, Uber is still looking for approaches to keep drivers and customers on its own platform, to integrate them into related ecosystems such as public transport, to leverage the regionally created added value beyond the regions, and to compile its operations into sustainable profits. This special breed of a platform business model entails many challenges for digital entrepreneurs to develop and validate their platform business model. Ghezzi (2019) highlights that most digital startups use the lean startup approach in the early phases of their existence. However, Ghezzi (2019) also points out that the same digital startups struggle to define proper tests and to design appropriate minimum viable although having a validated toolset at hand. In this chapter, we align a structured process to validate/invalidate different facets of a business model with the unique characteristics of a platform business model in order to help digital entrepreneurs when developing and validating a platform business model. We base our thoughts on the developments in the previous chapter of Göcke and Weninger (2020) with regard to the development and validation process of new venture ideas.

2 Background

2.1 Platform Business Models

The concept of a platform has come a long way from being a rather fuzzy concept that is sometimes understood as making companies more efficient through leveraging economies of scale and scope to the understanding of platform business models that are characterized by a multi-sidedness of value creation (Gawer 2014). Airbnb, for example, needs to be attractive to guests (demand side), as well as to hosts (supply side). Facebook has developed a six-sided platform in the past with friends and businesses (each with roles as sender and receiver), as well as advertisers and app developers (Evanas and Schmalensee 2016). This fundamental characteristic of multi-sidedness is critical to the understanding of platform business models (Evanas and Schmalensee 2016) and goes in hand with the dynamics of network effects (Shaprio and Varian 1999). These dynamics provoke chicken-egg problems as they require companies to establish a critical mass of users on a platform in order to unleash a virtuous cycle (Pan Fang et al. 2019). At the same time, network effects can lead to winner-takes-most/-all situations in which companies create a strong competitive advantage through the size of the network and a lock-in through the attractiveness of network effects to both market sides (Cennamo 2019). The platform characteristics of multi-sidedness, the impact of network effects, as well as the associated chicken-egg problem and the winner-takes-all logic play a particularly important role in the development and validation of digital platforms as the central topic of this chapter (Evans 2003; Rochet and Tirole 2003). After a general introduction, these characteristics will be explained in more detail and placed in the context of the platform framework.

A common classification of digital platforms according to (Gawer 2014; Cusumano et al. 2019) describes transaction-oriented, innovation-oriented, and hybrid platforms. **Transaction-oriented platforms**, generally referred to as marketplaces, offer the technical architecture to bring together supply-creating and supply-demanding actors in order to carry out transactions of different value units. The platform itself is mostly not involved in individual transactions but only creates the framework through defined functions and mechanisms. The primary value proposition of this platform type is the facilitation of a simplified matching of the mentioned actors under the premise of significantly reduced transaction costs. This means that the respective platform, through its role as a single point of contact, combines supply and demand more efficiently as this would be possible without a platform. Popular examples for companies operating transaction platforms are eBay (used things), SoundCloud (audio files), or Deliveroo (food deliveries). **Innovation-oriented platforms** are understood as a basic architecture on which different actors come together to create new products and services (Gawer and Cusumano 2002; Parker et al. 2016). Examples are operating systems for personal computers and mobile devices. Microsoft Windows still functions as the underlying innovation platform on which third parties develop a broad spectrum of different applications for personal computers. However, Internet browsers driven by Google, which does not control a major PC operating system but a gradually dominant browser, are becoming increasingly important as an innovation platform for Web-based applications. A further increase in the importance of Web applications significantly threatens the supremacy of operating system providers—in this case, Microsoft—as an independent ecosystem develops around the browser as an innovation platform. If companies operate a combined or several closely interlinked transaction and innovation platforms, this is referred to as a **hybrid platform**.

The technology giants from the USA known under the acronym GAFA: Google, Amazon, Facebook, and Apple, all generate a large part of their market value by operating hybrid platforms. The same applies to the Chinese counterparts BAT: Baidu, Alibaba, and Tencent. Apple, for example, offers developers for mobile applications an innovation platform for apps with the iOS environment. These apps will then be offered and monetized to iPhone users via the AppStore transaction platform. Transaction platforms (e.g., eBay) and innovation platforms (e.g., Android) share the common feature that functionalities and mechanisms control the activities of the actors on the respective platform and influence the benefits for the respective actors. In general, platforms all function similarly as different actors exchange certain value units within an existing architecture. These actors can be buyers and sellers or social media users, among other roles. The architecture can be a development environment or a marketplace, and value units are, e.g., goods, services, money, or information.

In each of the mentioned scenarios, the platform sponsor has three possibilities to control the ecosystem of the actors, the platform, and the platform mechanisms through his dominant role (Adner 2017; Jacobides et al. 2018). With these activities, a platform owner needs to ensure the value-added for the platform users and the value capture for the platform owner. The adaptation of the platforms' technical infrastructure can be described as **platform manipulation**. The sponsor can, for example, significantly intervene in the actors' scope of action by adding or removing features or functionalities (Ozalp et al. 2018). A high degree of technical specifications for the use of the architecture, for example, contributes to raising the entry barriers for new actors into the ecosystem. At the same time, such a policy often reduces the possibilities of multi-homing; i.e., the actors create the same offer on different platforms, since the individual requirements have a negative effect on an agnostic application design (Cennamo et al. 2018). Amazon is a popular example of a platform sponsor who acts as an active market participant (= **market interaction**) on his own platform and selectively competes with complementors (Zhu and Liu 2018). Even if in some cases this leads to the displacement of complementary actors, in other cases unsatisfied demands from certain users can be met and cross-side network effects on the platform strengthened. Using Amazon as an example, displacement can manifest itself in the platform owner offering batteries on the marketplace under its own AmazonBasics brand and thus taking over market shares from independent battery dealers. Through **ecosystem governance**, platform sponsors can intervene in the rules and regulations of the platform and thereby model the value propositions and, in particular, the possibilities of value capture for different actors. In addition, governance-driven quality controls, such as peer-to-peer reviews, have a positive effect on the confidence-building character of the intermediate platform model (Jacobides et al. 2018) (Fig. 1).

Platform manipulation, as well as market interaction and ecosystem governance, is interdependent with the aforementioned platform characteristics: multi-sidedness, network effects, and winner-takes-all. **Multi-sidedness** describes the market conditions in which digital platforms play an interdependent role. Both the supply side and the demand side have to be managed. In the dimension of platform

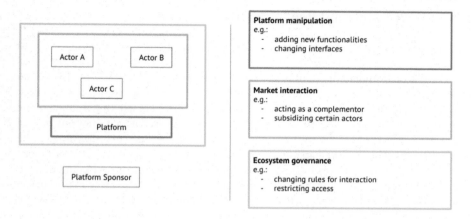

Fig. 1 Three dimensions of platform control

manipulation, these characteristics must be given high importance because technical changes in architecture must always be approached from the perspective of different actors on the platform. Through so-called **network effects**, the value that the platform creates for individual actors through other actors is increased. This is valid for additional and existing actors (Farrell and Klemperer 2007; Katz and Shapiro 1994). A distinction is made between the same-side and cross-side network effects. Same-side network effects describe the value-added effects on the same platform side, e.g., by additional users in a social network. With cross-side network effects, on the other hand, the value-added of the platform for one side increases through additional actors on another side. This can be observed, for example, in the relationship between supply and demand on eBay (Eisenmann et al. 2006). At its launch, every startup with a platform business model that builds on same-side or cross-side network effects faces a chicken-egg problem. Both users and suppliers/complementors to a platform alike do not want to see the platform thrive because their value is increasing with every additional user. Platform companies need to establish a critical mass that is attractive to both sides of the market (Shaprio and Varian 1999). Through the design of market interactions, platform sponsors themselves can act as supplier/complementor and thereby drastically increase the customer benefit through indirect network effects, especially in an early phase where there is still little supply on a platform. Driven by the network effect logic, the establishment of platforms in multi-sided market environments often leads to **winner-takes-all** situations. "Winner-takes-all" means that only one or a few platform sponsors serve and dominate a market. This mechanism can, for example, be strengthened by systematic action by the platform sponsor to increase market entry barriers within the ecosystem governance dimension.

2.2 Developing and Validating a Venture Idea

In the past ten years, the concept of a lean startup, where entrepreneurs and intrapreneurs alike validate or invalidate their riskiest business assumptions, has become a predominant thought in entrepreneurship literature (Ries 2011; Blank and Dorf 2012; Bland and Osterwalder 2020). Every venture idea can be seen as a bulk of interconnected assumptions. Some of the assumptions are existing right from the start, and others will evolve during the venturing process. The assumptions impact every decision and conversation, e.g., the design of business operations, the negotiations with venture capitalists, or the hiring of team members. The basic idea of the lean startup is to systematically test the most critical business assumptions to avoid premature scaling of the business since premature scaling is one major reason for startup failure (StartupGenome 2011; CBInsights 2018). It includes developing a product without even knowing if the customer has a problem that is worth solving or shows interest in the envisioned solution. Without the validation of demand and willingness to pay, the initiation of, e.g., an app development comes at high risk (StartupGenome 2011). Following Ries (2011), Blank and Dorf (2012), and Frederiksen and Brem (2017), the entrepreneur identifies a critical assumption to test, designs an experiment, runs the experiment, and creates learnings. Also in this book, Göcke and Weninger (2020) discussed the venture pyramid to structure the search process to a replicable and scalable business model as a response to the findings of Ghezzi (2019) that digital startups need. The venture pyramid (see Fig. 2) allows a focused experimentation of a business idea. It is structured into six levels of venture validation/invalidation. The questions next to the pyramid indicate the critical questions at every level. Every level of the pyramid builds on the former level. The assumptions with the highest magnitude of impact to the business reside at the bottom. Entrepreneurs are supposed to work upward the pyramid to validate or invalidate the most critical assumptions at the beginning of their startup journey. The assumption that a solution is attractive to potential users is located at the problem–solution fit. An entrepreneur can develop an experiment to test this critical assumption. The development of a minimum viable product (MVP) would be based on the validated assumption that users demand the product and are also willing to pay for it.

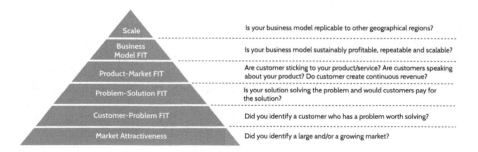

Fig. 2 Venture pyramid (reference Göcke 2017)

Entrepreneurs use the venture pyramid to structure the dynamic search process for a product market and business model fit, to run experiments, and thus to improve the decision making in circumstances of high uncertainty. At every level of the venture pyramid, an entrepreneur has multiple options to design an experiment (see also Göcke and Weninger 2020). The specific characteristics of platform business models add a new complexity to the validation/invalidation of a business idea (Table 1).

3 Conceptual Model and Empirical Insights

The development and validation of platform business models go hand in hand with a couple of specific challenges for a digital entrepreneur. In the following section, we apply the specific characteristics of platform business models to the venture pyramid. Furthermore, we look at the dynamics of platform business models and alternatives to develop a minimum viable platform to validate the product market fit.

3.1 Venture Pyramid for Platform Business Models

The venture pyramid has been discussed as a structured approach to develop and test an entrepreneurial venture. As discussed before, there are four specific characteristics of a platform business model that distinguish this type from a pipeline business: multi-sidedness, network effects, chicken-egg-problem, and winner-takes-all/-most situation.

Considering the **multi-sidedness** of a platform business, a startup needs to create value for at least two sides of the platform. Following the Airbnb example, we have guests representing the demand side (Side A) and hosts representing the supply side of the business (Side B). Both sides need to demand the platform to connect them either to sellers/buyers (transaction platform) or to connect them to complementors/users (innovation platform). The validation of the demand from both sides is central to the success of the platform business model. Therefore, a

Table 1 Special characteristics of platform business models impact the experimentation of a venture idea

Multi-sidedness	More than one actor on a platform requires experimentation with different market sides
Network effects	Utility for a customer depends on the number of users from the other market side. Experiments to test the importance and strength of network effects are required
Winner-takes-all/-most	Tendency to single-homing or multi-homing to be tested

platform entrepreneur needs to run experiments for both sides. To illustrate this, we have split the discussed venture pyramid to allow entrepreneurs to test the different market sides separately in the early phases of idea and concept validation (Fig. 3). The demand for a solution is primarily tested on the level of problem–solution fit, e.g., via smoke tests or qualitative interviews. To reach the level of problem–solution fit, platform entrepreneurs can run smoke tests or conduct interviews with the different sides of a platform. These developments should be built on a validated market attractiveness and customer problem fit for each side to avoid premature scaling. Both assumptions on the size of the target group and the relevance of the problem need to be true for the different sides of the platform. The separation into the two sides indicates that the existence of a customers' problem and demand can be tested in isolation for both sides. This again is essential to reduce the probability of premature scaling of the company. At the level of platform market fit, digital entrepreneurs' objective is to achieve not only onetime activation but ongoing usage, revenue, and word of mouth. This is the first moment when both sides of the platform need to be considered together. Thus, we describe a *platform market fit* as a situation where a platform continuously attracts and satisfies the demand from both sides. This platform market fit can be induced by the aforementioned actions of platform manipulation, market interaction, and ecosystem governance. We suggest experimenting with different alternatives, e.g., changing structures or rules, on the way to identify platform market fit. For an innovation platform (e.g., AppStore), this entails, for example, the decisions on the openness of interfaces or the design of the review/acceptance process (Tiwana 2014). The partial split of the venture pyramid illustrates that a platform market fit can be built on a product market fit where only one side of the platform is validated. An example of this is the validation of the Zappos platform business model by leveraging a Wizard of OZ MVP (Göcke and Weninger 2020). In its early days, Zappos creates an e-commerce Web site to buy shoes online. When launching the Web site, the supply side was purely handpicked shoes without any direct connection to the shoe manufacturer (Ries 2011). It was an early experiment on the demand side of the platform, without testing the intention of shoe companies to connect to the platform.

In businesses with a **network effect,** utility and demand are dependent on the number of users on the platform. As discussed before, network effects can take the form of same-side or cross-side network effects. For the success of the platform, digital entrepreneurs need to validate the critical assumptions on the existence of network effects to ignite growth for the business. See Table 2 for an outline of these assumptions.

We see the level of problem–solution fit as an initial stage to validate risky assumptions on the network effects in the business. User attraction in an early stage can be best evaluated through direct feedback in qualitative interviews or metrics like the conversion rate or customer acquisition cost in landing page tests. Early split tests with prototypes or landing pages can help to validate/invalidate the strength of same- or cross-side network effects. In these experiments, a user can be confronted with different signals on the number of users on a platform. The generated information guides the design of a minimum viable product and the startups'

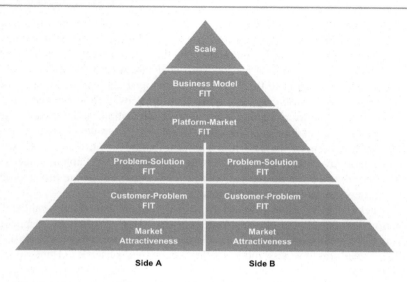

Fig. 3 Venture pyramid for platform business models

Table 2 Risky assumptions on network effects

	Side A (demand side)	Side B (supply side)
Same-side network effects	1. We believe that users of Side A are attracted by the number/quality of relevant users of Side A	2. We believe that users of Side B are attracted by the number/quality of relevant users of Side B
Cross-side network effects	3. We believe that users of Side A are attracted by the number/quality of relevant users of Side B	4. We believe that users of Side B are attracted by the number/quality of relevant users of Side A

market entry. It helps furthermore to cope with the **chicken-egg problem** because it indicates what side needs to be addressed first to gain traction on the platform. In addition, early evidence on the strength of the network effects can help to design the platform accordingly to reach a critical mass.

The stronger the dependency of one user side on the other, the greater is the chance of a lock-in situation where users are kept in the system because of its inherent attractiveness. These lock-in situations can turn into **winner-takes-all/-most situations** where one company dominates the market. Conditions of winner-takes-all or -most scenarios can be characterized by single-homing on a market side (e.g., Google for search engines). Here, users of the platform (applies to all sides) only use one platform to get their job done. In a multi-homing scenario, users use different alternatives to fulfill their jobs (e.g., fashion e-commerce). It is very important for a platform business to know whether it provides its service to single-homing users or multi-homing users as it impacts the company's need for capital, the market entry strategy, and the characteristics of its competitive positioning. In the stage of problem–solution fit, the platform entrepreneur has the opportunity to explore existing alternatives of the solution with qualitative interviews or based on a search engine keyword analysis. After the validation of the solution, the MVP version of the platform is developed and early adopters can be interviewed to identify use cases that make them turn away from the platform. As suggested before, platform manipulation, market interaction, and ecosystem governance are essential actions to create and capture value from the platform business model. The validation of the design of platform manipulation, market interaction, and ecosystem governance to not only create value but also to capture value is the missing step to achieve a business model fit. This is not a onetime fitting process but a continuous optimization of the business model (Fig. 4).

After achieving a business model fit, every entrepreneur should validate the international scalability of the platform business. Due to different competitive landscapes or environmental conditions (e.g., legal, political, or cultural), the scaling of platform business models often encounters obstacles. Here, too, the multi-sided platform character contributes to complexity. When entering new markets and regions, it is therefore also important to meet different requirements. While the user behavior of mobility seekers in Germany is presumably very similar to the user behavior in San Francisco, the supply side is much more regulated. In addition, in the case of Uber, different cityscapes influence the localization of passengers and drivers, and the algorithms working in San Francisco can lead to problems in Berlin.

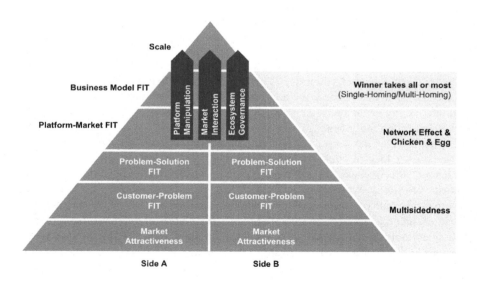

Fig. 4 Location of platform characteristics and platform control mechanisms on venture pyramid

3.2 Case Studies of Early-Stage Platform Startups

In order to illustrate our thoughts with some practical insights, we have created three different case studies with early-stage startups that are based in Germany. We conducted structured interviews for each case study, which followed a semi-structured interview guideline. The respective companies have been selected because they recently developed and implemented a platform business model. All three are still in an early stage but already report revenue and a growing user base as metrics for traction.

3.2.1 Anyyogi: The Yoga Community Platform

Anyyogi connects yoga teachers, students, and a space where the class can take place on one platform. The founder Natalie Pompe, herself a passionate yoga teacher, spotted the opportunity for creating Anyyogi in 2018 when she intensively explored the economics of the yoga market. After the completion of the training, there are basically two ways for yoga teachers to practice what they have learned. As a trainer, you can either sign up in a yoga studio or organize classes under your own name. Both paths offer advantages and disadvantages. It is difficult to be accepted as a trainer in a studio because the competition is high. In addition, the studio keeps a strong control over the timing and content of the course program and it extracts a large part of the revenues. For independent trainers, on the other hand, the problem is how to find a suitable room for the class and how to find and address potential students. Many do not manage to keep the frequency of courses or the number of participants as high as to make it profitable in the long run. Anyyogi addresses, in particular, the independent trainers and takes on the role of the studio in a particular capacity as the platform provides space on the one hand and sufficient participants and reach on the other. Due to the platform structure, the trainers retain a significantly higher share of the generated revenue as rooms are only used temporarily and the operation of extensive infrastructure is no longer necessary. In the platform design process, Anyyogi explicitly relies on an existing community of selected trainers and solves the chicken-egg problem by guaranteeing a high-quality offer on the platform. Students and new trainers are actively integrated into the community through networking during events and communication activities through the platform to maintain the initial momentum. At the time of the interview in mid-2019, Natalie was still managing many classes herself, which enabled her to gain a very detailed understanding of the desires and needs of all the groups involved, which she then translated into an automated software platform. High loyalty of trainers and students, identification with the platform and the brand, as well as user-driven marketing are some of the advantages of the community-driven approach of the Anyyogi platform. In the context of technical implementation and scaling, Natalie works in particular on questions concerning the automatic quality assurance of the service and the user-friendly design of the platform interfaces. To answer these questions, she is currently iteratively developing different versions of the platform, which get tested and optimized with selected users.

3.2.2 kawaloo: The Airbnb for Storage Space

The startup kawaloo was founded in 2019 as Airbnb for storage space by the two founders Marcel Wipijewski and Jan-Michael Steiner. Users have the chance to rent out space in their garage or basement with flexible durations to users who need additional storage space. kawaloo is a bootstrapped business that iteratively tested the business idea. In the early stages of customer problem fit and problem–solution fit, the kawaloo founders conducted a survey to validate the demand of both— landlords and tenants. Participants of the survey were invited to test mock-ups of the platform and to become lead users. The multi-sidedness was thus addressed simultaneously with a single experiment. For the minimum viable product, the kawaloo founders chose to develop a platform out of different available components —e.g., Web site builder or payment solution (piecemeal MVP). The supply side of storage space has been identified by the founders as the critical side of the business model to initiate the network effect. Especially, the optimized user experience through an integrated booking and payment process differentiates kawaloo from alternatives (e.g., Forum, eBay, Classifieds). kawaloo focuses on matching supply and demand in a relatively small geographical area, e.g., one neighborhood. Since proximity is at the heart of the business model, storage space is marked on a map. kawaloo aims to address the chicken-egg problem by extending the piecemeal MVP with a concierge component where the founders actively contact potential users of competing platforms to convert these users to early evangelists. This active conversion is conducted in strategic important launch regions and based on direct customer inquiries. In addition, social media and offline campaigns as well as publishing relevant content and articles help to further increase reach and awareness of the brand.

3.2.3 LogCorp: The Uber for Courier Services

The analyzed logistics startup can be defined as Uber for courier services. Founded in 2019, the startup currently works predominantly in Berlin and on its platform. It brings courier drivers together with companies and private individuals who are looking for a courier service. The driver network is fueled by individual drivers and vendors. The focus on the demand side is clearly on the B2B. Courier drivers have a lot of effort with current services. For example, there is no integrated navigation system, individual invoicing is required, and pickup forms must be carried in paper form. The startup digitizes and automates all these and other processes and also offers the best conditions on the market for courier drivers. The founding team discovered in the competition analysis that pure P2P models have failed and therefore initially built on the supply side through partnerships with professional driver agencies in order to meet the demand of the addressed B2B customers in any case. This demand (problem–solution fit) was validated in interviews and via landing page testing with Google AdWords. After generating relevant volumes in predominantly manual work on both the supply and demand sides, the startup's current challenges lie in process automation and increasing customer value. The latter goes hand in hand with testing and prioritizing new features on the platform. However, the team always keeps an eye on the balance between the two sides and, if necessary, activates driving agencies. The startup's developers implement new features in the product and get firsthand feedback from the drivers or carry out orders themselves. For the acquisition of B2B customers, the offensive communication of existing customers has proven to be the most successful approach.

3.3 Approaches to Design Minimum Viable Platforms

In the analyzed case studies, we identified three specific and one general approach to minimum viable platform design. All named startups start with the identification and implementation of a core transaction between actors. With kawaloo, for example, this is the provision of storage space by a supplier in exchange for a fee from the customer. Parker et al. (2016) and Cusumano et al. (2019) already describe the relevance of early focus on a core transaction in relation to the successful development of digital platforms. We empirically underline this finding in the examined case studies. Basically, the concept of the minimum viable product is applied to the more complex context of a multi-sided market. The core transaction is, therefore, to be understood as the simplest way of representing the value proposition of the platform for the addressed actors. All further services, offers, or additional transactions are to be understood as complementary features to the core.

The special approaches can be explained on the basis of procedures for each of the studied startups. The first approach, called **immersion**, describes a high manual effort of a platform sponsor, in our case Anyyogi, to deepen the understanding of the supply and demand side. The platform sponsor takes on the role of a market participant and engages on the platform to create a high level of learning in the early days of the venture development. YCombinator founder Paul Graham describes this procedure in a blog article published in 2013 with the title "Do Things that Don't Scale" using the example of the platform startups Airbnb. Anyyogi provides further evidence of the added value in prioritizing early-stage learning and improving the value proposition over automation. The main advantage of the immersion approach is that startups can reduce their early effort of building, e.g., supply-side relations when testing the experiences of the demand side. Although the immersion into a demand-side/supply-side actor enables the startup to test the covered role, the generated insights are biased.

LogCorp is initially building on the supply side of its delivery services platform itself by keeping drivers available, independent of demand, and in order to be able to immediately serve any requests that may arise. This approach of serving one side of the platform as a sponsor is called **anticipation**. Thus, the startup initially concentrates on testing the assumptions made on the demand side and focusing the knowledge gained on this side. At the same time, demand can be built up through the self-created offer, making the platform more attractive for independent providers in a second step. This approach comes at high risk, without an early problem–solution fit test of the customer demand,

kawaloo leverages other platforms to create the necessary reach to test its minimum viable platform assumptions. Called **piggybacking**, this could already be seen in the development of PayPal, which used the reach of eBay to build traction. Through active participation as buyers and sellers, PayPal employees actively convinced eBay users to use its service for financial processing during the transactions. Thereby, PayPal used the scale of eBay and the value-added of their service for eBay users as a leverage effect.

4 Practical Implications for Digital Entrepreneurs

The development of a platform business brings unique challenges (e.g., multi-sidedness and chicken-egg problem) for digital entrepreneurs. These challenges are contingent on the platform business model, but independent from the type of entrepreneurs, whether they are startup entrepreneurs or corporate entrepreneurs. We have adapted the venture pyramid to the characteristics of platform businesses and suggest to test the risky assumptions associated with multi-sidedness and network effects very early in the venturing process. For digital entrepreneurs, this means that a venture idea for a platform business model needs to be tested for both sides in order to get insights on the fundamental dynamics of platform business models. We want to encourage digital entrepreneurs to walk the extra mile to validate the demand side, as well as the supply side. It is tempting to focus only on the validation of the demand side of the business when time constraints and limited resources accompany the entrepreneurial journey. But the exclusive validation of one side of the platform comes at high costs. The development of a minimum viable platform based on wild guesses for these characteristics is accompanied by great risks to the venture process. From the state of platform market fit on, digital entrepreneurs should not only validate their assumptions on the single-homing vs. multi-homing characteristics but also on the design of the platform control mechanism in order to create and capture value. We see potential to conduct further research on the venturing process for platform business models, especially in terms of validation of risky business assumptions.

References

Adner, R. (2017). Ecosystem as structure: an actionable construct for strategy. *Journal of Management, 43,* 39–58.
Blank, S., & Dorf, B. (2012). *The startup owners manual: The step-by-step guide for building a great company.* K&S Ranch.
Bland, D. J., & Osterwalder, A. (2020). *Testing Business Ideas.* Wiley.
CBInsights. (2018). *The top 20 reasons startups fail.* https://www.cbinsights.com/research/startup-failure-reasons-top/. Retrieved October 09, 2019.
Cennamo, C. (2019). Competing in digital markets: A platform-based perspective. *Academy of Management Perspectives.* https://doi.org/10.5465/amp.2016.0048.
Cennamo, C., Ozalp, H., & Kretschmer, T. (2018). Platform architecture and quality trade-offs of multihoming complements. *Information Systems Research, 29*(2), 461–478.

Cusumano, M. A., Gawer, A., & Yoffie, D. B. (2019). The business of platforms: Strategy in the age of digital competition, innovation, and power. harperbusiness.

Eisenmann, T. R., Parker, G., & Van Alstyne, M. W. (2006). Strategies for two sided markets (October 1, 2006). Harvard Business Review, Vol. October 2006.

Evanas, D. S., & Schmalensee, R. (2016). *Matchmakers*. Boston: Harvard Business Review Press.

Evans, D. S. (2003). Some empirical aspects of multi-sided platform industries. *Review of Network Economics, 2,* 191–209.

Farrell, J., & Klemperer, P. (2007). Coordination and lock-in: Competition with switching costs and network effects. *Handbook of Industrial Organization, 3,* 1967–2072.

Frederiksen, D. L., & Brem, A. (2017). How do entrepreneurs think they create value? A scientific reflection of Eric Ries' lean startup approach. *International Entrepreneurship and Management Journal, 13,* 169–189.

Gawer, A. (2014). Bridging differing perspectives on technological platforms: Toward an integrative framework. *Research Policy, 43*(7), 1239–1249. https://doi.org/10.1016/j.respol. 2014.03.006.

Gawer, A., & Cusumano, M. A. (2002). *Platform Leadership: How Intel, microsoft and cisco drive industry innovation.* Boston, MA: Harvard Business School Press.

Ghezzi, A. (2019). Digital startups and the adoption and implementation of lean startup approaches: Effectuation, bricolage and opportunity creation in practice. *Technological Forecasting and Social Change, 146,* 945–960.

Göcke, L. (2017). *Why the Venture Pyramid changes how you think aboutinnovation.* https://www.swan.ventures/blog/2017/8/22/venture-pyramid. Retrieved July 15, 2020.

Göcke, L., & Weninger, R. (2020). Business development and validation in digital entrepreneurship. In M. Soltanifar, M. Hughes, & L. Göcke, L. (Ed.), *Digital entrepreneurship.* Wiesbaden: Springer.

Gründerszene (Ed.) (2018). Die 50 Wachstumssieger 2018. https://www.gruenderszene.de/awards/content/gewinner. Retrieved January 10, 2019.

Handelsblatt. (2018). Das sind die zehn wertvollsten Unternehmen der Welt. https://www.handelsblatt.com/finanzen/anlagestrategie/trends/apple-google-amazon-das-sind-die-zehn-wertvollsten-unternehmen-der-welt/22856326.html?ticket=ST-24231724-cc0GNWJucOFSehQhfxAT-ap5. Retrieved May 10, 2019.

Jacobides, M. G., Cennamo, C., & Gawer, A. (2018). Towards a theory of ecosystems. *Strategic Management Journal, 39,* 2255–2276.

Katz, M. L., & Shapiro, C. (1994). Systems competition and network effects. *Journal of Economic Perspectives, 8*(2), 93–115.

Ozalp, H., Cennamo, C., & Gawer, A. (2018). Disruption in platform-based ecosystems. *Journal of Management Studies, 55,* 1203–1241.

Pan Fang, T., Clough, D. R., & Wu, A. (2019). From chicken-or-egg to platform ecosystem: Mobilizing complementors by CReating Social Foci. *Academy of Management Proceedings, 2019*(1), 14047. https://doi.org/10.5465/AMBPP.2019.76.

Parker, G. G., Van Alstyne, M. W., & Choudary, S. P. (2016). *Platform revolution: How networked markets are transforming the economy–and how to make them work for you.* New York: WW Norton & Company.

Ries, E. (2011). *The lean startup: How constant innovation creates radically successful businesses.* Penguin Random House.

Rochet, J. C., & Tirole, J. (2003). Platform competition in twosided markets. *Journal of the European Economic Association, 1,* 990–1029.

Shaprio, C., & Varian, H. R. (1999). *Information rules: A strategic guide to the network economy.* Harvard Business School Press.

StartupGenome. (2011). Startup genome report. A new framework for understanding why startups succeed. https://s3.amazonaws.com/startupcompass-public/StartupGenomeReport1_Why_ Startups_Succeed_v2.pdf. Retrieved June 10, 2019.

Tiwana, A. (2014). *Platform ecosystems. Aligning architecture, governance, and strategy.* Waltman: Morgan Kaufmann.

Zhu, F., & Liu, Q. (2018). Competing with complementors: An empirical look at Amazon.com. *Strategic Management Journal, 39*, 2618–2642.

Blockchain as an Approach for Secure Data Storage on Digital Consulting Platforms

Sebastian Gerth and Lars Heim

Abstract

This chapter examines the concept of data security in a society increasingly shaped by digital technologies. We show how secure data storage can be optimised regarding digital documentation in the implementation of health-related service offers based on established procedures. Security and privacy of data are therefore particularly important in this subject area since highly sensitive data is stored and processed during health-related online consultations. The advent of blockchain technology provides a valuable opportunity to create trust in digital platforms. After relevant concepts and terms have been clarified, the functionality of the blockchain in general, as well as the different types, will be discussed. From this, options for the use of online consulting are developed and illustrated on the basis of three use cases.

1 The Relevance of Digital Consulting Platforms for Entrepreneurs Considering Blockchain Technology

Due to its decentralised mode of operation, blockchain technology enables data to be stored more securely than the centralised methods of data storage that have been widely used up to now. Existing uncertainties have been publicly demonstrated by recent data scandals: For example, the so-called Doxing Gate at the end of 2018, in which the online user "0rbit" or "G0d" made celebrities' data publicly accessible as

S. Gerth (✉)
University of Erfurt, Thuringian Competence Center Economy 4.0, Erfurt, Germany
e-mail: sebastian.gerth@uni-erfurt.de

L. Heim
Clausthal University of Technology, Clausthal-Zellerfeld, Germany

© The Author(s) 2021
M. Soltanifar et al. (eds.), *Digital Entrepreneurship*, Future of Business and Finance,
https://doi.org/10.1007/978-3-030-53914-6_6

in a kind of advent calendar. Just as well known is the Cambridge Analytica scandal in 2016, when millions of Facebook data were illegally evaluated for Donald Trump's election campaign (Gerth and Heim 2020). These incidents show that we live more in an age of trust than in an information age. While information on electronic news, social media and knowledge platforms is continuously available and is exponentially growing in volume (Demary 2016; Jaekel 2017; de Reuver et al. 2018; Zehir et al. 2020), trust is a commodity that the players must either first strategically acquire or laboriously recapture when they hope to gain the favour of the users for digital services such as digital consulting platforms (DIVSI 2017a, b; Diekhöner 2018).

The range of *digital services* is extremely diverse and extends from the (partially) public provision of information or communication options such as chats, e-mail or similar, to online banking, billing and payment systems, for example, in the case of e-commerce solutions, to e-learning and concrete personal advisory services (Hanekop et al. 2001; Bruhn and Hadwich 2017; Stich et al. 2019). The borders between services are often blurred, since social media platforms, for example, allow multimedia communication between at least two parties, money transfer, discussions in forums and so on. However, all digital services generally have in common that they are provided by centralised institutions, which themselves have a high degree of digitisation and are represented via digital platforms (Jaekel 2017; Kofler 2018). As a result, the business models are highly scalable, and corresponding organisations can have considerable market power (Gundlach 2009; Täuscher et al. 2017). Thus, in this chapter, a digital service is understood to be a service offered on an online platform to solve a socially or individually relevant problem, in the course of the use of which personal data is collected, stored and processed by the offering institution. As already indicated, the collection of personal data demands a certain level of data security. This is where blockchain technology can provide a remedy.

There is still disagreement in the scientific literature about a generally valid definition of blockchain, as different scientific directions, such as economics, computer science and law, meet and deal in parallel with the common terms used in the practical application of the technology (Gerth and Heim 2020).[1] In a comprehensive, interdisciplinary analysis, Meijer (2017) summarises all relevant definition components from the scientific, but also from the application-oriented literature. This results in the following definition, which is used in this chapter:

'Blockchain technology is a distributed, shared, encrypted, chronological, irreversible and incorruptible database and computing system (public/private) with a consensus mechanism (permissioned/permissionless), that adds value by enabling direct interactions between users' (Meijer 2017, p. 39).

---

[1]Blockchain technology is a comparatively young technology, which has been used mainly for online or open access publications to date. This is reflected in the consequent selection of sources.

In other words, a blockchain is a digital accounting system in which several actors —first and foremost transmitters, receivers and operators (of the nodes) of the decentralised network—are involved (Burgwinkel 2016; Drescher 2017).

In the following, this chapter aims to highlight the contribution of blockchain technology in creating trust in digital service and consulting offerings through data security.

2 Underlying Concepts: Data Security and Data Protection in Online Consulting and Blockchain Technology

Online consulting, as a specific form of digital services, can be described as an exchange of information between at least two parties via digital channels based on natural and/or artificial intelligence. On the level of content, the counterpart takes care of a (e.g. physical) problem of one or more clients individually in order to improve the (e.g. health) state. Such a consultative institution can be a human being on the one hand, and a digital counterpart, such as an artificial intelligence in the form of an algorithm (e.g. a bot), on the other.

2.1 Data Security and Data Protection

The handling of data in communication and storage, especially against the background of individual problems, is highly relevant. Discretion can, for example, be ensured by a self-imposed duty of confidentiality, the existence of which and the mandatory compliance with which should be publicly communicated. Ultimately, this is a way of establishing anonymity towards third parties. It appears useful if those seeking help always have the same contact person, although complete digital documentation in the form of a customer administration—for example, by means of a personalised e-filing system (also known as EHR systems, electronic health records; Ströher and Honekamp 2011; Karg 2013)—provides the possibility that colleagues can also offer their help in an emergency. Furthermore, several consultations are often necessary to solve a problem and a future request for help can be based on the solution history of the respective client. Availability can be controlled via cloud applications and the allocation of appropriate access rights to the personal e-file. While this dimension focuses on the management of an organisation, the protection against manipulation, disclosure and loss of relevant data mainly concerns the underlying IT infrastructure. Privacy is an essential umbrella for both aspects: on the one hand regarding the consultant/intermediary–client relationship, and on the other hand of course regarding to data security and data protection (Grimm and Bräunlich 2015). While *data security* should protect data, *privacy* protects people. Data security concerns the protection of data against abuse, falsification and loss or non-availability. Data protection concerns the use of personal data by authorised persons. Data protection is primarily of interest from the perspective of the data subject, while data security is primarily considered from the perspective of the data processor and owner (Bühler et al. 2019). Data security is thus aimed at IT systems and therefore at the technical component of digital services, while data protection refers to stored content and hence the legal component. The latter is usually regulated by specific directives such as the European Data Protection Regulation (GDPR) and must be implemented by intermediaries or organisations involved in online consulting. The former, however, requires consideration because of the relevance of blockchain technology for digital consulting platforms.

In order to securely archive long-term data in digital form (Hackel and Roßnagel 2008), it is possible to work with local systems, i.e. software installed on local computers and/or storage on individual data carriers. Modern working environments, on the other hand, use certain cloud systems as a de facto standard. The advantage is, above all, the ability to work independently of time, location and device, as well as collaborative work due to the constant availability of the owing to its storage on servers that are usually provided externally. These are usually operated in computer centres, which in turn are specialised in their operation, administration, security and access protection as a business model. Hardware acquisition and maintenance are therefore no longer necessary if external services are used; the services provided can be easily adapted to the organisational development and, if necessary, several existing or new company locations can be easily integrated; SaaS models for, for example, specific CRM systems for documenting customer contacts also allow reliable cost calculation based on monthly invoices. The only requirement for its use is sufficiently fast Internet access. Employees are then given access to the files relevant to their work, which can sometimes also be edited collectively.

The points mentioned above already show that not only clients must have confidence in the provider in order to use it, but also the management of the organisation itself must trust in cloud providers with regard to data security, sovereignty, access and processing as well as storage location, maintenance, failure protection and so on (Walterbusch and Teuteberg 2012; Buch et al. 2014; Backhaus and Thüring 2015), which provide and ensure the technological basis for the work on the client. In addition, dependence on the cloud or SaaS provider also has a significant impact, as non-compliance with data protection and security standards ultimately falls back on the institution. This can not only result in image problems but also sometimes lead to immense downtime costs in the event of the cloud provider's insolvency.

The current practice of data processing and the reasons mentioned above motivate entrepreneurs and their teams, as same as individuals to think about alternatives and/or possible solutions. Trust in centralised systems can be created, for example, through anonymisation (e.g. through onion routing, as in the TOR service), encryption technologies (Schulz 2016; Petrlic 2017), digital signatures (Kumbruck 2000; Bertsch 2002), VPN connections and/or legally and audit-proof archiving (Hackel and Roßnagel 2008). In addition to these instruments, the blockchain also serves to increase not only data security, but also data protection, as described in the following section.

2.2 Foundations, Advantages and Disadvantages of Blockchain Technology

The technological basis of a blockchain is formed by the so-called data blocks: each block contains at least one data record (e.g. digitally recorded contents of a consultation), a timestamp (date and time of the conversation), transaction data (in the form of addresses of the parties involved, e.g. from consultant to client) and a cryptographically secure, so-called hash value of the previous block as well as the verification sum of the entire blockchain. The hash value is a character string of a certain length that acts as a check value: the blocks that build on each other are cryptographically linked using the hashes to form a chain (e.g. to map the course of a consultation over a longer period of time). This is where the name of the technology is derived from (Swan 2015; Mougayar and Buterin 2016) (Fig. 1).

The entirety of these signed and sealed blocks is called a blockchain. It is stored on several network computers or nodes; thus, it is decentralised and hence a neutral system of information processing (Burgwinkel 2016). To participate in the blockchain, a software access, the so-called wallet, is required. Access is gained via digital keys: the public key is comparable to the international bank account number (IBAN) known from the banking sector, and the private key is like the secret personal identification number (PIN). The public key can, therefore, be easily communicated to third parties as an address for transactions, while the private key serves as an access password to the wallet and for transaction verification: in order for the participants in the public blockchain to agree on an identical version of the same block, a consensus must be reached—for this purpose, there are various mechanisms for signing or creating blocks.[2] This process is called mining. Those actors who are involved in this process are called miners—in the above metaphor, these are, so to speak, the accountants of the blockchain.

The *advantages* offered by blockchain are numerous. First, the technology creates a new level of transparency, as all transactions can be monitored. Furthermore, the code of the blockchain is often freely available. Decentralisation

---

[2]*Proof of work* (PoW) means that the miners must prove that they have made a certain amount of effort in the verification process. The idea is that the miner demonstrates a conscious willingness to actively participate in the blockchain by using his own energy—i.e. electricity to operate one or more computers, as well as time and equipment. In the PoW, numerous arithmetic operations are performed to create a chain of predefined length from a chain of characters of any length using mathematical hash functions. In this way, the legitimacy of the transaction is checked using resources. The first miner to find the solution is then rewarded (e.g. with a certain value of a cryptocurrency). In the case of PoW, the blockchain is vulnerable to the so-called 51% attacks: If an actor succeeds in controlling 51% of the nodes or computing power for mining, the transaction history can be manipulated—for example, by using the same money several times for purchases, e.g. of Bitcoin. This is not possible with the proof of stake methodology. In *proof of stake* (PoS), the blockchain network itself uses a weighted random selection to reach a consensus on who can create a new block. Moderating aspects of the weighting are, for example, the duration of participation and/or the ability to participate ('stake') measured by the network resources applied. The PoS thus can do without mining. In any case, the consensus algorithms enable each participant to check whether his or her stored blockchain complies with the rules of the whole.

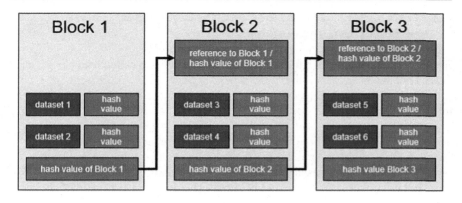

Fig. 1 Illustration of the block generation of a blockchain. *Source* Own illustration according to Burgwinkel (2016)

ensures that each participant (e.g. consultants and clients involved in the network) has equal rights and always a synchronised, validated and up-to-date version of the blockchain. This also means that decisions (e.g. on code updates) must be made by a majority. By storing the blocks in the distributed network, the verification of the transactions by numerous nodes as well as the cryptographic encryption and the complex consensus mechanisms, a high degree of integrity and manipulation security is generated in a blockchain (Hooper 2018). This makes it highly reliable and trustworthy (e.g. for verification to a third party, such as a health insurance company).

Decentralised data processing with many replications also leads to a high degree of reliability (Burgwinkel 2016). This redundancy is thus effective protection against attacks and data loss. Furthermore, the interlinking of the individual data blocks with the help of transparent hashing in the distributed network ensures good traceability of the permanently traceable transaction history (e.g. in the form of a medical history; Consultancy UK 2017). The blockchain also enables transactions to be processed faster and more efficiently than previous methods. This can lead to an increase in quality at lower costs compared to other IT systems. The technology also ensures disintermediation, i.e. the streamlining of value chains, which can prevent dominant market positions (Song et al. 2016). Particularly, (fee-based) intermediary players are affected, which could be eliminated by using a blockchain (Düring and Fisbeck 2017).[3]

However, the advantages are also countered by several *disadvantages* (Cap 2019; Kossow 2019). Currently, the scaling of blockchains is problematic: since each node of the network has to store all data, large amounts of data of several terabytes can accumulate in a short time, especially with numerous transactions

---

[3]For a direct transfer, for example, banks would no longer be necessary or notaries for the confirmation of contracts. In this way, corruption can be prevented, which makes the blockchain not only technologically economical but also socially relevant.

(e.g. payments), as the blockchain increases in size with each block. It is therefore difficult for many new users to join a blockchain at short notice. With the current broadband and storage capacities, participation is therefore difficult, especially for private individuals, or involves great demands on the technical infrastructure. Ultimately, this also limits the lifetime of a blockchain if the expansion of memory and network speed is lagging behind the resource requirements of a blockchain, and thus successive nodes will disappear, since for instance the expensive hardware is no longer affordable.

Concerning the transactions, there are two noticeable features in particular: on the one hand, the actual transaction must also be signed and synchronised, which is why a blockchain has a significantly lower performance about the speed of the transactions compared to a classic database, which only stores the final state and not the entire transaction history as does a blockchain. It should be mentioned, however, that the difficulty of capacity and confirmation delays is an increasingly less weighty argument against the blockchain, mainly due to the lighting network.[4] On the other hand, revising transactions is virtually impossible—the stability postulated above as an advantage is thus also a weakness. This applies in particular to public-permissionless blockchains (see the following subchapter, in particular, Table 1); in blockchains with a restricted consensus, this may be possible because the group of validators is clearly defined and they can decide on a rollback by majority vote (Baumann et al. 2017). The above-mentioned advantageous transparency ensures, especially in the case of public blockchains, that everyone can use the public key to view the transaction history—i.e. income, expenses and prices— via an explorer, which is not desirable for every potential participant and is therefore disadvantageous at the same time. This is particularly relevant for automated big data analyses, for example, regarding systematics of transaction flows. An additional problem is access to the blockchain: if a user loses the private key required for validation, he also loses irretrievable access to his wallet and thus to the blockchain (Dasu et al. 2018). While this problem mainly affects individual participants, another problem arises on a collective level: if the actors involved in a blockchain do not have a consensus on the future of a blockchain project since the majority decision process can sometimes be difficult for actors unknown to each other due to a lack of trust (which is why majority voting is both an advantage and a disadvantage), it can lead to the so-called forks, i.e. to splits and thus fragmentation of one and the same blockchain. This can lead to uncertainty among users, as they may then no longer know which blockchain is the one with the more promising future. Another difficulty can be the integration of a blockchain into existing IT

---

[4]This is a protocol that allows scaling, especially of the Bitcoin blockchain, although the idea also seems to be applicable to other blockchains: here, the concept is that after a start signal, the so-called funding transaction, transactions made within a channel, are not stored in the blockchain. This results in a relief and thus potential scalability. After each payment, the current account balance is temporarily stored in the so-called commitment transaction and all transactions are only written to the blockchain when one of the participants closes the channel with a finalising signal, the so-called settlement transaction (Sixt 2017).

Table 1 Types of blockchain technology

Dimension		Validation		
		Permissionless	Permissioned	
			Single organisation (single authority blockchain)	Consortium (federated blockchain)
Access	**Public**	Public-permissionless	Public-permissioned	Public-permissioned
	Private	Private-permissionless	Private-permissioned	Private-permissioned

Source Own illustration

infrastructures. This applies equally to hardware and software at the technical level and change management at the employee level.

3 Blockchain Typology and Its Usage for Consulting Platforms

The use of blockchain technology in connection with online consulting is often discussed in the medical field (Hölbl et al. 2018; Agbo et al. 2019). However, from the advantages and disadvantages explained in the previous section, it is clear that not all kinds of blockchains are suitable for documenting data of digital consulting platforms in a data protection-compliant manner and thus sufficiently protecting privacy, as these data would be visible to every participant of the blockchain (Pesch and Böhme 2017; Bogdan 2018). Nevertheless, one can distinguish between different blockchain types which offer different application possibilities due to their different configuration (Meijer 2017; Meier and Stormer 2018). According to Kudra (2018), two essential dimensions are used for this purpose:

The '*access*' *dimension*: User rights regarding read and write rights and the execution of transactions (public vs. private)

The '*validation*' *dimension*: User rights regarding participation in the consensus mechanism (permissionless vs. permissioned)

These two dimensions can be combined, allowing four blockchain types to be distinguished and defined (BitFury Group 2015; Kravchenko 2016; Meijer 2017; Carson et al. 2018; Kudra 2018). These are summarised in the following table.

Public blockchains are therefore intended more for the use by individuals: they retain control over their personal data and can carry out transactions of various data, such as information, financial resources, etc., quickly and cost-effectively without being dependent on a central agency. Private or federated blockchains are predestined for private companies and externally segregated, closed groups, which have to limit the activities in their network to a certain group of people. They offer the efficiency and transparency of blockchain technology in a protected environment that cannot be seen by outsiders. On a private blockchain, access to it—for example, through a digital consultation request with subsequent consultation—is approved by the operator or consultant and thus ultimately by a specific institution. At the same time, it can be defined within the organisational structure which employee can perform specific tasks based on the stored data. For example, a consultant needs information on content, while the payment for the service used is mainly of interest to the finance department.

An institution using a private blockchain retains complete control of the system because all users and all operators of the consensus mechanism are known. In contrast to a public blockchain, trust in the validators is therefore necessary (Buterin 2015). Another significant difference is the reduced transparency: the code of the blockchain cannot usually be seen by the users (Wüst and Gervais 2017). External parties—such as health insurance companies, the employer, or friends and acquaintances of the person seeking help—cannot access the system either. On the one hand, this serves to protect the blockchain and the data it contains, but it also prevents the blockchain from being developed further by a majority of users. The question in each individual case is always whether this is necessary. Just like the validation of transactions, the further development and updating of the blockchain falls to the limited group of validators (Baumann et al. 2017). According to Buterin (2015), an extension or improvement of the blockchain is thus much easier to achieve, since, for example, reconciliation processes can be streamlined. The revision of transactions is also possible in this environment through a rollback, since the group of validators is clearly defined (Baumann et al. 2017). This may be necessary if transactions have been incorrectly validated, e.g. if software errors or attacks have resulted in incorrect prices for the services provided.

Private blockchains use different types of consensus mechanisms than public blockchains, which can validate at a much higher speed than, for example, the above-mentioned proof-based consensus mechanisms (Wüst and Gervais 2017). Particularly noteworthy here are the Byzantine fault tolerance (BFT) based consensus protocols, such as the pBFT (Wüst and Gervais 2017; Castro and Liskov 1999). This is mainly due to the fact that only a few, very powerful network nodes are required for validation: both data transfer rate and loading time are significantly faster with these consensus mechanisms.[5] The resilience of this blockchain type against hacker attacks, data loss and system failures is much higher when compared since they store data only on a selected set of computing systems (Baumann et al. 2017). Private blockchains are also very scalable and can be easily extended if necessary. Therefore, it is also well possible to test them initially on a small scale and if successful in expanding them (Carson et al. 2018). Legal framework conditions can also be clearly defined, as the blockchain can be unambiguously assigned to a company or another user group (Bogensperger and Hinterstocker 2018). These aspects speak in favour of using private blockchains when setting up

---

[5]For example, in the public-permissionless Bitcoin blockchain, the validation time of a transaction can be up to two hours. In private-permissioned blockchains, it is usually only about 15 seconds (Baumann et al. 2017).

digital consulting platforms; however, their centralisation is problematic on top of the disadvantages mentioned above.

In order to break up the centralisation of private blockchains, the so-called federated blockchain can be considered as an extension of the latter (Gerth and Heim 2020). In such a case, more than one institution is responsible for the maintenance of the network or validation. This results in mutual control since the majority of the institutions makes decisions for the benefit of the network. Accordingly, such a consortium reaches a consensus if the majority votes for a certain action (e.g. a change of code, access rights, etc.). Wrong decisions or manipulations by individuals can thus be prevented as far as possible, and the advantages of (limited) decentralization can still be used. In case of establishing online consulting platforms, such a regulative acting consortium should accordingly be composed of experts who are involved in the added value of online consulting: representatives from civil society, professional associations and professional federations and ultimately, for example, market active companies, medical and/or psychological associations and/or health insurance companies, provided that they contribute a share of the financing. The blockchain then serves as a digital instrument that creates trust between all parties involved in the consulting process and at the same time enables the progress of this technology.

4 Case Studies: Telemedicine, Patientory and Medblock

Practical implementations of digital consulting platforms based on the blockchain technology are still rare due to the novelty of the technology and its areas of application. In the following sections, three relevant cases will be presented.

4.1 Telemedicine—COVID-19-Pandemic

One possible use of blockchain-based digital consulting platforms in the context of the healthcare system and healthcare provision is the remote diagnosis of disease symptoms by medical personnel. The relevance of such services seems to be high, especially against the background of the COVID-19-pandemic (Khan et al. 2020). Due to the exponential, worldwide spread of the disease and its typical symptoms, which are similar to those of common influenza, the short-term need for diagnoses increased rapidly. In order to reduce the risk of infection for other patients and the medical staff involved, a remote diagnosis option appears to be highly appropriate.

Such a service not only helps to counteract panic but also to collect valuable data that can be used to contain the disease. A system of this kind also makes sense because of the containment measures that came with the COVID-19-pandemic, such as the quarantine of individuals and curfews that were imposed in many places. It could not only assist in the initial diagnosis, but also serve as a basis for further monitoring of quarantined patients. Especially for efforts to contain such epidemics and pandemics, early detection and, as a result, the quality of the data obtained is important (Williams et al. 2013). In addition, patients must be certain of the anonymity and purpose of their patient data and the qualifications of the medical staff treating them. A solution based on a federated blockchain, as described above, could guarantee data quality and security. Accordingly, not only patients would benefit, but also forecasts with higher reliability could be made. A consortium that could oversee the consensus mechanism of such a blockchain could consist of government institutions, hospitals and family physicians. The authors are not aware of any telemedicine company that already relies on the blockchain technology.

The Swedish start-up Kry (kry.de), however, is pursuing an approach that moves in this direction (Blix and Jeansson 2018). Founded in 2015, the company first tested the marketability of telemedicine in Sweden. It entered the German market in December 2019, prompting patients to book a video consultation hour in the smartphone app and answer a few questions about their complaints (Stübner 2020). Such questions are intended to help the doctor prepare for the video chat. At the latest, after 20–30 min—as promised by the start-up—a doctor will get in touch. The company works together with physicians who can issue a prescription, a sick note, or a referral to a specialist. The company also cooperates with the online pharmacy DocMorris, which can deliver the required medication to the patient on prescription if required (Stübner 2020). Although the company is not yet using blockchain technology at the time this text was written, such technology could be used in the future. This could, for example, also make the issuing of prescriptions via the service to patients more secure. During the COVID-19-pandemic, Kry used its existing infrastructure to provide free video consultations to patients with COVID-19-symptoms (KRY 2020).

4.2 Patientory

Patientory (patientory.com) is one of the first providers of distributed apps (dApps) and blockchain-based software solutions for the healthcare industry, which meet the complex challenges of the healthcare sector (Warner 2019). The purpose of such apps is to enable consumers to better manage their own health information and thereby improve their quality of life and health while providing benefits to all stakeholders in the healthcare industry. In order to offer such solutions, the PTOYNet blockchain was launched and additionally, the Patientory Association was founded in 2017 as a global non-profit organisation consisting of institutions of the healthcare industry. The members of the Patientory Association form the consortium to monitor the consensus mechanism of the federated PTOYNet blockchain (Patientory Association 2019).

On the one hand, patientory's dashboard software provides institutions, service providers and insurance companies with a simple and secure means of storing and better managing health information. It thus serves the health management of a population by regulating and protecting the patient data in the blockchain while providing easy, secure access to actionable health information and administrative decision support. It also enables physician-coordinated patient care that can be fully managed through the platform. On the other hand, the mobile app enables consumers to efficiently track and manage information about their own health and any costs associated with it. Furthermore, the secure transfer of the users' medical information, which is secured within the PTOYNet blockchain, is facilitated. With these services and benefits, patientory seeks to revolutionise the relationship between patients, physicians and healthcare institutions by utilising blockchain technology (Patientory 2018). It is critical to note that there is still no generally recognised blockchain for the healthcare sector. Nevertheless, patientory has taken an important step in this direction by founding the Patientory Association as a supervisory consortium.

4.3   Medblock

The London-based company MedBlock (medblock.co.uk) intends to store patient data using blockchain and integrate it into the medical treatment process. The company is focusing on a b2b business model which not only allows secure and decentralised data storage and exchange but also wants to enable (predictive) analyses of the available data. The company connects existing EHR systems onto the blockchain network enabling the automation of arbitrary business processes using the data. It, however, does not explain the exact process of data analysis. This is particularly regrettable because the use of artificial intelligence should certainly offer added value here, while the communication between the blockchain and the algorithm would be worth discussing. Regardless of the procedure, the evaluation of the data should always be carried out under the control of a physician who is supported by modern technology.

Particularly against the background of increasing globalisation, it seems to make sense to store health data securely and at any time worldwide for quick comparison during treatments. This is especially true for emergencies, as rapid data availability can be crucial for targeted and successful treatment. For the patient, a transparent insight into the data is relevant for an overview of their own health and correct billing. They are informed about updates on the blockchain by e-mail. Doctors can avoid multiple documentation of the same diseases and thus bureaucratic effort by updating existing entries. Insurance companies can make data retrieval more efficient and coordinate any difficulties with all parties involved on the same data basis.

MedBlock promises to connect existing electronic health record (EHR) systems with the blockchain, without specifically addressing the technical implementation of the interfaces. The company relies on a private blockchain and uses technologies from IBM Bluemix, the IBM Cloud and IBM Watson Health. Against the background of the points discussed above, this seems to be the best solution so far. According to the company's information, the blockchain is based on the Hyperledger Fabric v.1.4 platform (as of April 2020), as the following figure shows. MedBlock cooperates with Altoros (Sunnyvale, CA, USA) on the development side.

It should be critically noted that there is not yet a standard for storing patient data in the blockchain and that this can probably only be developed by a consortium of relevant, globally active players in the health industry or even the WHO. In this case, a federated blockchain would have to be used. It is therefore fundamentally questionable whether individual companies without certification—it may be that MedBlock will receive one in the future—will achieve a high reach in the field of healthcare and blockchain.

Given the disadvantages of a blockchain, as discussed above, it is debatable why the business model should not be implementable with a cloud-based, encrypted database; this would simplify the desired data analysis in particular, but would possibly be less performant. It is also questionable what happens to patient data if the private keys are lost. MedBlock itself provides a solution by enabling patient-side authentication via fingerprint. The combination of data analysis—whether blockchain-based or not—and treatment methods seems particularly interesting: evaluated data could possibly also contain information on more precise (surgical) procedures that robots would be able to perform much better than humans. A major advantage of a blockchain-based solution is that intermediaries are no longer necessary, thereby strengthening the direct doctor–patient relationship. All in all, the company appears to be still at the beginning of its business activities, which is not unusual given the novelty of the technologies and the associated problems to be solved.

5 Conclusion

The topic of digital services has already been established in social and scientific discourse for several years, and the blockchain technology is increasingly gaining profound interdisciplinary attention. The growth in interest in the blockchain technology is shown for instance by the worldwide patent applications with blockchain reference per year, which are rapidly increasing since 2013 and have tripled from 2017 to 2018 (IPlytics 2019). So far, however, a linking consideration of these two technological currents has been largely overlooked. This chapter counters this desideratum by highlighting relevant terms using the example of online consultations, especially in the healthcare sector and the possibilities of creating and maintaining data security through the blockchain. This new technology makes it possible for the first time in history to increase the security level through a technically (or at least organisationally) decentralised solution, as security no longer needs to be centrally placed in an institution (Wildhaber 2016; Tapscott and Tapscott 2018). Transparent end-client communication regarding the functionality of the system, the technical background, and the various user groups that have access to the data are essential in this context. Most importantly, the system must be easily accessible for a user, trivially usable (UX) and highly trustworthy. Ultimately, it is particularly the users who are strengthened by the inclusion of a blockchain in digital services: they are given more control over their personal data and the transactions themselves and thus over their own privacy—provided they understand what opportunities and risks the technology as a whole brings with it (Bogdan 2018). This is also reflected in the three cases presented. The users of patientory, for example, get increased control over their health data. In the same way, the users of MedBlock and of Kry or other telemedicine providers are also strengthened—for example, by the gain in flexibility and confidence in their data security.

Users are currently accustomed to centralised control systems in various areas of social life. This is mainly because responsibilities can be assigned directly. With a blockchain, this is not the case. Participants should, therefore, always be aware that the risk ultimately lies with each user himself or herself. Conversely, this means that, especially in a transitional period, online consulting organisations must ensure that users can make use of both blockchain-based and "traditional" forms of data processing. On the platform side, the question of integrating previous data processing into the blockchain arises. Furthermore, questions of digital ethics (Capurro 2017; Grimm et al. 2019) will also have to be discussed—especially regarding the unavoidable permanence of the information stored on the blockchain. Governments should also create legal models and instruments to provide a legal framework for the management of digital assets. Regulatory supervision and thus also centralisation, however, are controversial, as it takes the idea of decentralisation, which underlies the blockchain technology, to absurdity.

Overall, it can be stated that private (and sometimes federated) blockchains appear to be particularly suitable for data processing in digital services by companies: these types of blockchains combine all the following advantages which allow those seeking and receiving help to interact with each other as best as possible without the risk of data being leaked to third parties: integrity, manipulation and failure safety through transparency, decentralisation, majority principle and cryptography.

References

Agbo, C. C., Mahmoud, Q. H., & Eklund, J. M. (2019). Blockchain technology in healthcare: A systematic review. *Healthcare*. https://doi.org/10.3390/healthcare7020056.

Backhaus, N., & Thüring, M. (2015). Trust in cloud computing: pro and contra from the user's point of view. *i-com*. https://doi.org/10.1515/icom-2015-0001.

Baumann, C. et al. (2017). TeleTrust-Bundesverband IT-Sicherheit. https://www.teletrust.de/fileadmin/docs/publikationen/broschueren/Blockchain/2017_TeleTrusT-Positionspapier_Blockchain__.pdf. Accessed 14 April 2020.

Bertsch, A. (2002). *Digitale signaturen*. Heidelberg, Germany: Springer.

BitFury Group. (2015). Public versus private blockchains part 1: permissioned blockchains. *BitFury Group*. https://bitfury.com/content/downloads/public-vs-private-pt1-1.pdf. Accessed 14 April 2020.

Blix, M., & Jeansson, J. (2018). Telemedicine and the welfare state: The swedish experience. *Research Institute of Industrial Economics*. Working Paper Series 1238.

Bogdan, B. (2018). *MedRevolution—Neue technologien am Puls der Patienten*. Heidelberg, Germany: Springer.

Bogensperger, A., Zeiselmair. A., & Hinterstocker, M. (2018). *Die Blockchain-Technologie—Chance zur Transformation der Energieversorgung?* Forschungsstelle für Energiewirtschaft e.V. https://www.ffe.de/attachments/article/803/Blockchain_Teilbericht_Technologiebeschreibung. pdf. Accessed 14 April 2020.

Bruhn, M., & Hadwich, K. (2017). Dienstleistungen 4.0—Erscheinungsformen, Transformationsprozesse und Managementimplikationen. In M. Bruhn, & K. Hadwich (Eds.), *Dienstleistungen 4.0* (pp. 1–39). Wiesbaden, Germany: SpringerGabler.

Buch, M. S., Gebauer, L., & Hoffmann, H. (2014). Vertrauen in cloud computing schaffen—Aber wie? *Wirtschaftsinformatik & Management*. https://doi.org/10.1365/s35764-014-0424-6.

Bühler, P., Schlaich, P., & Sinner, D. (2019). *Datenmanagement: Daten—Datenbanken—Datensicherheit*. Berlin, Germany: SpringerVieweg.

Burgwinkel, D. (2016). Blockchaintechnologie und deren Funktionsweise verstehen. In D. Burgwinkel (Ed.), *Blockchain Technology: Einführung für Business- und IT Manager* (pp. 3–50). Basel, Switzerland: De Gruyter Oldenbourg.

Buterin, V. (2015). On public and private blockchains. *Ethereum Blog*. https://blog.ethereum.org/2015/08/07/on-public-and-private-blockchains/. Accessed 14 April 2020.

Cap, C. (2019). Grenzen der blockchain. *Informatik Spektrum*. https://doi.org/10.1007/s00287-019-01179-w.

Carson, B., Romanelli, G. Walsh, P., & Zhumaev, A. (2018). Blockchain beyond the hype: What is the strategic business value? *McKinsey & Company—Our Insights*. https://www.mckinsey. com/business-functions/digital-mckinsey/our-insights/blockchain-beyond-the-hype-what-is-the-strategic-business-value. Accessed 14 April 2020.

Capurro, R. (2017). Digitization as an ethical challenge. *AI & Soc, 32*, 277–283. https://doi.org/10.1007/s00146-016-0686-z.

Castro, M., & Liskov, B. (1999). Practical byzantine fault tolerance. In *OSDI '99: Proceedings of the Third Symposium on Operating Systems Design and Implementation* (pp. 174–186). New Orleans, USA: USENIX Association.

Consultancy UK. (2017). *Blockchain technology: How it works, Main advantages and challenges*. Consultancy UK. https://www.consultancy.uk/news/13484/blockchain-technology-how-it-works-main-advantages-and-challenges. Accessed 14 April 2020.

Dasu, T., Kanza, Y., & Srivastava, D. (2018). Unchain your blockchain. *Proceedings of Symposium on Foundations and Applications of Blockchain, 1*, 16–23.

de Reuver, M., Sørensen, C., & Basole, R. C. (2018). The digital platform: A research agenda. *Journal of Information Technology*. https://doi.org/10.1057/s41265-016-0033-3.

Demary, V. (2016). Der Aufstieg der Onlineplattformen: Was nun zu tun ist. *IW-Report, 32.*, Köln, Germany: Institut der deutschen Wirtschaft (IW).

Diekhöner, P. K. (2018). *The trust economy. Warum jedes Unternehmen eine Vertrauensstrategie braucht, um im digitalen Zeitalter zu überleben*. Heidelberg, Germany: Springer.

DIVSI. (2017a). Digitalisierung—Deutsche fordern mehr Sicherheit. *Deutsches Institut für Vertrauen und Sicherheit im Internet*. https://www.divsi.de/wp-content/uploads/2018/02/DIVSI-Studie_Digitalisierung_Deutsche-fordern-mehr-Sicherheit_2017–08.pdf. Accessed 14 April 2020.

DIVSI. (2017b). Vertrauen in Kommunikation im digitalen Zeitalter. *Deutsches Institut für Vertrauen und Sicherheit im Internet*. https://www.divsi.de/wp-content/uploads/2017/12/DIVSI-Vertrauen2018.pdf. Accessed 14 April 2020.

Drescher, D. (2017). *Blockchain Grundlagen: Eine Einführung in die elementaren Konzepte in 25 Schritten*. Frechen, Germany: Mitp.

Düring, T., & Fisbeck, H. (2017). Einsatz der Blockchain-Technologie für eine transparente Wertschöpfungskette. In A. Hildebrandt, & W. Landhäußer (Eds.), *CSR und Digitalisierung. Der digitale Wandel als Chance und Herausforderung für Wirtschaft und Gesellschaft* (pp. 449–464). Berlin, Germany: SpringerGabler.

Gerth, S., & Heim, L. (2020). Trust through digital technologies: Blockchain in online consultancy services. In *The 2nd International Conference on Blockchain Technology*. https://doi.org/10. 1145/3390566.3391662.

Grimm, R., & Bräunlich, K. (2015). Vertrauen und Privatheit. Anwendung des Referenzmodells für Vertrauen auf die Prinzipien des Datenschutzes. *Datenschutz und Datensicherheit—DuD*. https://doi.org/10.1007/s11623-015-0415-7.

Grimm, P., Keber, T., & Zöllner, O. (2019). *Digitale Ethik. Leben in vernetzten Welten: Reclam Kompaktwissen XL*. Ditzingen, Germany: Reclam.

Gundlach, H. (2009). Marktmacht und Meinungsmacht digitaler Plattformen. In J. Krone (Ed.), *Fernsehen im Wandel. Mobile TV & IPTV in Deutschland und Österreich* (pp. 53–77). Baden-Baden, Germany: Nomos.

Hackel, S., & Roßnagel, A. (2008). Langfristige Aufbewahrung elektronischer Dokumente. In D. Klumpp, H. Kubicek, A. Roßnagel, & W. Schulz (Eds.), *Informationelles Vertrauen für die Informationsgesellschaft* (pp. 199–207). Heidelberg, Germany: Springer.

Hanekop, H., Tasch, A., & Wittke, V. (2001). „New Economy" und Dienstleistungsqualität: Verschiebung der Produzenten- und Konsumentenrolle bei digitalen Dienstleistungen. *SOFI-Mitteilungen Nr., 29*(2001), 73–91.

Hölbl, M., Kompara, M., Kamišalić, A., & Zlatolas, L. N. (2018). A systematic review of the use of blockchain in healthcare. *Symmetry*. https://doi.org/10.3390/sym10100470.

Hooper, M. (2018). Top five blockchain benefits transforming your industry. *IBM*. https://www. ibm.com/blogs/blockchain/2018/02/top-five-blockchain-benefits-transforming-your-industry/. Accessed 14 April 2020.

IPlyticts. (2019). Anzahl der weltweiten Blockchain-Patentanmeldungen pro Jahr von 2008 bis 2019. Statista. https://de.statista.com/statistik/daten/studie/1062733/umfrage/anzahl-der-weltweiten-blockchain-patentanmeldungen-pro-jahr/. Accessed 14 April 2020.

Jaekel, M. (2017). *Die Macht der digitalen Plattformen. Wegweiser im Zeitalter einer expandierenden Digitalsphäre und künstlicher Intelligenz*. Wiesbaden, Germany: SpringerVieweg.

Karg, M. (2013). Datenschutzrechtliche Anforderungen an die E-Akte. *Datenschutz und Datensicherheit—DuD*. https://doi.org/10.1007/s11623-013-0297-5.

Khan, N., Fahad, S., Faisal, S., & Naushad, M. (2020). Quarantine role in the control of corona virus in the world and its impact on the world economy. *SSRN*. https://doi.org/10.2139/ssrn. 3556940.

Kofler, T. (2018). *Das digitale Unternehmen. Systematische Vorgehensweise zur zielgerichteten Digitalisierung*. Berlin, Germany: Springer Vieweg.

Kossow, N. (2019). Blockchain: viel Potential, begrenzte Umsetzbarkeit. In: S. Skutta, & J. Steinke (Eds.), *Digitalisierung und Teilhabe. Mitmachen, mitdenken, mitgestalten!* (pp. 97–112). Baden-Baden, Germany: Nomos.

Kravchenko, P. (2016). Ok, I need a Blockchain, but which one? Medium. https://medium.com/ @pavelkravchenko/ok-i-need-a-blockchain-butwhich-one-ca75c1e2100. Accessed 14 April 2020.

KRY. (2020). Symptom-Check für COVID-19—Tracke deine Symptome mit einem täglichen Check-up bei KRY. kry.de. https://www.kry.de/magazin/coronavirus/kostenfreier-covid-19-symptom-check/. Accessed 14 April 2020.

Kudra, A. (2018). Blockchain trifft Digital Identity. *Informatik Aktuell*. https://www.informatik-aktuell.de/betrieb/virtualisierung/blockchain-trifft-digital-identity.html. Accessed 14 April 2020.

Kumbruck, C. (2000). Digitale Signaturen und Vertrauen. *Arbeit*. https://doi.org/10.1515/arbeit-2000-0203.

Meier, A., & Stormer, H. (2018). Blockchain = Distributed Ledger + Consensus. *HMD, 55*, 1139–1154. https://doi.org/10.1365/s40702-018-00457-7

Meijer, D. B. (2017). *Consequences of the implementation of blockchain technology*. Delft: Delft University of Technology.

Mougayar, W., & Buterin, V. (2016). *The business blockchain: Promise, practice, and application of the next internet technology.* New York, USA: Wiley & Sons.

Patientory. (2018). Making healthcare accessible. *Patientoryinc.* https://patientory.com/features/. Accessed 14 April 2020.

Patientory Association. (2019). Advancing healthcare interoperability. *Patientory Association.* https://patientoryassociation.org/. Accessed 14 April 2020.

Pesch, P., & Böhme, R. (2017). Datenschutz trotz öffentlicher Blockchain? Chancen und Risiken bei der Verfolgung und Prävention Bitcoin-bezogener Straftaten. *Datenschutz und Datensicherheit – DuD.* https://doi.org/10.1007/s11623-017-0735-x.

Petrlic, R. (2017). Wunderwaffe Verschlüsselung? *Datenschutz und Datensicherheit—DuD.* https://doi.org/10.1007/s11623-017-0780-5.

Sixt, E. (2017). Bitcoin und die Finanzindustrie. In: Bitcoins und andere dezentrale Transaktionssysteme. Springer Gabler, Wiesbaden. https://doi.org/10.1007/978-3-658-02844-2_14.

Schulz, J. (2016). Ist Verschlüsselung der Schlüssel zur digitalen Souveränität? In M. Friedrichsen, & P. J. Bisa (Eds.), *Digitale Souveränität. Vertrauen in der Netzwerkgesellschaft* (pp. 161–167). Wiesbaden, Germany: SpringerVS.

Song, W., Shi, S., Xu, V., & Gill, G. (2016). Advantages and Disadvantages of Blockchain Technology. *Blockchain Technology.* https://blockchaintechnologycom.wordpress.com/2016/11/21/advantages-disadvantages/. Accessed 14 April 2020.

Stich, V., Schumann, J. H., Beverungen, D., Gudergan, G., & Jussen, P. (2019). *Digitale Dienstleistungsinnovationen. Smart Services agil und kundenorientiert entwickeln.* Berlin, Germany: SpringerVieweg.

Ströher, A., & Honekamp, W. (2011). ELGA—die elektronische Gesundheitsakte vor dem Hintergrund von Datenschutz und Datensicherheit. *Wiener Medizinische Wochenschrift, 161* (13–14), 341–346.

Stübner, J. (2020). Schwedisches start-up bringt Videosprechstunde nach Deutschland. *Welt.de.* https://www.welt.de/wirtschaft/gruenderszene/article204792286/Schwedisches-Start-up-Kry-bringt-Videosprechstunde-nach-Deutschland.html. Accessed 14 April 2020.

Swan, M. (2015). *Blockchain. Blueprint for a new economy.* Sebastopol, USA: O'Reilly and Associates.

Tapscott, D., & Tapscott, A. (2018). *Die Blockchain-Revolution. Wie die Technologie hinter Bitcoin nicht nur das Finanzsystem, sondern die ganze Welt verändert.* Kulmbach, Germany: Plassen.

Täuscher, K., Hilbig, R., & Abdelkafi, N. (2017). Geschäftsmodellelemente mehrseitiger Plattformen. In D. Schallmo, A. Rusnjak, J. Anzengruber, T. Werani, M. Jünger (Eds.), *Digitale Transformation von Geschäftsmodellen. Schwerpunkt: Business Model Innovation* (pp. 179–211). Wiesbaden, Germany: SpringerGabler.

Walterbusch, M., & Teuteberg, F. (2012). Vertrauen im Cloud Computing. *HMD Praxis der Wirtschaftsinformatik.* https://doi.org/10.1007/BF03340757.

Warner, C.D. (2019). The Future of Healthcare: "We will use blockchain, AI/ML to bring together siloed health data" with Chrissa McFarlane, CEO of Patientory Inc. Thrive Global. https://thriveglobal.com/stories/the-future-of-healthcare-we-will-use-blockchain-ai-ml-to-bring-together-siloed-health-data-with-chrissa-mcfarlane-ceo-of-patientory-inc/. Accessed 14 April 2020.

Wildhaber, B. (2016). Kann man blockchains vertrauen? In D. Burgwinkel (Ed.), *Blockchain Technology: Einführung für Business- und IT Manager* (pp. 149–158). Basel, Switzerland: De Gruyter Oldenbourg.

Williams, S., Fitzner, J., Merians, A., & Mounts, A. (2013). The challenges of global case reporting during pandemic A(H1N1) 2009. *Bulletin of the World Health Organization.* https://dx.doi.org/10.2471%2FBLT.12.116723.

Wüst, K., & Gervais, A. (2017). Do you need a blockchain? *Department of Computer Science*, ETH Zurich: https://eprint.iacr.org/2017/375.pdf.

Zehir, C., Zehir, M., & Zehir, S. (2020). New strategies for evolution of business ecosystems: platform strategies. In Ü. Hacıoğlu (Ed.), *Handbook of research on strategic fit and design in business ecosystems* (pp. 98–122). Hershey, Pennsylvania: IGI Global.

AI-Enhanced Business Models
for Digital Entrepreneurship

Wolfgang Pfau and Philipp Rimpp

Abstract

The world of AI offers new opportunities for companies and is therefore of particular interest to entrepreneurs at potentially every level impacting their business. The following article therefore tries to classify the roles of artificial intelligence (AI) applications on the strategic level and their influence on business models. By means of case studies, current business practice will be examined to give entrepreneurs and researchers an understanding of this technology, by providing practical examples so that they can pursue their own AI path. The analysis is based on case studies that examine the role of AI in a company's business model, both for new market participants in the form of start-ups and incumbents such as the tech giants. By means of case studies, both sides of the extremes are covered in order to provide a picture of the scope of the applications. Insights from these case studies are processed to develop a classification scheme of the influence of AI on business models. Furthermore, the interaction of the different innovation possibilities of AI is compared and with that the importance for the innovative power of companies. Additionally, strategy types are developed on the basis of the presented classification scheme, but give entrepreneurs a suggestion for their own AI path in terms of AI applications to consider. Further, research could consider the influence of the presented AI roles in business models, especially the AI-driven business model is of interest here.

W. Pfau · P. Rimpp (✉)
Clausthal University of Technology, Clausthal-Zellerfeld, Germany
e-mail: philipp.rimpp@tu-clausthal.de

© The Author(s) 2021   121
M. Soltanifar et al. (eds.), *Digital Entrepreneurship*, Future of Business and Finance,
https://doi.org/10.1007/978-3-030-53914-6_7

1   The Relevance of AI for Digital Entrepreneurs

The technology of artificial intelligence (AI) is already considered to be a ground-breaking technology that has the potential to fundamentally change markets, industries and in general business activities. Its disruption and innovation potential is considered to be of a magnitude that cannot be compared to any known technology. And yet the threshold for research and use of AI is still ongoing (cf. Marr and Ward 2019, pp. 1–3). This opens the opportunity to participate in this pioneering technology and make it available for usage by entrepreneurs at every market level. At the same time, this also increases the pressure not to fall behind. For entrepreneurs as well as companies the question arises as to how much influence AI can have on their business now and in the future and how they can leverage the technological potential for themselves. Against this background, it is essential that entrepreneurs consider the consequences of AI in their business model.

AI technology is not a new phenomenon, neither in science nor for companies. However, recent developments, e.g. in machine learning (ML), lead to breakthroughs in the applicability of AI in many areas. These changes and improvements in usability now allow many companies to use this technology in various applications.

The idea that AI is not yet or only to a small extent present in the entrepreneurial world and that it is rather a theoretically phenomenon would be a misconception that an entrepreneur could succumb to. In fact, AI or algorithms that come close to it have already penetrated many areas of everyday life. Many of these examples are currently familiar to users, while others often remain hidden. Examples are shopping suggestions, face recognition or speech assistants (cf. Intel Corporation 2020). Some voices even go a step further and speak of a new age of AI, in which human abilities and talents are challenged by AI, thus changing the question of the long-term changes in human life, including in the corporate and new venture sector (cf. Iansiti and Lakhani 2020, pp. 17–18). Due to the fact, that AI is already used in many and diverse areas, the question arises how this technology can influence the business and especially the business model (BM) of an entrepreneur. Furthermore, the use of AI naturally requires technological investments and access to the relevant data for the operating of AI. In particular, the output quality of AI depends on the quality and quantity of available data (cf. Agrawal et al. 2018, pp. 98–99).

All these developments illustrate not only the potential, but also the already dominant influence and opportunities that AI can offer companies. From this point of view, it is of interest for entrepreneurs to know what general possibilities are available to them. Especially the effects on a strategic level more precisely the innovation of the business model through AI applications are the focus of this article. Finally, the range of innovation possibilities shall be shown so that entrepreneurs become aware of this potential and can use it.

2 Theoretical Background for Entrepreneurs

2.1 The Technological Aspect of AI

A unitary definition of artificial intelligence (AI), and thus when it can be attributed to a machine, has so far been omitted because it differs according to the point of view. Essentially, the approaches to definition differ in their determination of intelligence, how this intelligence manifests itself and at what point a machine can be considered intelligent (cf. Legg and Hunter 2007, pp. 7–8).

Nevertheless, it is possible to distinguish two forms of AI that are generally different in the way these programs work. First, the **symbolic AI** is a learning program that focuses on symbols as operating ground for its learning progress. A rule-based thinking presented in the symbols, e.g. numbers, drives this form. The major advantage of this type of artificial intelligence is its practicability for the human users. Because its logic is quite easy to understand for a human, it can be useful as a support system. This may provide a user or company with an advantage over another non-user, if used correctly. Their potential often lies in the automation of processes, which are usually consuming intense amounts of time and knowledge. On the other hand, the symbolic AI is a program that needs a lot of programming work done into it. This is why the symbolic AI gets quite expensive (cf. Lee et al. 2019, pp. 2–3). The other major form of intelligence is the so-called **neural AI**, which is enabled by the usage of machine learning. This method uses algorithm of improved learning by using practice or sample data as learning material for generating patterns that it can later rely upon. The goal of this method is that the AI should function like a human brain, in the sense that even complex problems can be solved, similar to neural work. Thus, neural AI is not needing actual training embraced by humans in the form of teachers. Its objective is to learn by itself from data sources it is given access to (cf. Lee et al. 2019, p. 4). Especially, ML and its subfield deep learning are known from this area, due to major breakthroughs of these research fields especially in the field of image and voice processing (cf. Skilton and Hovsepian 2018, pp. 132–134). This field is receiving more and more attention from researchers and companies, because it has the potential to learn from raw data. Conversely, this means that less human work has to be done in advance. While both methods or types of AI still face problems in terms of scalability and reasoning, much hope is put into the combination of both types. The combination creates the hope of solving tasks related to fundamental problems in the applicability of the technology. Examples of these challenges are insufficient data for operations or the solution of the black-box appearance of AI to a human observer. While this research stream is still in its infancy, entrepreneurs should pay attention to future opportunities (cf. Lee et al. 2019, pp. 4–5).

Beyond the basic understanding of how AI can be differentiated from a technological view, it is important for the entrepreneur, to know what AI can do for his or her business. An approach to understand the way AI works in the practical context is to understand it as a prediction machine. This logic focuses on the very basic principle of an AI output. If AI is used, it is trained in advance based on data. In the subsequent application, the AI uses its learning chains to evaluate the situation it is to consider. This process is described as prediction, as the AI uses given data to indicate the missing information. Therefore, this technology cannot only make statements about current problems, but also about past and future. This of course requires that the AI has a sufficient amount of data (cf. Agrawal et al. 2018, pp. 23–30). This brief overview of the technical background and the practicable interpretation of AI show that entrepreneurs should have at least a superficial knowledge of the technology when using it or even considering to use it in the future.

2.2 The (Current) Role of AI in Developing Business Models

Given the research approaches to AI and entrepreneurship, a variety of paths can be identified. In the sense of this article, the primary goal is to identify the effects of AI on a strategic corporate level. This is accompanied by an examination of the business model and the effects on it. There are also numerous research streams and definitions for the business model. At this point, the business model definition of Osterwalder and Pigeur, who define it as the "rationale of how an organization creates, delivers and captures value" (Osterwalder and Pigneur 2010, p. 14), will be used as a basis for continuing research here. Furthermore, the effects of the use of AI on the business model will be examined, especially in its effects on the business model canvas.

The world of business models under the influence of AI is not a new research phenomenon but has already received some attention. On the one hand, research has already been conducted on the influence of AI applications on the individual elements of the business model (cf. Metelskaia et al. 2018, pp. 38–40). Such comprehensive views open up the possibility for the entrepreneur to estimate which influences they can use for their own innovation of the business model. On the other hand, there are already approaches for long-term planning of the integration of AI into the company. Such strategic developments are fossilized on a path that the company takes to integrate AI applications into its own business. Examples for such planning methods can be general plans for the adaptation of AI applications in the company (cf. Rao 2017, pp. 9–10), or portfolio planning like the 3 Horizon framework for AI (cf. Kreutzer and Sirrenberg 2020, pp. 235–238). In the area of these planning methods and procedures, there are various examples of literature on this topic. It can therefore be concluded that the current role of AI in the development of business models is limited to their influence on the elements and their planning for future business models. However, an important question, regarding AI as a technology in general, which both views tend to neglect, is still lingering. The question of methodologies is determining the strategic direction of AI applications and their impact on business models. This includes how AI applications influence business models through innovation, respectively, implementation. This is accompanied by the role of AI in the innovation of the business model, independent of the desired state or form of the business model. In this way, it should be clarified for entrepreneurs how these AI applications can be differentiated from a strategic perspective in order to be able to shape their visions by means of the corresponding AI performance in the business model. A study of the business world is therefore necessary at this point.

2.3 Method of Investigation

For the exploration of the current and partly future use of AI applications in the business context, the first question is how this should be investigated. In the context of this chapter, an attempt is made to give a picture of the landscape of AI use in the entrepreneurial context. Especially the effects on a strategic level are of interest. For this to happen within a certain framework, a limitation is necessary. The range of enterprises and the related examples of use are numerous in the real world. From innovative start-ups to medium-sized companies and large incumbents, a broad spectrum is opening that presents a challenge. Therefore, the research approach is divided into two parts. First, start-ups are to be investigated and thus how these firms design AI applications and make them available to the market. In the second part, established, preferably innovative companies will be examined, which have a clear focus on AI solutions and, if possible, show a broad range of applications. This should not only show which application possibilities are already established and therefore practicable, but also which possibilities exist for companies that want to acquire them. Furthermore, this will be done with a focus on explorative case studies, which will be able to give an insight into the use of the technology (cf. Siggelkow 2007, pp. 20–23). Subsequently, the usage and especially the strategic possibilities for innovation through AI will be shown. All this is done in the context of the business model and its innovation. A connection to the business model should therefore be considered at every point.

Table 1 Strategies for AI applications

	Outsourcing	Incremental	Profound	Disruptor
Performance/ Awareness	Common	Standard	Unique/Unrivalled	Unchallenged
Development	Outsourcing	Outsourcing/In-house-development	In-house-development	In-house-development
Change potential	Minor	Minor—moderate	Moderate—Profound	Profound—disruptive
Type of business model innovation	Support	Support	Support/Driver	Driver

3 Development of a Schema from Practice

When analysing start-ups in the AI field, it can be quickly determined that a wide range of existing companies with very different focuses on the application of AI prevails. Therefore, a narrowing down is mandatory. First, the scope of applications of AI should be narrowed down. For a fundamental examination of the influence of AI services on business models, it is particularly useful to focus on core elements of the organization. This means that the applications should be as independent as possible from the industry sector in which a company is active. On the other hand, existing market services which are already established and thus available to as many user companies as possible are of interest. At the same time, the effects of such a start up on the market, in terms of changes to the business model, are to be investigated. This means that not only the elements of the business model canvas that would be changed by such a service should be identified, but also the role of innovation that the change would bring. Due to the large number of start-ups in the AI field, a further narrowing down is necessary here as well. At this point, the research approach will concentrate on companies in the German area (cf. Table 2: References of AI start-ups).

The limited investigation of the German start-up world in the field of AI reveals several indications. First, the companies appear as providers of AI software and usually market it as AI-as-a-Service (**AIaaS**), based on the business models of the software-as-a-service industry. An AIaaS provider is thus a vendor of a finished and usable product or service that is made available to the customer by the provider, for regular payment (Metelskaia et al. 2018, p. 36). In this way, AI becomes a product on which a company builds its business model and brings their type of AI to market. The path away from a per-seat model to a model of utilization is already clearly recognizable or predominant in the area of AIaaS in the cases considered here. Additionally, the role of AI for the user of these AIaaS products can be defined in terms of their impacts on the BM. First assisting functions and supporting functions as the following can be identified.

AI-assisted: Business processes that are improved or supported by AI, but do not directly contribute to strategic elements and therefore do not affect any element of the business model. The focus remains on operational tasks.

AI-supported: AI services that directly influence one or more elements of a company's business model and modify it without fundamentally changing the established business model.

While these definitions give an understanding about the strategic impact on the lower end of the BM spectrum, further research on major impacting roles should be made. Those impactful AI services/roles are to be identified in real-world examples.

Furthermore, clear differences can be identified in the target applications of the AI, which relate to the core functions of the company. A distinction can be made here between applications that focus on the company's own activities and those that focus on customer-specific activities. Company activities refer to the way the company carries out activities, such as partnerships or cost structures. On the other hand, customer-specific activities which focus on activities related to the customer, such as communication or channels. This differentiation in two directions of the influence of an AI service allows a classification for the company, when considering it. Of course, not every AI application is equally influential in terms of its orientation and impact. Furthermore, a differentiation regarding the direction of orientation also suggests that one or both directions can be present simultaneously to varying degrees. This means that a distinction can be made regarding the influence. Applications that have no influence on an orientation side would be listed accordingly in this scheme on the zero line of the axis. The classification of such an application will be illustrated by the following figure (Fig. 1).

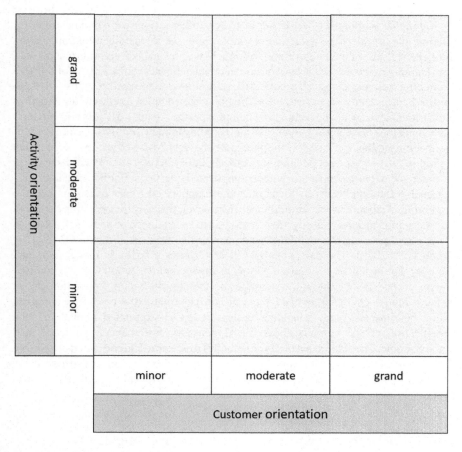

Fig. 1 Classification scheme for AI applications

For additional illustration of this classification scheme, the following case studies serve as examples in their usage of AI applications. Moreover, additional investigations in this chapter are to be made based on the classification scheme.

4 Examples from Practice: Investigating Newcomers and Incumbent Enterprises

4.1 Illustrating a Newcomer: The Case of E-Bot7

The German company of e-bot7 is a start-up founded in mid-2016 and located in the city of Munich. The product the company is offering is based around an AI-driven algorithm that is oriented towards automated customer response communication. It is offering its customers the reduction of employee usage in customer communication through the usage of their algorithm. This is achieved by an NLP algorithm, that is not only learning on given use cases of customer contact, but also constantly evolving due to ongoing business cases (cf. e-bot7 2020a). It aims at automated responses to standardized customer questions and the sorting of more complex queries to the expected professional in between the company. Their product the Agent + KI® Hybrid Model is confirming the correctness of given answers by being trained through the employees of the operating company. That way the purchaser of e-bot7 AI-based product can train the algorithm for their service operations (cf. e-bot7 2020b). At best automated answers can be generated to handle repeating and uncomplicated questions. For the purchaser, this can enable the employees to focus on more complex customer questions and the preserving of labour that can be automated. Moreover, that way the operating company shall be getting an advantage by a less cost-intensive customer care service. Customers of the e-bot7 products are well-known company's like Deutsche Bahn or O2 (cf. DIA Group B.V. 2020). The case of e-bot7 clearly shows a business model as AIaaS provider. The product a customized AI for customer communication with its promised human needed labour through automation is thereby the value proposition of the business model. On the other hand, the usage of the product of e-bot7s by a company within their business model can rather be classified as **AI-supported**. In relation to the classification scheme presented above, the AI focuses on customer communication and thus a customer orientation that has a (potentially) **moderate** degree of intensity. On the activity side of the scheme, however, it can be assumed that the more cost-oriented and personnel-reducing activities of the AI have a **minor** inflow. This is particularly given by the possible automation of communication.

4.2 Incumbents Innovation Through AI: Case Studies from Amazon

Amazon is serving as the first case study of an incumbent, consisting of three examples, on how Amazon uses AI in different ways for different objectives in between their company structure. As a first example, Amazon Web Services is a product and service platform for Internet-based technologies that Amazon offers its customers. The range of services offered extends from analytical services, blockchain, databases and storage to tools for developers (cf. Amazon.com Inc. 2020a). Against the background of this study, the machine learning offer is of interest. With this service, Amazon offers its customers the possibility of AI applications. At this point, this means that Amazon offers the infrastructure and the service of development and thus provides the customers the possibility to develop AI services at lower costs. These costs can not only be of a direct monetary nature but can also be reflected in the personnel area. By that companies using this offer need less personnel with the skills in machine learning or AI to carry out their own developments in this area. Thus, this service from Amazon Web Services is not only to be understood as an **Infrastructure-as-a-Service** but also as an AI-as-a-Service. Secondly, Amazon Go and Amazon Go Grocery should serve as another example for the use of AI. This represents a separate mainstay of Amazon in the grocery retail sector. The essential concept of this store model is the shopping experience without queues at the checkout. This is achieved by dispensing the physical checkout. This so-called checkout-free shopping is attained by using AI to record the products taken by the customer. By the aid of sensors, the AI can monitor the status of the products in the market permanently. When the customer leaves the shop, an invoice is automatically sent to the Amazon customer's account (cf. Amazon.com Inc. 2020b). With the use of the AI, a value creation for the customer is operated in this BM. The transaction costs for the customer are minimized by the elimination of the checkout. This not only improves customer service, but also creates a completely new value creation service (cf. Clickatell Inc. 2020). On the other hand, this BM also changes the usual structure of the shop operator. By using AI, personnel costs for the checkout are omitted. Furthermore, this BM is only made possible by using AI. It represents the fundamental component that not only makes the innovation of the BM possible, but also operates this model. The business model can therefore be described as **AI-driven**. Additionally, the orientation in terms of the BM is to be considered **moderate to grand** on both sides. As a final example, the concept of anticipatory shipping has to be mentioned. Amazon has been thinking about radically changing its retail business model with the use of AI and has even patented this (cf. Google Patents 2012). Under the term "anticipatory shipping", the company developed an idea where the shipping of a product should take place before the actual sale. Based on the prediction of an AI, products that are expected to be desired by the customer should be shipped without their order. Subsequently, the customers could then decide whether to return or keep the product. There are different interpretations of whether the product should be shifted anticipatory into a closer environment or delivered directly to the customer (cf. On Marketing 2014), (cf. Lomas 2014). Regardless of the interpretation of such a model, it shows a phenomenon in the way Amazon would change the way it does business. The customer would no longer be the sole executor of a purchase, but the AI would also. The arguments for such a drastic change of the BM are in the way the value creation should take place after the change. It is assumed that value is created for the customer by taking over the activity of selecting and buying. This is intended to relieve the burden on the customer and at the same time strengthen the relationship with the company. It is also assumed that such an innovation of the BM would have an impact on all areas of the BM (cf. Agrawal et al. 2018, pp. 16–17). Ultimately, it is essential for the context considered here that the AI would make the new business model possible in the first place. The execution and efficiency of the prediction of the AI used thus determine the business activities, and therefore, such a business model can be considered **AI-driven**. Furthermore, such a BM innovation would be a significant change in the market. In the context of innovation categorization, this could certainly become out as a disruptive BM and the orientation would be **grand** in each side of the orientation.

4.3   Incumbents Innovation Through AI: Case Studies from Uber

The first case of AI used by Uber is the company's own AI platform Michelangelo. It enables the internal teams of Uber machine learning to use it in a scalable way. This means that Uber provides itself with an AI platform so that all developers and designers in the company have a uniform infrastructure for their development projects. Through this unified infrastructure, all participants should have the same development opportunities, an ability to grow the AI projects in the company and also a cost-saving is achieved through the standardization. With this, Uber has created a service to support own processes in the company (cf. Hermann 2017). The service can be seen as AIaaS and developed by the company for the own company. From the user's point of view, it is a support of the development processes and is therefore not a core element of the BM. Rather, it assists in the development of potentially supporting or value-adding AI services in the future. Thus, the AI platform can be classified as **AI-assisted** and has an internal focus, in the context of innovations through AI. The second case study at Uber is about Uber Marketplace, which is intended to illustrate the use of AI within this business form. Uber Marketplace is a platform where passengers and drivers are brought together. Uber acts here as an intermediary between both parties, for a fee. In this platform business model Uber has integrated AI to improve the platform's own performance. With the help of AI, the usage behaviour of customers is predicted in order to achieve the capacity utilization of the drivers on the one side and the optimal provision of trips for the customer on the other side. The use and integration of the AI into the platform model enable the company to offer its own services more efficiently and at the same time maximize the benefit for the customer by ensuring the highest possible reliability. While it can be assumed that the value creation has the same goal as before and is strengthened if possible, this AI use achieves a mutual focus on both the company and the customer side (cf. Uber 2020). In the context of the classification of AI performance for the business model, it is therefore to be described as **AI-supported**. The impact on the business model can be described as **moderate** in both directions of the classification scheme at this point. However, by focusing on both halves of the business model, the value creation is possibly increased.

5 Implications for Practice

5.1 Differentiation of the Effects of Innovation

The preceding case studies not only distinguish the AI's rollers in terms of potential assisting or supporting services for the business model, but also showed the driving potential of these within a BM. The Amazon case shows here in two different configurations that AI-driven business models can be theoretically and practically possible, or that this is already established. The possibility of such a business model based on the performance of the AI turned out to be new business models on the market in the two cases presented here.

Nevertheless, there is a certain hierarchy with concerning the improvement of business models with AI. As a basis, the Infrastructure-as-a-Service or the AI-as-a-Service is shown. The infrastructure is necessary for self-development while AIaaS allows the direct use or implementation of AI. One of the two services is therefore necessary to make AI usable in any form for the BM. The previous definitions are in line with this within their potential of influence, starting from the assisting to the supporting service to the driving factor, the influence of the AI on the business model increases. The extent cannot be scaled at this point, as it depends on the practical design of the BM. Nevertheless, such a dimensioning of the influence can be shown. All this is of course done in the context of an improvement of BM by means of AI. Thus, the entrepreneur has the choice of the role of the AI from the options presented here for the enhancement of his own business model (Fig. 2).

AI-enhanced		
AI-assisted: Business processes that are improved or supported by AI, but do not directly contribute to strategic elements and therefore do not affect any element of the business model. The focus remains on operational tasks.	**AI-supported:** AI services that directly influence one or more elements of a company's business model and modify it without fundamentally changing the established business model.	**AI-driven:** AI services that enable the introduction and performance of a new type of business model. A key factor is the necessity of the AI to drive the business model.
Increasing influence of AI		

Fig. 2 Roles of AI in enhancing the business model

Furthermore, the case studies carried out can be prescribed within the "innovation matrix". The cases here illustrate the scope of AI applications on a strategic level. Not only one-sided fossilized application possibilities, but also double-sided, partly varyingly pronounced combinations are possible.

In addition, it has been shown that AI cannot only be developed in-house but is also available to companies in the form of market services. Noticeably, not every conceivable form of AI for companies is available on the market, but many functions are already offered that can be related to core functions of a company. Nevertheless, there are already providers who offer development assistance with their services for AI-based services. The offers on shown here are mostly AIaaS and play an assisting or supporting role the user organizations. These applications have an innovative character, which can have a moderate but sustainable impact on business models, especially in the area of supporting services. On the other hand, completely new BM is already emerging through AI, which is only made possible using this technology. Such innovations have the strongest character on the strategic level for companies, in the sense that they can potentially be built on an increased or unique creation of value. Whether a resulting business model will have a disruptive nature cannot usually be assessed in advance but is a phenomenon that only occurs in the long term. The following diagram is intended to illustrate the previous results for the classification of the AI performance, described in the case studies. At this point, AIaaS and IaaS services are excluded, since they may be an essential component for the development of own AI applications. They are rather of secondary importance for the innovation potential concerning the implementation in the BM. Especially, the interface between activity and customer focus in a high (grand) level of innovation is of interest at this point. If both characteristics can be achieved by an AI application, it appears in the examples considered here as if this could lead to far-reaching changes in the BM. In theory, these changes have the potential to be disruptive (Fig. 3).

Finally, another assumption can be made regarding the disruptive nature of new business models in the field of AI. It is possible that AI-driven business models may have disruptive potential, provided that they can demonstrate a sufficiently strong focus on the activity and customer side in the business model. While the two cases presented here are merely intended to serve as an indicator for such an idea, further case studies as well as long-term studies about these business models are necessary.

5.2 Derivation of the Dynamic Interaction and Resulting Strategies

The question arises as to what insights entrepreneurs can draw from the findings derived here regarding the role of AI in the innovation of business models. First, it becomes clear that such a differentiation of AI applications as that made here is not a planning method for the development of AI within the company. Rather, this view opens a possibility to classify AI ideas and applications with respect to their influence on the business model using the presented matrix and roles. It can be

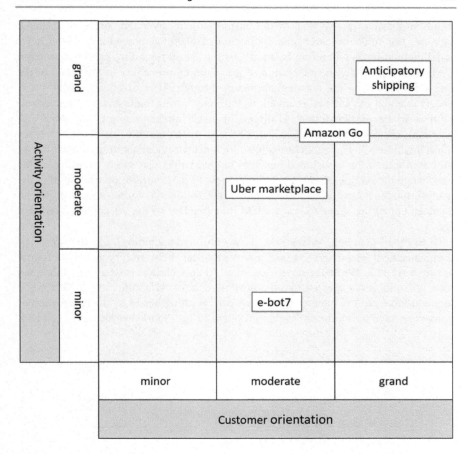

Fig. 3 Classification of presented AI applications cases

assumed that both assisting and supporting services will cause a rather incremental impact of innovation in the business model, whereas a driving force of AI in the business model would cause a profound change.

Furthermore, it is quite conceivable that different AI applications will coexist in the same enterprise. One such example is the case of Uber in a sense, which uses two of these types, Michelangelo and Uber Marketplace. However, while this only covers the lower end of the definition of the roles of AI, it is quite conceivable that a similar application is possible on the other end of the ladder. A resulting presumption would be the independence of the roles of AI within a company, in terms of their application. This would mean that companies could incorporate any form into their business model, independent of the other roles at hand. For planning the innovation of a company's business model, the awareness of independence and the influence of the respective AI performance are therefore central. An innovation of the business model would thus not be limited to one of the roles, but each role would be possible in any state of the business model over the course of strategic planning. For future research, the adaptation of planning procedures for business model innovation can therefore be an interesting aspect regarding the differentiation of AI roles. Especially the adaptation of the planning procedure to the needs of the companies regarding the own enhancement through AI is of interest. While it is conceivable that incremental innovations will only have a major impact when added up, it is to be expected that AI-driven business models cannot only represent completely new business models, but can also hold potential for deeper changes within the industry. This reduction allows for a deeper understanding of what the AI will contribute to the envisioned business model, while also solely focusing on the core change the AI does. Such a simplified view of the contribution of AI within the business model innovation is illustrated in the following figure, which shows an enhancement of the states (S) of the BM, independent of the AI applications used (Fig. 4).

Thus, the question arises on how an understanding of the role of AI-enhancement in business model innovation can help entrepreneurs to follow their own AI path. While the development of AI applications is becoming more and more dynamic, it is expected that the development of AI applications will become more and more rapidly in enterprises. This can be strengthened by the application of approaches such as minimum viable products or test-and-learn mentalities, which

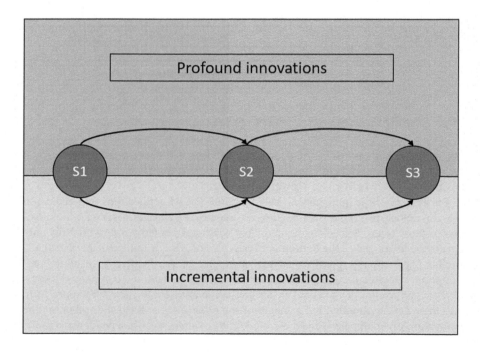

Fig. 4 Dynamic inventing states of BM

allow to shorten the development time (cf. Fountaine et al. 2019, p. 5). A more dynamic view on business model enhancement could thus offer the option of not committing to long-term static plans, but rather to dynamized developments of AI according to the necessary role of AI in business model innovation. The proprietary AI path could thus be seen as a permanent innovation loop, modified by the selected AI performance.

In view of the different applications and their various effects, the question arises as to which derivations entrepreneurs can derive for their company in order to follow their own AI path. By means of the presented classification scheme, a derivation of general or standard strategies for entrepreneurs shall be derived. The previous studies of start-ups and incumbents show a possibility not only to pre-scribe the AI applications with respect to their extent in the classification scheme, but also to divide them into zones in order to imply a standardization strategy based on their strategic potential for the company. These standardization strategies should give the entrepreneur suggestions for action, based on the zones in which an AI application is located or has been identified by the user of the scheme. The fol-lowing strategic implications could be fund by the investigations carried out in this chapter and are to be seen as suggestions for the own AI path of the entrepreneur.

Outsourcing:

Applications that have a (one-sided or two-sided) weak influence on the business model should be procured, if possible, through offers on the market, i.e. external providers. By outsourcing, the focus of AI's in-house development is directed to more influential applications and is released in their favour. Outsourcing should be chosen in particular when considering scarce resources.

Incremental:

Applications with a minor up to moderate influence on the business model can improve it incrementally. At this point, companies must weigh up between in-house development and outsourcing. Especially from a short-term perspective, incre-mental improvements to the business model are achievable in many ways and should therefore be constantly monitored.

Profound:

Applications have the potential to leave behind major changes in the business model. Such applications can give the company a competitive advantage and should therefore be the long-term goal with regard to the own AI path. Such AI solutions are usually not offered by external providers, and the focus should be on in-house development.

Disruptor:

Applications have the greatest potential to change entire industries in the long term and profoundly. The focus here is exclusively on in-house development and innovation of the own business model.

These standardization strategies differ significantly in their potential for change at the business model level. In addition, it can be assumed that a distinction is made with regard to the performance of the application or the awareness of the competitors with regard to this application. Especially the differences between ordinary and unique or unchallengeable applications may be tempting, but this is again to be seen under the independence and simultaneous applicability of the applications. The previous distinction regarding supporting and driving AI services is also applicable here (Table 1).

These strategy fields for the applications are to be seen in dependence on the classifications schema presented before. The strategies do not appear as rigid boundaries within which one must think, but as blurring borders that show a flowing transition between the adjacent strategies and can thus be used depending on the respective situation and the assessment by the entrepreneur (Fig. 5).

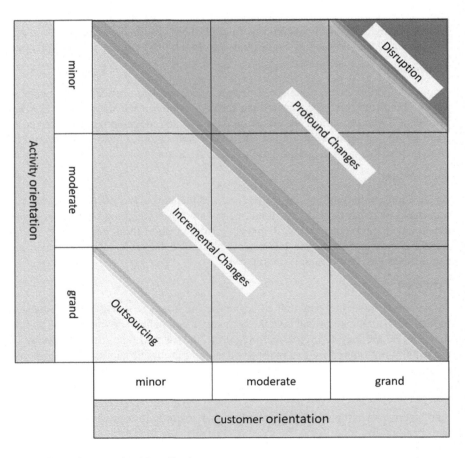

Fig. 5 Strategic zones for AI applications

6 Conclusion

AI plays an increasingly important role for businesses. Researchers and entrepreneurs are becoming more and more aware of this topic, which is reflected in the number of research topics in this area.

In this chapter, we explored a strategic view of AI applications and their influence on the innovation of business models. The investigation of start-ups and incumbents opened the distinction of AI roles in business model innovation. The results showed that AI not only assists or supports but also has the potential to drive business models. Furthermore, a classification scheme was developed that allows to prescribe the impact of AI on the business model in terms of its inflow and orientation. This allows to identify interactions within the business model and to evaluate AI applications with respect to their innovation potential. In addition, the standardization strategies allow the entrepreneur to make proposals for action that can make his own AI path more accessible.

It is therefore essential that companies become aware of the diversity and range of AI applications and their potential. The AI roles, classification schemes and standardization strategies presented here are intended to provide a better understanding and to provide the entrepreneur with tools for strategic consideration.

New opportunities for entrepreneurs and researchers are related not only to the development of supporting applications, but also especially to the theoretical and practical design of AI-driven business models. The novelty of these business models can give rise to completely new business relationships, organizational structures and business processes that could lead to companies of a kind not seen before. Potential future research could therefore focus on the field of AI-driven enterprises, based on an AI-driven business model.

The challenges for entrepreneurs who want to pursue their own AI path are manifold. Data management, development costs and talents, operational and strategic changes are only a part of what can happen to companies now and in the future. Nevertheless, the AI path is already being taken by many companies, in the knowledge that this class of technology will change many areas of the economy forever. The advantage of going down the AI path as an entrepreneur is not only the elimination of a potential competitive disadvantage, but rather the possibility to develop and break new ground.

Appendix

See Table 2.

Table 2 References of AI Start-ups, (companies from: UnternehmerTUM GmbH 2020)

Startup (KI)	Enterprise function	Service objective	Targeted BMC-Element	AI-function	Information at
I2x	Customer service	Customer comprehension	Segments	AI-supported	https://i2x.ai/
cognigy	Customer service	Automated communication	Channels	AI-supported	https://cognigy.com/
Botfriends	Customer service	Chatbot/ Automated communication	Channels	AI-supported	https://botfriends.de/en/
Kauz	Customer service	Chatbot /automated communication	Channels	AI-supported	https://kauz.net/en/
solvemate	Customer service	Chatbot /automated communication	Channels	AI-supported	https://www.solvemate.com/en/
tywla	Customer service	Chatbot /automated communication	Channels	AI-supported	https://www.twyla.ai/
virtualQ	Customer service	On-hold loop improvements	Channels	AI-supported	https://virtualq.io/en/
Mercury	Customer service	Chatbot /automated communication	Channels	AI-supported	https://www.mercury.ai/en/
Voixen	Customer service	Customer comprehension	Segments	AI-supported	https://www.voixen.ai/en
e-bot7	Customer service	Chatbot /automated communication	Channels	AI-supported	https://e-bot7.co.uk/
parlamind	Customer service	Automated communication	Channels	AI-supported	https://parlamind.com/en/
Fraugster	IT & Security	Fraud detection	Cost structure	AI-supported	https://fraugster.com/
Dedrone	IT & Security	Protection against drones	Resources	AI-assisted	https://www.dedrone.com/
Xccelo	IT & Security	Safety technology	Resources	AI-assisted	https://xccelo.com/en
Neurocat	IT & Security	AI system security	Resources	AI-assisted	https://www.neurocat.ai/
Zeitgold	Finance & Accounting	Automated Accounting	Cost structure	AI-supported	https://www.zeitgold.com/?lang=en
candis	Finance & Accounting	Automated Accounting	Cost structure	AI-supported	https://www.candis.io/
taxy	Finance & Accounting	Automated taxation	Cost structure	AI-assisted	https://www.taxy.io/
troy	Finance & Accounting	Debt collection management	Cost structure	AI-supported	https://www.troy-bleiben.de/en/kategorie/general/
Bunch	H & R	Manager management	Cost structure	AI-assisted	https://bunch.ai/
Joblift	H & R	Job platform management	Cost structure	AI-supported	https://joblift.co.uk/
jobpal	H & R	Chatbot for recruiting interviews	Cost Structure	AI-asissted	https://jobpal.ai/en/
Mindmatch	H & R	Job ad distribution	Cost structure	AI-supported	https://mindmatch.ai/
retorio	H & R	AI video recruiting	Cost structure	AI-assisted	https://www.retorio.com/
rfrnz	Legal	Automated contract analysis	Cost structure	AI-assisted	https://www.rfrnz.com/
synergist	Legal	Automated recurring contracts	Cost structure	AI-assisted	https://synergist.io/
risk methods	Supply chain management	Riskmanagement of supply chains	Cost structure	AI-assisted	https://www.riskmethods.net/
kinexion	Supply chain management	Tracking of goods	Activites	AI-assisted	https://kinexon.com/de
intranav	Supply chain management	3D-localization of goods	Activities	AI-assisted	https://intranav.com/
CrossEngage	Sales & Marketing	AI Multi-Channel Marketing	Channels	AI-supported	https://www.crossengage.io/
2Txt	Sales & Marketing	Text generation for product descriptions	Channels	AI-assisted	https://2txt.de/
admetrics	Sales & Marketing	AI marketing experimentation	Channels	AI-supported	https://www.admetrics.io/en/start/
Upcue	Sales & Marketing	AI sales assistant	Channels	AI-supported	https://www.upcue.com/
Blackout	Sales & Marketing	conversional AI tools	Channels	AI-supported	https://blackout.ai/
Network insight	Sales & Marketing	Cloud infrastructure	Key ressources	AI-assisted	https://www.vmware.com/de/products/vrealize-network-insight.html
Sensape	Sales & Marketing	Interactive Marketing (VR-based)	Channels	AI-supported	https://www.sensape.com/en/
Simplaex	Sales & Marketing	User targeting	Segments	AI-supported	https://www.simplaex.com/

Styla	Sales & Marketing	AI content creation	Channels	AI-assisted	https://www.styla.com/
Adtriba	Sales & Marketing	Cross-channel management	Channels	AI-supported	https://www.adtriba.com/
Attention Insight	Sales & Marketing	AI design analytics	Channels	AI-assisted	https://www.attentioninsight.com/
Ubermetrics	Sales & Marketing	AI multichannel marketing	Channels	AI-supported	https://www.ubermetrics-technologies.com/
Wonderwerk	Sales & Marketing	AI sales training	Channels	AI-assisted	https://www.wonderwerk.co/
Scoutbee	Procurement	Procurement Database für transparency	Activities	AI-assisted	https://scoutbee.com/
Pricefx	Sales & Pricing	Pricemanagement	Activities	AI-assisted	https://www.pricefx.com/
Iplytics	Market Data & Information	Market data management	Activities	AI-assisted	https://www.iplytics.com/
Mapegy	Market Data & Information	Innovation information management	Resources	AI-assisted	https://www.mapegy.com/
Vencortex	Decison Making	Design augmentation	Resources	AI-assisted	https://www.vencortex.com/
Neuroflash	Marketing	Content Creation	Channels	AI-assisted	https://neuro-flash.com/

References

Agrawal, A., Gans, J., & Goldfarb, A. (2018). *Prediction machines. The simple economics of artificial intelligence*. Boston, Massachusetts: Harvard Business Review Press.

Amazon.com Inc. (2020a). *Amazon Web Services (AWS)—Cloud Computing Services*. With assistance of. Available online at https://aws.amazon.com/?nc1=h_ls. Updated on 2/19/2020, checked on 3/12/2020.

Amazon.com Inc. (2020b). Amazon.com: Amazon Go. Available online at https://www.amazon.com/b?language=en_US&node=16008589011&tag=bisafetynet-20. Updated on 3/12/2020, checked on 3/12/2020.

Clickatell Inc. (2020). *Will Amazon Go's AI put an end to thousands of retail jobs?—Clickatell*. Available online at https://www.kungfu.ai/wp-content/uploads/2019/07/HBR-Building-the-AI-Powered-Org.pdf. Updated on 3/12/2020, checked on 3/12/2020.

DIA Group B.V. (2020). *e-bot7: Artificial Intelligence for Customer Service|Digital Insurance Agenda|Accelerate Innovation in Insurance*. Available online at https://www.digitalinsuranceagenda.com/304/e-bot7-artificial-intelligence-for-customer-service/. Updated on 3/10/2020, checked on 3/10/2020.

e-bot7. (2020a). *About Us|We are building the next generation AI-based communication platform*. Available online at https://e-bot7.co.uk/about-us/. Updated on 3/10/2020, checked on 3/10/2020.

e-bot7. (2020b). *Customer service use cases*. Available online at https://e-bot7.de/kundenservice/. Updated on 3/2/2020, checked on 3/2/2020.

Google Patents. (2012). *US8615473B2—Method and system for anticipatory package shipping—Google Patents*. Available online at https://patents.google.com/patent/US8615473B2/en. Updated on 3/8/2020, checked on 3/8/2020.

Hermann, J. (2017). *Meet Michelangelo: uber's machine learning platform*. Available online at https://eng.uber.com/michelangelo-machine-learning-platform/. Updated on 3/12/2020, checked on 3/12/2020.

Iansiti, M., Lakhani, K.R. (2020). *Competing in the age of AI. Strategy and leadership when algorithms and networks run the world*. Boston, MA: Harvard Business Review Press.

Intel Corporation. (2020). *Examples of artificial intelligence in everyday life*. Available online at https://www.intel.de/content/www/de/de/analytics/artificial-intelligence/ai-in-your-pocket-infographic.html. Updated on 3/7/2020, checked on 3/7/2020.

Kreutzer, R., Sirrenberg, M. (2020). *Understanding artificial intelligence. Fundamentals, use cases and methods for a corporate AI journey.* Cham: Springer (Management for professionals).

Lee, J., Suh, T., Roy, D., & Baucus, M. (2019). Emerging technology and business model innovation: The case of artificial intelligence. *JOItmC, 5*(3), 44. https://doi.org/10.3390/joitmc5030044.

Legg, S., Hutter, M. (2007). A collection of definitions of intelligence. In *Frontiers in Artificial Intelligence and Applications.* Available online at http://arxiv.org/pdf/0706.3639v1.

Lomas, N. (2014). Amazon patents "Anticipatory" Shipping—To start sending stuff before you've bought it—TechCrunch. Available online at https://techcrunch.com/2014/01/18/amazon-pre-ships/. Updated on 3/8/2020, checked on 3/8/2020.

Marr, B., Ward, M. (2019). *Artificial intelligence in practice. How 50 successful companies used artificial intelligence to solve problems.* Chichester, West Sussex: Wiley.

Metelskaia, I., Ignatyeva, O., Denef, S., Samsonowa, T. (2018). A business model template for AI solutions. In L. Moutinho, X.-S. Yang (Eds.), *Proceedings of the International Conference on Intelligent Science and Technology - ICIST '18. The International Conference. London, United Kingdom* (pp. 35–41), 30.06.2018–02.07.2018. New York, USA: ACM Press.

On Marketing. (2014). *Why Amazon's anticipatory shipping is pure genius.* Available online at https://www.forbes.com/sites/onmarketing/2014/01/28/why-amazons-anticipatory-shipping-is-pure-genius/#9f115b84605e. Updated on 3/8/2020, checked on 3/8/2020.

Osterwalder, A., Pigneur, Y. (2010). *Business model generation. A handbook for visionaries, game changers, and challengers.* 2. print. Toronto: Flash Reprod.

Rao, A. (2017). A strategist's guide to artificial intelligence. As the conceptual side of computer science becomes practical and relevant to business, companies must decide what type of AI role they should play. In *strategy + business* (87), pp. 1–12. Checked on 4/14/2020.

Siggelkow, N. (2007). Persuasion with case studies. *AMJ, 50*(1), 20–24. https://doi.org/10.5465/amj.2007.24160882.

Skilton, M., Hovsepian, F. (2018). *The 4th Industrial Revolution. Responding to the Impact of Artificial Intelligence on Business.* Cham: Springer International Publishing.

Uber. (2020). *Marketplace| Uber.* Available online at https://kthexecutiveschool.se/wp-content/uploads/2018/10/sb87_17210_Strategists_Guide_to_Artificial_Intelligence.pdf. Updated on 3/13/2020, checked on 3/13/2020.

UnternehmerTUM GmbH. (2020). *Startup Landscape 2020—AppliedAI.* Available online at https://appliedai.de/startup-landscape-2020/. Updated on 3/17/2020, checked on 3/17/2020.

Settings/Contexts of Mobilising Digital Entrepreneurship

The Role of an Entrepreneurial Mindset in Digital Transformation- Case Study of the Estonian Business School

Mari Kooskora

Abstract

This chapter focuses on entrepreneurial mindset in digital transformation and presents a short case study about leading the digital transformation in one Estonian private business school, where the ongoing digital process has changed the organisation itself and also the ways how students are taught and trained for coping and leading in the digital world. In order to better understand the context and environment, a brief introduction to the digitalisation topic and slightly more detailed overview of digitalising in higher education sector is provided first.

1 Introduction

We can argue that among different transformations taken place within entrepreneurial activities, there has been a major shift to digitalisation that has rapidly intensified especially during the last decade. Different authors have conceptualised and described digitalisation in different ways, but they all have agreed that digitalisation has and still is one of the major transformations which has changed the ways how work and business are done and that affects basically everything around us. Today digitalisation and the need for digitally savvy people is present everywhere. This also applies to the universities, both as organisations and as teaching institutions. Universities need to transform themselves to become more digital and they also need to help their students to cope and lead these digitalisation processes within their own organisations. Estonia is a country that is known for its digital

M. Kooskora (✉)
Estonian Business School, Tallinn, Estonia
e-mail: mari.kooskora@ebs.ee

M. Soltanifar et al. (eds.), *Digital Entrepreneurship*, Future of Business and Finance,
https://doi.org/10.1007/978-3-030-53914-6_8

143

development and in very many areas digital services have already practically replaced the traditional paper-form and person-to-person interactions among state, people and businesses and digitalisation in all areas has even become a norm and normative need in the society. Education sector is no different and 'the educational revolution in Estonia aims to implement modern digital technology more efficiently and effectively in learning and teaching' (Education e-estonia 2018). However, digitalisation and digital technologies are just tools, to help people and make interaction and services better and easier for them; the success of the transformation always depends on the culture and mindset, values and ethical considerations of people, especially of those who lead this change. This chapter focuses on entrepreneurial mindset and presents a short case study about leading the digital transformation in one Estonian private business school, where the ongoing digital process has changed the organisation itself and also the ways how students are taught and trained for the changes needed to be coped and lead in the digital world. In order to better understand the context and environment, a brief introduction to the digitalisation topic and slightly more detailed overview of digitalising in higher education sector are provided first.

2 Importance and Impact of Digitalisation

In today's highly competitive business environment, it is vital for organisations, both public and private (Grönroos 2006), to change as the environment and people's needs have already changed significantly and keep changing in the future, and therefore focusing on change processes is extremely important. One of the major transformations of today's world is digitalisation and together with globalisation these have brought along a much faster and less predictable environment whereas today's technology accelerates the speed at which companies make decisions and process information (see Earley 2014).

When trying to create the understanding of digitalisation, we see that it is a wide topic where multiple definitions exist. For example, Patel and McCarthy (2000) were among the first people to mention the concepts of digitalisation and digital transformation, however they did not conceptualise either of the terms. More recently, Ilmarinen and Koskela (2015) describe digitalisation to be the biggest transformation of our generation and see digitalisation as a process where digital technology is used in order to benefit all parts of life, thus enabling both the societies and organisations to create new opportunities to grow, improve, change and renew themselves.

Westerman et al. (2014) define digitalisation as the usage of different digital technologies to change existing business models or provide new revenue and value-producing opportunities, whereas the authors find that replacing workers with automation processes can save significant amounts of time (Westerman and Bonnet 2015). Several authors (e.g. Kvist and Kilpiä 2006; Ilmarinen and Koskela 2015; Matt et al. 2015) see digitalisation as a transformation process, which involves changing organisation's key business operations into a digital form, while affecting products and processes, but also organisational structures and management concepts.

Digitalisation was made possible by rapid technological progress and devices with increased computing power performing more demanding tasks and enabling digital services of higher quality (Mollick 2006) have accelerated its speed. Besides the higher quality and computing power of devices, the prices of smartphones with complex technological attributes have decreased 50 times from 2007 to 2014 (Ismail 2014). Furthermore, the declining cost of storing, processing, replicating and distributing digits has given the organisations ability to shift their products and services to digital format (Grover and Kohli 2013) and ultimately implement new business strategies that can utilise the opportunities created by digitalisation.

The Internet already plays an indispensable role in the everyday life of billions (Bock et al. 2015). Being connected on the web has became a societal phenomenon and about 3 billion connected consumers and businesses (as well as governments and other organisations) search, shop, socialise, transact, and interact every day using personal computers and, increasingly, a broadening range of mobile devices. The digital economy is growing at 10 per cent a year, significantly faster than the global economy as a whole (ibid). Due to the rapidly increasing number of smartphones and tablets, billions of individuals and organisations have been able to fully take advantage of this digital revolution. Either purchasing music, books, newspapers, or any other item online, making banking transactions, being a communicator, whether through personal email, texting, watching published videos or providing digital services by themselves.

The impact of digitalisation is seen everywhere around the world. Digital technologies have changed operations in organisations and enabled far-reaching social and political changes. Today the digital economy is an increasingly important source of jobs, however also the reason of job losses for millions globally. Rapid and continuous technology developments are transforming the skills required for most existing jobs and creating completely new types of roles, and changing current job functions. Already more than 47% of people, even in remote areas, are online and the development of blockchain, advanced robotics, and the Internet of things presents a profound shift for the future (DMCC 2019). According to Snabe (2015), digitalisation provides a unique opportunity for global leaders to shape our future, however at the same time, also places a momentous responsibility on their shoulders to ensure these transformations will have a positive impact on business and society.

Acknowledging the increased competitiveness of the business world, Day-Yang et al. (2011) state that digital transformation has become increasingly essential for organisations that seek to survive and attain competitive advantage. Furthermore, according to Mok and Leung (2012), digitalisation enhances peoples' economic, political and social lives and thus it is fundamental for organisations to focus on the new trends it brings. While studying the strategies related to digital technology Fitzgerald et al. (2014) found most managers to believe in technology bringing transformative change to businesses and concluded that accomplishing digital transformation is critical for companies wishing to survive.

Therefore as complicated transformations take place, companies need to create management practices to oversee them and as above mentioned authors agree (e.g. Kvist and Kilpiä 2006; Ilmarinen and Koskela 2015; Matt et al. 2015) coordination, prioritisation and implementations of digital transformation can all be done successfully when a digitalisation strategy exists. According to Fitzgerald et al. (2014) technology opens routes to new ways of doing business and a clear plan helps the organisation to avoid mistakes in that process. In addition, Westerman (2016) also points out the new opportunities that digitalisation brings along and lists three technology-driven forces that are transforming the nature of management. These are automation, data-driven management and resource fluidity, whereas technology helps businesses to increase efficiency and productivity as well as innovation and customer satisfaction.

We can discuss further that digitalisation results from multiple different aspects. According to Tolboom (2016), one reason for digitalisation is the changing customer behaviour and demand. Customers today expect to get service faster and this had led organisations to offer online services that are constantly available for customers. Kvist and Kilpiä (2006) found one of the reasons for digitalisation to be companies' willingness and need to be more customer-centric, wanting to focus more on customers' relationships and making customers' lives easier. Ilmarinen and Koskela (2015) state similarly that with the possibilities digitalisation creates, companies can focus more on customer wishes and preferences. Another reason behind digitalisation is that organisations want to end using multiple services and channels for doing business and with digital services, all can be found in one place.

Additionally, Pagani (2013) highlights the competitive advantage, added value and higher profits that can be attained with the use of a digital business strategy. Fosic et al. (2017) acknowledge that while companies have had IT strategies for decades already, these were only to support the business strategy, and propose that companies should no longer have separate IT and business strategies, but just one digital business strategy that applies for both, the IT and business side. Thus by utilising a digital business strategy organisations can be more competitive in today's challenging business world.

3 Opportunities and Threats of Digitalisation

Several authors and also practitioners agree, that digital solutions can simplify systems, provide improvement in services, facilitate trade and make business activities faster and easier. According to Matt et al. (2015), the benefits of digitalisation include increases in sales and productivity and innovations in value creation. With digitalisation stakeholder interaction often increases as well and organisations can spend more time on customers, clients and other stakeholders when certain processes are digitalised. This was also affirmed in Berman's (2012) study which showed that companies wishing to gain opportunities from digitalisation should focus on reshaping customer value propositions and transforming their operations to offer more customer interaction and collaboration. Furthermore, the research indicated that engaging with customers at every value creation point in the relationship, companies can differentiate themselves from competitors.

However, there are also threats related to digitalisation and one of these is losing customers in this process (Matzler et al. 2015) as not everyone is satisfied with transformation of traditional services into digital ones. The switching costs related to customer changing the supplier can be divided into three categories: financial costs, procedural costs and relationship costs. These switching costs can originate from financial aspects, and time and effort related matters or from old relationships ending and new ones beginning. Multiple studies (e.g. Hsu et al. 2011; Molina-Castillo et al. 2012) found that switching costs occur when a customer changes from one product to another, and customers considering to switch compare the revenue and costs of switching, and decide to stay when the costs of changing would become higher than the original costs. Additionally, Burnham et al. (2003) relate switching costs to switching intentions and behaviour. Further, it is proposed that companies can avoid switching costs by strategic planning and trying to minimise the negative affects of the change on customers.

According to Bentley (2012) modern economies, different industries and governments as well as societies rely on the help of computers and the digital format of text, audio and pictures and the modern world could not operate in the way it does without digitalisation any more. Grönroos (2006) sees one of the threats of digitalisation in the low level of knowledge that regular employees have of the technology they use. As the using new technology and computers have become so easy and intuitive, most people are unaware of the science behind them. Furthermore, Bentley (2012) claims that when technology related problems occur, ordinary employees are unable to fix them and while people with special IT skills are required to help it often takes time and means costs for the organisation. Related concerns are expressed by Fosic et al. (2017), who state that IT and Internet are not sufficient by themselves and that human capital is needed for operating with these devices.

Besides many important opportunities discussed above digitalisation makes people more dependent on technology and thus also more vulnerable. The risk of cyber incidents increases significantly and highlights the importance of cybersecurity. The Internet of things, big data, altering working and business environments, fundamental changes in value-added processes and business as such and the integration of digital and physical worlds in a so-called Industry 4.0 bring along new type of risks and threats. There is the fear of interruption and disruption due to the business and human challenges brought upon us by new business models and increasing competition, often coming from non-traditional players and 'disruptive' newcomers. With market entry barriers coming down and (the impact of) digitalisation speeding up, organisations find themselves with the challenge to perform in a volatile, uncertain, complex and ambiguous environment (I-Scoop 2016), and therefore businesses have no option but to be innovative and agile.

4   Entrepreneurial Mindset for Digital Transformation

To better cope with the new challenges related to various changes in the environment there is also a need for a new type of mindset, the way how and why we think about things we do and how we interpret the world, and new set of skills. The uncertainty around us creates high level of risks, but also great opportunities. Innovation starts with the right mindset (Meyers 2016) and according to McGrath and MacMillan (2000), uncertainty can be used for one's benefit when a person employs and develops an entrepreneurial mindset. Furthermore, Morris and Kuratko (2002) emphasise the need for entrepreneurial mindset especially in the current business environment and believe that for sustaining the competitiveness people must unlearn traditional management principles, be creative and innovative and have the ability to rapidly sense, act and mobilise.

Thus, the entrepreneurial mindset can be understood as a person's specific state of mind which orientates towards entrepreneurial activities and outcomes (Financial Times 2019), often in the pursuit of opportunity with scarce, uncontrolled resources. For Senges (2007) people with an entrepreneurial mindset are those who passionately seek new opportunities and facilitate actions aimed at exploiting these opportunities and according to Koe et al. (2012, 198) entrepreneurial people recognise opportunities, take risks, seize opportunities, and ultimately feel satisfaction. In doing so, these opportunities exist for business ideas and individuals who are able to identify them and exploit the ideas through the creation of new businesses to pursue their goals (Bygrave 1997), Kuratko and Hodgetts (2004) also interpret this as a dynamic process of vision, change and creation.

Digital transformation is one of the major changes in current business environment that gives people with entrepreneurial mindset the opportunity to enter the marketplace and provide innovative, often web- or data-based solutions, new products and services. The movement being stimulated by the fast pace of progress in the fields of mobile technology, big data, predictive analytics, cloud infrastructure, self-learning algorithms, personalisation and the growing dominance of information and communication technologies (Digital Transformation Initiative 2015) enables also new, but digitally minded entrepreneurial players to start up their companies and achieve great success, often relatively fast.

However, not all the people with entrepreneurial mindset become successful entrepreneurs, but only those who are really able to launch, manage, grow and promote new business (Humbert and Drew 2010). According to Maltsev (2016), entrepreneurs create and develop their own business using their own expertise and abilities and their own or externally borrowed resources. In doing so, the entrepreneur has to fulfil a wide variety of roles and activities in the creative and development process—from establishing a business development concept to running business processes (such as product manufacturing or customer service). While Coulter (2001) views entrepreneurship as a process in which a person or a group of people uses common efforts and measures to grow and pursues opportunities and goals, to create value through innovation and originality and thereby fulfil their desires and needs then according to Timmons (1994) an entrepreneur can be considered a person who has the ability to create and construct a vision from virtually nothing and to make it work for his own benefit.

Although becoming a digital entrepreneur seems to be easier than so-called traditional entrepreneur and may be very attractive opportunity for many, it requires certain characteristics that all people with entrepreneurial mindset may not possess. Even when each entrepreneur is unique there are several common features that can be highlighted. Among these, Costin (2012, 14) has listed intelligence, independence, high motivation, energy, initiative, innovation orientation, creativity, desire for success, originality, optimism, self-confidence, dedication, ambition, perseverance, activity, good leadership and leadership qualities, and the willingness and courage to take risks. However, entrepreneurs with right entrepreneurial mindset and required leadership skills and characteristics have better chance to succeed than those without, whether in digital or non-digital businesses.

Moreover, entrepreneurs are increasingly confronted with different precarious situations, while also experiencing a great deal of time stress, fatigue and strong emotions. Even in these intensive circumstances, they are more susceptible to mistakes, both in their decision-making process and in their judgment and reasoning (Baron 1998). This, in turn, may culminate in ethically questionable or unethical behaviour (Rutherford et al. 2009). According to Shane (2003), such tensions when entrepreneurs are more likely to exhibit unethical behaviour are most likely to arise during the foundation or start-up phase of companies, because starting entrepreneurs do not yet have the necessary social connections and feel pressure to prove and establish themselves as successful entrepreneurs.

Payne and Joyner (2006) believe that the propensity to face ethical dilemmas may also stem from the need to balance one's own values, customer needs, employee expectations, and responsibilities towards stakeholders, including shareholders. Likewise, (especially start-up) entrepreneurs can be self-centred and inclined to self-interest (Baron 1998), with a degree of self-justification due to their strong passion and high commitment to their business idea. Being a digital entrepreneur requires strong leadership, focus and discipline, moreover the only way businesses can succeed at digital transformation is to create digital entrepreneurs, people who have the necessary skills and mindset.

Furthermore, the concepts of right principles, values, ethics and responsibility have become even more important with the fast emerging digital transformation (see also Kooskora 2013; BBVA 2012). During the time of great changes it is utmost important to define what is right and wrong, good and bad, acceptable and not acceptable and both in theory and in practice, generally and in specific circumstances. For that people need clear guidelines, that can be helpful in dealing with ethical issues such as fairness, safety, transparency (Kooskora 2012) and the upholding of fundamental rights related to digitalisation. Moreover, especially the digital leaders who are making decisions having great impact on many around them have to consider and stand for the right values that are often at risk and know what must be done to preserve them. With the help of digital ethics, we can ensure that human beings, not technology, remain our primary consideration during this digital age.

Discussing further it should be pointed out that this digital transformation requires new leadership roles, skills and also digitally minded leaders with high level of integrity. Moreover, digital leadership is much more than a job title, it is an entirely new mindset (Kaganer et al. 2013). According to Kerr (2019), the digital mindset requires open mindedness and today's leaders have to be aware and understand all the capabilities that technology has to offer and put it in use. These leaders have focus on better future and constantly seek and find new ways to use technology in order to enhance employee engagement, drive customer satisfaction and unleash competitive advantage.

However, the digital world is not about technology, but people (Becerra 2017). Digital leadership is about empowering others to lead and creating self-organised teams that optimise their day-to-day operations. Leadership today is no longer hierarchical—it needs participation, involvement and contribution from everyone (Dubey 2019), and leaders need to create a compelling vision and communicate with clarity so that everyone understands what the team is trying to achieve and why. Great leaders know that people can achieve great things when they are driven by a strong purpose and find work meaningful. They understand that when people know the why, they figure out the how and can achieve remarkable results.

Furthermore, when organisations create a culture of learning, failures and experiments lead to inventions and innovations, therefore digitally minded and entrepreneurial leaders provide support and energise everyone and inspire them with an inclusive vision. Digital leaders are adaptable and able to handle pressure and constant changes, and to take decisions with agility (Dubey 2019), they understand the value of diversity, inclusion and open-mindedness and can navigate the challenges of technological disruptions.

According to The World Economic Forum's 2018 Future of Jobs (2018) report no less than 54% of all employees will require significant re- and up-skilling by the year 2022 and of these about 35% are expected to require additional training of up to six months, while 9% will require re-skilling lasting 6–12 months and 10% will require additional skills training of more than a year. Therefore, the digital leadership will need to address the skill gaps, prepare themselves and their teams to face the future by creating an environment of lifelong learning and with the adoption of new technology and solutions, new professions, skills and industries will emerge. This is why it is important for companies to identify, develop and place future-oriented innovative, entrepreneurial, critical thinking leaders who are able to create a long-term sustainable value for all stakeholders.

To conclude this brief overview, it can be said that digitalisation is the use of digital technology to provide new opportunities for people and organisations. Smith (2004) views technology as a division of knowledge that deals with the creation and use of technical means and their interrelation with life, society, and the environment. According to Mäkkylä (2017), digitalisation has enabled new concepts, procedures and new agents into different fields and changed people's behaviour. With the help of the Internet, people have become more aware of their preferences, their requirements have increased and knowledge of the available alternatives is greater. Cherif and Grant (2014) suggest that digitalisation has initiated the

Internet's ability to conveniently display information and therefore the communication between service providers and potential customers has changed and improved. Industries' services have been transferred into digital services which has enabled newcomers into the field and forced traditional agents to renew themselves.

5 Case Study

5.1 Leading Digital Transformation at Estonian Business School

5.1.1 Digitalisation in the Higher Education Sector

Similarly to various other sectors, the role of universities in the society and economy and the ways how education is delivered is changing and continues to change in the next decades. Compared to other sectors, the impact of global change is even more present in higher education and the whole nature of higher education changes significantly (Coskun 2015; Bridgstock and Cunningham 2016) as universities need to become more digital learning institutions. Whereas the market has become global everywhere, universities are also competing globally for students, academics and funding, and it is believed that only those that stay relevant and leverage new digital capabilities will benefit in this digital age (PwC 2015; McKinsey 2015).

In order to overcome challenges related to technological changes, universities have to respond digitalisation in a quick and effective way and develop strategies that help to benefit from these changes. Therefore, many universities all over the world are developing digital strategies and invest heavily in IT systems (Jones 2016; Newman and Scurry 2015). Being digitally well-equipped to ensure effective use of modern technology is required for achieving a successful digital transformation, and the whole university including students, staff and academics has to be prepared to work with digital tools and techniques. Universities that efficiently follow a digital framework are equipped with the competencies to drive innovation and disruption approaches (Tapscott and Williams 2010; Khalid et al. 2018).

Whereas twenty-first century students have many expectations of universities, their experiences and expectations of future employability after university education are now more critical and require universities to change. The digital age brings along new challenges and opportunities for university leaders and faculty as teaching methods, ways of learning and research techniques are all changing fast. A digitally sophisticated generation is expecting to learn and to be taught using methods in accordance with their personal preferences, which requires implementing modern technologies, including smart mobile, cloud-based IT, wearable devices and advanced analytics (Kirkwood and Price 2013; McKinsey 2015). Digital technologies are considered as vital elements of student education and linked with substantial changes to the ways students learn and experience (Coskun 2015; Henderson et al. 2017). Moreover, adapting educational institutions and training providers to the digital age can be regarded as a cornerstone of any long-term strategy to foster digital skills, as formal schooling is still considered the main way how people acquire and develop digital skills.

A core function of academic institutions is to continually update and advance their management and learning process and for a digital success, the right balance and connectivity among students, staff and departments are the key elements for survival. However, the role of senior management in supporting and helping to take most out the substantial benefits linked with the digital change is essential. Khalid et al. (2018) argue that in order to meet the needs of the knowledge society, students' learning preferences, as well as technological development of faculty members, university leaders must be aware of a growing imperative to reshape their structures and processes, pedagogic and curricula practices. Digital skills are developed through life-long learning programmes while adding new techniques and capabilities, and inhibiting culture to accepting modern technologies and development (Hill et al. 2015). The knowledge, skills and competences that such programmes deliver help to shape digital leadership skills and entrepreneurial mindset.

Digital literacy includes skills, knowledge and confidence to use advanced technology and while digitalisation has enabled various innovative teaching techniques, for instance, richer distance learning, flipped classroom and hybrid teaching models, not all universities and faculty members have welcomed these changes. Being omnipresent in social media and active use of innovative interactive techniques for teaching is not too appealing for all academics. Another reason behind this lies in the technological development and required infrastructure, implementing new technologies and digital tools need investing a lot of time and money and supporting leaders with digital mindset.

Nevertheless, e-learning is already widespread and MOOCs (Schuwer et al. 2015) have become popular among students around the world, therefore most universities are interested in developing and creating online learning opportunities. However, some of the leading universities, including Cambridge and Oxford (Berger and Frey 2016), have found more useful and implement blended learning models, where online learning is complemented with face-to-face interaction helping students to develop relevant skills while tackling real-world challenges. Problem-based learning (PBL) is often used to foster critical thinking, problem-solving, and interpersonal skills (Frey and Osborne 2013), the skills needed to compete in the twenty-first century labour market and MOOCs to improve the learning experience rather than wholly shifting the provision of education online.

Moreover, the senior management must consider that universities those are not adopting new digital change will not be able to fully compete in the contemporary digital era. Therefore, to implement this change within the universities, it is critical to create a high level of digital awareness, develop digital vision and determine how to gain the necessary digital capabilities and develop entrepreneurial mindset. To avoid falling behind competition, universities must rethink how they should operate in the evolving digital era.

Digitalisation is deeply embedded also in the Estonian educational sector. The educational digital revolution in Estonia aims to implement digital technology more efficiently and effectively in learning and teaching, and to improve the digital skills of the entire nation (e-Estonia 2019). Estonia can be happy for its developments in this sector, with being first in Europe in the OECD PISA test, having 100% of schools using e-school solutions, and every 10th student studying IT every year. Digital solutions and tools are widely used in all other educational forms and it is ensured that every student receives the necessary knowledge and skills to access modern digital infrastructure for future use. One example of the digital transformation in the education system is that by 2020 all study materials in Estonia will be digitised and available through an online e-schoolbag.

In 2005, Estonian state created a database named Estonian Education Information System (EHIS) that brings together all the information related to education in Estonia (ehis.ee). The database stores details about education institutions, students, teachers and lecturers, graduation documents, study materials and curricula. The service is intended for anyone in education, whether students enrolled in general, vocational, higher or hobby programmes, or the teachers and academic staff providing that education. It is also possible to access information on the qualifications and further training completed by teachers and academics. EHIS is also part of monitoring the education system so that the authorities can make sure it prepares people for the labour market of the future. Higher education is free in Estonia at public universities and applying for university studies by simply transferring one's details to the desired university is the most common use of the EHIS database (EHIS 2019). Availability of numerous of education e-solutions is definitely very helpful for Estonians as most of them believe that raising smarter kids is the smartest investment a country can make and for staying smart life-long learning is a must.

5.2 Leading the Digital Transformation at Estonian Business School

5.2.1 Brief Introduction to Estonian Business School

Founded in 1988, Estonian Business School (EBS) is the oldest privately owned business university in the Baltics (see ebs.ee) educating and training current and future managers in the areas of business administration, leadership and entrepreneurship and conducting research in related fields. With more than 1500 students, EBS's goal is to provide enterprising people with academic knowledge, skills and values for its successful implementation and offering degrees at Bachelor's, Master's as well as Doctoral levels. When EBS was founded in 1988, it was the first institution in Estonia to introduce diploma business education and since business administration did not exist in soviet universities, there was no teaching tradition, no faculty and no textbooks: a difficult starting position.

However, the size of the country and its orientation towards the West has meant that EBS has stressed the international and innovation perspectives from the start, and the rapidly changing environment has encouraged EBS to respond and adapt at an adequate speed. Starting from the scratch can also be seen as an advantage since the university was and still is not tied down by outdated procedures and over-whelming traditions from the past, which also makes its digital transformation as a logical and natural step ahead.

Adapting to the Estonian context has meant, for example, that EBS uses many practitioners and higher-level managers as lecturers in its courses, revising tradi-tional programmes to fit actual needs from the industry, and applying management theories and best business practices in the running of the institution itself as well. EBS also acknowledges and appreciates most of its students working full-time or part-time in addition to studying, encouraging and shaping their entrepreneurial mindset. By using both English and Estonian as languages of instruction, EBS is preparing students for the Estonian market and beyond. Today more than 30% of students come from abroad, from 12 different countries and 20% of faculty mem-bers are foreigners.

In year 2011, EBS was the first university to establish its subsidiary in neigh-bouring country Finland. The goal of EBS Helsinki Branch is to provide Finnish students with the possibility to study international business administration by way of session-based learning in English in the students´ home country. EBS Helsinki is located in the modern and innovative Technopolis Ruoholahti business park, ben-efitting from various digital solutions and tools. Along with developing high-quality learning environment in Helsinki, EBS has significantly increased the investments into transformation to more innovative and digital solutions also in Tallinn's main campus and now these tools are more widely and rapidly implemented in teaching and training activities and being daily used by all students, staff and academics.

5.3 Study Methodology

For getting more information about the digital transformation at Estonian Business School and for illustrating this discussion with real-life examples, I conducted personal in-depth interviews with EBS owner and chancellor Mart Habakuk (hereafter M.H.), who coming from real estate industry took over the university's management after his father's Madis Habakuk's sudden death in 2016. Prof. Madis Habakuk was the founder and owner and also long-time rector of EBS who was actively involved in management until the day he passed away. He also kept EBS constantly updated and adapted to the changes in the environment and several big changes were made rather often, moreover, several e-solutions were available from the beginning, including WebCT, Moodle, online study system (ois), free use of electronic databases, etc. However, his son Mart Habakuk, coming from business sector and having much more radical views and readiness for innovation and digitalisation, started a new digital transformation process immediately after becoming the chancellor of the university.

For gathering the material for this empirical case study (Yin 2012), I conducted personal unstructured in-depth expert interviews (Saunders et al. 2009) in August 2019.

My purpose of having these interviews was to have open conversation and therefore indicated just the main topics and areas related to a more general view on digitalisation, digitalisation in the university, future of learning and teaching, leading the digital transformation, and values and mindset of the digital leader.

The interviews took place in an open atmosphere, and after I had explained him the purpose of this study, the chancellor was willing and ready to openly share his views and thoughts about these topics. The interviews were conducted in EBS Tallinn campus, in Estonian language. These were recorded, wholly transcribed and translated into English, I also took notes during the interviews to keep an eye on the process, and to be able to ask additional questions for drawing attention to some topics needed to be covered. The recordings lasted for 59 min and the amount of transcribed text was 30 pages.

The chancellor was chosen as the respondent with a clear purpose (see Creswell 2009) to get rich data, to know more about his views and experiences, and especially about his entrepreneurial mindset as being the digital leader, whereas he is the person who initiated the digital transformation and makes most important decisions related to digitalisation at EBS. The information collected from these interviews enables to better understand the importance of entrepreneurial mindset in digitalisation process taking place at EBS and know what were and are the reasons behind decisions related to digitalisation. For analysing I used the case-by-case qualitative content analysis (Frechtling and Sharp 1997), searching for meaningful patterns and creating categories, drawing relations between different topics and focusing on the values and entrepreneurial mindset. The transcribed texts were read several times and different categories marked, during the analysis inductive open in vivo coding was used, in order to create the detailed understanding and decode meanings.

5.4 Digitalisation

The first topic was about conceptualising digitalisation in general. It can be said that here his view goes in line with the ideas of authors discussed previously (Matt et al. 2015; Ilmarinen and Koskela 2015; Westerman et al. 2014). For M.H., digitalisation means using technology in order to do things better and more efficiently, or as he put it in words: *'When looking from more distant, digitalisation might seem to be the use of digital documents or some kind of new program, however with more inside look we realise that it means implementing new products and technology that often is new hard- and software, to make things better and more efficiently'.*

M.H. also made an interesting comparison to the innovation related to steam engine and new technology back then, emphasising that everything starts with the purpose, and why these new applications are needed and he also indicated that today the tools and equipments are just more developed, saying that *'however the purpose has remained the same, to do things better and more efficiently and when this new technology includes software, then it can be also called as digitalisation'.*

5.5 Digitalisation in the University

Next I wanted to know what is the meaning of digitalisation for the university. In his answer, M.H. stated that digitalisation for the university is not as purpose per se, but in order to make its products and services better, it is possible to set up several hypothesis. In his view, learning has to take place over long time, *not like one-two-days sprints*; it is important to learn several things at one time, in order to create connections between different subjects; he also highlighted the importance of learning and teaching from each other, based on own experiences and that has been read from some books or other forms of courses. *Learning about something and then sharing this with the others.*

Similarly with Henderson et al. (2017) he also emphasised the role of experimenting and trying different solutions. The role of technology and digital tools was just seen as helping people, both students and faculty in this process. *Digitalisation of university means a range of different trials and experiments, what might work and what not, and it is also clear, that what works with one might not work with the other, and this depends on the student, on the subject, the instructor and relatively little on the technology.*

M.H. told also more specifically about the EBS's experiences and what has been done in the university during this new digital transformation process. What was really interesting to hear was that there are several trials and experiments taking place at the same time and the success of these is mainly determined by the facts whether these help students and whether corporate customers will buy these for their employees. '*... from the digi- and start-up world (that is also indirectly related to the digital world) it can be seen how new things are done, first there is an idea, then you can look for best practices from the world, put together the brief overviews, find people to test these with, which ones would they buy ... and when the majority would buy the same you have selected, you are on the right track and can use these with students. These should be relevant and specifically meeting the students' needs'.*

5.6 Future of Learning and Teaching

Learning together and sharing the knowledge was emphasised several times during these interviews. The chancellor also argued from the student's perspective, saying that '*in today's high pace environment ... it would be more faster and efficient doing it individually, and thus* via *different forms of online and on-demand courses, where you can learn the basics and which might not be so exiting, but need to be known'.* He also found it possible and even necessary to have group works in the virtual world, where students do not need to be physically present, but also expressed his concerns stating that: '*there's not yet enough evidence that it will replace meetings with others. And there are things which have been and also will stay, these are face-to-face meetings, working in groups and learning from each other'.*

When talking about teaching at the university, he called the lectures with 500 students *edutainment*, which are meant for the superstars, '*who come and do something awesome*', but added, '*when you look at the learning process as a whole, when you learn some tools or skills, then these big lectures are not so optimal choices*'. Helping to develop certain skills and entrepreneurial mindset, to learn how to use new and innovative tools were topics that seemed to be very important for him as he returned to these several times and considered these as the main purpose and role of the university in the twenty-first century. As the same ideas are also found from Frey and Osborne's (2013) studies, then the importance of digitally minded entrepreneurial people in academic sector cannot be underestimated.

Looking at the whole learning process and helping students there was something that M.H. considered especially relevant for the future: '*... but what I believe that may emerge is the personal learning cloud and big qualitative change in online courses, that are not courses any more, but learning paths*'. The importance of life-long learning and university's role facilitating the process was another topic that was repeated several times: '*... and the new role of the university is being a place where people do these things which are more efficient done as face-to-face, where someone helps when one is stuck. Thus it's possible to ask either from the fellow student or from a faculty member.*' (see also Hill et al. 2015). M.H. views faculty members as facilitators, mentors, who help the students to achieve their purposes, and who need to be present when students need help, in most cases in teams and sometimes also individually. '*... it's is more like a mentor—student relationship and the traditional belief, that a faculty member is the most knowledgeable person is outdated today. A faculty member should help students to achieve their purposes and can suggest what skills are needed and in which order*'.

Turning their head towards customers (as also discussed by Tolboom 2016; Ilmarinen and Koskela 2015; Edelman 2010), creating a supporting infrastructure (Matt et al. 2015) and encouraging atmosphere for recognising opportunities and taking risks (Koe et al. 2012) and developing entrepreneurial mindset have been also considered significant during transformation processes. According to M.H., the digitalisation transformation activities are directly related to the investments made into the infrastructure and providing new spaces where students can work in teams (either in real life or by using new digital tools and solutions) on the assignments faculty members have given them. '*...this (our digitalisation activities (M.K.) ... relates to the experiments we are making with the infrastructure right now, creating more learning spaces outside the auditoriums, there were no such places earlier and now there will be about 10% of the whole area for informal learning spaces. ... It's an experiment now, and it will be interesting to see how students will adopt it and start using it. It also should change the whole image and mindset of people to study together more, also when using online learning...*'. With this statement, M.H. once again gave proof that the whole digitalisation process is carried through with the purpose to increase sheared (online) learning, make things better and more efficient especially for the students, who represent the paying customers for a private university like EBS.

Interesting examples and ideas were expressed by M.H. especially about the future learning opportunities and methods. Some of these solutions are already existing, others being currently developed and constantly improved. *'...Today the big companies such as Amazon and Google have their own academias, where with very reasonable price and constantly improving quality courses are offered and those who want and are able to motivate themselves, can create even groups from people with similar mindsets, and able to get the same education within the same time, at 10 times lower price. But of course universities have several arguments against it, for example the public sector is a thankful customer, who thinks that people should be taught and motivated to learn...'* Here we can argue, that according to M.H. the future learning activities should not take place at the university at all, although this can be considered true and rather probable, however this also endangers the future perspectives of universities as such.

5.7 Leading the Digital Transformation

As Mart Habakuk is really a person with an entrepreneurial mindset, being the initiator and brain behind the digital transformation process at EBS, it was interesting to know more about his experiences when leading this change. Khalid et al. (2018) have emphasised the role of university leaders and hearing how the process is lead at our university enabled to understand certain decisions and choices much better. Although at first M.H. considered this topic more complicated, the answers showed that in case of EBS and for himself personally as well the vision of the leader and encouraging others to work towards that vision (e.g. Kouzes and Posner 2012) are the main leading principles in this digital transformation process. M.H.: *'...basically it is telling your stories, and making sure that you can help to remove the obstacles, that do not allow people to do things they are able to do if they want ... and as the things that can be done are so many, and it's not possible to do them all, even half of these not, then to filter out the single ones where it's feasible to make an effort and put recourses in, looking where the impact is the biggest and always measuring on what ... so we also like to deepen the way of thinking, shape the mindset, that we are not here to become the best university in the Eastern Europe, but for helping our students to achieve their purposes'.*

Here again, his concerns about helping the students to achieve their purposes were heard: *'...and everything we do or leave undone, we need to think whether it helps our students to achieve their purposes or not ... and when not, then what can help them ... and making this way of thinking to become prevailing'.* The same idea was also mentioned when talking about main obstacles in this process as often faculty members are relaying too much on what they are used to do and may be hesitant when implementing new solutions and digital tools (see Fosic et al. 2017): *'... but a big thing is whether we can get our faculty members to integrate the world-class content and solutions into their own courses. So that also the content not produced by themselves is ok, and should be used in order to help students to achieve their purposes. So in principle to offer solutions to overcome the skill caps students might have...'*

5.8 Values and Mindset of the Digital Leader

Final interesting and relevant topics that were discussed were related to the values and mindset of the leader in the digital transformation process. The answers again gave proof to the ideas expressed by several authors who have analysed the digital leaders' activities and principles (e.g. Kaganer et al. 2013; Becerra 2017; Dubey 2019; Khalid et al. 2018). The values were expressed in the best way through M. H.'s views how to measure success and what are the principles behind decisions that are made in the university. Working together on the common purpose, sharing ideas and information was repeated several times, also the ideas how to support our students in the best way and even why is it important to help others in the same field. According to M.H.: '... *values* ... *mainly how to make people do things that are needed, make sense and get agreements that we are going to achieve these together ...our main success measurement is the number how many persons do not leave the university after graduation, but come back for different courses and events, keeping in touch with us ... this also shows that they are interested and want to learn more ... and so we can offer special modules, at multiple levels ... (it's not yet) not so acknowledgeable, but our main purpose should really be to help students ... and when doing things well, money will follow, it's the result ... (we have also to consider) ... availability is not only the privilege of wealthy ... we can help our students to get the best on the market ... and when doing something and creating something, helping also the others, sharing information and best practices, helping the others to succeed as well (is important) ... as the goldsmiths are all on the same street, when everyone succeeds, then all will be successful ... (and our main purpose is) ...to wake up the 21 century persons, and make them valuing themselves, so that also the others will benefit from it'.* All these ideas were something that I really liked to hear and now hope that these values (e.g. Kooskora 2012, 2013; BBVA 2012) will start playing even bigger role in the university's activities as well.

To conclude this case study, it is just one example how digitalisation transformation is lead in one Estonian private university. It highlights some most important aspects and shows what are the ideas and thoughts behind decisions made during the process and emphasises the role of entrepreneurial mindset. It attempts to look and make sense of the choices that the digital leader has made, not to generalise to other universities in Estonia nor anywhere else, but to advance theory and conceptualisation. Although all cases are different depending on the environment and certain situations as well as concrete persons, their views and values, this case study still presents some certain aspects and patterns that can be also considered characteristic for the twenty-first century organisations. Turning the head towards the customers, hearing their voice, considering the needs and expectations of different stakeholders, involving own organisation's members in the process, leading them by shared vision and telling stories, creating the supportive environment and encouraging entrepreneurial atmosphere, empowering people and valuing their skills are just some of these. Formulating the overall purpose to help their customers, understanding that right and good activities make the money to follow and helping others to succeed as well can definitely be considered as values that may help to succeed in the changed environment of the twenty-first century. Moreover, while developing relevant online and blended courses there is a need to collaborate closely with different stakeholders. Identifying the skills that are demanded by employers and designing course content to facilitate the development of skills that are aligned with industry demand need considerable input from many stakeholder groups and development of entrepreneurial mindset. Furthermore adapting the curriculum should go beyond the infusion of digital skills to also address the role of digital leadership skills, the skills required of an individual to initiate and achieve digital transformation across companies and industries, and develop digital leadership mindset.

6 Concluding Remarks

The discussion about digitally minded leaders with entrepreneurial mindset and short case study about digitalisation and leading the digital transformation process showed clearly, that although the new solutions and tools gained through digitalisation are helpful they do not have any value without the people. Digitalisation just gives the tools that should make people's lives better and their activities and work more effective, however how successful the process is and will be depends on the people and especially those who are leading it. In order to compete in the much-changed environment, organisations need to succeed in merging their activities and technology. Whereas while facing some of the greatest challenges as well as greatest opportunities from the digital transformation, much depends on people with entrepreneurial mindset and the vision of the leaders.

References

Baron, R. A. (1998). Cognitive mechanism in entrepreneurship: Why and when entrepreneurs think differently than other people. *Journal of Business Venturing, 13,* 275–294.

BBVA. (2012). *Values and ethics for the 21st century.* e-book https://www.bbvaopenmind.com/wp-content/uploads/2012/01/BBVA-OpenMind-Book-2012-Values-and-Ethics-for-the-21st-Century.pdf. Accessed 10 Sept 2019.

Becerra, J. (2017). *The digital revolution is not about technology—It's about people.* World Economic Forum. https://www.weforum.org/agenda/2017/03/the-digital-revolution-is-not-about-technology-it-s-about-people/. Accessed 10 June 2019.

Bentley, P. J. (2012). *Digitized.* New York, USA: Oxford University Press Inc.

Berger, T., & Frey, B. (2016). *Digitalisation, jobs and convergence in Europe: Strategies for closing the skills gap* (Vol. 50). Oxford Martin School.

Berman, S. J. (2012). Digital transformation: Opportunities to create new business models. *Strategy & Leadership, 40*(2), 16–24.

Bock, W., Vasishth, N., Wilms, M., & Mohan, M. (2015). *The infrastructure needs of the digital economy*. https://www.bcg.com/publications/2015/infrastructure-needs-of-the-digital-economy.aspx. Accessed 10 June 2019.

Bygrave, W. D. (1997). *The portable MBA in entrepreneurship*. New York: Wiley.

Bridgstock, R., & Cunningham, S. (2016). Creative labour and graduate outcomes: Implications for higher education and cultural policy. *International Journal of Cultural Policy, 22*(1), 10–26. https://doi.org/10.1080/10286632.2015.1101086.

Burnham, T., Frels, J., & Mahajan, V. (2003). Consumer switching costs: A typology, antecedents and consequences. *Academy of Marketing Science Journal, 31*(2), 109.

Cherif, E., & Grant, D. (2014). Analysis of e-business models in real estate. *Electronic Commerce Research, 14*(1), 25–50 (New York).

Creswell, J. (2009). *Research design: Qualitative, quantitative and mixed methods approaches*. USA: Sage Publications.

Coskun, Y. D. (2015). Promoting digital change in higher education: Evaluating the curriculum digitalisation. *Journal of International Education Research, 11*(3), 197–204.

Costin, G. (2012). The profile of an entrepreneur in a modern society. *Valahian Journal of Economic Studies, 3*(4), 13–16.

Coulter, M. K. (2001). *Entrepreneurship in action*. NJ: Prentice Hall.

Day-Yang, L., Shou-Wei, C., & Chou, T.-C. (2011). Resource fit in digital transformation. *Management Decision, 49*(10), 1728–1742 (London).

Digital Transformation Initiative. (2015). *World Economic Forum* http://reports.weforum.org/digital-transformation/. Accessed 15 Sept 2019.

DMCC. (2019). *The impact of digitalisation, future of trade*. https://futureoftrade.com/the-impact-of-digitalisation. Accessed 30 July 2019.

Dubey, A. (2019). This is what Great Leadership looks like in the digital age. *World Economic Forum*. https://www.weforum.org/agenda/2019/04/leadership-digital-age-leader/. Accessed 15 June 2019.

Earley, S. (2014). The digital transformation: Staying competitive. *IT Professional Magazine, 16*(2), 58 (Washington).

Edelman, D. C. (2010). Branding in the digital age you're spending your money in all the wrong places. *Harvard Business Review, 88*, 63–69. https://depositioneerders.nl/wp-content/uploads/2017/01/Branding-in-the-Digital-Age-HBR.pdf. Accessed 15 June 2019.

Education e-estonia. (2018). https://e-estonia.com/solutions/education/. Accessed 10 Aug 2019.

E-Estonia. (2019). *Building blocks of E-Estonia e-estonia.com*. Accessed 10 Aug 2019.

EHIS. (2019). *Estonian Education Information System (EHIS)*. http://www.ehis.ee. Accessed 10 Aug 2019.

Financial Times. (2019). *Term—Entrepreneurial mindset*. http://markets.ft.com/research/Lexicon/Term?term=entrepreneurial-mindset.

Fitzgerald, M., Kruschwitz, N., Bonnet, D., & Welch, M. (2014). Embracing digital technology: A new strategic imperative. *MIT Sloan Management Review, 55*(2), 1–12. (Cambridge).

Fosic, I., Trusic, A., & Sebalj, D. (2017). Digital organizational strategy—Ticket for competitiveness on the international market. *Strategic Management, 22*, 3–10.

Frechtling, J., & Sharp, L. (1997). *User-friendly handbook for mixed method evaluations*. Diane Publishing.

Frey, C. B., & Osborne, M. A. (2013). *The future of employment: How susceptible are jobs to computerisation?* https://www.oxfordmartin.ox.ac.uk/downloads/academic/The_Future_of_Employment.pdf. Accessed 13 June 2019.

Future of Jobs. (2018). Future of jobs report. *World Economic Forum's 2018*. https://www.weforum.org/reports/the-future-of-jobs-report-2018. Accessed 15 June 2019.

Grover, V., & Kohli, R. (2013). Revealing your hand: Caveats in implementing digital business strategy. *MIS Quarterly, 37*(2), 655–662.

Grönroos, M. G. (2006). *Mahdollisuuden Aika kohti Virtuaalista Organisaatiota*. Tampere: Tammer-Paino Oy.

Henderson, M., Selwyn, N., & Aston, R. (2017). What works and why? Student perceptions of 'useful' digital technology in university teaching and learning. *Studies in Higher Education, 42*(8), 1567–1579.

Hill, R., Betts, L. R., & Gardner, S. E. (2015). Older adults' experiences and perceptions of digital technology: (Dis)empowerment, wellbeing, and inclusion. *Computers in Human Behavior, 48*, 415–423.

Hsu, C., WengWang, D., & Xing, P. (2011). Switching costs and influence on customer loyalty in the online shopping market. *Sansia, 8*(3), 295–314.

Humbert, A., & Drew, E. (2010). Gender, entrepreneurship and motivational factors in an Irish context. *International Journal of Gender and Entrepreneurship, 2*(2), 173–196.

Ilmarinen, V., & Koskela, K. (2015). *Digitalisaatio*. Finland: Talentum.

I-Scoop (2016). *The risks of digitalization*. https://www.i-scoop.eu/the-risks-of-digitalization-and-disruption-for-2016-and-beyond/. Accessed 30 June 2019.

Ismail, S. (2014). *Exponential Organizations: Why new organization are ten times better, faster and cheaper than yours (and what to do about it)*. New York: Diversion Books.

Jones, A. (2016). *Digital technology and the contemporary university: Degrees of digitization*, Taylor & Francis.

Kaganer, E., Zamora, J., & Sieber, S. (2013). 5 skills every leader needs to succeed in the digital world. In *IESE Insight*, 18 https://www.ieseinsight.com/doc.aspx?id=1509. Accessed 30 June 2019.

Kerr, J. (2019). Today's best leaders all share these 5 traits—A digital mindset. https://www.inc.com/james-kerr/every-business-leader-needs-a-digital-mindset-to-succeed-and-it-starts-with-these-5-things.html. Accessed 30 June 2019.

Kirkwood, A., & Price, L. (2013). Examining some assumptions and limitations of research on the effects of emerging technologies for teaching and learning in higher education. *British Journal of Educational Technology, 44*(4), 536–543.

Khalid, J., Ram, B. R., Soliman, M., Ali, A. J., Khaleel, M., & Islam, M. S. (2018). Promising digital university: A pivotal need for higher education transformation. *International Journal of Management in Education, 12*(3), 264–275.

Koe, W. L., Sa'ari, J. R., & Majid, I. A. (2012). Determinants of entrepreneurial intention among millennial generation. *Procedia-Social and Behavioral Sciences, 40*, 197–208.

Kooskora, M. (2012). Ethical leadership: The role of the leader. *Cases of Organizational Ethics*, Vilnius University, pp. 23–38.

Kooskora, M. (2013). The role of (the right) values in an economic crisis. *Journal of Management & Change, 2*(1), 49–65.

Kouzes, J., & Posner, B. (2012). *The leadership challenge* (5th ed.). San Francisco: Jossey-Bass Publishers.

Kuratko, D. F., & Hodgetts, R. M. (2004). *Entrepreneurship: Theory, process, and practice* (6th ed.). Mason, OH: Thomson/South-Western.

Kvist, H., & Kilpiä, T. (2006). *Muutosaskeleita*. Jyväskylä: Gummerus Kirjapaino Oy.

Mäkkylä, M. (2017). *Kiinteistönvälitysalan nykyaikaisen konseptin vaikutus toteutuneisiin myyntihintoihin*. Turun Ammattikorkeakoulu, 42.

Maltsev, E. (2016). Dynamics of the entrepreneur's role composition. *Amity Global Business Review, 11*, 7–14.

Matt, C., Hess, T., & Benlian, A. (2015). Digital transformation strategies. *Business & Information Systems Engineering, 57*(5), 339–343. (Berkeley).

Matzler, K., Strobl, A., Thurner, N., & Füller, J. (2015). Switching experience, customer satisfaction and switching costs in the ICT industry. *Journal of Service Management, 26*(1), 117–136.

McGrath, R. G., & MacMillan, I. C. (2000). Assessing technology projects using real options reasoning. *Research-Technology Management, 43*(4), 35–49.

McKinsey. (2015). *A labour market that works: Connecting talent with opportunity in the digital age.* McKinsey Global Institute, June 2015. https://www.mckinsey.com/ ~ /media/McKinsey/ Featured%20Insights. Accessed 10 June 2019.

Meyers, A. (2016). *Innovation starts with the right mindset.* https://www.linkedin.com/pulse/ innovation-starts-right-mindset-arlen-meyers-md-mba/.

Mok, K. H., & Leung, D. (2012). Digitalisation, educational and social development in the greater China. *Globalisation, Societies and Education, 10*(3).

Morris, M. H., & Kuratko, D. F. (2002). *Corporate entrepreneurship.* Mason, OH: South-Western College Publishers.

Molina-Castillo, F.-J., Rodriquez-Escudero, A.-I., & Munuera-Aleman, J.-L. (2012). Do switching costs really provide a first mover advantage? *Marketing Intelligence & Planning, 30*(2), 165–187.

Mollick, E. (2006). Establishing Moore's law. *IEEE Annals of the History of Computing, 28*(3), 62–75.

Newman, F., & Scurry, J. E. (2015). Higher education and the digital rapids. *International Higher Education, 26.*

Pagani, M. (2013). Digital business strategy and value creation: Framing the dynamic cycle of control points. *MIS Quarterly, 37*(2), 617–632.

Patel, K., & McCarthy, M. (2000). *Digital transformation: The essentials of e-business leadership.* McGraw-Hill Professional.

Payne, D., & Joyner, B. E. (2006). Successful US entrepreneurs: Identifying ethical decision-making and social responsibility behaviors. *Journal of Business Ethics, 65,* 203–217.

PwC. (2015). The 2018 university—Making the right choices, making it happen. www.pwc.co.uk/ 2018university.

Rutherford, M., Buller, P., & Stebbins, J. (2009). Ethical considerations of the legitimacy lie. *Entrepreneurship Theory and Practice, 33*(4), 949–964.

Saunders, M., Lewis, P., & Thornhill, A. (2009). *Research methods for business students* (5th ed.). Harlow: Pearson Education Limited.

Schuwer, R., Jaurena, I. G., Aydin, C., Costello, E., Dalsgaard, C., Brown, M., Jansen, D., & Teixeira, A. (2015). Opportunities and threats of the MOOC movement for higher education: The European perspective. *The International Review of Research in Open and Distributed Learning, 16*(6).

Shane, S. (2003). *A general theory of entrepreneurship: The individual-opportunity Nexus.* Cheltenham, UK: Edward Elgar.

Senges, M. (2007). Knowledge entrepreneurship in universities: Practice and strategy of internet based innovation appropriation (Doctoral dissertation, Universitat Oberta de Catalunya).

Smith, B. (2004). Computer-mediated negotiated interaction and lexical acquisition. *Studies in Second Language Acquisition, 26,* 365–398.

Snabe, J. H. (2015). What will digitalisation do to the future? *World Economic Forum.* https:// www.weforum.org/agenda/2015/11/what-will-digitalization-do-to-the-future/. Accessed 9 June 2019.

Tapscott, D., & Williams, A. D. (2010). Innovating the 21st-century university: It's time. *Educause Review, 45*(1), 16–29.

Timmons, J. A. (1994). *New venture creation.* Homewood, IL: Irwin.

Tolboom. I. (2016). *The impact of digital transformation.* https://repository.tudelft.nl/islandora/ object/uuid:d1d6f874-abc1-4977-8d4e-4b98d3db8265/datastream/OBJ. Accessed 10 June 2019.

Westerman, G. (2016). Why digital transformation needs a heart. *MIT Sloan Management Review, 58*(1), 19–21 (Cambridge).

Westerman, G., & Bonnet, D. (2015). Revamping your business through digital transformation. *MIT Sloan Management Review, 56*(3), 10–13 (Cambridge).

Westerman, G., Bonnet, D., & McAfee, A. (2014). Leading digital: Turning technology into business transformation. *Harvard Business Review Press.*

Yin, R. K. (2012). Case study methods. In H. Cooper, P. M. Camic, D. L. Long, A. T. Panter, D. Rindskopf, & K. J. Sher (Eds.), *APA handbook of research methods in psychology, Vol. 2. Research designs: Quantitative, qualitative, neuropsychological, and biological* (pp. 141–155). Washington, DC, US: American Psychological Association. http://dx.doi.org/10.1037/13620-009.

Digital Creativity: Upgrading Creativity in Digital Business

Edin Smailhodžić and Denis Berberović

Abstract

Creativity has become one of the most important driving factors of today's digital business environments. Businesses are increasingly looking for creative employees who can offer new and out-of-the-box solutions to existing problems. Companies go through the process of digital transformation by increasingly changing the ways in which they employ digital technologies and develop new digital business models that help to create and to capture value. Combined with a creative approach, companies have experienced a surge in creative digital solutions. However, the creative process is not a self-perpetuating mechanism. It must be initiated and supported by organizations. This is done by understanding the creative process itself and by making small but fruitful adjustments to the work environment and the overall management of the workforce. As three chosen real-life examples will illustrate, such approach results in unleashing powerful creative energy that offers new services to the market, new approaches to solving existing problems, or as seen in the case of Uber—bringing in a completely new business model based on creative solutions and innovative approaches to different aspects of business operations.

E. Smailhodžić (✉)
University of Groningen, Groningen, The Netherlands
e-mail: e.smailhodzic@rug.nl

D. Berberović
University of Sarajevo, Sarajevo, Bosnia and Herzegovina

© The Author(s) 2021
M. Soltanifar et al. (eds.), *Digital Entrepreneurship*, Future of Business and Finance,
https://doi.org/10.1007/978-3-030-53914-6_9

1 Introduction

1.1 Digital Transformation and Creativity

In this chapter, we would like to outline the process of digital transformation and the increasing importance of creativity in the new digital age. Our economy is transforming, and the ways in which we create, communicate, work, and collaborate are changing (Rogers 2016). Today's society and business landscape are characterized by trends such as pervasive connectivity, improved performance of information technologies, information abundance, and emergence of big data (Bharadwaj et al. 2013). Accordingly, digital transformation and new business models have also changed consumers' expectations imposing pressure on traditional companies (Verhoef et al. 2016). In this new digital age, creativity and innovation play an important role in creating value for businesses (Sousa and Rocha 2019). Although creativity and innovation have always been important, their nature is changing in the digital business context (Hinings et al. 2018). Competition between companies is now not only based on the quality of products or efficiency in satisfying consumer needs but rather how innovative products are, how well they are designed and how well they solve a consumer problem in a creative manner. This becomes especially important as digital transformation cuts across industry boundaries (Hopp et al. 2018). Competitors are not only traditional companies in an industry, but also digital companies who are using their digital resources to enter the new markets. For example, apps, such as Google Maps, are competing with traditional navigation companies such as Garmin and TomTom, which led Garmin to lose 70% of its market capitalization two years after the navigation apps were introduced (Downes and Nunes 2013).

New digital businesses are one of the examples of the digital transformation era. In line with this, the behavior of customers is also changing. They often become co-producers of the products through, for instance, crowdsourcing campaigns. Furthermore, their expectations have changed. Consumers have the intention to buy and have access to products and services in an easier and more convenient way than ever before. They want to order products online and receive them the next day; this is resulting in an increasing trend for electronic commerce. For example, 69% of Internet users in the European Union shopped online in 2018 (Eurostat 2018). Changes like this are creating the shift in the economy, and companies need to adjust to this or they often go bankrupt. And platforms, like Netflix, are transforming industries, driving big players such as Blockbuster to bankruptcy.

Due to these changes in the economy, the workforce is also affected and must adjust. Employers now require employees to have different skills than before. It seems no longer to be important how much employees know, but rather how well they can apply their knowledge. In the digital era, skills that are essential are higher-order thinking and creative problem solving, as companies increasingly depend on the creation of new products, services, and processes in order to remain competitive. These skills rely on the fact that we must find meaning or patterns in big data. We have to be creative and find insights that will help to solve problems in a different way than usual (Brinson 2017). For example, big data can be used as a digital asset in order to personalize products and services (Verhoef et al. 2016)

This implies that the digital age is in a way extension and elaboration of the twentieth-century knowledge age. The world is moving toward the right-brained intuitive and creative world instead of a left-brained logical thinking world. The rising automation resulting in increased productivity means that there might be less need for labor in the future. This further leads to more time for other activities, and one of the alternatives is creative work. At the same time, the world experiences a greater need for innovative ideas. The current business environment features a fast strike mentality of companies that aim to disrupt competitive advantage of market leaders, which makes competitive advantage of companies no longer sustainable in the long run (D'Aveni 2010). Thus, this illustrates the increasing importance of creativity and reinvention to remain competitive. Along with this, there is an increasing need for creative people in the workforce, not only for artists and designers (Areete 2018). A creative approach is also needed in business management and strategic planning. Due to the shift of the digital era, jobs for creative people have also changed as they are needed in the more traditional roles within a business in order to help change companies that seek to be competitive in this era of change.

All these changes in the process of digital transformation point to the importance of new skills such as strategic imagination and creative problem solving (Mills 2015). In particular, it is important to have the skill of thinking outside of the typical roles and tasks that one does on a daily basis. Actually, employees should be supported in thinking outside of their tasks and how they can make it more efficient. In an increasingly changing environment enabled by digital transformation, creative problem solving becomes of utmost importance in regard to problem solving and finding new entrepreneurial opportunities. Creativity and critical thinking are not only important today but also projected to be the skills in most demand in the future (World Economic Forum 2018).

2 Theoretical Background on Creativity and Digital Business

2.1 Creativity

Before we can start linking creativity to digital entrepreneurship, we need to define what creativity is and why it is important. Simply defined, creativity is the act of turning new and imaginative ideas into reality (Naiman and Naiman 2017). According to Amabile (1988), it applies to both idea generation and problem solving. However, Amabile et al. (2005) also emphasize that these ideas should not only be novel but also useful. In the context of organizations and workplaces, creativity is seen as the creation of new and useful products, services, and processes by employees (Woodman et al. 1993). Creative people have the ability to perceive the world in new ways, to find hidden patterns and find connections between unrelated issues. This all makes it possible to generate new solutions.

Creativity should not be seen only as a form of art or an idea. Those are outcomes of a creative process. Creativity itself is a process that takes multiple steps to create the results (Scy 2016). It all starts with a problem that we think of. If this problem does not contain the formula to solve itself, we have to use our creativity to come up with a solution to this problem. We are not able to objectively measure creativity because it is mostly subjective. Outcomes to the problems are usually based on two principles; the idea is most useful or unique. If an idea is useful, it is relevant to the task it needs to be solved. When an idea is unique, it is different from other ideas and not experienced before. To be creative, it is important to not stop at a useful idea. Most people can come up with this. The hard part is to keep thinking and creating an idea that is unique. The creative process takes time and patience, especially to learn the art of being creative. With creativity, there is no guarantee that you come up with new, creative ideas every time that is useful for your project. So, the creative process is guaranteed but the outcomes are not (Scy 2016).

In addition, research has shown that there may be different types of creativity. The types of creativity are based on either emotional or cognitive and spontaneous or deliberate (Al Balooshi 2016).

1. *'Thomas Edison'* type of creativity. It is called Thomas Edison because he ran experiment after experiment before he came up with an invention.

   - Based on deliberate and cognitive.
   - Comes from continuous work.
   - Implies putting together existing information in new ways.

2. *"Aha moments"* type of creativity.

   - Based on elaborate but emotional parts.
   - "Aha moments" have to do with the emotions and feelings and are not continuously focusing on one work.

3. *"Isaac Newton Eureka moments"* type of creativity.

   - Occurs suddenly.
   - Spontaneous and cognitive creativity.
   - It implies working on a problem for a long time and not be able to find solutions. Then when doing something else, flash-insight arises with a solution for the problem.

4. *"Epiphanies"* type of creativity.

   - Spontaneous and emotional type.
   - Mostly used by musicians and artists.

- It is not cognitive, but mostly a skill is needed to perform this kind of creativity such as playing guitar or writing skills.

Another type of categorization of creativity concerns the type of people and the approach to creativity. This is also relevant as people are very different in the level of creativity and in the manner of how they express creativity. In this respect, we can divide people into adaptors and innovators. Adaptors are people who are trying to improve things but within the general system. They are trying to find ways to do things better and more efficiently. Adaptors often work in professions that have stability and order. They link ideas they have to the problem they have and pertain persistent in this. They could be somewhat linked to the process of exploitation, which is described by March (1991). He describes the process of exploitation as focused on refinement, efficiency, selection, and implementation. The second type of creative person is innovators. They like to do things differently than ordinary businesses and people do it. Innovators challenge the status quo. They often come up with radical changes and plans, whereas adaptors like to do things better, innovators like to do things differently. The ideas that innovators come up with are often related to bringing new elements in the problems and changing the formulation of the problem. Same as with adaptors, the role of innovators can be linked to March's (1991) process of exploration, which is focused on concepts such as risk-taking, discovery, and innovation.

Although people can be categorized in these two groups, there are some other factors that both groups should have to be successful in creating creative solutions for problems. Some of the most important ones are motivation, curiosity, and social network. Specifically, motivation represents a crucial part of creativity. Motivation is the measure of emotional investment that makes people break with the old situation and move into a direction with a situation that they actually want (Kim 2018). This desire to move to something new starts the process of creativity. So, to start the creative process, every person needs at least motivation to start it and create something new. After feeling motivated, people get curious about searching for unknown information that can be useful. Curiosity can be frightening due to the fact that something that can be potentially dangerous one has to transform into something manageable and interesting. When fear arises, curiosity is hard to sustain (Kim 2018). An issue often neglected is the social nature of creativity. The power of an unsupported mind is often overrated. A lot of intelligence and creativity results come from interaction and collaboration with other people. Creativity does not develop in people's minds but in the interaction between people's thoughts and a sociocultural context (Kim 2018). For example, supportive supervision and perception that an employee's supervisor is supportive of new ideas have always been an important condition for creativity (Oldham and Cummings 1996). Furthermore, a positive peer group and the participation of others within the company are also important requirements for employees to excel at creativity (Hunter et al. 2007).

2.2   Digital Business

Due to new technological innovations, new ways of conducting business, connecting, and collaborating have been established. The new technologies, such as social media, are building bridges between people, which makes connecting with each other much easier. Digital technologies also have challenged companies forcing them to continuously innovate in order to achieve competitiveness in this new landscape as business models evolve and companies experience immense pressure to stay on track (Fenwick 2016).

Business models have changed, and companies are challenged to keep up. Digital business is about the creation of new value chains and business opportunities that traditional businesses cannot offer. It is the creation of new businesses where the lines between digital and physical worlds are blurred or not even visible. For example, most start-ups these days are digital businesses that solve a problem or have a solution to make day-to-day tasks easier and more convenient. Examples of digital start-ups that have become successful are companies such as Uber, which makes it easier to go to places for a lower price than conventional cabs; or Airbnb, which provides a place for people who want to rent their house and people who are looking to rent a house for the vacation of other purposes. Both of these companies are digital businesses and do not have any physical products.

Wirtz (2018) defines digital business as the initiation, transaction, and maintenance of the service exchange process between economic partners through information technology. Some of the most important elements in the digital business are mobile technologies, social media platforms, analytics, and cloud computing technologies (Fischer and Lopez 2019). Some examples that make these of key importance for digital business are that mCommerce has an increasing part in the total of electronic commerce, social media platforms such as LinkedIn and Facebook have changed the ways in which people meet and collaborate and big data analytics enable businesses to uncover hidden patterns, which lead to reduction of costs and better decision making. Overall, the digital business helps to eliminate barriers that now exist among industry segments while creating new value chains and business opportunities that traditional businesses cannot offer (Fenwick 2016).

However, digital businesses also face challenges such as pervasive connectivity, which challenges companies with their speed of product launches and decision making (Bharadwaj et al. 2013). Fast product launches by digital natives such as Facebook, Google, and Amazon are putting pressure on companies to introduce their products fast. Furthermore, the same platforms and big data pose challenges to react in real time as well as to access, process, and analyze data that become available in a digitally connected world. Such developments enable hyper-connections among customers, companies, processes, and things. Taken together, digital contributes to the hypercompetitive digital economy. With hypercompetition, no competitive advantage is sustainable in the long term (D'Aveni 2010), which emphasizes a need for businesses and individuals to be creative and continuously reinvent and innovate.

2.3   Toward Digital Creativity

2.3.1   How Is Creativity Related to Digital Business Ideas?

For the purpose of this chapter, we define digital creativity broadly as all forms of creativity driven by digital technologies (Lee 2012). Understanding and adopting digital innovation have become more important for existing businesses. For example, banks need to keep up with the latest financial technology to keep being relevant for customers and universities need to change the way they educate students. Keeping up-to-date with the latest digital innovations is not easy, and creativity plays an important role in this adapting phase (Medium 2017). Digital innovations need individuals who are thinking differently and can change the business. Innovators are crucial for developing new digital innovations that will keep businesses up-to-date with the latest trends. The creative process of digital innovations is a structured process that needs guidance and a clear goal. People need to think differently about the possibilities and impossibilities of new technologies. In addition to this, it is important for companies to embrace the creative process and look for new opportunities as well as risks.

In today's world, creativity can facilitate the creation of value, and therefore, it is an important aspect for companies. Due to the fact that the world is changing and is becoming more digital, customers expect this from companies as well. The customer wants to do everything online, and therefore, companies have to adjust. With this adjustment, creativity plays an important role. But how does a manager create value for customers and what makes it different from other companies? Companies should be creative and innovative in the way they adapt to the digital business age because it can create a lot of value for the company. Companies who stay behind will lose customers and eventually will not survive. Thus, companies have to focus on the digital age and provide creative and innovative solutions for existing problems that conventional companies cannot solve (Solomon 2018).

Although creativity has been traditionally regarded as a key in search of innovative ways for generating revenues (Amabile et al. 1996), it is especially important in the age of digital. Digital increases the importance of business agility and speed to market (Luftman and Derksen 2012), and it has been suggested to pay attention between digital and creativity (Yoo 2010). Digital enables individuals to have access to the Internet and other technologies anytime and anywhere allowing them to stimulate their creative thinking (Bal 2013). Given that the employees can achieve creative products through communication and collaboration (Amabile et al. 1996), the link to digital stimulates the creative process in the creation of new digital businesses.

2.3.2   How Can Organizations Develop and Strengthen Digital Creativity?

Digital creativity in businesses can be strengthened mostly due to the culture that lies within a company. Creativity and creative thinking should be encouraged; even if mistakes occur, employees should be motivated to further pursue their creative approach. As already pointed out, inspiration is needed for a creative mindset. The workplace should encourage inspiration and therefore offer an environment that is boosting the inspiration (Magitti 2018).

Some of the traditional ways on how businesses should boost creativity (Noice 2019) can also be applied to digital context as follows:

- *Search for new experiences and perspectives.* Discussions with people from different departments, work with clients from different industries, or receiving help from non-profit organizations. This helps in critically approaching defined problems and enhances creative solutions.
- *Spending time to think about new ideas on a daily basis.* Even if it is only for 15–20 min, it will help with the creative process because individuals are aware of the time they spend on bringing up new ideas. Detaching from daily routines has a positive effect on finding new ways of solving specific issues.
- *Making weekly goals.* Planning how many ideas one wants to come up with and stick to it. In this way, one will be motivated to keep the creative brainstorming sessions useful.

However, Rogers (2016) suggests a more specific enabler for digital creativity and transformation, specifically rapid experimentation. In particular, he suggests that the firms must change their strategic assumptions from those that apply to the analog era to those that apply in the digital era. These concern being able to make decisions based on testing and validating rather than on intuition, considering that the testing ideas can be done in a cheap, fast, and easy way rather than seeing it as expensive, slow and difficult process, conducting experiments constantly by everyone and not only by experts infrequently, and focusing on minimum viable prototypes and iterations after lunch and only focusing on 'finished' product.

Finally, it is important for an employer to promote creativity by creating a work atmosphere where effort and failure are respected and not punished. It takes brave and open-minded employees to come up with new ideas and pitch them to supervisors; therefore, respect is highly important even when an idea does not appear to be great. Employees should feel motivated to find another idea or improve the existing one. In cases where employees are being punished for erroneous attempts (ideas), a decrease in motivation may result in lower creativity and even worse ideas.

Difference between traditional companies, digital businesses, and start-ups is that traditional companies usually do not apply such encouraging workspace. Start-ups often offer more flexibility and promote the creative process with greater passion. The biggest difference between working in a digital start-up or a traditional company is that working tasks change very quickly in a start-up when the organization is successful and growing. Usually, employees in a start-up have more responsibilities, and therefore, more creativity is required to solve problems that emerge with a growing business. Due to such problems that need to be solved, there are many opportunities to experiment with new ideas. If a failure occurs, another idea from the pool of ideas is selected and implemented. In a traditional company, this is more difficult due to hierarchical layers and due to the fact that employees are accountable to their supervisors.

2.4 Critical Perspective on Digital Creativity

Digital creativity can bring a plethora of positive outcomes regarding business ideas and solutions for current problems. However, there are several challenges in regard to the creative process of companies. The main issue is the fact that the transition to a more creative economy carries significant costs for an existing business (Lehrer et al. 2018). Businesses have to keep up with the newest innovations to keep competing with new start-ups which usually appear with creative solutions for an existing problem.

Creative people are a good asset to the company; however, people are hired to work. If they do not deliver what they are hired for but keep coming up with new ideas, companies will not run smoothly and work will not be done. In addition to this, one cannot always apply new ideas. Sometimes, it seems best to first focus on one new idea and then after it has been implemented or refused, to look for additional innovations (Lehrer et al. 2018).

Another point is that not all ideas or innovations are useful (Soulsby 2019). Therefore, it is important to have a good look at which innovations need to be implemented and which are not worth the time and money. A good working system to decide which innovations are relevant can save a lot of money and time for the company. If companies focus on an innovation that is not relevant and do not add any value to the company, it can lose the competition with other companies who choose another innovation (Sherman 2019).

Sometimes it is better to be cautious with the company's decisions and not taking high risks. When there is economic uncertainty, it might be better to not implement creative ideas with the risk that it will fail and increase costs. In such situations, it might be better to be cautious and not experiment with creativity (too much).

A more in-depth risk of implementing creative and innovative ideas is that a certain idea or project takes too long to implement. This is a very costly occurrence, and businesses can run out of money which results in insolvency risk for the business. This can cause problems with the future existence of the company. The new innovative product can face the fact that it is more difficult to produce and therefore not produced on a large scale which results in higher production costs (Soulsby 2019). The return on investment is not guaranteed which then can anger investors and stakeholders (Sherman 2019). Another downside of innovative products is that quality can be received as poor and then damages the reputation of the whole company. This has consequences not only for that product but also for the company. The company can be facing lower sales levels which then would affect the financial position of the company.

There are multiple examples of innovation that went wrong. But there are two types of innovations that went wrong. One is a new product or service that was not received well by the market. The second is the lack of innovation in which companies stayed behind their competitors which resulted in a loss of market share. When this happened, it is usually too late to catch up.

A good example of a failed innovation is Google Glass. This product was developed by Google in 2014. It was supposed to be a great innovation with a computer that was always on and always provided real-time information. It displayed information in a smartphone-like way, and it was also hands-free. Wearers could communicate via voice commands and so command Google Glass to implement commands (Kariff 2019). When Google started selling the glasses, it got significant criticism, where the main critique was that it violated the privacy laws. After the criticism and the fact that it flopped, Google announced to stop the production of the glasses in 2015. In 2017, they again started with the production with an adjusted version but this time more focused on usage within companies and in the medical sector (Williams 2019).

One of the world's most famous examples of failure to innovate and therefore lose the complete market is Nokia. This mobile phone brand refused to make the innovative leap from phones to smartphones. Nokia was the best-selling phone brand in the world. When Apple became a serious competitor of Nokia, it failed to respond in a proper way. The technological innovations of Nokia were nothing compared to those of Apple. The top managers were arrogant and refused to change their strategy and invest more in innovation (Doz 2019). The failure of Nokia can not only be assigned to not innovating well enough because there were many internal problems within the company. The organizational structures were dysfunctional and managers were competing and thwarting each other. This was the ground for the poor strategic decisions the company made. For example, they used an operating platform for their smartphones called Symbian. At the beginning of smartphones, this operating system gave Nokia an advantage but eventually caused delays because for every different phone new code had to be developed and tested. The management was struggling with finding proper solutions and made crucial strategic mistakes. The software was becoming more important in the smartphone market than hardware. Due to the struggles with the operating system Symbian, Nokia could not keep up with this change and lagged behind. Additionally, the applications became more important but Nokia lacked the skills to develop these applications and struggled again with keeping up with their competitors. By 2010, it became clear that Nokia had fallen behind due to the usage of their operating system and the lack of skills to develop applications. Nokia missed these innovations and stood still in a rapidly changing and developing market.

3 Conceptual Model

3.1 Digital Creativity Process

The creativity process consists of five different stages, with each of them having a distinct length. Depending on the organization, this process can be altered, but it usually does go through all these stages. Some of the phases can even happen simultaneously, such as immersion and incubation. Leaps from one stage to the

Fig. 1 Conceptual model

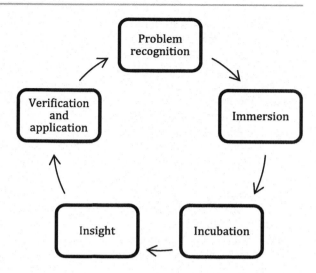

next are sometimes difficult to distinguish as lines between different stages are not always clear, such as between incubation and insight (Gannett 2018) (Fig. 1).

Stages in the creativity process are as follows:

1. *Problem recognition*—when facing challenges in the digital business environment, both organizations, as well as employees, initiate a problem resolution process. This phase implies considering the challenge and starting a creative process whose final output is a solution for the emerged issue. In terms of the digital business environment, this is an often occurring process; in fact, the digital business environment is a challenge in its own right, and most of the digital businesses emerged actually as responses to these challenges. It is further important to emphasize that in terms of starting the creative process, it is highly important that the emerged problem is being approached as an opportunity and not as a threat. That leads to creativity being unleashed to its fullest extent. It must also be noted that 'problems' in digital business are not necessary situations that represent an obstacle. It might well be those common situations, activities, operations, etc., in the real world that represent a valuable territory for creative digital solutions. (Weill and Woerner 2018).

2. *Immersion*—after the challenge has been detected and defined, even vaguely, employees will start to gather information in order to be able to approach the issue from different angles. By doing so, they delve deeper into understanding the challenge. This is a crucial phase as it not only helps to understand the challenge from different perspectives, but it also immediately initiates possible solutions. Digital creative solutions are in most cases focused on finding IT solutions; however, there has been a slight shift from finding pure IT solutions to creating solutions that are focused on finding the more comfortable, artistic, fast, or easiest option.

3. *Incubation*—collecting information in order to encompass all aspects of a challenge does not go forever. When the point of saturation has been reached, creative minds usually stop collecting information and even stop thinking about it. Usually, they engage in completely different activities, the ones that are not related to the challenge. Employees would be well advised to stop thinking about the new app they are currently trying to develop, or about the possible solution to the defined IT problem. By 'cooling down' the mind, employees actually move from an active to a passive state of finding a solution. Namely the task of finding a solution with all the gathered data is assigned to the subconsciousness, which keeps working even during the state of mind's rest. This is the reason why most companies nowadays, particularly IT companies, actively support employees in taking time off and resting their minds and bodies. By helping them take the pressure from everyday activities at work, the room is made for creativity.

4. *Insight*—it is exactly in moments of rest and relaxation when suddenly solutions to existing challenges arise from the subconscious to the conscious level. Therefore, creative minds, such as artists, copywriters, and designers, usually have small books by their side, or apps to help them catch sudden ideas and insights. This phase is also called the 'Aha!' or 'Eureka' moment, as it is characterized by a sudden surge of solution. As we live in times of portable devices that offer the opportunity to implement the newly emerged idea instantly, it is no surprise that a sharp rise of experimentation and implementation of newly emerged digital ideas has been noted.

5. *Verification and application*—finally the creative solution needs to be tested—does it work? Does it need an alteration? An immediate upgrade? Due to its nature, digital business is particularly prone to these instant and immediate tests. It is important to note that such tests often lead to emerging of additional challenges or problems. This sparks the creative process again, starting with the first phase—problem recognition. This is the reason why the creative process has been depicted in this chapter as a circle, without a definitive beginning and end.

3.2 Boosting Creativity in Digital Businesses

In order to support creativity in digital businesses, companies have several tactical tools at their disposal.

(a) Diversity—it has been for decades now that companies have realized that diversity opens new ways for creativity. Diversity in organizational culture brings in new approaches, fresh insights, and different, sometimes even unthinkable, perspectives to existing problems. Seen through the lens of creativity, for digital businesses nowadays this implies a set of different solutions to one existing problem.

(b) Breaks—as discussed in the section on the creative process, rest and relaxation play an important part in supporting the creative process. Pushing creativity to the edge can and often is counterproductive. What seems rather lazy, such as having several short breaks, is, in fact, a better way to improve creative productivity. It is often the calm moments that precede important creative breakthroughs.

(c) Reduced time pressure—this builds on the previous point. Breaks help in taking some time off, mostly taking pressure from employees. Time pressure gives people the adrenaline shot to finish operational tasks in the most efficient way. However, it is rather poisonous for creative solutions which for the most part need a strategic approach.

(d) Change the scene—this builds also on one of the previous points. While diversity implies different psychological and cultural perspectives, there is a rather simple way to achieve diversity (although somewhat superficial). By simply rearranging the work environment, or including the lately famous work-from-home approach, employers can boost creativity in their businesses.

(e) Embrace failure—failure is certainly the first step to success. Failing implies learning; failing implies realizing what does not work; failing narrows down options; failing might lead to solutions to other problems; failing leads even to the improvement of the solution which will work.

4   Examples from Practice

Case 1: Tesco in South Korea

South Korea has been a hard market for large retail companies such as Walmart. Tesco Homeplus has been founded by Tesco and Samsung, and it has grown into the second-largest retailer in South Korea. Homeplus has always aspired to become the leader in the market but was hesitant to increase the number of its retail shops. In line with this, they conducted research on the style of life and shopping habits of South Korean customers. Findings of this market research indicated that the people were working long hours and found their time very important. On the one hand, time devoted to shopping for groceries did not have a high priority. On the other hand, South Koreans are heavy users of technology and 95% of the population own smartphones (Taylor and Silver 2018). Combining these two findings, Homeplus decided to think out of the box and be more creative than just setting up physical stores to compete with other retailers. They decided to start the concept of the virtual store. Homeplus created virtual stores in subway stations with the displays that matched exactly the ones in the actual stores. Customers were able to use their smartphone app to scan a product they would like to buy and complete the order. Their order would then be delivered to their home the same day. This creative move by Homeplus largely increased their sales and made them leading in the online market and second in the offline market for groceries. Online shopping is not a new phenomenon, but Homeplus used its insights into a very creative way to make it extremely convenient and appealing for the customers. The customers found the idea appealing to them because it met their shopping needs, but also turned their waiting time at subway stations into productive shopping and maximized their free time. In 2011, they won the Grand Prix award for mobile creativity emphasizing success in changing the way the people used mobile technologies. Homeplus was able to do this as they looked at its organization and competition in a different way than its competitors. They creatively created a novel and useful solution that mimicked real store shelves with digital displays. In addition, they brought together marketing and sales as the marketing of their company and products directly became sales. Their creativity in this process was expressed through the creative combination of two existing products, namely smartphone app and digital displays.

Case 2: Benchvertising

When Nermin Velagić, the founder of Benchvertising.com, started working in the advertising industry, he did not really plan to introduce innovations that would take advertising to a whole new level. His first business venture within this industry was focused on installing classical benches in parks and main pedestrian zones in the City of Sarajevo, Bosnia, and Herzegovina. When not in use, part of the bench used for sitting would fold, thereby exposing a highly visible surface to anyone walking nearby. Being installed in places with high frequency, these benches became a very attractive communication medium. Several hundreds of such benches were installed and advertisements of major Bosnian–Herzegovinian advertisers were highly exposed. It was a win-win-win situation for municipalities, advertising agencies, and the public, i.e., (potential) consumers.

However, as consumers embraced digitalization in every aspect of their everyday lives, Mr. Velagić was aware that he had to follow. Instead of starting a completely new (digitalized) business idea, he decided to do something extraordinary with the current business. He decided to digitalize the bench! A very traditional, simple artifact has been around for centuries in more or less the same shape and with a very basic function.

Meanwhile, very much as the whole of Europe, Bosnia and Herzegovina faces the demographic trend of an aging population. For local communities, among other things, this implies an increasing need for benches—in parks, pedestrian zones, around medical, and administrative facilities. In terms of costs related to benches, local authorities face rising costs of purchasing, installing, and maintaining them. In times of increasing pressure to achieve high-cost efficiency, financing benches represent a growing challenge for local authorities with anyhow tight budgets.

Having in mind the need to 'go digital' and finding out the problem of long-term financing the rising need for benches, Mr. Velagić, again, came to the idea to create a win-win-win business concept. He created digital benches labeled as 'Benchvertising' which provides a web, cloud-based, communication tool that allows owner/user to upload content, create, and schedule campaigns, to manage execution as well as to control screens on benches. It is an advertising display on a city bench, used to present an advertiser's product or service. It is a new and innovative way of digital-out-of-home (DOOH) advertising venture. Mr. Velagić claims that Benchvertising's social influence is immense, as it not only revolutionizes the traditional bench by bringing people together, but it also brings dynamics to usually calm areas in local communities where benches are installed. And finally, not least important, it tackles the issue of financing benches as it represents a profit source for bench owners/vendors.

In order to enhance the spread of these benches around the world, Mr. Velagić and his partners have decided to approach this business initiative by applying a well-known business model—franchising. Benchvertising.com is franchising their expertise to allow franchisees an opportunity to share their vision of the future of advertising, which helps local community growth and brings a substantial income to the franchisee. Only Benchvertising.com franchisees are entitled to strategically position and manage benches in their local community and to sell advertising slots to other businesses. To conclude in Mr. Velagić's words: 'We think this is the best way to combine a global-born digital initiative with local knowledge and expertise.'

Case 3: Uber

Another case in point when thinking about digital business and creativity is Uber. Uber was founded 10 years ago and was one of the fastest-growing companies in the world. In those years, Uber created over 160.000 jobs in the USA (Siu 2016).

The idea of Uber arose from the cab problem in San Francisco. Inhabitants thought of a simple way to solve the problem and avoid waiting on the streets of San Francisco and avoid getting stranded. They came up with the Uber app that helped connecting local drivers and passengers. It was initially launched in San Francisco but already a year later it expanded to New York which proved that it was a good and convenient alternative to the public transport and often more expensive cabs (Hyder 2017).

Uber quickly became very popular due to its simplicity and convenience. It matched the problem of the cabs in San Francisco with the upcoming mobile technology, thus offering solutions with new approach to digital creativity. Namely Uber makes use of GPS systems to locate the drivers and passengers making it easy for both parties to see where the other is. It uses also digital payment opportunities via mobile phones, creating thereby not only a unique service experience for the user but also a highly safe service offer for drivers because no cash is involved (Hyder 2017). Uber relies on digital solutions for service quality feedback, as its application also offers driver feedback which improves the experiences for the customers. This transport service is available by charging a 20% fee over each ride. However, the app can be used for free. Even though customers' overall feedback appears to be highly positive, the company and its application are continuously changing as new features are added. For example, the latest feature makes it possible to choose the type of vehicle that you want (Siu 2016).

This creative digital solution to solving an intense cab problem leads to a large company emerging based on a rather simple digital solution. Furthermore, it disrupted not only the cab service industry but also the whole car industry as Uber has changed the concept of owning a car (Siu 2016). Uber fares are comparatively cheaper to rivals and sometimes lower than cab fares, and passengers can always order an Uber. Therefore, it disrupts the car industry in the sense that people do not find it necessary anymore to own a car on their own (Hyder 2017).

5 Practical Implications

The new technologies are building bridges between people and make connecting with each other easier. It is important to emphasize that creativity is being encouraged in businesses to support employees to come up with new ideas and solutions for problems that have arisen. Due to an increasing interest in the creative process by people and companies, and the fact the economy is shifting toward a new digital era, new digital businesses and start-ups are booming. New ideas to make our lives simpler are being thought of every day, and this will continue for years to come. This era is mainly focused on making people's lives easier and more convenient since people are increasingly busy and do not have time to do other things. Of course, shifting to this digital era also has its drawbacks and carries new threats, such as hackers. Data can be stolen and manipulated, thereby affecting people's privacy. On the other hand, this problem creates not only new jobs but whole new industries, such as IT security, offering opportunities for new digital businesses to emerge.

References

Al Balooshi, M. (2016). *There are 4 types of creativity*. Retrieved from https://www.linkedin.com/pulse/4-types-creativity-maryam-al-balooshi/.

Amabile, T. M. (1988). A model of creativity and innovation in organizations. *Research in organizational behavior, 10*(1), 123–167.

Amabile, T. M., Barsade, S. G., Mueller, J. S., & Staw, B. M. (2005). Affect and creativity at work. *Administrative Science Quarterly, 50*(3), 367–403.

Amabile, T. M., Conti, R., Coon, H., Lazenby, J., & Herron, M. (1996). Assessing the work environment for creativity. *Academy of Management Journal, 39*(5), 1154–1184.

Areete. (2018). *Conceptual age—Knowledge, skills and attitudes*. Retrieved from https://areete.wordpress.com/2011/11/02/conceptual-age/.

Bal, S. N. (2013). Mobile web—Enterprise application advantages. *International Journal of Computer Science and Mobile Computing, 2*(2), 36–40.

Bharadwaj, A., El Sawy, O. A., Pavlou, P. A., & Venkatraman, N. (2013). Digital business strategy: Toward a next generation of insights. *MIS Quarterly*, 471–482.

Brinson, S. (2017). *The conceptual age: The importance of higher order thinking*. Retrieved from https://www.diygenius.com/higher-order-thinking/.

Bullas, J. (2015). *3 digital start-ups that that made it big*. Retrieved from https://www.jeffbullas.com/3-digital-start-ups-that-that-made-it-big/.

D'Aveni, R. A. (2010). *Hypercompetition*. Simon and Schuster.

D'Aveni, R. A. (1994). *Hypercompetition: Managing the dynamics of strategic maneuvering*. New York: Free Press.

Doz, Y. (2019). *The strategic decisions that caused Nokia's failure*. Retrieved from https://knowledge.insead.edu/strategy/the-strategic-decisions-that-caused-nokias-failure-7766.

Downes, L., & Nunes, P. (2013). Big bang disruption. *Harvard Business Review*, 44–56.

Eurostat. (2018). https://ec.europa.eu/eurostat/statistics-explained/index.php/E-commerce_statistics_for_individuals.

Fenwick, N. (2016). *Digital business: Transformation, disruption, optimization, integration and humanization*. Retrieved from https://www.i-scoop.eu/digital-business/.

Fischer, K., & Lopez, J. (2019). *What is digital business and why it matters?* Retrieved from https://www.dvt.co.za/news-insights/insights/item/97-what-is-digital-business-and-why-it-matters.

Gannett, A. (2018). *The creative curve: How to develop the right idea, at the right time*. New York, USA: Penguine Random House.

Hinings, B., Gegenhuber, T., & Greenwood, R. (2018). Digital innovation and transformation: An institutional perspective. *Information and Organization, 28*(1), 52–61.

Hopp, C., Antons, D., Kaminski, J., & Oliver Salge, T. (2018). Disruptive innovation: Conceptual foundations, empirical evidence, and research opportunities in the digital age. *Journal of Product Innovation Management, 35*(3), 446–457.

Hyder, Y. (2017). *Uber's evolution: From San Francisco to international disruption*. Retrieved from http://soumyasen.com/IDSC6050/Case15/Group15_index.html.

Jaffe, E. (2017). *The key to creative insight can be simpler than you think*. Retrieved from https://www.fastcompany.com/3035811/the-key-to-creative-insight-interrupt-yourself.

Kariff, O. (2019). *Bloomberg—Are you a robot?* Retrieved from https://www.bloomberg.com/news/articles/2015-08-20/google-glass.

Kim, L. (2018). *9 ways to dramatically improve your creativity*. Retrieved from https://www.inc.com/larry-kim/9-ways-to-dramatically-improve-your-creativity.html.

Lee, K. C. (ed.). (2012). *Digital creativity: Individuals, groups, and organizations* (Vol. 32). Springer Science & Business Media.

Lehrer, J., Baker-Whitcomb, A., Oberhaus, D., Simon, M., Gertner, J., & Harrison, S. (2018). *The cost of creativity*. Retrieved from https://www.wired.com/2012/03/the-cost-of-creativity/.

Lipscomb, W. *What are the main characteristics of creativity?* Retrieved from http://www.icreate-project.eu/index.php?t=179.

Luftman, J., & Derksen, B. (2012). Key issues for IT executives 2012: Doing more with less. *MIS Quarterly Executive, 11*(4).

Magitti, P. (2018). *Creativity requires a culture that respects effort and failure*. Retrieved from https://www.businessinsider.com/how-to-build-creativity-in-business-2013-3?international=true&r=US&IR=T.

March, J. G. (1991). Exploration and exploitation in organizational learning. *Organization Science, 2*(1), 71–87.

Medium. (2017). *Working at a startup vs. working at a large, established company: What to expect*. Retrieved from https://medium.com/office-hours/working-at-a-startup-vs-working-at-a-large-established-company-what-to-expect-d1b5e21a420.

Mills, F. (2015). *The conceptual age and right-brain skills*. Retrieved from https://www.icmi.com/resources/2018/The-Conceptual-Age-and-Right-Brain-Skills.

Naiman, L., & Naiman, L. (2017). What is creativity? (And why is it a crucial factor for business success?). Retrieved from https://www.creativityatwork.com/2014/02/17/what-is-creativity/.

Noice, M. (2019). *5 ways to boost creativity in your business*. Retrieved from https://www.entrepreneur.com/article/270157.

Rogers, D. L. (2016). *The digital transformation playbook: Rethink your business for the digital age*. Columbia University Press.

Scy, Z. (2016). *Is creativity a skill or an innate quality?* Retrieved from https://www.quora.com/Is-creativity-a-skill-or-an-innate-quality.

Sherman, F. (2019). Retrieved from https://bizfluent.com/info-8471685-advantages-disadvantages-innovators.html.

Siu, E. (2016). *10 lessons startups can learn from Uber's growth.* Retrieved from https://www.singlegrain.com/blog-posts/business/10-lessons-startups-can-learn-ubers-growth/.

Solomon, Y. (2018). *2 reasons why creative people work in startups.* Retrieved from https://www.inc.com/yoram-solomon/2-reasons-why-creative-people-work-in-startups.html.

Soulsby, T. (2019). *Advantages & disadvantages of innovation.* Retrieved from https://getrevising.co.uk/grids/advantages-and-disadvantages-of-innovation.

Sousa, M. J., & Rocha, Á. (2019). *Strategic knowledge management in the digital age.* JBR Special Issue Editorial.

Taylor, K., & Silver, L. (2018). *Smartphone ownership is growing rapidly around the world, but not always equally.*

Verhoef, P. C., Kooge, E., & Walk, N. (2016). *Creating value with big data analytics: Making smarter marketing decisions.* Routledge.

Weill, P., & Woerner, S. L. (2018). *What's your digital business model? Six questions to help you build the next-generation enterprise.* Boston, USA: Harvard Business Review Press.

Williams, R. (2019). *Google glass will make 'privacy impossible' warn 'Stop The Cyborgs'.* Retrieved from https://www.independent.co.uk/life-style/gadgets-and-tech/news/google-glass-will-make-privacy-impossible-warn-stop-the-cyborgs-campaigners-8550499.html.

Woodman, R. W., Sawyer, J. E., & Griffin, R. W. (1993). Toward a theory of organizational creativity. *Academy of Management Review, 18*(2), 293–321.

World Economic Forum. (2018). *The future of jobs report 2018.* Geneva, Switzerland: World Economic Forum.

Yoo, Y. (2010). Computing in everyday life: A call for research on experiential computing. *MIS quarterly,* 213–231.

Zucker, M. (2015). *Transforming your business with digital creativity.* Retrieved from https://www.forbes.com/sites/matzucker/2015/04/27/transforming-your-business-with-digital-creativity/#3bc127825b75.

Corporate Digital Entrepreneurship: Leveraging Industrial Internet of Things and Emerging Technologies

Swapan Ghosh, Mathew Hughes, Paul Hughes, and Ian Hodgkinson

Abstract

Industrial firms are under severe pressure to innovate by leveraging the industrial Internet of things (IIoT) and emerging digital technologies. Digital entrepreneurship for existing organizations (corporate digital entrepreneurship) is a key differentiating factor in a highly competitive and disruptive environment. However, there is limited guidance for corporate digital entrepreneurship and industrial managers do not have a conceptual framework to navigate their organizations for new product and process innovation. This paper discusses the importance of emerging digital technologies for digital entrepreneurship and presents a conceptual framework of corporate digital entrepreneurship highlighting three elements—business model transformation, operating model transformation, and cultural transformation—which is necessary for fostering digital entrepreneurship in organizations. The chapter presents three case studies and discusses practical implications for the future.

S. Ghosh (✉)
Menlo College, Atherton, California, USA
e-mail: swapan.ghosh@menlo.edu

M. Hughes · I. Hodgkinson
Loughborough University, Loughborough, UK

P. Hughes
De Montfort University Leicester, Leicester, UK

© The Author(s) 2021
M. Soltanifar et al. (eds.), *Digital Entrepreneurship*, Future of Business and Finance,
https://doi.org/10.1007/978-3-030-53914-6_10

1 The Relevance of the Topic

Innovation and entrepreneurship are intertwined and most often entrepreneurship starts with innovation by an individual or group of people (Gustavsson et al. 2018). The great economist Schumpeter suggested that entrepreneurship by individuals or by a large firm could drive the innovation and growth of a firm (Schumpeter 1934). In corporate entrepreneurship terms, acts of entrepreneurship (or intrapreneurship within the boundaries of the firm) and innovation are needed to perpetuate and sustain an organization over time (Kraus et al. 2018; Hughes and Mustafa 2017). Despite considerable scholarly discussion about entrepreneurship, we must increasingly pay attention to digital technologies and its profound impact on entrepreneurship (a phenomenon termed "digital entrepreneurship") (Nambisan et al. 2017) as we traverse the new industrial revolution. The practitioners have started multiple digital transformation initiatives; however, they have limited guidelines for fostering entrepreneurship in a large organization.

The Fourth Industrial Revolution (Industry 4.0) and the industrial Internet of things (IIoT) are fundamentally changing the industrial landscape, and digitization of businesses is driving innovation and change in organizations (Kagermann et al. 2014). We are also moving from the Fourth Industrial Revolution to the Fifth Industrial Revolution (Industry 5.0), where man and machine will be integrated seamlessly to deliver business outcomes and artificial intelligence (AI) will bring the Fifth Industrial Revolution.[1] Digital (corporate) entrepreneurship in large organizations using digital technology is more important now than a decade ago. For example, businesses must anticipate and address digitization in business and corporate strategies (Mithas et al. 2013; Kohli and Grover 2008), revise organizational design (Sund et al. 2016), and must implement new digital technologies (Setia et al. 2013) and generate new capabilities (Tripsas and Gavetti 2000) to innovate new value propositions (Krotov 2017), or else be left behind. As appropriately surmised by Bill Ruh, former CEO of GE Digital,[2] "if you cannot master the idea of digital inside your business, you are opening the door for commoditization." By leveraging industrial IoT and other digital technologies such as artificial intelligence (AI), machine learning (ML), blockchain, big data/analytics, managers, and corporate entrepreneurs can accelerate business transformation, which in turn will optimize the organizational productivity and increase customer satisfaction. Industrial IoT requires new business models and the concepts of digital entrepreneurship and traditional entrepreneurship are merging together for industrial businesses.

This chapter discusses how large and established companies are accelerating corporate digital entrepreneurship by leveraging industrial IoT and emerging technologies.

---

[1]https://www.robotics.org/blog-article.cfm/What-is-Industry-5-0-and-How-Will-Industrial-Robots-Play-a-Role/99.
[2]https://www.forbes.com/sites/maribellopez/2018/01/24/ge-digital-ceo-shares-insights-on-digital-transformation-in-industrial-markets/#23e4b1fe3385.

2   Background

There is a plethora of academic studies positioning the meaning and intent behind entrepreneurship Schumpeter (1934) viewed the entrepreneur as a leader and contributor to the process of creative destruction. Kirzner (1985) suggested that entrepreneurs mostly fulfill unsatisfied needs in the market or improve operational efficiency by detecting and closing gaps in the marketplace. In recent times, views have emerged that highlight the uncertainty under which entrepreneurs must make judgments about assembling resources and mobilizing partners and markets (Foss, Klein and Bjørnskov 2018). Digitization and Industry 4.0 are symptomatic of a context characterized by fundamental uncertainty and asymmetric information. Perhaps the most significant challenge to large organizations in this context is the inability to foresee which business models will be the most profitable, what capabilities are needed into the long-term, and what the customer and competitive landscapes will consist of. This is all the more apparent which are industry boundaries blur, and non-traditional entities become modern-day competitors (e.g., consider Apple, Dyson, and Google) all making investments in autonomous vehicles versus the classic top car manufacturers (VW, Toyota, Renault Nissan, GM, Hyundai Kia, Ford, Honda, Fiat Chrysler, Suzuki, PSA Peugeot Citroen, BMW, and Mercedes-Benz).

Digital entrepreneurship can be thought of as an extension of the traditional entrepreneurship model; however, there are some distinct differences. The process of marketing products and services, workplaces and coordination between stakeholders are different in the digital entrepreneurship model (Hafezieh et al. 2011). E-commerce business models exist for a couple of decades (Turban et al. 2006; Mahadevan 2000) where business models support business-to-business (B2B) and business-to-consumer (B2C) models and most of the companies developed their own e-commerce platforms (e.g., ebay.com, Alibaba.com, etc.). However, with technological advancements and cloud computing, platform-based business models have emerged and platform owners have more power than the factory owners in the early industrial revolution. For example, Amazon Web Services (AWS), Salesforce.com, and other platform vendors provide software platforms to build different e-commerce solutions quickly for a larger customer base. The platform economy has helped a new set of entrepreneurial companies like Airbnb, Uber, Lyft to connect consumers with service providers.

According to Hull et al. (2007), value creation is the core purpose of entrepreneurship, where digital entrepreneurship is a subcategory of entrepreneurship where most or all of the products and services are digitized. Hair et al. (2012) suggested that market orientation is important for digital entrepreneurship and electronic community and communication play an important role for successful digital ventures. Giones and Brem (2017) further divided entrepreneurship into three categories: *Technology Entrepreneurship* characterized by new products based on innovative and breakthrough research and development, *Digital Technology Entrepreneurship* where new products are based on information and communication technology (ICT), and *Digital Entrepreneurship* where new products and services are developed by leveraging the Internet, Cloud, Big Data/Analytics and other emerging technologies. Sussan and Acs (2017) believe that digital entrepreneurship is any venture (social, government, or corporate) where digital technologies are used for developing products and services for customers.

2.1 Corporate Digital Entrepreneurship/Intrapreneurship

Corporate entrepreneurship is implemented in the firm either through corporate venturing (internal, cooperative, or external corporate venturing) or through strategic entrepreneurship, where a company invests in innovation activities for competitive advantage; however, these innovations may or may not result in new business (Morris et al. 2010). Other researchers suggest that corporate entrepreneurship includes a firm's innovation activities, venturing, and renewal activities (Ling et al. 2008). Corporate entrepreneurship is also a higher-order capability/construct based on a firm's ability in innovation, venturing, and renewal activities (Ling et al. 2008).

Corporate entrepreneurship is typically used synonymously with Intrapreneurship and is defined as entrepreneurship within an existing organization (Antoncic and Hisrich 2001), commensurate with innovation practices within an organization by which employees undertake and pursue different business opportunities (Ward and Baruah 2014). Ping et al. (2010) suggest that intrapreneurship fosters every aspect of business innovation and create new business benefits for organizations. Intrapreneurship initiatives can help a company to develop new businesses by innovating new products and services (Knight 1997; Stopford and Baden-Fuller 1994; Zahra 1993) or by entering new markets and customer segments (Zahra 1991) or both. These efforts can alter the course of the business and revitalize its business performance.

For the remainder of this chapter, corporate digital entrepreneurship is used in lieu of corporate entrepreneurship and intrapreneurship from a digitization viewpoint. Corporate digital entrepreneurs play important roles in bringing industrial Internet of things (IIoT) and emerging technology-based business applications to the market and create new business models using their technical knowledge, business expertise, and relationships with ecosystem partners. These entrepreneurs connect the dots between technological, business, ethical and legal issues and create a business environment where they can develop new products and services (Krotov 2017). As with any other innovation, technology-based innovations can be classified into three categories: incremental, revolutionary (integrative), and disruptive (Christensen et al. 2005). For example, GE Healthcare developed GE Centricity™ imaging collaboration suite in the cloud.[3] This is an example of incremental

---

[3]https://www.gehealthcare.com/products/healthcare-it/enterprise-imaging/centricity-imaging-collaboration-suite.

innovation over GE's in-hospital Centricity imaging solution. Now, the hospital can store healthcare-related images in the cloud and clinicians (general physicians, radiologists, specialists) and patients can share and collaborate effectively in a cloud-based environment. The scope of the incremental innovation is mostly restricted to existing customers and markets. On the other hand, GE Healthcare also developed a GE health cloud,[4] where hospitals, patients, and related services can store comprehensive health information (imaging, monitoring, electronic medical record, etc.) for patients. This is an example of a revolutionary (integrative) innovation. This type of integrative innovation is enterprise-wide and mostly creates new customers and markets. GE Healthcare also developed a handheld pocket-sized ultrasound machine[5] using a smartphone and intelligent probes. This machine can collect ultrasound images for a patient and securely transfer the image to a health cloud or in-house hospital imaging system. This is a moderately low cost, high utility machine for developing countries and represents an example of disruptive innovation, which creates new markets and expands the business rapidly. Corporate digital entrepreneurs in large organizations develop products and services by leveraging these three categories of innovations. These innovative solutions use IoT-based applications and digital technologies for data management and analysis.

2.2 Impact of Industrial IoT and Emerging Technologies

Application of industrial IoT and digital technologies is disrupting industrial businesses, and this external pressure can stimulate entrepreneurship within incumbent organizations. "Industrial Internet" is a term coined by General Electric (GE) (Leber 2012) and comprises of connecting together industrial machines to share information on a real-time or near real-time basis and to make proactive and predictive business decisions based on machine analytics. Leber (2012) further suggests that the industrial Internet can change the entirety, or at least substantially, the business paradigms of industrial businesses, which in turn will help a company to develop new products and processes faster, improve productivity, and increase customer satisfaction. There is a convergence of industrial systems with the power of advanced processing and analysis capabilities, the emergence of low-cost cloud-based data sharing environments, and low-cost sensing and machine data sharing. These business solutions are transforming the industrial world and in turn will change our daily lives, including the ways we do our jobs and business. For example, GE aviation and Pivotal have created a data analytics solution where they can track 3 million flights, gather 300 terabytes of data and analyze the data 2000 times faster than the previous methods and reduce cost tenfold (Schneider 2014).

---

[4]https://www.gehealthcare.com/products/health-cloud-platform.
[5]https://www.gehealthcare.com/products/ultrasound/vscan-family/vscan.

Siemens healthcare has developed a digital ecosystem store in the cloud where Siemens and its partners are sharing healthcare applications and the customers can subscribe to those applications on a pay-per-use basis.[6]

This holds the promise of greater productivity, a higher standard of living and a safe and secure industrial environment. The savings from interconnected and intelligent machines will be substantial for the global market. For example, in fifteen years globally, improving fuel savings by just one percent in the aviation industry could save $30 billion, one percent of fuel savings in power generation equipment could save $66 billion, one percent of operation costs of hospitals could save $63 billion, one percent increase in transportation efficiency could save $27 billion, and one percent improvement in capital utilization in upstream and downstream oil exploration and development could save $90 billion (Evans and Annunziata 2012). So, the power of just one percent improvement is substantial for industrial companies and these five industries alone could save $276 billion globally in fifteen years. The corporate entrepreneurs can utilize the digital ecosystems and develop new products and services and bring those to the market much faster than their competitors.

The problems facing firms are twofold, though. First, which companies will gain as technologies shift, new technologies emerge and are implemented, and new business models emerge is uncertain. Established, incumbent businesses are struggling with historical investments in capabilities and ways of doing business that has developed a dependency and reinforced by years if not decades of investments. Second, established, incumbent businesses must embrace entrepreneurial and digital mindsets to set a willingness to innovate into new, non-traditional technologies, the ability to both do so and execute on which requires hitherto undefined capabilities. As firms cannot make infinite investments, strategic decisions on markets and capabilities are judgments couched in uncertainty, which calls on incumbent firms to embrace corporate digital entrepreneurship. For example, Pitney Bowes Inc. (www. pitneybowes.com) is a nearly century-old office postage meter company in Stamford, CT, USA. The company's annual revenue is around $3.5 billion. In 2014, Pitney Bowes realized that office postage meter and printing businesses were changing and customers were more interested in digital transactions. The corporate digital entrepreneurship initiative was started by Roger Pilc, then chief innovation officer,[7] who realized that Pitney Bowes should reposition itself as a technology company and should leverage emerging technologies such as IoT, big data, mobile, and cloud technologies. They developed a commerce cloud (software-as-a-service, SaaS) solution and diversified their business in cross-border e-commerce. In 2018, half of the revenue came from commerce services.[8]

---

[6]https://www.siemens-healthineers.com/press-room/press-releases/pr-20180306009hc.html.
[7]https://www.forbes.com/sites/peterhigh/2016/08/09/roger-pilc-awakens-pitney-bowes-innovation-engine/#1a32078f603d.
[8]https://www.investorrelations.pitneybowes.com/static-files/faba498e-408f-4085-87ae-fc815edbc061.

2.3 Elements of Digital Entrepreneurship

From the above discussion, we can infer that digital technologies and interconnected ecosystems have a profound impact on digital entrepreneurship as companies are developing new ways to do business, manage their internal operations differently, and have developed new ways to interact with their partners. For example, disruptive technologies such as 3D printing technologies could help in business model innovation as it allows rapid prototyping and mass customized products based on unique fulfillment requirements for the customers (Rayna and Striukova 2016). These mass customized products could initiate new enterprise ventures. In the dotcom era, business model innovations were started by the start-up companies by developing advertisement-based business models as digital technologies changed the value creation models (Abd Aziz et al. 2008), however in the current situation, established companies must transform their business models and initiate new ventures by developing new products and services so that they can compete in the connected ecosystem (Burmeister et al. 2016).

As companies are changing their business models, they need to change their operating models as well as needing the next-generation operating models for the digital world (Bollard et al. 2017). As business models are changing, companies are developing new operating models to support their business models (Berman and Hagan 2006). Researchers (Reijnen et al. 2018) have suggested an operating model canvas (OMC) approach such as based on business model innovation. A company can develop an OMC model that visualizes value proposition, primary and supporting business activities, channels and actors responsible for such activities. Thus, digital technologies are impacting existing operating models and by realigning operating models with business models, companies can be engaged in the new ventures.

Other than business models and operating models, the mindsets of the managers, which transform organizations culturally, are equally important to be successful as digital entrepreneurs. The mindsets of the executives and top managers influence strategic changes (Adner and Helfat 2003). As industrial businesses are expanding their digitization efforts, companies are redrawing their industry boundaries and developing new and innovative ways to deliver services to their customers (Kaganer et al. 2014). According to these authors, digital leadership is not a job title or a role, but a mindset of managers responsible for digital entrepreneurship. The cognition capability is an important attribute of top managers (Finkelstein et al. 2009). Smith and Tushman (2005) suggest that top managers need to build "paradoxical cognition" that enables them to pursue exploration and exploitation simultaneously.

Digital disruptions and emerging technologies are influencing a firm's ability to change its business models, operating models, and culture which is in turn fostering digital entrepreneurships, and these transformations lead to new ventures.

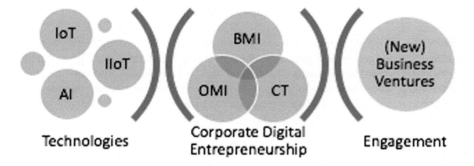

Fig. 1 Conceptual framework for corporate digital entrepreneurship

3 Conceptual Model/Empirical Findings

Emerging digital technologies (Industrial IoT, AI/ML, Blockchain, etc.) foster digital entrepreneurship by providing a disruptive solution development paradigm so that new and existing companies develop new products and services across multiple industries by leveraging these technologies (Lee and Lee 2015). IoT provides new opportunities for innovation (Krotov 2017), whereas artificial intelligence (AI) has a significant impact on the economy as it is being considered a "method for invention" which positively changes the innovation processes within an organization and the roles of R&D within that organization (Cockburn et al. 2018). AI/ML-based technologies are helping digital entrepreneurship in medical technologies including expert system guided medical diagnosis (Cockburn et al. 2018), home health care (Augusto et al. 2007), intensive care unit applications (Hanson and Marshall 2001). Outside healthcare, AI/ML-based applications are accelerating digital entrepreneurship in manufacturing, retail, and other industrial businesses. By utilizing IoT, AI/ML, and other Internet technologies, manufacturers have developed proactive preventive maintenance solutions for their machines and they are offering product-as-service business models to their customers.[9] IoT and AI/ML serve as a boon for retail companies as they collect huge amounts of customer data from different customer interactions, analyze the data using machine learning techniques, and provide new and enhanced customer-centric solutions including highly structured web shops, intelligent in-store bots, and online chatbots (Fig. 1).[10]

---

[9]https://www.forbes.com/sites/insights-intelai/2018/07/17/how-ai-builds-a-better-manufacturing-process/#38a799f01e84.
[10]https://medium.com/datadriveninvestor/how-ai-will-change-the-retail-industry-in-2019-c817091c6306.

As mentioned in the previous sections, industrial organizations are changing their business models and developing outcome-centric business models, which are possible due to technological advancements. Since organizations are venturing into new markets and customers, they are transforming their operating models by integrating business systems and processes with internal systems and with ecosystem partners. Finally, organizations are transforming their cultures and developing digital cultures for entrepreneurship. However, external factors such as competitive turbulence, market turbulence, technology turbulence, and internal factors such as path dependency and digital commitment influence these factors. The following sections describe these three factors and influencers.

3.1 Business Model Transformation

Corporate digital entrepreneurs are developing new products and services by transforming existing business models and introducing new ones. Value creation and value capture are two fundamental functions of a business model. Teece (2010) suggests that the purpose of a business model is to define how the company delivers value to its customers, entices its customers to pay for those perceived values, and converts those payments to profit for the company. Teece further suggests that business model innovation can be a path to competitive advantage if it is sufficiently differentiated from its competitors and cannot be replicated easily. Hui (2014) highlights the importance of digital business model innovation for IoT businesses. The author emphasizes that in the connected world, companies need to rethink how values are created and captured for their customers. Hui (2014), in the *Harvard Business Review* article entitled "How the Internet of Things Changes Business Models", describes the value creation and capture model and identifies the capabilities needed to create and capture values for IoT business. Value creation is related to the offerings provided by companies to their customers so that they are encouraged to use the service and to pay for those services. Earlier competition was based on features and, since new features add incremental value for customers, most of the business models were based on price. However, in the connected world, products are never sold once as the companies collect the usage of the products on a continuous basis and tweak the products based on customer requirements. This is a continuous improvement process and one that embraces services aligned to products. As with value creation, Hui suggests that the value capture model is changing. Companies are not relying on the one-time value of their products and services, but on recurring values captured from their customers. This is becoming possible due to real-time connectivity with customers. Table 1 (adapted from Hui 2014) describes the model and how emerging technologies are helping to transform the business models.

A business model developed by one company in one market segment can be implemented in another company in a different segment (Teece 2009). For example, a subscription-based software services model pioneered by Salesforce.com's platform is being adopted by GE Digital in its Predix, Industrial Internet platform.

Table 1 Value creation/capture analysis

Value models	Factors for value creation/capture	Traditional business model	IoT and technology-based business model
Value creation	Customer needs	To solve existing problems (reactive)	To address the current and future needs proactively
	Offerings	To market products with service contracts	To market products as-a-service
	Role of data	To maintain customers by collecting data periodically for future product enhancements	To enhance customer satisfaction by continuous monitoring of customers
Value capture	Path to profit	To develop and maintain sales capabilities for one-time sale of the product and service	To enhance sales capabilities for recurring pay-per-use revenue
	Control points	To protect using IP protection, brand values, and customer support	To protect using personalization and network effects
	Capability development	To leverage core competencies and existing resources and capabilities	To work with alliance partners to develop products and fill the gaps with customers

Source Hui (2014)

Though business model studies have gained importance, some scholars (Zott et al. 2011) observe that: (i) the definition of a business model is not clear, (ii) the researchers are interested in business models for e-business/digital business and how business models are creating competitive advantages, and (iii) researchers are considering a business model as a new unit of analysis and partners play an important role. For industrial businesses, firms must develop value creation capabilities (such as offering service-based business models, freemium-based subscription models) and business models must include contributions from partners. Though industrial businesses are going through technological innovation, they do not guarantee business success; the new product development efforts should be coupled with a new business model to capture value for its customers (Teece 2010).

Digital technologies have led to the disruption of existing business models (Weill and Woerner 2015). Corporate digital entrepreneurs in innovative companies take advantage of new business opportunities and enhance or disrupt the existing business models (e.g., Instagram, a Facebook company, disrupted Kodak's business model of capturing, sharing, and storing photography, Lucas and Goh 2009). Similarly, a big retailer, Ikea is implementing digital technologies (augmented reality AR, virtual reality VR, big data analysis, etc.) and developing new customer-centric business models (Milne 2018). Ibarra et al. (2017) suggested four different ways in which digital entrepreneurs in existing companies are transforming their business models by leveraging digital technologies: internal and external process optimization by applying digital technologies in existing businesses; improving customer interfaces with digital technologies and offering new business models; developing new ecosystems and value networks by integrating companies' business processes with ecosystem partners and offering new products and services; developing disruptive new smart products and services and creating new business models.

Based on these discussions, we propose that digital technologies lead to business model transformations, which in turn influence corporate digital entrepreneurs to develop new products and services for their organizations.

3.2 Operating Model Transformation

Business model transformation may not be enough for corporate digital entrepreneurship and companies need to transform their existing operating models or develop new operating models for innovation and operational efficiencies. The digital operating model is a new way of running business functions, processes, and structures that combines digital technologies and operational capabilities of an organization so that it can achieve its mission (WEF 2018). Companies can achieve operational efficiencies and competitive advantages by understanding current and emerging business processes, models and current and emerging digital technologies (Andriole 2017). Organizations should develop the following capabilities to transform their operations digitally (WEF 2018) to initiate new ventures.

- **To sense disruption and extend industry boundaries**: Since physical and digital worlds are converging, companies should develop an operating model that will expand beyond their current industry. Corporate digital entrepreneurs should explore business opportunities outside their current business boundaries. As firms now have temporary competitive advantages (McGrath 2013) as more competitors are entering the business from multiple industries, to remain competitive, a firm needs to transform its operating model and expand its industry boundaries.
- **To experiment with ideas and launch them faster**: Corporate digital entrepreneurs should launch their ideas faster and should try to get early mover's advantage with their products and services. Digital entrepreneurs should take advantage of platform-based innovations and open systems (Hsieh et al. 2019).
- **To understand and leverage data**: Corporate digital entrepreneurs should understand their data and should come up with operating models to monetize data in new ways and which may lead to new business. The data monetization capability is gaining importance. Data monetization is the conversion of the intangible value of data into real value by selling the data, and it can also be monetized in other forms, like data-driven advertising or discounts and reduction in IT costs (Najjar and Kettinger 2013). For example, GE and Pivotal created a

data lake for the airline industry by storing flight data from the aircraft and providing analytics to airlines.[11] Thus, a data-driven operating model may foster corporate digital entrepreneurship.

- **To build a competent digital team**: Companies should assess their digital capabilities and acquire new or retrain existing workforce in digital technologies. The managerial cognitive capability (Helfat and Peteraf 2014) is essential for managers who are faced with strategic changes for corporate digital entrepreneurship. The role of Chief Digital Officer (CDO) is critical for corporate digital entrepreneurship, and this person is responsible for digital initiatives in large organizations (Singh and Hess 2017).
- **To develop ecosystem partnerships**: Corporate entrepreneurs should develop ecosystem partnerships to provide comprehensive solutions to their customers. Also, companies should partner for non-core activities. The firm with stronger technological capabilities likes to enter an emerging technological field through internal development, whereas the firm with weaker technological capabilities will enter through strategic alliances (Anand et al. 2010). In order to successfully launch new products and services, a firm often cannot fulfill all the requirements from customers on its own, so the strategic partnership is key for success and corporate digital entrepreneurs should take advantage of that.
- **To organize for speed**: Companies should have digitally savvy executives who can lead corporate digital entrepreneurship. The role of CDO reporting to the CEO could be ideal for companies. In a hyper-competitive environment (digital disruption), the mere presence of adequate resources is not enough and the firm's ability to mobilize its resources and organizational capabilities and align them dynamically with the changing opportunities in the environment is vital to maintain competitive advantage (Liao et al. 2009). The role of the CDO to bring changes using digital technologies is a key for corporate digital entrepreneurship (Rickards et al. 2015).
- **To design a user-friendly experience for its customers**: Corporate digital entrepreneurs should design multi-channel user experiences for their customers, which should include web, mobile, and other digital assistants. Omni-channel marketing capabilities are gaining importance to connect with the customers and becoming a key success factor for developing new products and services for a firm (Mirsch et al. 2016).

Industry 4.0 or the Fourth Industrial Revolution refers to the next phase of the digitization of manufacturing where emerging technologies, such as IoT, play a significant role which has the potential to develop low volume highly personalized products and services cost-effectively (Bahrin et al. 2016). According to Fonseca (2018), Industry 4.0 fosters newer production systems and business models impacting the overall manufacturing value chain, society, and environment. The Fourth Industrial Revolution will empower consumers and will foster new business models, and digitally enabled consumer-obsessed companies must change their

---

[11]https://www.ge.com/reports/post/94170227900/angling-in-the-data-lake-ge-and-pivotal-pioneer-4/.

operating models to satisfy the consumers' needs.[12] One of the significant changes in the operating model is driven by digitization across vertical and horizontal functions of an organization. Industrial businesses are digitizing and integrating their vertical value chains, from design, manufacturing, sales and service functions. All operational process information is available on a real-time basis, and it is supported by emerging technologies such as augmented reality (AR), virtual reality (VR), artificial intelligence, and machine learning (AI/ML). The horizontal integration spans across partners, suppliers, and customers in the digital ecosystem. The corporate digital entrepreneurs are developing new operating models to support pay-per-use business models. For example, Baker Hughes (a GE Company) has developed digital twins in their Minden plant to optimize supply chain and factory operations.[13] Digital Twins are virtual models of physical assets or business processes that learn continuously from the data; they provide proactive business decisions and use emerging digital technologies such as IoT, Big Data, AI/ML, 3D simulation, and other technologies. The corporate digital entrepreneurs are also forging strategic alliances and bringing new products and services to the market. For example, GE Aviation and Microsoft are developing a new outcome-centric business model, "TrueEngine", where GE Aviation will use Microsoft's Blockchain technology and offers a cloud-based service so that airline companies can get better visibility of their entire supply chains, which in turn will improve their operational efficiencies (Allison 2019). Thus, strategic ecosystem-centric operating models are helping digital entrepreneurs to develop new products and services.

Based on these discussions, the framework proposes that digital technologies influence operating model transformation and foster corporate digital entrepreneurship.

3.3 Cultural Transformation

Business model transformation and operating model transformation are two key factors for corporate digital entrepreneurship. However, another key factor is cultural transformation. To implement Industry 4.0, the companies will face organizational challenges related to digital culture and training as all employees need to think and act like digital natives, should have the willingness to experiment with new technologies and new ways to do their work (Lee et al. 2017). In the new digital age, business leaders must have the ability to reimagine their businesses with clear digital strategies and to foster digital cultures in their organizations (Kane et al. 2015).

Most companies are facing digital talent and skill challenges, and they need to develop digital workforces by improving their company culture and offering

---

[12]https://www.accenture.com/_acnmedia/pdf-72/accenture-strategy-wef-operating-models-future-consumption-full-report.pdf.
[13]https://gereportsbrasil.com.br/how-digital-twin-is-making-machines-and-processes-more-productive-a4d1b6ef4ddc.

suitable incentives and growth opportunities for their digital workforce. Corporate digital entrepreneurs should pay special attention to the following challenges for developing new products and services:

- **Attracting and retaining talent**: Corporate digital entrepreneurs should develop proper recruitment and retention strategies for their employees. Companies also need to have transparent hiring policies because digitally savvy applicants receive information from different online channels, such as Glassdoor and Linkedin.com, and any negative comments might impact on selecting and retaining talent. Employee satisfaction is also associated with long-term returns, profitability, and valuation of the companies in countries with high labor market flexibility (Edmans et al. 2014). Creating and sensing opportunities are not uniformly distributed among employees or throughout the organization, and employees need to have the capability and knowledge to recognize and execute these opportunities (Teece 2007; Nonaka and Toyama 2007). Thus, a digitally savvy and knowledgeable workforce possesses the necessary capabilities for sensing and seizing opportunities and works with internal and external partners to execute those opportunities.
- **Creating a digital workforce**: Due to the shortages of the digitally skilled and digitally equipped workforce, companies should develop strategies and capabilities to acquire digitally trained employees from within and outside their companies. Digital success is not all about technology. However, organizations with digital maturity are four times more likely to provide the necessary digital skills to their employees for DT (Kane et al. 2015). Organizations should assess their digital needs and develop proper training and development programs for their employees, including digital boot camps, in-house training and should encourage employees to participate in the educational courses outside the company. Companies should also prepare an inventory of existing employee skills and encourage hidden talent within the company to pursue corporate digital entrepreneurships (WEF 2018).
- **Bringing in a digital leadership team**: Companies may not have digitally skilled and equipped managers and need to hire digital managers from within or outside the organization so that they can initiate changes in the organization; these individuals should be placed in different functions in the organization to enable changes on a broader scale, not restricted to one business function. The top managers in a company must work as catalysts for digital corporate entrepreneurship. Top managers' entrepreneurial and leadership skills can help an organization in its transformation journey (Teece 2010).
- **Moving away from a risk-averse culture to more entrepreneurial approaches**: Due to digital disruption, companies should experiment with newer and bolder ideas to bring changes. According to Teece (2009), risk-averse managers tend to discount outcomes that are improbable and go after certain outcomes. For corporate digital entrepreneurship, entrepreneurial capability, such as risk-taking, is becoming a necessity as more digital companies are taking risks to venture into new areas of business (Kane et al. 2015). The role of middle

managers is also important for driving innovation in an organization. Middle managers must allocate resources for innovative projects in organizations, and they play innovative roles in these organizations (Engle et al. 2017).

Digital technologies are forcing existing organizations to change their organizational cultures and develop a nimbler entrepreneurship-focused organization (Porter and Heppelmann 2015). Bilgeri et al. (2017) have identified three organizational and cultural issues for corporate digital entrepreneurship in large organizations: the role of new corporate entities, the role of traditional information technology (IT) functions, and business unit (BU) collaborations. More and more large organizations are creating a Chief Digital Officer (CDO) role as a key executive leadership role to drive corporate digital entrepreneurship. The role of IT is changing and the role of Chief Information Officer (CIO) is to help the CDO in new innovative projects. The business units incorporate customer success management mandates in their corporate objectives as companies and customers are collaborating for new business ventures. Most of the major organizations have CDOs as executive management roles. For example, Samsung, Nike, GE, Hitachi, etc., have CDO roles in their executive organizations. A CDO in a large organization works as a digital entrepreneur and is supported by a proper organization structure and digital culture to accelerate new digital business opportunities.

Based on these discussions, the framework proposes that digital technologies are influencing cultural transformation in the organizations and facilitating corporate digital entrepreneurship.

3.4 Factors Affecting Corporate Digital Entrepreneurship

The framework suggests that environmental turbulence (technology turbulence and market turbulence) influences the relationship between digital technologies and corporate digital entrepreneurship because environmental turbulence creates new digital business opportunities. Some scholars (Wilden and Gudergan 2015) suggest that technological capabilities such as implementing digital technologies enhance performance in stable competitive environments and marketing capabilities such as developing new business plans, go-to-market strategies, and enhance performance in highly competitive environments. Huang et al. (2012) find that technology turbulence positively affects the relationship between external technology acquisition and firm performance and not external technology exploitation and firm performance. So, digital disruptions and rapid technological changes affect corporate digital entrepreneurship as it helps organizations to develop new products and services. Environmental turbulence also influences cultural transformation. A top management team can be considered as the information processing center of an organization (Thompson 1967). Haleblian and Finkelstein (1993) suggest that the degree of environmental turbulence or stability greatly influences the information processing requirements of a top team (managers). So, environmental turbulence influences the use of managerial capabilities of top managers in a turbulent technology and market environment and their capability for corporate digital entrepreneurship. Another important characteristic of a digital manager is the manager's perception of the need for change as in a stable environment a manager perceives the environment as predictable and that there is less need for change, whereas, in a turbulent environment, the manager perceives it as fast-paced, unpredictable and that the need for change is very high (Ambrosini et al. 2009). In his book, *The Innovator's Dilemma*, Christensen (1997) argues that the organization needs to align differently when faced with technology disruption and changing market conditions. Christensen further suggests that corporate digital entrepreneurs need to have exploration and exploitation strategies in these disruptive situations. However, the firm needs to consider its existing capabilities and systematically develop new strategies and capabilities for exploration and exploitation for developing new products and services. Competitive turbulence refers to the degree of competition in an industry (Porter 1985). When the market is highly competitive, the companies must watch out for their competitors and their relative positioning in the market (Han et al. 1998). The digital business is highly competitive, and companies are coming from different industries to get a share in digital businesses. Based on these discussions, it could be suggested that the external environment influences the relationship between digital technologies and corporate digital entrepreneurship.

Internal factors, such as path dependency and digital commitment, affect corporate digital entrepreneurship. Path dependency is a property of a system where the outcomes over a period are determined by the initial set of conditions (Goldstone 1998). Path dependency can speed up, slow down or halt construction of capabilities which could better position the firm for corporate digital entrepreneurship (Sydow et al. 2009). Path dependency is developed when contingent events trigger self-reinforcing paths (i.e., the set of positive and negative mechanisms which increase the attractiveness of a path related to other paths) (Vergne and Durand 2011). These scholars also suggest that path dependency creates a lock-in within a firm. A firm may not be able to sense the opportunity and may remain on its historic path during this disruption. For example, though Blackberry realized that the mobile application market was changing drastically from a mobile phone for the conversation to a multi-purpose mobile device for conversation, audio and video, due to path dependency it did not change its original path/business and lost business. So, path dependency for Blackberry created a negative effect on corporate digital entrepreneurship. Strategic focus and intent create digital commitment for a firm, and it accelerates the development of corporate digital entrepreneurship. For example, the Board of Directors of GE, including the previous chairman Jeff Immelt,[14] were committed to the digital transformation of GE's businesses by leveraging digital technologies and they established GE Digital as among the top ten software companies in the world. Adner and Helfat (2003) propose that within a single industry, where managers face

---

[14]http://www.cnbc.com/2017/02/15/ge-ceo-jeff-immelt-tells-cramer-hes-betting-on-the-industrial-internet.html.

the same external environment, time-varying corporate effects for managerial decisions are statistically significant. By extending this concept to digital commitment, it can be said that faced with digital disruptions, the commitment of managers and allocating resources will have a significant impact on corporate digital entrepreneurship. Digital commitment from the top, especially the CEO and CDO, should enable commitment to transformation initiatives by digital technologies, and they should allocate the necessary resources to achieve that; otherwise, the transformation will be sporadic (Bendor-Samuel 2017). Thus, it is proposed that digital commitment positively influences the relationship between digital technologies and corporate digital entrepreneurship.

4 Examples from Practice/Case Studies from Practice

4.1 Rolls Royce—Power by the Hour

Rolls Royce's civil aerospace business is the leading manufacturer of aircraft engines for commercial aircraft, regional jets and the business aviation market. The company's aircraft business has a 35% market share and revenue of 7.3B Euro in 2018. The company transformed its business model by changing a product-centric business model to an outcome-centric model, where customers pay by the operating hours of the engine.[15] Previously, a customer used to pay a one-off large amount for the engine and bought a service contract for ongoing maintenance. In the engine value-based pricing model, the payment is based on flight performance hours achieved with the engine and customers do not have to buy the engines and pay the maintenance costs, thus allowing low-cost airlines to sign contracts with Rolls Royce. This innovative business model has increased its customer base and provides better benefits for customers as they only pay for engine performance.

Rolls Royce started their "Total Care" business model in the mid-1990s when the company introduced a new venture, "Total Care Term", where customers signed up for coverage over a fixed fee per engine flight hours. The fees were charged based on the expected number of shop visits and related costs divided by the expected number of flight hours. Though there were uncertainties about the engine conditions at the end of the contract, customers chose this term for the lowest cost. In 2007, Rolls Royce enhanced the existing maintenance service venture and introduced "Total Life". As the company gained more and more experience in servicing aircraft, it introduced a new service business model to increase its market share in the aircraft maintenance business. In the "Total Life" model, Rolls Royce provides aircraft maintenance for life (as long as the aircraft is in operation) and the flying hours are considered for per-hour cost; the service can be transferred to other aircraft operators in case of any changes in ownership. In 2015, Rolls Royce introduced the "Total Care Flex" business model, where a customer can pay a

---

[15]https://www.rolls-royce.com/media/our-stories/discover/2017/totalcare.aspx.

higher per -hour cost for flexibility. The business model "Total Care" helps the company to reduce waste and optimize resource efficiency while it enables customers to maximize the flying hours of their aircraft. Rolls Royce monitors the performance of the aircraft engines by implementing an IoT-based real-time data collection and analysis system and utilizing AI/ML and big data analytics technologies for proactive maintenance of the engines. Rolls Royce in turn has constant revenue streams by charging by the flying hours of the engines. Business model transformation such as "Total Care" drives new business ventures as Rolls Royce can provide other value-based services to the airlines and the airports.

Thus, Rolls Royce's new business models align with customers' business requirements and it can create powerful circular business models. With the usage of emerging technologies, a company can gain meaningful insights about the businesses of its customers which can lead to new business models and business ventures. This example illustrates how a company such as Roll Royce utilizes transformation technologies available at a particular time and has developed new business models, which in turn facilitated new business ventures.

4.2   Siemens Healthineers Digital Ecosystem

Siemens Healthineers is a healthcare company based in Munich, Germany, and is a division of Siemens AG. The company provides a wide range of imaging and diagnostic medical devices including X-ray systems, radiation oncology systems, laboratory diagnostics, and other diagnostic medical devices. In 2018, the revenue of Siemens Healthineers was 13.4B Euro with a profit of 2.3B Euro. Though the healthcare diagnostic and imaging systems collect a lot of data and most data is stored in the individual machines, it is difficult for a healthcare provider to analyze all these data together to provide a comprehensive 360-degree view of a patient. There is a lack of interoperability between different healthcare systems and machines from different vendors may not share information. Siemens initially developed a new service venture by participating in Integrating the Healthcare Enterprise (IHE) and providing healthcare data integration services to its customers. However, the service business realized that instead of providing individual integration services, Siemens could change its operating model and provide a healthcare data platform for interoperability with multiple partners and customers. Thus, Siemens Healthineers started a new venture, Healthcare Digital Ecosystem. Siemens Healthineers imaging equipment, in-vitro solutions and associated software and services cover more than 200,000 patients per hour globally; the data from the patients could be collected in a cloud-based digital ecosystem and analyzed using emerging technologies such as AI/ML, big data and IIoT for better patient diagnosis. The digital platform-based economy is not new and companies such as Amazon, eBay, Facebook, Google, Salesforce, and others have developed new businesses leveraging digital platforms. The platforms are frameworks that allow multiple parties to collaborate, most often creating a de-facto standard and form an ecosystem for value creation and culture (Kenney and Zysman 2015). The digital service providers can scale internationally by leveraging digital platforms and can develop new business ventures in different geographies (Täuscher and Laudien 2018). The healthcare digital platform links healthcare experts together, and they can communicate with their peers worldwide and exchange views and expertise for medical diagnostics, which in turn help patients and healthcare providers since population health could improve by such collaboration. A platform is successful once it has a critical mass of partners who use the platform to develop new business ventures by leveraging data from the platform. The healthcare digital ecosystem platform allows healthcare device manufacturers, healthcare payers, providers, and service providers to integrate their services seamlessly into the platform. Siemens has signed up a large number of partners to collaborate effectively in the digital platform. Currently, the platform supports data transparency across imaging systems, maintenance and performance of assets, laboratory process automation, actionable analytics from diagnosis, and imaging software platforms for multimodality reading.

Siemens has transformed its service operating model by leveraging emerging technologies such as cloud, IoT, AI/ML, big data and developed new platform-based service operations, and it helped to create new business ventures not only for Siemens but also for its ecosystem partners. The influence of emerging technologies initiates operating model transformation of an existing business and fosters entrepreneurship within the organization.

4.3   GE Digital

Cultural transformation is another key component for corporate digital entrepreneurship, and it is highly influenced by digital disruptions and digital technologies. Business model transformation and operating model transformation influenced by emerging technologies may not be sufficient for digital entrepreneurship without transforming the culture of the organization. The GE Digital example illustrates that.

Digital transformation is not about the digitization of existing business but rather to transform products and services to software-defined assets and to utilize these digital assets to redefine the business (Govindarajan and Immelt 2019). GE is a big industrial conglomerate, and in 2010, it operated major businesses such as aviation, healthcare, energy, oil and gas, transportation, home and business solutions and GE Capital, with a revenue of $149.59B. GE businesses sold industrial equipment and service contracts (to maintain that equipment) to their customers. The contribution of service revenue from those contracts was 58.5% in 2010 (GE Annual Report 2011). GE's executives realized that GE could increase their earnings from service contracts by making their machines "Smart Machines". However, the software service business was dominated by software service providers such as IBM, Toshiba, HP, and industrial businesses such as GE, Siemens, and others were not aggressively engaged in digital initiatives. Most of the industrial companies were relying on software service providers, and they outsourced their digital operations to many software vendors. Also, the average gross profit margin from the manufacturing industry is around 10–15%,[16] whereas for the software industry, the median gross profit margin is around 30–40%.[17] By analyzing the trend, GE management decided that investing in digital initiatives would be a game-changer for them as it could take the company to the next level of higher profitability and revenue. GE management also realized that GE was an industrial company, and though it had significant software revenues from different businesses, the culture of the company was not suitable for a pure-play software company. To transform the business culturally and to transform the company into a digital industrial company by leveraging IIoT, GE decided to create a new business venture, GE Digital in Silicon Valley, California, far away from its headquarters in upstate New York. GE also launched an advertising campaign, where a recent college graduate (Owen) was breaking the news to his parents and friends that he had joined GE. In one advertisement, Owen's friends were very excited and in another advertisement, Owen's father told Owen that he was not macho enough to work for an industrial manufacturing company (Winig 2015). GE wanted to reposition itself to recruit Millennials. As industrial Internet footprints were expanding in GE, the management decided to create a new role, Chief Digital Officer (CDO), in all GE businesses. The CDOs of the respective business groups reported to the group CDO of GE, and he was also the CEO of GE Digital. This matrix structure allowed the CDO of GE to influence each business in its digital ventures. Since there was a strong strategic focus and intent to transform GE businesses digitally, all business CDOs started implementing GE's digital platform "Predix" as their base digital platform for new businesses. Thus, GE implemented a strong digital culture and developed new business ventures for its different business groups.

5 Conclusion and Implications

Emerging digital technologies are disrupting businesses, and companies are increasingly accelerating their corporate digital entrepreneurship initiatives. This is not only true for start-up or small companies but equally important for large organizations as they need to transform their businesses and remain competitive in the market. Managers can develop new business, and operating models by leveraging digital technologies and coming up with new products are services that were not possible earlier. Cultural changes are critical to orchestrating structural changes in the organization. A proper sensing strategy is a prerequisite to understanding the internal and external environments for corporate digital entrepreneurship opportunities which are influenced by digital technologies. Once opportunities are identified, digital commitment is necessary to support these initiatives by allocating proper resources and implementing suitable operating models to seize those

---

[16]https://smallbusiness.chron.com/average-manufacturers-gross-profit-percent-15827.html.
[17]https://www.inc.com/graham-winfrey/the-5-most-profitable-industries-in-the-us.html.

opportunities. Companies should also provide learning and development opportunities for their employees to become digital employees. Ecosystem partnership is very important and a company cannot provide the entire business solution, so strategic alliances and customer management are critical for corporate digital entrepreneurship.

As larger organizations are implementing digital technologies to foster corporate digital entrepreneurship, they can identify potential business ventures to strengthen their competitive positioning in the market. For industrial businesses, product-as-service business models could be piloted for newer products and services. The organizations can develop joint go-to-market (GTM) strategies with alliance partners to address customer requirements. Corporate digital entrepreneurship must be a corporate mandate and a proper organization structure, headed by a CDO or Chief Information Officer (CIO), could foster corporate digital entrepreneurship.

References

Abd Aziz, S., Fitzsimmons, J. R., & Douglas, E. J. (2008). Clarifying the business model construct.

Adner, R., & Helfat, C. E. (2003). Corporate effects and dynamic managerial capabilities. *Strategic Management Journal, 24*(10), 1011–1025.

Allison, I. (2019). Codename 'TrueEngine:' GE aviation and microsoft reveal aircraft parts certification blockchain. From https://finance.yahoo.com/news/codename-truengine-ge-aviation-microsoft-153044786.html.

Ambrosini, V., Bowman, C., & Collier, N. (2009). Dynamic capabilities: An exploration of how firms renew their resource base. *British Journal of Management, 20*(S1), S9–S24.

Anand, J., Oriani, R., & Vassalo, R.S. (2010). Alliance activity as a dynamic capability in the face of a discontinuous technological change. *Organization Science*, 1213–1232.

Andriole, S. (2017). Is digital privacy a right or a privilege? *MIT Sloan Management Review*, Spring 2017 issue.

Antoncic, B., & Hisrich, R. D. (2001). Intrapreneurship: Construct refinement and cross-cultural validation. *Journal of Business Venturing, 16*(5), 495–527.

Augusto, J. C., McCullagh, P., McClelland, V., & Walkden, J. A. (2007, November). Enhanced healthcare provision through assisted decision-making in a smart home environment. In *2nd Workshop on Artificial Intelligence Techniques for Ambient Intelligence*.

Bahrin, M. A. K., Othman, M. F., Azli, N. N., & Talib, M. F. (2016). Industry 4.0: A review on industrial automation and robotic. *Jurnal Teknologi, 78*(6–13), 137–143.

Berman, S. J., & Hagan, J. (2006). How technology-driven business strategy can spur innovation and growth. *Strategy & Leadership, 34*(2), 28–34.

Bilgeri, D., Wortmann, F., & Fleisch, E. (2017). How digital transformation affects large manufacturing companies' organization.

Bendor-Samuel, P. (2017). How to eliminate enterprise shadow IT. CIO.

Bollard, A., Larrea, E., Singla, A., & Sood, R. (2017, March). The next-generation operating model for the digital world. *Digital McKinsey*.

Burmeister, C., Lüttgens, D., & Piller, F. T. (2016). Business model innovation for Industrie 4.0: Why the "Industrial Internet" mandates a new perspective on innovation. *Die Unternehmung, 70*(2), 124–152.

Christensen, C. (1997). *The Innovator's Dilemma: When new technologies cause great forms to fall* (p. 1997). Boston, MA: Harvard Business School Press.

Christensen, C. M., Anthony, S. D., Roth, E. A., & Kaufman, R. (2005). Seeing what's next: Using the theories of innovation to predict industry change. *Performance Improvement, 44*(4), 50–51.

Cockburn, I. M., Henderson, R., & Stern, S. (2018). *The impact of artificial intelligence on innovation* (No. w24449). National Bureau of Economic Research.

Edmans, A., Li, L., & Zhang, C. (2014). *Employee satisfaction, labor market flexibility, and stock returns around the world* (No. w20300). National Bureau of Economic Research.

Engle, R. L., Lopez, E. R., Gormley, K. E., Chan, J. A., Charns, M. P., & Lukas, C. V. (2017). What roles do middle managers play in implementation of innovative practices? *Health Care Management Review, 42*(1), 14.

Evans, P.C., & Annunziata, M. (2012, November). *Industrial Internet: Pushing the boundaries of minds and machines.* From http://www.ge.com/docs/chapters/Industrial_Internet.pdf.

Finkelstein, S., Hambrick, D. C., & Cannella, A. A. (2009). *Strategic leadership: Theory and research on executives, top management teams, and boards.* Strategic Management (Oxford U.).

Fonseca, L. M. (2018, May). Industry 4.0 and the digital society: Concepts, dimensions and envisioned benefits. In *Proceedings of the international conference on business excellence* (Vol. 12, No. 1, pp. 386–397). Sciendo.

GE Annual Report. (2011). From https://www.ge.com/sites/default/files/GE_AR11_EntireReport.pdf.

Giones, F., & Brem, A. (2017). Digital technology entrepreneurship: A definition and research agenda. *Technology Innovation Management Review, 7*(5).

Goldstone, J. A. (1998). Initial conditions, general laws, path dependence, and explanation in historical sociology. *American Journal of Sociology, 104*(3), 829–845.

Govindarajan, V., & Immelt, J. R. (2019). The only way manufacturers can survive. *MIT Sloan Management Review, 60*(3), 24–33.

Gustavsson, A. K., Petrov, P. N., Lee, M. Y., Shechtman, Y., & Moerner, W. E. (2018). 3D single-molecule super-resolution microscopy with a tilted light sheet. *Nature Communications, 9*(1), 123.

Hafezieh, N., Akhavan, P., & Eshraghian, F. (2011). Exploration of process and competitive factors of entrepreneurship in digital space: A multiple case study in Iran. *Education, Business and Society: Contemporary Middle Eastern Issues, 4*(4), 267–279.

Hair, N., Wetsch, L. R., Hull, C. E., Perotti, V., & Hung, Y. T. C. (2012). Market orientation in digital entrepreneurship: advantages and challenges in a Web 2.0 networked world. *International Journal of Innovation and Technology Management, 9*(06), 1250045.

Haleblian, J., & Finkelstein, S. (1993). Top management team size, CEO dominance, and firm performance: The moderating roles of environmental turbulence and discretion. *Academy of Management Journal, 36*(4), 844–863.

Han, J. K., Kim, N., & Srivastava, R. K. (1998). Market orientation and organizational performance: Is innovation a missing link? *The Journal of Marketing,* 30–45.

Hanson, C. W., & Marshall, B. E. (2001). Artificial intelligence applications in the intensive care unit. *Critical Care Medicine, 29*(2), 427–435.

Helfat, C. E., & Peteraf, M. A. (2014). Managerial cognitive capabilities and the microfoundations of dynamic capabilities. *Strategic Management Journal (Early View)* 1–20.

Hsieh, Y. J., & Wu, Y. J. (2019). Entrepreneurship through the platform strategy in the digital era: Insights and research opportunities. *Computers in Human Behavior, 95,* 315–323.

Huang, P. Y., Ouyang, T. H., Pan, S. L., & Chou, T. C. (2012). The role of IT in achieving operational agility: A case study of Haier. *China. International Journal of Information Management, 32*(3), 294–298.

Hughes, M., & Mustafa, M. (2017). Antecedents of corporate entrepreneurship in SMEs: Evidence from an emerging economy. *Journal of Small Business Management, 55,* 115–140.

Hui, G. (2014, July). How the Internet of Things changes business models. *Harvard Business Review.*

Hull, M. E., Farmer, F. R., & Perelman, E. S. (2007). *U.S. Patent No. 7,269,590*. Washington, DC: U.S. Patent and Trademark Office.

Ibarra, D., Igartua, J. I., & Ganzarain, J. (2017). Business model innovation in industry 4.0: the case of a university-industry experience in SMES. In *Inted 2017 Proceedings*.

Kaganer, E., Sieber, S., & Zamora, J. (2014). The 5 keys to a digital mindset. IESE. From http://www.forbes.com/sites/iese/2014/03/11/the-5-keys-to-a-digital-mindset/2/#47c6c5e94f5f.

Kagermann, H., Riemensperger, F., Hoke, D., Helbig, J., Stocksmeier, D., Wahlster, W., et al. (2014). *Smart service welt: Recommendations for the strategic initiative web-based services for businesses*. Berlin: Acatech-National Academy of Science and Engineering.

Kane, G. C., Palmer, D., Phillips, A. N., Kiron, D., & Buckley, N. (2015, July). Strategy, not technology, drives digital transformation. *MIT Sloan Management Review*.

Kenney, M., & Zysman, J. (2015, June). Choosing a future in the platform economy: The implications and consequences of digital platforms. In *Kauffman Foundation New Entrepreneurial Growth Conference* (Vol. 156160).

Knight, G. A. (1997). Cross-cultural reliability and validity of a scale to measure firm entrepreneurial orientation. *Journal of Business Venturing, 12*(3), 213–225.

Kirzner, I. (1985). *Discovery and capitalist process*. Chicago: The University of Chicago Press.

Kohli, R., & Grover, V. (2008). Business value of IT: An essay on expanding research directions to keep up with the times. *Journal of the Association for Information Systems, 9*(1), 1.

Kraus, S., Burtscher, J., Vallaster, C., & Angerer, M. (2018). Sustainable entrepreneurship orientation: A reflection on status-quo research on factors facilitating responsible managerial practices. *Sustainability, 10*(2), 444.

Krotov, V. (2017). The Internet of Things and new business opportunities. *Business Horizons, 60*(6), 831–841.

Leber, J. (2012). General Electric Pitches an Industrial Internet. *MIT Technology Review*, November 2012.

Lee, I., & Lee, K. (2015). The Internet of Things (IoT): Applications, investments, and challenges for enterprises. *Business Horizons, 58*(4), 431–440.

Lee, M. X., Lee, Y. C., & Chou, C. J. (2017). Essential implications of the digital transformation in industry 4.0.

Liao, J., Kickul, J. R., & Ma, H. (2009). Organizational dynamic capability and innovation: An empirical examination of internet firms. *Journal of Small Business Management, 47*(3), 263–286.

Ling, Y. A. N., Simsek, Z., Lubatkin, M. H., & Veiga, J. F. (2008). Transformational leadership's role in promoting corporate entrepreneurship: Examining the CEO-TMT interface. *Academy of Management Journal, 51*(3), 557–576.

Lucas Jr, H. C., & Goh, J. M. (2009). Disruptive technology: How Kodak missed the digital photography revolution. *The Journal of Strategic Information Systems, 18*(1), 46–55.

Mahadevan, B. (2000). Business models for internet-based E-commerce: An anatomy. *California Management Review, 42*(4), 55–69

McGrath, R. G. (2013). *The end of competitive advantage*. Boston, MA: Harvard Business Review Press.

Milne, R. (2018). Ikea vows "transformation" as it reshapes business models. From https://www.ft.com/content/1a66c838-3cc1-11e8-b7e0-52972418fec4.

Mirsch, T., Lehrer, C., & Jung, R. (2016). Channel integration towards omnichannel management: A literature review.

Mithas, S., Tafti, A., & Mitchell, W. (2013). How a firm's competitive environment and digital strategic posture influence digital business strategy. In *MIS quarterly* (pp. 511–536).

Morris, M. H., Kuratko, D. F., & Covin, J. G. (2010). *Corporate entrepreneurship & innovation*. Cengage Learning.

Nambisan, S., Lyytinen, K., Majchrzak, A., & Song, M. (2017). Digital innovation management: Reinventing innovation management research in a digital world. *MIS Quarterly, 41*(1).

Najjar, M. S., & Kettinger, W. J. (2013). Data Monetization: Lessons from a retailer's journey. *MIS Quarterly Executive, 12*(4).

Nonaka, I., & Toyama, R. (2007). Why do firms differ? The theory of the knowledge-creating firm. In: *Knowledge creation and management. New challenges for managers* (pp. 13–31).

Ping, W. L., Jie, J., Naiqiu, L., & Zhengzhong, X. (2010). A review and prospects of research on human resource management of intrapreneurship. In *2010 IEEE International Conference on Advanced Management Science (ICAMS 2010)*.

Porter, M. E. (1985). *Competitive advantage: Creating and sustaining superior performance*. New York: Free Press, 43, 214.

Porter, M. E., & Heppelmann, J. E. (2015). How smart, connected products are transforming companies. *Harvard Business Review, 93*(10), 96–114.

Rayna, T., & Striukova, L. (2016). From rapid prototyping to home fabrication: How 3D printing is changing business model innovation. *Technological Forecasting and Social Change, 102,* 214–224.

Reijnen, C., Overbeek, S., Wijers, G. M., Sprokholt, A., Haijenga, F., & Brinkkemper, S. (2018). *A shared vision for digital transformation: Codification of the operating model canvas approach.*

Rickards, T., Smaje, K., & Sohoni, V. (2015). *Transformer in chief: The new chief digital officer.* McKinsey&Company.

Setia, P., Setia, P., Venkatesh, V., & Joglekar, S. (2013). Leveraging digital technologies: How information quality leads to localized capabilities and customer service performance. *MIS Quarterly*, 565–590.

Schneider, S. (2014). GE Shores Up Saving with a Data Lake. VmWare Tanzu Blog. From https://tanzu.vmware.com/content/blog/ge-shores-up-savings-for-aviation-with-a-data-lake.

Schumpeter, J. A. (1934). Change and the entrepreneur. *Essays of JA Schumpeter.*

Singh, A., & Hess, T. (2017). How chief digital officers promote the digital transformation of their companies. *MIS Quarterly Executive, 16*(1).

Smith, W. K., & Tushman, M. L. (2005). Managing strategic contradictions: A top management model for managing innovation streams. *Organization Science, 16*(5), 522–536.

Stopford, J. M., & Baden-Fuller, C. W. (1994). Creating corporate entrepreneurship. *Strategic Management Journal, 15*(7), 521–536.

Sund, K. J., Bogers, M., Villarroel, J. A., & Foss, N. (2016). Managing tensions between new and existing business models. *MIT Sloan Management Review, 57*(4), 8.

Sussan, F., & Acs, Z. J. (2017). The digital entrepreneurial ecosystem. *Small Business Economics, 49*(1), 55–73.

Sydow, J., Schreyögg, G., & Koch, J. (2009). Organizational path dependence: Opening the black box. *Academy of Management Review, 34*(4), 689–709.

Täuscher, K., & Laudien, S. M. (2018). Understanding platform business models: A mixed methods study of marketplaces. *European Management Journal, 36*(3), 319–329.

Thompson, E. P. (1967). Time, work-discipline, and industrial capitalism. *Past & Present, 38,* 56–97.

Teece, D. J. (2007). Explicating dynamic capabilities: The nature and microfoundations of (sustainable) enterprise performance. *Strategic Management Journal, 28,* 1319–1350.

Teece, D. J. (2009). *Dynamic capabilities and strategic management: Organizing for innovation and growth*. Oxford University Press on Demand.

Teece, D. J. (2010). Business models, business strategy and innovation. *Long Range Planning, 43*(2–3), 172–194.

Turban, E., King, D., Lee, J., Warkentin, M., & Chung, M. H. (2006). E-commerce: A managerial perspective. *Low Price Edition*, 180–183.

Tripsas, M., & Gavetti, G. (2000). Capabilities, cognition, and inertia: Evidence from digital imaging. *Strategic Management Journal, 21*(10–11), 1147–1161.

Vergne, J. P., & Durand, R. (2011). The path of most persistence: An evolutionary perspective on path dependence and dynamic capabilities. *Organization Studies, 32*(3), 365–382.

Ward, T., & Baruah, B. J. (2014, September). Enhancing intrapreneurial skills of students through entrepreneurship education: A case study of an interdisciplinary engineering management programme. In *13th International Conference on Information Technology based Higher Education and Training (ITHET)* (pp. 1–6). IEEE.

Weill, P., & Woerner, S. L. (2015). Optimizing your digital business model. MIT Sloan Management Review 53(3), 28–36.

Wilden, R., & Gudergan, S. P. (2015). The impact of dynamic capabilities on operational marketing and technological capabilities: investigating the role of environmental turbulence. *Journal of the Academy of Marketing Science, 43*(2), 181–199.

Winig, L. (2015, February). GE's Big Bet on data and analytics. *MIT Sloan Management Review*.

World Economic Forum. (WEF, 2018, May). The future of jobs: Employment, skills and workforce strategy for the fourth industrial revolution. From URL: http://reports.weforum.org/digital-transformation/wp-content/blogs.dir/94/mp/files/pages/files/dti-executive-summary-20180510.pdf.

Zahra, S. A. (1991). Predictors and financial outcomes of corporate entrepreneurship: An exploratory study. *Journal of Business Venturing, 6*(4), 259–285.

Zahra, S. A. (1993). A conceptual model of entrepreneurship as firm behavior: A critique and extension. *Entrepreneurship theory and practice, 17*(4), 5–21.

Zott, C., Amit, R., & Massa, L. (2011, May). The business model: Recent developments and future research. *Journal of Management*.

New Sources of Entrepreneurial Finance

Theo Lynn and Pierangelo Rosati

Abstract

Digital technologies are transforming entrepreneurial finance. Near-ubiquitous access to the Internet, platformisation, and advances in cloud computing, machine learning and artificial intelligence, and blockchain are changing the sources, basis, and quantum of funding in ways that were unimaginable at the turn of the century. This chapter outlines the changes to the market for entrepreneurial finance from the perspective of structure and participants. The key sources and characteristics of alternative sources of finance available to entrepreneurs, including start-ups, are presented. Two online alternative finance sources, crowdfunding and token offerings, are discussed in greater detail. These are illustrated with case studies. This chapter concludes with recommendations and a discussion of practical implications.

1 Introduction

Entrepreneurs are typically defined by their risk taking, innovation, and opportunity-seeking behaviour (Wennekers and Thurik 1999). Their contribution to economic growth is widely accepted. Entrepreneurship provides employment and income to a wide range of citizens and contributes to increased innovation, productivity, and competitiveness (OECD 2017; Wennekers and Thurik 1999). Despite this, the nascency of entrepreneurial ventures presents challenges for entrepreneurs in attracting the resources needed to survive and achieve and sustain economic success. This is particularly the case in sourcing finance. Limited credit histories,

T. Lynn (✉) · P. Rosati
Irish Institute of Digital Business, DCU Business School, Dublin, Ireland
e-mail: theo.lynn@dcu.ie

© The Author(s) 2021   209
M. Soltanifar et al. (eds.), *Digital Entrepreneurship*, Future of Business and Finance,
https://doi.org/10.1007/978-3-030-53914-6_11

cash flow, under-collateralisation, lack of sophisticated financial statements, and higher default risks are just some of the factors that impede access to credit (Bhide 2003; Hall and Lerner 2010; OECD 2013). While entrepreneurs and SME owners report that credit conditions have improved in recent years, they also report that access to finance is a major concern (OECD 2019).

Entrepreneurs are exploiting new technologies to develop, market, and sell traditional and new products and services in new ways to global markets 24/7/365. At the same time, these technologies are changing how entrepreneurs access funding and from whom. As a result, a large number of new channels to investors have been introduced to the market mobilising new sources of capital. Entrepreneurs have never had so much choice with respect to sources of funding. The remainder of this chapter outlines the changing landscape of entrepreneurial finance and discusses two Internet-enabled sources of entrepreneurial finance in greater detail—crowdfunding and token offerings. These are illustrated with two case studies on Jolla Software and AspenCoin. The former raised over US$1.8 million from over 13,000 contributors in 21 days using the IndieGoGo crowdfunding platform (Jolla 2014c), while the latter raised over US$18 million through a security token offering (Carroll 2018b). The chapter concludes with a summary of the key takeaways for entrepreneurs.

2   The New Alternatives for Entrepreneurial Finance

Up until the turn of the century, the traditional sources of entrepreneurial finance were the so-called three "Fs"—friends, family, and fools—and then as a venture evolved, additional finance was sourced from business angels, venture capital firms, and capital markets (Bellavitis et al. 2017). Over the last twenty years, the market for entrepreneurial finance began to change in terms of both its structure and, relatedly, its participants (Harrison and Mason 2019). Table 1 summarises the structural changes and the implications of these changes for entrepreneurial finance.

Alongside the structural changes highlighted in Table 1, Harrison and Mason (2019) note that a large number of new actors have entered the market mobilising new sources of capital. To some extent, these new actors (presented in Table 2) mitigate the negative effects of structural changes by providing funding at formative stages (e.g. university or government venture capital), reactivating the three Fs, and providing a wider geographic reach for fundraising (e.g. crowdfunding), and democratising venture capital (e.g. token offerings—initial coin offerings (ICOs) and security token offerings (STOs)).

These new actors are re-conceptualising the funding cycle by introducing new peculiarities and dynamics (Brown et al. 2019; Martino et al. 2019). Rather than a relatively linear funding cycle, new sources of entrepreneurial finance can be used interchangeably and revisited many times (Bellavitis et al. 2017). Furthermore, they may not have financial goals or require equity at all. The peculiarities of these new

Table 1 Major structural changes in the market for entrepreneurial finance in the last twenty years

Structural change	Description	Implication
Demise of "classic venture capital"	Withdrawal of institutional venture capital from the start-up and early-stage capital market due to the economics of managing and investing increasingly larger funds	Smaller number of larger transactions thus affecting business development and economic growth
Closure of the IPO market	The IPO market is only available to all intents and purposes to larger companies	Has resulted in "second equity gap" and growing importance in long-term angel investors
Emergence of formally organised angel groups	The development, often with government support, of business angel networks (BANs) which act as matchmaking services for entrepreneurs and investors	Emergence of formal managed angel syndicates, syndicate managers/gatekeepers, formal and informal alliances of angel investors Demise of traditional funding escalator and replacement with a bundling model involving angel groups co-investing with other funds
Identification of a "scale-up" problem	The displacement of individual business angels by BANs and the requirement for larger long-term investment commitments may result in a "first equity gap"	Downward management of entrepreneurs' growth aspirations to match the availability of capital
Changing geography of venture capital	Venture capital investment tends to be concentrated in a relatively small number of the world's major cities	Venture capital has an uneven impact on urban and regional economic development

Adapted from Harrison and Mason (2019)

sources of alternative funding reflect the heterogeneity of the stakeholders behind them. Their goals may be financial, non-financial, or a blend of both financial and non-financial in the case of government, university, and social venture capital funds. In other cases, funding may be provided by stakeholders who just like the idea or consider themselves fans (Block et al. 2018). Similarly, the benefits to firms include not only access to finance but infrastructure, customers, or legitimacy (Bellavitis et al. 2017).

3 The Digital Alternatives: Online Alternative Finance

Not all of the new sources of alternative finance are Internet-enabled. Online alternative finance involves soliciting funds from the public for a project or venture through an Internet-based intermediate platform. Like traditional financing, these may be debt or equity-based. The two most prominent categories of online alternative finance are crowdfunding (including peer-to-peer lending) and token offerings (including ICOs and STOs). The Global Crowdfunding Market was valued at

Table 2 New sources of entrepreneurial finance

Sources of finance	Description	Debit/equity	Investment approach	Investment goal	Examples
Accelerators	A fixed-term, cohort-based program for start-ups, including mentorship and/or educational components, that culminates in a graduation event (Cohen et al. 2019)	Varies	Active	Varies	Y Combinator, Techstars
Business Angel networks	A structured network which offers business angels the possibility to access projects in need of financing (Lange et al. 2003)	Equity	Active	Financial	Tech Coast Angels (US), HALO (Ireland)
Contests	Contests between start-ups and founders where business plans are presented to a panel of judges where the prize may be funding, investment, mentoring, or other supports	Varies	Passive	Varies	Start-up World Cup, Disrupt SF
Crowdfunding	An open call, mostly through the Internet, for the provision of financial resources from a group of individuals or organisations either in the form of donation or in exchange for the future product or some form of reward to support initiatives for specific purposes (Belleflamme et al. 2014; Lynn et al. 2017)				
– Debt-based (Peer-to-peer lending)	A type of crowdfunding where funds are provided as a loan, with the expectation of a rate of return on capital invested (Mollick 2014)	Debt	Passive	Financial	Prosper.com, Funding Circle

(continued)

Table 2 (continued)

Sources of finance	Description	Debit/equity	Investment approach	Investment goal	Examples
– Donation-based	A type of crowdfunding that is used to collect funding in support of charitable or social causes and projects (Lukkarinen et al. 2016)	NA	Passive	Social	Crowdrise, GoFundMe
– Reward-based	A type of crowdfunding where funders receive non-monetary rewards in exchange for their support (Lukkarinen et al. 2016)	NA	Varies	Product-related	IndieGoGo, Kickstarter
– Equity-based	A type of crowdfunding where funders receive a share of future profits or equity securities in exchange for their support (Belleflamme et al. 2014)	Equity	Passive	Financial	IndieGoGo, Kickstarter
Corporate venture capital	The investment of corporate funds directly in external start-up companies for financial or strategic reasons (Chesbrough 2002)	Equity	Active	Financial, technological, strategic	Google Ventures, Intel Capital, Comcast Ventures
Family offices	A private company that manages investments and trusts for a single family (Single Family Office) or a form of financial services to management investments for multiple families (Multi-family Office)	Equity	Mostly passive	Financial	Omidyar Network, Kapor Capital

(continued)

Table 2 (continued)

Sources of finance	Description	Debit/equity	Investment approach	Investment goal	Examples
Governmental venture capital	The investment of government funds directly or indirectly in external start-up companies for financial or policy reasons	Debt or equity	Mostly passive	Financial, governmental	Yozma (Israel), Innovation Network Corporation (Japan)
Incubators	A program that provides a physical office space, networking opportunities, and basic business services to start-up companies. Incubators may offer accelerator programs	Varies	Mostly passive	Financial	Academpark Incubator, ActivSpaces (See Accelerators)
Initial coin offerings	Open calls for funding promoted by organisations, companies, and entrepreneurs to raise money through cryptocurrencies, in exchange for a "token" that can be sold on the Internet or used in the future to obtain products or services and, at times, profits (Adhami et al. 2018)	Equity	Passive	Financial	Telegram, Filecoin
IP-based investment funds	Patent-based investment funds acquire intellectual properties such as patents or patentable inventions at an early stage of development (Gredel et al. 2012)	NA	Passive	Financial	Altitude Capital, Rembrandt IP Management

(continued)

Table 2 (continued)

Sources of finance	Description	Debit/equity	Investment approach	Investment goal	Examples
IP-backed debt funding	Provision of finance for IP owners, either directly or as intermediaries, usually in the form of loans (debt financing), where the security for the loan is either wholly or partially IP assets (i.e. IP collateralisation) (Millien and Laurie 2007)	Debt	Passive	Financial	Bowie Bonds, Singapore IP Financing Scheme (IPFS)
Micro-loans	Provision of debt financing to entrepreneurial projects on a small scale (Heller and Badding 2012)	Debt	Passive	Financial, social	Grameen Bank, BRAC
Mini-bonds	Fixed income debt securities (bonds) that can take advantage of a simplified issuing mechanism (Altman et al. 2018)	Debt	Passive	Financial	Crowdcube
Security token offering	Open calls for funding promoted by organisations, companies, and entrepreneurs to raise money in exchange for a "token" that is fully regulated and approved within at least one jurisdiction	Equity	Passive	Financial	AspenCoin, BoltonCoin
Social venture funds/social venture capital	These funds invest in companies that manufacture or sell socially beneficial products, utilise a management approach that benefits employees and customers, or in companies created to support non-profit organisations or to pursue primarily social objectives (Rubin 2009)	Debt and equity	Active	Financial, social	Better Ventures, Acumen Fund

(continued)

Table 2 (continued)

Sources of finance	Description	Debit/equity	Investment approach	Investment goal	Examples
University-managed/university-based funds	The investment of university funds directly or indirectly in external and internal start-up companies for financial or strategic reasons	Primarily equity	Active	Financial, university-related	The House Fund (Berkeley), NYU Innovation Venture Fund
Venture debt lenders or funds	Loan origination to start-ups who may lack positive cash flow or securities	Debt	Passive	Financial	Clearbanc, Columbia Lake Partners

Adapted and extended from Block et al. (2018)

10.2 Billion US$ in 2018 and is expected to reach 28.8 Billion US$ with a CAGR of 16% by 2025 (Valuates Reports 2019). More recently, token offerings have gained traction providing more than $26 billion in funding through more than 1700 thousand successful offerings (ICObench 2019a).

3.1 Crowdfunding

3.1.1 Equity, Reward, and Donation Crowdfunding

Crowdfunding enables entrepreneurs to attract external finance and develop their business idea by sourcing small amounts of money from a large number of individuals, typically non-professional, i.e. the "crowd" instead of relatively small group of professional investors (Ordanini et al. 2011; Belleflamme et al. 2014; Brown et al. 2019). Crowdfunding platforms exploit the power of the Internet and platformisation to create a two-sided market that links capital-seekers (crowdfunders) and capital givers (investors) generating revenues for themselves through a commission on funds (Haas et al. 2014; Zvilichovsky et al. 2013; Zaggl and Block 2019).

Figure 1 provides an overview of the typical process for a crowdfunding campaign. Promoters submit their project idea to a crowdfunding platform describing the idea, the amount of capital sought, the team, the reward promised, and the length of the campaign. Platforms typically allow promoters to upload interactive material. This may include images or video. A properly designed narrative is quite important for the success of crowdfunding campaigns and is considered an effective way of building legitimacy around new ventures and mobilising diverse and dispersed actors like crowdfunders (Frydrych et al. 2014; Manning and Bejarano 2017). Properly designed communication strategies, both pre and post-launch of a campaign are key elements for its success as they help creating awareness for the project (Gierczak et al. 2016). Furthermore, crowdfunding campaigns typically heavily rely on social media and online communication in order to reach a wide and dispersed audience and in particular potential investors unknown to the promoters (Agrawal et al. 2011; Lynn et al. 2017). Most of the funds tend to be collected during the first and the last weeks of campaigns, therefore, it is important to sustain communication and engagement efforts until the end of a campaign to maximise the amount of capital collected (Kuppuswamy and Bayus 2018).

Crowdfunding platforms do not borrow, pool, or lend money on their own account but enable investors to pledge funds, often on an or all-or-nothing or keep-it-all basis (Cumming et al. 2015; Haas et al. 2014) (see Table 3). The economic model for these platforms is typically a commission based on funds raised or donations received. As such, when a campaign ends, promoters receive the amount of capital raised net of the platform fee. A key differentiation of these platforms is that they cater for a wide range of projects including products, experience goods, social initiatives, and more recently, research projects. Since its emergence in 2010, crowdfunding has expanded in terms of the volume, variety, and value of

Fig. 1 Crowdfunding process

Table 3 All-or-nothing versus keep-it-all (Cumming et al. 2020)

All-or-nothing	Entrepreneurial firms set a capital raising goal below which the entrepreneurial firm does not keep any of the pledged funds and the crowd does not receive any reward
Keep-it-all	Entrepreneurial firms can keep the entire pledged amount regardless as to whether or not the stated capital raising goal is reached

transactions to which it is applied (Agrawal et al. 2015). Massolution (2015) reported that crowdfunding investments worldwide grew to US$34.4 billion in 2015 from over 1250 crowdfunding platforms.

Crowdfunding differs from traditional VC investments by the characteristics of investors, the investment model, and indeed the type of relationship the investors have with the investee. First, as mentioned earlier, unlike traditional investment, the overwhelming majority of crowdfunders are not professional but rather comprise friends, family, and those motivated by preferential access to products or feelings of connectedness to a community or a social cause (Gerber et al. 2012; Brown et al. 2019). Second, crowdfunding investment models are more varied than traditional investment and include crowdinvesting (lending and equity-based crowdfunding) and crowdsponsoring (donation, reward, and pre-purchase) (Griffin 2012). Third, the relationship between investors and investees in crowdfunding models differs from traditional investment (Ley and Weaven 2011). Due to the nature of crowdfunding, the ability to mitigate risk through deal screening, deal referrals, information sensitivity and due diligence before investment are limited. Similarly, ex-post risk mitigation through contractual rights, board representation, value adding capability, economic life, and exit options are also limited (Ley and Weaven 2011). In the case of donation and reward, and pre-purchase crowdfunding models, these may not even be relevant.

Conducting a crowdfunding campaign can be particularly beneficial for entrepreneurs as it provides them with access to capital but also generates a community effect around the project. Research suggests that many crowdfunders are motivated by early or preferential access to innovative products/services and feelings of connectedness to a community (Gerber and Hui 2013). As discussed earlier, crowdfunding also has the potential to eliminate geographical boundaries between entrepreneurs and investors therefore providing them access to a larger pool of resources and projects, respectively. This may result in more investment opportunities for capital givers and in more business and innovation, business and growth opportunities for entrepreneurs. However, cross-border opportunities have not been fully exploited by investors yet (Wardrop et al. 2015), and therefore, entrepreneurs should still focus on developing and leveraging their own local personal network. Critically, local investors tend to invest early, and this may represent an important signal to the other funders in the initial phase of campaign (Agrawal et al. 2011).

3.1.2 Peer-to-Peer Lending

Lending-based crowdfunding, typically referred to as peer-to-peer (P2P) lending, has attracted most of the crowdfunding investment so far. P2P lending platforms are typically quite targeted as they mostly focus on either personal or business lending with very few exceptions (e.g. LendingClub[1]). Table 4 provides an overview of the funding provided through P2P lending platforms by region and segment.

Zopa was the first P2P lending platform to be launched back in 2005 (Cummins et al. 2019). Two other large US-based platforms, Prosper.com and LendingClub, followed in 2006 and 2007, respectively (Greiner and Wang 2009). However, the amount of capital channelled through P2P lending started growing significantly only post-2009, in the aftermath of the financial crisis. In fact, the combined effect of the crisis and the introduction of stricter banking regulations (e.g. Basel II) made access to capital extremely difficult for small enterprises and entrepreneurs. On the other hand, low interest rates made bonds and other traditional financial instruments unattractive for investors. In this context, P2P lending platforms started to prosper as they represented suitable alternatives to traditional channels for both businesses and investors.

P2P lending is anything but new. Entrepreneurs have traditionally leveraged their personal network to raise capital (Berger and Udell 1998; Kotha and George 2012; Robb and Robinson 2014; Cummins et al. 2019). Small loans are often provided by family members or friends on the basis of personal relationships rather than formal due diligence. These informal transactions carry undeniable risks for both borrowers and lenders. Online P2P lending platforms have improved this process by providing online marketplaces that enable borrowers and lenders to transact directly with defined rules of engagement and by providing due diligence services that reduces the risk of default (Cummins et al. 2019). In exchange for this, platforms charge a fee, typically a small percentage of the funded amount, paid by borrowers.

A brief outline of the funding process for business loans on LendingClub is as follows.[2] A potential borrower registers to the platform, provides verifiable contact and bank details together with the desired loan amount and duration. Then, the borrower provides additional background information about the business and its current financial status (e.g. last year's revenues and profits, ownership, and other existing financial commitments such as loans or leases). The approval process takes on average seven days, and the platform sets the interest rate based on its own risk

---

[1]https://www.lendingclub.com/.
[2]https://help.lendingclub.com/hc/en-us/articles/360001352047-Business-loan-application-walk through.

Table 4 Size of P2P lending funding by region and segment

Region	P2P consumer lending	P2P business lending
2015		
The Americas	18.00	2.60
Asia Pacific and China	52.78	39.99
Europe	0.40	0.23
Middle East and Africa	0.01	0.02
2016		
The Americas	21.10	1.30
Asia Pacific and China	137.02	58.51
Europe	0.73	0.37
Middle East and Africa	0.03	0.03
2017		
The Americas	14.90	1.50
Asia Pacific and China	225.26	98.05
Europe	1.39	0.47
Middle East and Africa	N/A	N/A

Notes All figures are reported in USD/billions
Sources Cambridge Centre for Alternative Finance (2017a, b, 2018a, b, c, d), Cummins et al. (2019)

assessment. If the borrower accepts the offered the proposed conditions, the funds are transferred to the provided bank account, and the borrower repays the loan to the platform on a monthly basis. The platform collects the monthly payments and transfers them to each backer on the basis of the amount funded. A key differentiator of online P2P loans when compared to traditional banking loans is that borrowers have the flexibility to make lump sum payments or repay their loans early at no extra cost. This flexibility, together with short approval times, is particularly valuable for businesses that face temporary liquidity needs.

The interest rates charged by P2P lending platforms are on average higher than the ones offered by traditional financial institutions. This reflects the fact that P2P loans are typically riskier than the ones funded by banks (de Roure et al. 2016). P2P loans are mostly unsecured, and the access requirements for businesses are not as strict as the ones imposed by banks. For LendingClub, for example, a company would need to have been in business for a minimum of 12 months with at least $50,000 in revenues.[3] As such, P2P lending platforms are complementary to traditional financial institutions as it allows riskier borrowers, which could not be served by banks, to obtain access to capital (de Roure et al. 2016). However, P2P lending platforms are also competing with traditional financial institutions for low risk borrowers (Tang 2019). In fact, investors (i.e. lenders) bear all the risk in P2P lending, and a key metric for them to evaluate platforms is default rate. As a result,

---

[3]https://www.lendingclub.com/business/?utm_source=LC&utm_medium=link&utm_campaign=pl_top_nav&u=1.

the rejection rate at the application stage is quite high for risky borrowers, and capital is more likely to flow towards borrowers who are already "bankable" (Tang 2019).

3.1.3   Case Study: Jolla—The Power of the Crowd

In February 2010, Intel and Nokia merged their efforts to develop a Linux-based mobile operating system (OS), MeeGo, and agreed to work together to drive a broad ecosystem of partners (Grabham 2010). For a short time, this partnership seemed to make progress, attracting companies like Novell, AMD and Aminocom to the MeeGo development effort. This all came to a shuddering stop exactly one year later when Nokia abandoned the partnership to switch to Windows Phone 7 (Reuters 2011). Intel soon followed and by October 2011 (Ricknas 2011), the MeeGo development effort had migrated to a new community effort named Mer (Mer Project 2011).

The switch to Windows Phone 7 was a major blow to Nokia. This strategy change contributed significant to nearly 24,000 job losses (Blandford 2012). To support those made unemployed, Nokia launched the Bridge programme. Under this programme, an ex-employee can potentially receive up to €25,000 in seed funding for a start-up company and up to four employees can come together for one start-up (Blandford 2012). One such group of former Nokia employees came together to form a new company, Jolla, to evolve the MeeGo/Mer OS. Jolla's plan was to license the new OS, Sailfish OS, to smartphone manufacturers, but this was not without challenges. Sami Pienimaki, cofounder of Jolla, told Engadget:

'We realised that we had to develop our own phone in order to bring life to the Sailfish operating system' (Summers 2018).

After suffering a number of setbacks, the Jolla phone launched in November 2013 to lukewarm reviews. Undeterred by the lacklustre reception, Jolla continued to market and sell its Sailfish-based smartphones. It also refocussed its efforts to demonstrate the capabilities of Sailfish OS in the emerging tablet market. A big question remained unanswered. How would it market and fund this new tablet effort?

On 19 November 2014, a year after launching its smartphone, the Jolla Tablet Indiegogo crowdfunding campaign was announced. Marc Dillon, the then CEO launched the campaign:

'Crowdsourcing has been the foundation of so many amazing, inspiring and independent products, and what it stands for taps directly into Jolla's ethos. We have a strong worldwide community supporting us, and we want to give people the opportunity to contribute early and take part in the Jolla Tablet campaign. By contributing you also have the opportunity to have your say in the actual development of the product' (Jolla 2014a).

As part of the Jolla Tablet campaign, the first thousand contributors were given the opportunity to get a Jolla Tablet for US$189 and assuming the campaign hit its target of US$380,000, product shipments would start in the second quarter of 2015.

The campaign was made available in all EU countries, Norway, Switzerland, the USA, India, China, Hong Kong, and Russia. Jolla supported the campaign with PR, online advertising, and social media but also by seeking feedback on product features from the community.

By 27 November, Jolla had pledges of nearly US$1.3 million, exceeding its original target by nearly 3X (Jolla 2014b). Riding the momentum, Dillon decided to use the feedback on product features to incentivise more investment. Jolla announced an extended phase of their crowdfunding campaign with the promise of new hardware and software features (3.5G HSDPA, extended memory card support, and split screen UI), if a new target of US$2.5 million was reached, nearly 6.5X the original campaign target (Jolla 2014b). Dillon announced:

'We are really excited to announce these new stretch goals, which we've carefully identified and discussed together with our community. We asked what our backers want, and we hope we get to fulfil these promises. The highest stretch goal, adding the 3.5G HSDPA connectivity, has been in our hopes for a while already, and now we're looking forward to build further partnerships with cellular operators across the markets' (Jolla 2014b).

Would they succeed? By the time, the Jolla IndieGoGo campaign ended on 10 December, Jolla raised over US$1.8 million from over 13,000 contributors in 21 days (Jolla 2014c). Including post-campaign contributions, Jolla raised over US $2.5 million from 21,633 contributors (IndieGoGo 2019). The campaign's original target was reached in two hours, and US$1 million in funding was raised in the first 24 hours. The campaign not only raised valuable funding but helped build a brand and international customer base in less than a month. Antti Saarnio, Chairman of the Board of Jolla commented:

'Involving fans and followers early through a crowdfunding campaign is a perfect way to launch a new product, and also to test the demand in advance. We are really pleased with the outcome, and are happy and thankful to see so many early contributors participating. Jolla has a strong worldwide community who believe in us and this campaign is one proof of that' (Jolla 2014c).

3.2 Token Offerings

3.2.1 Initial Coin Offerings

Initial token offerings, often referred to as initial coin offerings (ICOs), are, at first glance, similar to crowdfunding campaigns as they represent open calls for funding. However, they have critical differences in that they are completely disintermediated, typically are of orders of magnitude larger in terms of participants and value, and are established on blockchain-based smart contracts. Although token offerings represent a recent phenomenon, more than US$27 billion has been raised through ICOs since 2013, with exponential growth over the last two years (PwC 2019). Figure 2 provides an overview of how ICOs work.

The unencumbered nature of ICOs has attracted the attention of policy makers worldwide; in some countries (e.g. China), ICOs have even been deemed illegal

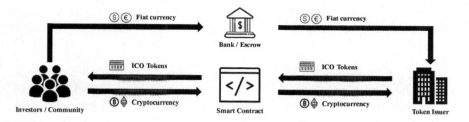

Fig. 2 ICO process (adapted from PwC 2019)

(Barsan 2017). As such, entrepreneurs aiming to launch an ICO should first verify the legal implications of conducting an ICO in the jurisdiction that they, and potential investors, are based in.

The token issuer, typically a start-up, defines the main characteristics of the tokens (e.g. the rights it will provide to token holders, number of tokens, protocol, etc.) and of the selling process (e.g. initial value, issuing platform, time period of token sale, type of investors, accepted methods of payment, etc.). There are three main types of tokens (Tasca 2019):

- Payment tokens which are essentially cryptocurrencies that are used as means of payment or value transfer;
- Utility tokens that allow token holders to access a specific digital application/service;
- Asset/debt tokens which represent for the investor assets such as a debt or equity.

From a project promoter's perspective, one of main benefits of token offerings is the opportunity to attract both capital and users, particularly with the issuance of utility tokens. This is particularly beneficial for platform promoters as reaching a critical mass of users is paramount for the success of the project. Unsurprisingly, platform-based businesses represent the majority of completed token offerings so far, followed by projects related to cryptocurrencies (ICObench 2019b). As this type of fundraising matures, the number of token offerings across other industries is expected to grow, particularly in the IT sector.

Once the token and the sale process have been designed, the entire project is then described in a "white paper". A white paper typically contains the technical details related to the token offering but also a detailed description of the project and the team. The white paper is a key element for the success of a token offering (Adhami et al. 2018), and its production typically involves considerable cost (Fisch 2019). The white paper then needs to be promoted to potential investors. In this phase, a properly built website, and a clear marketing and communication strategy can make the difference in terms of reaching potential target investors in the most effective way. This phase typically requires time and effort as awareness needs to be built around the proposed project.

Once launched, the duration of the sale depends on how attractive the project is to investors and how effective the pre-sale communication is. Gnosis' ICO, for example, concluded in 10 minutes[4]; others may last for weeks or months. Many do not reach the minimum threshold at all. If the token offering is successful, the next step is for the promoters to deliver on their promises. This includes delivering tokens to the buyers and getting the tokens listed on one or more exchanges. One of the advantages of token offerings compared to traditional VC investments or crowdfunding campaigns is that tokens can be traded in the secondary market (Benedetti and Kostovetsky 2018). Tokens' price fluctuates based on progress in product development and project's future prospects (Benedetti and Kostovetsky 2018). Despite all the hype around token offerings and the announcements of multi-million sales frequently reported in the media, the failure rate of token offerings is quite high. According to a recent report published by Satis Group LLC, only 15 percent of the ICOs launched so far managed to get to the listing stage, and approximately, 50 percent of them are deemed to be successful (Satis Group 2018).

3.2.2   Security Token Offerings

Although very attractive from a financial standpoint, token offerings face two main challenges. Firstly, ICOs suffer from legitimacy issues arising from 78% of past ICO initiatives being perceived or designated as scams (Satis Group 2018).[5] Unsurprisingly, many investors still look at token offerings with suspicion. This also relates to the second challenge—ambiguous regulation. As mentioned previously, ICOs were, and still are, completely unregulated in many countries. As such, investor protection is very limited at best or non-existent at worst. Some regulators have recently provided clearer frameworks by making asset/debt tokens comparable to more standard securities like debt or equities. This has enabled the development of more legitimate, transparent, and regulated token offerings (also known as security token offerings—STOs). What distinguishes STOs from ICOs is that STO tokens pass what is called "The Howey Test"—there is (i) an investment of money, (ii) profits are expected, (iii) money investment is a common enterprise, and (iv) any profits come from the efforts of a third party (Henning 2018). As such, unlike ICOs, STOs are defined as securities and therefore face the same regulation as equity shares while retaining the advantages of cryptocurrencies over traditional private markets in terms of liquidity, price discovery, and market makers. STOs are particularly attractive for profit-driven established investors who are looking to acquire a stake in these innovative ventures. From a promoter perspective, the process of launching and conducting an STO is similar to the one for ICOs presented previously with two key differences mostly related to compliance (Lee et al. 2019). Firstly, token issuers need to pay more attention to compliance with local security law requirements and to fully understand the legal implications of the STO for both the issuing company and investors. Secondly, token issuers must provide potential

---

[4]https://cointelegraph.com/news/fastest-ever-ico-ethereum-based-gnosis-creates-300-mln-in-minutes-raising-12-mln.
[5]https://medium.com/@sherwin.dowlat/ico-quality-development-trading-e4fef28df04f.

investors with a prospectus, a legal document which contains detailed information about the offering and the financial elements of your offering. The prospectus has to be approved by a financial regulator and is designed to protect investors from fraud.

3.2.3 Case Study: Aspen Coin—The First Real Estate STO

Aspen, Colorado is one of the most expensive towns in the USA. Founded as a mining town in the nineteenth century, the development of the Aspen area into a ski resort heralded unprecedented real estate investment into the area and a skyrocketing of property prices that has continued today. Reliable snow, a variety of ski terrains, historic neighbourhoods, year-round events, and celebrity cachet have resulted in a proliferation of second homes adding to the already superheated property market. In 2017, Aspen had the highest entry threshold for high-end properties across the USA (Block 2017).

The St. Regis Aspen Resort is a five-star luxury destination nestled at the base of Aspen Mountain managed by a subsidiary of Marriott International. It is owned by Aspen REIT, Inc. In November 2017, Aspen REIT announced its intention to be the first single-asset REIT to list on a national exchange by offering 1,675,000 shares at US$20 per share on the NYSE American stock exchange (Aspen REIT 2017). At the time, Aspen REIT CEO Stephane De Baets said:

> 'We plan to bring to the market a first-of-its-kind real estate offering that provides individual investors with the opportunity to own shares in a highly attractive, trophy asset in the St. Regis Aspen Resort. Historically, the chance to own a portion of an individual property of this calibre and stature was only available to institutions. With our offering, we are changing this model while at the same time providing individual investors with liquidity optionality for a single-asset investment. Our value proposition is innovative and, we believe, highly compelling' (Aspen REIT 2017).

However, in March 2018, Aspen REIT withdrew its common stock from listing on the New York Stock Exchange. It had other plans. De Baets told the Aspen Times:

> '…we believe many people secretly want to own a piece of the St. Regis Aspen hotel. Owning a digital token is the equivalent of owning a share, and is a digital security. We saw that doing an IPO was not scalable through the traditional route. Seeing where the blockchain market was heading, we saw the opportunity to be first-movers with our token offering for the St. Regis Aspen' (Carroll 2018a).

In August 2018, Templum Markets launched Aspen Digital, a tokenised asset offering (TAO), on Templum's trading platform. Aspen Digital is a digital Reg D 506c security offering open to accredited investors (Templum Markets 2018). Each token, called an Aspen Coin, represents, through indirect ownership, one share of common stock in the St. Regis Aspen Resort. Aspen Coins can be bought with US dollars, BitCoin or Ethereum. More important, all Aspen Coins are backed by the St. Regis Aspen Resort asset. De Baets clearly felt he had found a more efficient, cost-effective, and liquid means to raise funds:

'Asset backed coins like the Aspen Coin not only offer a transformative way to invest in real estate, but also establish a new way to store wealth by utilizing collateralized and income generating digital assets…we believe that the real estate tokenization model has tremendous potential in that it brings liquidity and disintermediation to the world's largest asset class' (Templum Markets 2018).

Reg D 506c offerings differ from public offerings, such as the Aspen REIT IPO on the NYSE. For example, investors do not obtain voting rights, something that favours the promoter. While Reg D 506c are open to the public to some extent, they are technically private placements that are only open to non-US persons or "accredited investors" in the US for the first year. Accredited investors must meet income, network, or asset thresholds as well as know your customer (KYC) and anti-money laundering (AML) requirements. However, this only applies to US investors; overseas investors do not need to meet these requirements. Standard ICOs do not have the same thresholds or requirements. Notwithstanding this, the offering can be advertised widely with no dollar limit on offering size and much lower disclosure thresholds. These lower compliance requirements reduce a perceived burdensome overhead while addressing legitimation issues associated with ICOs. Furthermore, participation is not limited to "those in the know". Indeed, the Aspen Coin offering was relatively self-service. Interested parties registered on the Templum Markets platform and provided documentation to verify accredited investor status and meet the KYC/AML requirements. Once verified, investors could participate in the offering; the minimum investment was US$10,000.

In addition to Templum's existing network of investors, the Aspen Coin offering was marketed to the nine million users of IndieGoGo, a first for the global crowdfunding platform. IndieGoGo co-founder Slava Rubin explained their motivation:

'We have always strived to foster innovation and provide our users access to some of the most novel and interesting products and ideas from around the world. With the blockchain revolution fully underway, we at Indiegogo are excited about the world-changing impact and potential of security tokens. Our goal is to [perform diligence for] each company and provide an access point to our growing network of millions of customers. And it's a privilege to work with the St. Regis Aspen Resort' (Wolfson 2018).

So was the Aspen Coin offering successful? On 9 October 2018, Aspen Digital announced 18.9% of the St. Regis Aspen Resort ownership through US$18 million in tokens (Carroll 2018b).

4 Conclusion

Entrepreneurs and SMEs have an unprecedented range of funding sources to draw from. Digital technologies are providing new opportunities for value creation, value capture, and value delivery for not only entrepreneurs but also investors. Online alternative finance is both disintermediating and democratising entrepreneurial finance transforming the access, relationship, and dynamics between supply and demand and providing valuable alternatives for entrepreneurial ventures at different stages of development. While P2P lending is better suited for both traditional and established businesses with existing revenue streams but need of small, short-term loans to meet monthly loan repayments or for small investments (Fenwick et al. 2018), other forms of crowdfunding are better suited for early-stage riskier ventures in need for capital to fund their prototype or initial growth (Harrison 2013). Similar to crowdfunding, token offerings are particularly attractive for early-stage ventures although mostly suited to platform-based businesses and have been adopted by start-ups aiming to avoid the complicated and costly auditing, and regulatory burden of traditional funding models (Tasca 2019), they are also typically larger in scale than traditional crowdfunding.

While new Internet-enabled funding mechanisms, such as crowdfunding and token offerings, have the potential to transform entrepreneurial finance and play a significant role in creating a level global playing field for access to funding, it remains concentrated in a small number of markets and raises a number of public policy issues, not least investor protection. The trajectory of these financing innovations is only going one way. Whether they will replace or complement the existing funding cycle remains to be seen.

References

Adhami, S., Giudici, G., & Martinazzi, S. (2018). Why do businesses go crypto? An empirical analysis of initial coin offerings. *Journal of Economics and Business, 100*, 64–75.

Agrawal, A., Catalini, C., & Goldfarb, A. (2015). Crowdfunding: Geography, social networks, and the timing of investment decisions. *Journal of Economics & Management Strategy, 24*(2), 253–274.

Agrawal, A. K., Catalini, C., & Goldfarb, A. (2011). *The geography of crowdfunding* (No. w16820). National Bureau of Economic Research.

Altman, E. I., Esentato, M., & Sabato, G. (2018). Assessing the credit worthiness of Italian SMEs and mini-bond issuers. *Global Finance Journal, 43*, 100450.

Aspen REIT. (2017, November 14). Aspen REIT, Inc. Files for Initial Public Offering; Targets NYSE American Listing. Press Release. https://www.businesswirechina.com/en/news/36375.html. Accessed 7 July 2019.

Barsan, I. M. (2017). Legal challenges of initial coin offerings (ICO). *Revue Trimestrielle de Droit Financier (RTDF), 3*, 54–65.

Bellavitis, C., Filatotchev, I., Kamuriwo, D. S., & Vanacker, T. (2017). Entrepreneurial finance: New frontiers of research and practice: *Venture Capital 19* (1–2), 1–16. https://doi.org/10.1080/13691066.2016.1259733.

Belleflamme, P., Lambert, T., & Schwienbacher, A. (2014). Crowdfunding: Tapping the right crowd. *Journal of Business Venturing, 29*(5), 585–609.

Benedetti, H., & Kostovetsky, L. (2018). Digital tulips? Returns to investors in initial coin offerings (May 20, 2018).

Berger, A. N., & Udell, G. F. (1998). The economics of small business finance: The roles of private equity and debt markets in the financial growth cycle. *Journal of Banking & Finance, 22*(6), 613–673.

Bhide, A. (2003). *The origin and evolution of new business*. New York: Oxford University Press.

Blandford, R. (2012, July 18). Nokia's Bridge program aims to ease pain of job losses. *All About Symbian*. http://www.allaboutsymbian.com/flow/item/15297_Nokias_Bridge_program_aims_to_php. Accessed 8 July 2019.

Block, F. (2017, July 27). Aspen, Colorado, has the highest entry price in the U.S. for luxury homes. *Mansion Global*. https://www.mansionglobal.com/articles/aspen-colorado-has-the-highest-entry-price-in-the-u-s-for-luxury-homes-69765. Accessed 7 July 2019.

Block, J. H., Colombo, M. G., Cumming, D. J., & Vismara, S. (2018). New players in entrepreneurial finance and why they are there. *Small Business Economics, 50*(2), 239–250.

Brown, R., Mawson, S., & Rowe, A. (2019). Start-ups, entrepreneurial networks and equity crowdfunding: A processual perspective. *Industrial Marketing Management, 80,* 115–125.

Cambridge Centre for Alternative Finance. (2017a). Hitting stride—The Americas Alternative Finance Industry Report.

Cambridge Centre for Alternative Finance. (2017b, September). Cultivating growth—The 2nd Asia Pacific Region Alternative Finance Industry Report.

Cambridge Centre for Alternative Finance. (2018a). Expanding horizons—The 3rd European Alternative Finance Industry Report.

Cambridge Centre for Alternative Finance. (2018b, June). The 2nd Annual Middle East and Africa Alternative Finance Industry Report.

Cambridge Centre for Alternative Finance. (2018c, November). The 3rd Asia Pacific Region Alternative Finance Industry Report.

Cambridge Centre for Alternative Finance. (2018d, December). The 3rd Americas Alternative Finance Industry Report.

Carroll, R. (2018a, September 2). Business monday: Digital tokens, blockchain technology and the St. Regis Aspen. *Aspen Times*. https://www.aspentimes.com/news/local/business-monday-digital-tokens-blockchain-technology-and-the-st-regis-aspen/. Accessed 7 July 2019.

Carroll, R. (2018b, November, 9). In $18 million deal, nearly one-fifth of St. Regis Aspen sells through digital tokens. *Aspen Times*. https://www.aspentimes.com/trending/in-18-million-deal-nearly-one-fifth-of-st-regis-aspen-sells-through-digital-tokens/. Accessed 7 July 2019.

Chesbrough, H. W. (2002). Making sense of corporate venture capital. *Harvard Business Review, 80*(3), 90–99.

Cohen, S., Fehder, D. C., Hochberg, Y. V., & Murray, F. (2019). The design of startup accelerators. *Research Policy, 48*(7), 1781–1797.

Cumming, D. J., Leboeuf, G., & Schwienbacher, A. (2015). Crowdfunding models: Keep-it-all vs. all-or-nothing. *Financial Management, 44,* 1–30.

Cummins, M., Lynn, T., Mac an Bhaird, C., & Rosati, P. (2019). Addressing information asymmetries in online peer-to-peer lending. In *Disrupting finance* (pp. 15–31). Cham: Palgrave Pivot.

Cumming, D. J., Leboeuf, G., & Schwienbacher, A. (2020). Crowdfunding models: Keep-it-all vs. all-or-nothing. *Financial Management*, 49(2), 331–360.

de Roure, C., Pelizzon, L., & Tasca, P. (2016). *How does P2P lending fit into the consumer credit market?* Bundesbank Discussion Paper No. 30/2016. Available at SSRN: https://ssrn.com/abstract=2848043.

Fenwick, M., McCahery, J. A., & Vermeulen, E. P. (2018). Fintech and the financing of SMEs and entrepreneurs: From crowdfunding to marketplace lending. In *The economics of crowdfunding* (pp. 103–129). Cham: Palgrave Macmillan.

Fisch, C. (2019). Initial coin offerings (ICOs) to finance new ventures. *Journal of Business Venturing, 34*(1), 1–22.

Frydrych, D., Bock, A. J., Kinder, T., & Koeck, B. (2014). Exploring entrepreneurial legitimacy in reward-based crowdfunding. *Venture Capital, 16*(3), 247–269.

Gerber, E. M., & Hui, J. (2013). Crowdfunding: Motivations and deterrents for participation. *ACM Transactions On Computer-Human Interaction (TOCHI), 20*(6), 34.

Gerber, E. M., Hui, J. S., & Kuo, P. Y. (2012, February). Crowdfunding: Why people are motivated to post and fund projects on crowdfunding platforms. In *Proceedings of the international workshop on design, influence, and social technologies: techniques, impacts and ethics* (Vol. 2, No. 11, p. 10). Northwestern University Evanston, IL.

Gierczak, M. M., Bretschneider, U., Haas, P., Blohm, I., & Leimeister, J. M. (2016). Crowdfunding: Outlining the new era of fundraising. In *Crowdfunding in Europe* (pp. 7–23). Cham: Springer.

Grabham, D. (2010, February 10). Intel and Nokia merge Moblin and Maemo to form MeeGo. *Techradar.com*. https://www.techradar.com/news/phone-and-communications/mobile-phones/intel-and-nokia-merge-moblin-and-maemo-to-form-meego-670302. Accessed 8 July 2019.

Gredel, D., Kramer, M., & Bend, B. (2012). Patent-based investment funds as innovation intermediaries for SMEs: In-depth analysis of reciprocal interactions, motives and fallacies. *Technovation, 32*(9–10), 536–549.

Greiner, M. E., & Wang, H. (2009). The role of social capital in people-to-people lending marketplaces. In *ICIS 2009 proceedings*, 29.

Griffin, Z. J. (2012). Crowdfunding: Fleecing the American masses. *Case Western Reserve Journal of Law, Technology & the Internet, 4*, 375.

Haas, P., Blohm, I. & Leimeister, J.M. (2014). An empirical taxonomy of crowdfunding intermediaries. In *Proceedings of Thirty Fifth International Conference on Information Systems*, Auckland 2014. AIS.

Hall, B. H., & Lerner, J. (2010). The financing of R&D and innovation. In *Handbook of the economics of innovation* (Vol. 1. pp. 609–639). Amsterdam: Elsevier.

Harrison, R. (2013). Crowdfunding and the revitalisation of the early stage risk capital market: Catalyst or chimera? *Venture Capital, 15*(4), 283–287

Harrison, R. T., & Mason, C. M. (2019). Venture Capital 20 years on: Reflections on the evolution of a field. *Venture Capital, 21*(1), 1–34.

Heller, L. R., & Badding, K. D. (2012). For compassion or money? The factors influencing the funding of micro loans. *The Journal of Socio-Economics, 41*(6), 831–835.

Henning, J. (2018). The Howey test: Are crypto-assets investment contracts. *University of Miami Business Law Review, 27*, 51.

ICObench. (2019a). ICO market monthly analysis, October 2019. Available at: https://icobench.com/reports/ICObench_ICO_Market_Analysis_October_2019.pdf. Accessed 3 Dec 2019.

ICObench. (2019b). Stats and facts. Available at: https://icobench.com/stats. Accessed 30 July 2019.

Indiegogo. (2019). *Jolla Tablet - world's first crowdsourced tablet*. Available at: https://www.indiegogo.com/projects/jolla-tablet-world-s-first-crowdsourced-tablet#/.

Jolla. (2014a, November 19). Introducing Jolla Tablet, the world's first crowdsourced tablet project. Press Release. https://jolla.com/wp-content/uploads/2017/02/41_JOLLATABLET_IGG_PRESSRELEASE_NOV2014_FINAL.pdf?x54860. Accessed 8 July 2019.

Jolla. (2014b, November 27). Jolla Tablet project has more than tripled its goal by raising nearly $1.3 M; now introducing 3.5G cellular data campaign goal and more. https://jolla.com/wp-content/uploads/2017/02/44_JOLLATABLET_UPDATE_PRESSRELEASE_NOV2014_FINAL.pdf?x54860. Accessed 8 July 2019.

Jolla. (2014c, December 11). Jolla successfully ends the Jolla tablet crowdfunding campaign and closes financing round B. https://jolla.com/wp-content/uploads/2017/02/46_JOLLATABLET_STRATEGY_PRESS_RELEASE_DEC2014_FINAL.pdf?x54860. Accessed 8 July 2019.

Kotha, R., & George, G. (2012). Friends, family, or fools: Entrepreneur experience and its implications for equity distribution and resource mobilization. *Journal of Business Venturing, 27*(5), 525–543.

Kuppuswamy, V., & Bayus, B. L. (2018). Crowdfunding creative ideas: The dynamics of project backers. In *The economics of crowdfunding* (pp. 151–182). Cham: Palgrave Macmillan.

Lange, J., Leleux, B., & Surlemont, B. (2003). Angel networks for the 21st century: An examination of practices of leading networks in Europe and the US. *The Journal of Private Equity, 6*(2), 18–28.

Lee, J., Li, T., & Shin, D. (2019). *The wisdom of crowds in FinTech: Evidence from initial coin offerings*. Available at SSRN 3195877.

Ley, A., & Weaven, S. (2011). Exploring agency dynamics of crowdfunding in start-up capital financing. *Academy of Entrepreneurship Journal, 17*(1), 85.

Lukkarinen, A., Teich, J. E., Wallenius, H., & Wallenius, J. (2016). Success drivers of online equity crowdfunding campaigns. *Decision Support Systems, 87,* 26–38.

Lynn, T., Rosati, P., Nair, B., & Mac an Bhaird, C. (2017). Harness the crowd: An exploration of the crowdfunding community on Twitter. In *ISBE Annual Meeting 2017*.

Manning, S., & Bejarano, T. A. (2017). Convincing the crowd: Entrepreneurial storytelling in crowdfunding campaigns. *Strategic Organization, 15*(2), 194–219.

Martino, P., Bellavitis, C., & DaSilva, C. M. (2019). *Blockchain and initial coin offerings (ICOs): A new way of crowdfunding*. Available at SSRN 3414238.

Massolution. (2015). Crowdfunding Industry Report.

Mer Project. (2011). Mer is back. http://mer-project.blogspot.com/2011/10/. Accessed 8 July 2019.

Millien, R., & Laurie, R. (2007, October). A summary of established & emerging IP business models. In *The Sedona Conference*, Phoenix, AZ.

Mollick, E. (2014). The dynamics of crowdfunding: An exploratory study. *Journal of Business Venturing, 29*(1), 1–16.

OECD. (2013). *SME and entrepreneurship financing: The role of credit guarantee schemes and mutual guarantee societies in supporting finance for small and medium-sized enterprises*. Paris: OECD Publishing. https://www.oecd-ilibrary.org/economics/sme-and-entrepreneurship-financing_35b8fece-en. Accessed 27 July 2019.

OECD. (2017). *Enhancing the contributions of SMEs in a global and digitalized economy*. Paris: OECD Publishing. https://www.oecd.org/mcm/documents/C-MIN-2017-8-EN.pdf. Accessed 8 July 2019.

OECD. (2019). *Financing SMEs and entrepreneurs 2019: An OECD scoreboard*. Paris: OECD. https://www.oecd.org/cfe/smes/financing-smes-and-entrepreneurs-23065265.htm. Accessed 8 July 2019.

Ordanini, A., Miceli, L., Pizzetti, M., & Parasuraman, A. (2011). Crowd-funding: Transforming customers into investors through innovative service platforms. *Journal of Service Management, 22*(4), 443–470.

PWC. (2019). 4th ICO/STO report—A strategic perspective. Available at: https://cryptovalley.swiss/wp-content/uploads/ch-20190308-strategyand-ico-sto-report-q1-2019.pdf. Accessed 30 July 2019.

Reuters. (2011, February 11). Nokia drops first MeeGo phone before launch—sources. https://www.reuters.com/article/nokia-meego/nokia-drops-first-meego-phone-before-launch-sources-idUSLDE7180X420110209. Accessed 8 July 2019.

Ricknas, M. (2011, September 28). Intel drops MeeGo mobile OS, backs Tizen against Android. *ComputerWorld*. https://www.computerworld.com/article/2511522/intel-drops-meego-mobile-os–backs-tizen-against-android.html. Accessed 8 July 2019.

Robb, A. M., & Robinson, D. T. (2014). The capital structure decisions of new firms. *Review of Financial Studies, 27*(1), 153–179.

Rubin, J. S. (2009). Developmental venture capital: Conceptualizing the field. *Venture Capital, 11*(4), 335–360.

Satis Group LLC. (2018). Cryptoasset market coverage initiation: Network creation. Available at: https://research.bloomberg.com/pub/res/d28giW28tf6G7T_Wr77aU0gDgFQ. Accessed 2 Aug 2019.

Summers, N. (2018, March 1). The Finns who refuse to give up on Sailfish OS. https://www.engadget.com/2018/03/01/jolla-sailfish-os-team-interview-mwc/. Accessed 8 July 2019.

Tang, H. (2019). Peer-to-peer lenders versus banks: Substitutes or complements? *The Review of Financial Studies, 32*(5), 1900–1938.

Tasca, P. (2019). Token-based business models. In T. Lynn, J. Mooney, M. Cummins, & P. Rosati (Eds.), *Disrupting finance* (pp. 135–148). Cham: Palgrave Pivot.

Templum Markets. (2018, August 8). Templum Markets launches digital security offering of St. Regis Aspen Resort. Press Release. https://www.businesswire.com/news/home/20180808005549/en/Templum-Markets-Launches-Digital-Security-Offering-St. Accessed 7 July 2019.

Valuates Reports. (2019). The global crowdfunding market was valued at 10.2 billion US$ in 2018 and is expected to reach 28.8 billion US$ with a CAGR of 16% by 2025. Valuates Reports. Available at: https://www.prnewswire.com/in/news-releases/the-global-crowdfunding-market-was-valued-at-10-2-billion-us-in-2018-and-is-expected-to-reach-28-8-billion-us-with-a-cagr-of-16-by-2025-valuates-reports-888819175.html. Accessed 4 Dec 2019.

Wardrop, R., Zhang, B., Rau, R., & Gray, M. (2015). Moving mainstream. The European Alternative Finance Benchmarking Report, 15–16.

Wennekers, S., & Thurik, R. (1999). Linking entrepreneurship and economic growth. *Small Business Economics, 13*(1), 27–56.

Wolfson, R. (2018, August, 23). Crowdfunding giant Indiegogo expands into crypto-security tokens with tokenized shares of stock. *Forbes*. https://www.forbes.com/sites/rachelwolfson/2018/08/23/crowdfunding-giant-expands-into-security-tokens-with-tokenized-shares-of-stock-in-st-regis-resort/. Accessed 7 July 2019.

Zaggl, M. A., & Block, J. (2019). Do small funding amounts lead to reverse herding? A field experiment in reward-based crowdfunding. *Journal of Business Venturing Insights, 12*, e00139.

Zvilichovsky, D., Inbar, Y. & Barzilay, O. (2013). Playing both sides of the market: Success and reciprocity on crowdfunding platforms. In *Proceedings of the Thirty Fourth International Conference on Information Systems*, Milan 2013. AIS.

Digital Intrapreneurship: The Corporate Solution to a Rapid Digitalisation

Gifford Pinchot III and Mariusz Soltanifar

Abstract

For decades, intrapreneurship has been, and is still, promoted to employees as a way to capture the creativity and excitement of entrepreneurship, albeit with more resources and less risk. Intrapreneurship creates opportunities for individuals to be innovative and entrepreneurial within and for the organisation that employs them. The ways in which intrapreneurs act have not changed, unlike the business context surrounding them. Digitalisation has opened the path for new intrapreneurial opportunities; however, the amount of attention paid to the role of digital intrapreneurs within existing organisations is limited. We present our own definition of digital intrapreneurship and position our definition in the digital landscape where modern companies operate. This chapter outlines numerous ways to foster digital intrapreneurship, including a set of practical methods for managers to identify, and empower digital intrapreneurs. The chapter presents three case studies and discusses their practical implications for entrepreneurs and their teams.

G. Pinchot III (✉)
Seattle, USA
e-mail: gp3@pinchot.com
URL: https://intrapreneur.com/

M. Soltanifar
Open University, Heerlen, The Netherlands

M. Soltanifar
Hanze University of Applied Sciences, Groningen, The Netherlands

© The Author(s) 2021
M. Soltanifar et al. (eds.), *Digital Entrepreneurship*, Future of Business and Finance,
https://doi.org/10.1007/978-3-030-53914-6_12

1 Introduction

PlayStation, iPod, Post-it® Notes, and Gmail are all products of intrapreneurship. Introduced by Pinchot in 1978, intrapreneurship has long been promoted to employees as a way to capture the creativity, sense of purpose, and excitement of entrepreneurship, albeit with more available resources and less risk (Corbett 2018; Pinchot and Pellman 1999). Intrapreneurs are not merely talented speakers and polished PowerPoint presenters. They are individuals capable of making quick prototypes, testing ideas with potential customers, learning what works and what does not work, redesigning their products, testing them again, and pushing through or around whatever barriers are in their way. They are self-motivated, proactive, and action-oriented employees who take responsibility for turning an idea into a profitable business reality for their employer.

Digitalisation and digital transformation have opened new intrapreneurial possibilities. Digital tools and technologies are transforming business strategies and processes, firm capabilities, and key interfirm and customer relationships. These changes are not exclusively relevant to organisations focussing on digital products and services; they also affect how firms in traditional industries do business. Digital technologies are creating or changing most jobs and future growth opportunities. Digitalisation even transforms creative industries like music and film. Fundamentally, digitalisation puts enormous pressure on companies and individuals to reflect on their current strategies and explore new business and career opportunities (Rachinger et al. 2018). This is the 'new normal'.

Intrapreneurs are as essential to corporate innovation as entrepreneurs are to start-ups, so most companies need many more intrapreneurs than they used to in the more stable times of the past. A firm's capacity to foster intrapreneurial talent significantly affects its ability to address the many opportunities and disruptions caused by the digital transformation. For that reason, nowadays, an understanding of how a firm can create a corporate environment within which digital intrapreneurs can thrive is an essential leadership capacity.

According to recent studies, although digital transformation offers organisations numerous opportunities to involve intrapreneurs in seizing the opportunities made possible by digital technology, many of the platforms, designs, and tools that corporations use to encourage intrapreneurship are limited and ineffective (Reibenspiess et al. 2020). However, if managers can suitably locate digital intrapreneurs and accommodate their needs, organisations can function more effectively in a digitally transforming environment. This requires decision-makers to adopt entirely new ways of thinking, leading, and managing rather than simply approaching new processes with the same old mindset.

This chapter discusses the importance of digital intrapreneurs and explores the ways of identifying, surfacing, and empowering them within established organisations.

2 The Relevance of Intrapreneurship to Digital Business

This section defines intrapreneurship and digital intrapreneurship, describes intrapreneurial roles and behaviour, elaborates on the growth of digital transformation, and provides an overview of the subject.

2.1 Defining Intrapreneurship

Definitions of intrapreneurship abound, each emphasising a different aspect of the term (e.g. Zahra et al. 2016). For example, intrapreneurship has been used to describe the following:

1. The entrepreneurial *initiatives* of a firm, viewing the firm as a whole as an individual actor
2. The *processes and structures* for managing intrapreneurs within an organisation
3. The *activities and behaviours* of intrapreneurs, their teams, and their sponsors.

In this chapter, to distinguish between these three aspects of intrapreneurship, we shall use the term *intrapreneurship* to refer to (a) the intrapreneurial activities of a firm as a whole and (b) the methods it uses to support and guide intrapreneurs. We use *intrapreneuring* to discuss the activities and behaviour of an intrapreneur and an intrapreneurial team as they work on developing and implementing innovative solutions. We will also use intrapreneurship as a general term to refer to all three abovementioned aspects.

Academic literature on intrapreneurship embraces innovative initiatives coming from employees when the initiatives come as responses to requests and challenges from a firm's leadership and when innovations align with its strategy. Studies also recognise initiatives that began as bottom-up ideas and eventually received management approval. According to Pinchot (1985):

> '[Intrapreneurs are] any of the 'dreamers that do'. Those who take hands-on responsibility for creating an innovation of any kind within an organization. The intrapreneur may or may not be the creator or inventor but is always the dreamer who figures out how to turn an idea into a profitable reality' (p. ix).

Pinchot later defines one particular kind of intrapreneurs (1987): the 'in-house entrepreneurs, those dreamers who can increase the speed and cost-effectiveness of technology transfer from R&D to the marketplace' (p. 14).

Our definition of intrapreneurship is somewhat broader than general usage. Writing about intrapreneurs often focusses on the people within an existing organisation who develop innovative products or services provided to external customers. However, people can use their intrapreneurial spirit for many things other than new externally focussed products and services, instead concentrating on developing better ways to make, improve, and sell products and services. Although Pinchot's perspective includes both the intrapreneurial actors (i.e. intrapreneurial leaders and teams and their sponsors) and the ways corporations could encourage intrapreneuring, most studies on intrapreneurship and the often interchangeably used term 'corporate entrepreneurship' have focussed on organisations and not individuals (Soltanifar 2016). Moreover, throughout the past decade, studies on intrapreneurship or corporate entrepreneurship have been dominated by analyses of firm-level contributions, that is, the instances where firms acted as entrepreneurs (e.g. Lumpkin et al. 2009; Rauch et al. 2009), with only a few exploring the individual-level or team-level perspectives.[1] Until now, no studies had expressly modelled the individuals' intrapreneurial behaviour within the context of digital intrapreneurship.

2.2 Intrapreneurial Roles and Behaviour in Organisations

Pinchot and Pellman (1999) recognise five distinct roles that are essential for managing innovation: (1) an idea generator, or an inventor, (2) an intrapreneur, (3) an intrapreneurial team member, (4) a sponsor, and (5) an innovation climate maker. Although all five roles need to coexist to result in successful innovation, the permitted space, unfortunately, does not allow us to discuss all of them; thus, in this chapter, we focus solely on the roles of the intrapreneur and the sponsor and their contributions to digital intrapreneurship.

Intrapreneurial activities range from large interventions, such as creating new business ventures and changing the strategic direction of a company, to smaller changes, such as developing new products, services, and technologies and improving existing products and processes. Intrapreneurs, like entrepreneurs, prefer to act without having to prove that their attempts will necessarily be a success (Pinchot and Pellman 1999). Instead, they want to find out what will work through a series of experiments, learning scenarios, and redesigns. They are prepared to encounter obstacles and setbacks, learn from them, and adjust their initial assumptions according to any new information. Intrapreneurs operate across the boundaries of organisational units, which is often necessary, since many new ideas require changes in more than one aspect (Pinchot 1985).

Intrapreneurs' anticipatory behaviour aimed at creating, and later implementing, new ideas for their organisation increases its capacity to respond to new opportunities and external developments (e.g. Gawke et al. 2017). According to Deloitte (2015), this action-oriented intrapreneurial behaviour is often combined with a strong business focus and a relationship-building skill set, enabling intrapreneurs to actively sell their ideas within their corporations and thus drive their implementation. Without such skills, intrapreneurs might lack internal sponsorship and, regardless of their creative spirit and vision, fail to convince management to let them proceed. Intrapreneurs operate within their respective companies and are thus acutely aware that they will never act as independently as entrepreneurs (Deloitte 2015).

---

[1]For exceptions, see Covin et al. (2020), Hughes et al. (2018), Kraus et al. (2019), Marvel et al. (2007), Monsen et al. (2010), Mustafa et al. (2018).

Like the role of intrapreneur, the role of the sponsor has been extensively discussed in the literature on innovation and corporate entrepreneurship. Sponsors serve to ensure that the intrapreneurial projects they finance are legitimate and supported (e.g. Hayton and Kelley 2006). They help intrapreneurs to gain access to any resources they need for their ventures (e.g. Day 1994). Good sponsors are able to distinguish the real intrapreneurs from the 'promoters' who look and sound good but fail to get the job done. Once they select an intrapreneur to support and trust, sponsors protect and coach them on future strategies (Garud and Van de Ven 1992).

This demands a lot of the sponsors' time for each intrapreneur, so if many innovations are needed, as they are in today's disruptive environment, many sponsors are needed to coach and protect the many intrapreneurs that drive those innovations. For this reason, it is important that executives delegate discretionary time and budget to lower-level managers so they can support the many needed intrapreneurs (Hayton and Kelley 2006).

2.3 The Growth of Digital Transformation and Its Implications for Intrapreneurship

Many emerging digital technologies are called exponential because every few years their capabilities are doubled. Because they are rapidly becoming impactful, exponential technologies like the Internet of things (IoT), artificial intelligence (AI), machine learning (ML), 3D printing, robotics, and blockchain are creating many new opportunities in most industries almost every year.

IoT, for instance, opens up new possibilities for product development, logistics, and improved business processes (Phaneuf 2020). IoT also provides powerful tools for tracking the quality, the ownership history, and the social and environmental attributes of the supply chain. This might greatly increase the capacity of organisations to manage their supply chains and address the sustainable development goals set by the United Nations.

AI enables users to process huge amounts of consumer data accumulated from various customer interactions to provide new and enhanced customer-centric insights, which are useful for idea generation, advertising, surveillance, and the invention process (Newman 2019). Machine Learning, a type of AI, lowers the costs of prediction and problem diagnosis, which are inherent to all business decisions (Forbes Technology Council 2019). Blockchain provides access to various markets, smart contracts, finance innovation opportunities, and enhanced security and competitiveness strategies (OECD n.d.). However, these powerful exponential technologies, despite their numerous benefits, may cause undesirable results. First, such exponential technologies might radically reduce consumer privacy and potentially induce totalitarian control through enhanced surveillance mechanisms. Second, they may also increase the criminals' ability to conceal illegal activity and transfer the right to create money away from governments to private entities, which might significantly impact the distribution of wealth. Both of these possibilities come with ethical and political issues that businesses will have to manage.

Although digital transformation is currently impacting a large variety of businesses, we have noticed a limited display of attention towards the role of digital intrapreneurship within traditional industries. Nevertheless, digital intrapreneurship plays a significant role in such industries by increasing production speeds, streamlining logistics, managing processes, lowering costs, handling supply chains, supporting low-cost customisation, managing risks, and allowing companies to build more responsive relationships with customers.

To seize these opportunities, even the most traditional manufacturing businesses must initiate systems and foster corporate cultures conducive to digital innovation. This is not just about coding or system design skills; rather, this transition requires an understanding of how digital natives live. Most digital natives are millennials or younger people, who are born after 1982. This is not to say that older people cannot drive digital innovation—many can; however, the volume of talent required to deal with the speed of contemporary digital transformation means that even mid-sized companies must recruit, motivate, and retain many young digital intrapreneurs. Digital natives understand the ways in which emerging technology can be, and is, used (Rossi 2019).

What are digital natives looking for? Deloitte (2019) has recently conducted another round of their 'Millennials Survey' and suggested that millennials have the following expectations:

1. Work that is aligned with their sense of purpose
2. A chance to make a significant contribution before they are 50
3. Freedom to choose what projects to work on
4. Freedom to act and make decisions about their work without frustrating delays caused by waiting for permission
5. Work that aligns with a desire to make the world better, as well as producing profit.

These demands do not fit well with command-and-control management approaches or shareholder-value-only objectives. However, these demands do not come from an unreasonable sense of entitlement by the young. They are what employees need to get the digital innovations and the other increasingly creative, intrinsically motivated and self-guided work of the twenty-first century done.

Older managers, not realising that the nature of work is changing, might think that the demands of the young are absurd; however, most talented digital natives will stay in an unsupportive company for only as long as it takes to establish a good résumé entry and then leave to work for another employer who will be more willing to accommodate their needs. Many older managers find it frustrating to manage these young people, who do not seem to behave 'the way the employees ought to'. And yet, these young people and many of their behaviours are essential for the development of a robust strategy of digital transformation.

2.4 Putting It All Together: Digital Intrapreneurship

The broadened definition of intrapreneurship presented under 2.1 is particularly pertinent to a discussion of digital intrapreneurship. Digital intrapreneurship is any intrapreneurship that uses digital means as a critical component of its innovation initiative. The innovation itself can be a new digital product like Google's email client or Amazon's cloud storage; however, it can also be exemplified by the use of digital technology to do what the company already does, but better, cheaper, and faster.

The latter kind of innovation is the most important form of digital innovation for companies in traditional industries. For such companies, digital innovation is not about new digital products or services but rather about the better ways to market, relate to customers, create operational efficiencies, and use exponential technologies such as 3D printing or genomics to perform the current processes much better, faster, and cheaper. For example, digital intrapreneurship includes using AI to optimise scheduling in a trucking firm or image interpretation in health care. It can also be used to market non-digital products, such as Amazon's online sales of physical products, or design a new physical product, such as a new medication or an airplane. Much of the innovation of Boeing 777 was done using digital tools, which allowed to rapidly design a better integrated airplane, thereby streamlining production.

Continual improvement of operational processes is still best done using the total quality method and its descendants like Six Sigma; however, breakthrough process improvements are mostly done by digital intrapreneurs. If one looks closely at continual improvement processes, one will often find that they create an environment where employees express a higher degree of initiative that resembles an intrapreneurial spirit.

Google's use of ML to improve their language translation services is good example of a radical product improvement made possible by digital intrapreneurship. Google was already delivering machine translation to customers; however, a small team of intrapreneurs overrode the traditional methods of its translation engines with a statistical ML approach. The outcome of this decision was an exponential improvement in the quality of translation, which was so striking that it caused Google to promptly stop working on improvements reliant on older methods (Lewis-Kraus 2016).

Quite often, digital intrapreneurship offers innovation opportunities that can create major transformations in terms of efficiency or customer relationship with a very modest investment. This creates a large number of high return-on-investment (ROI) intrapreneurial opportunities by developing personalised customer relationships, collaborating with suppliers, taking more data-driven decisions, automating diagnostics, managing natural resources like energy or water, and optimising logistics and process control.

Digital intrapreneurs are employees who use their entrepreneurial spirit for the benefit of their employer and simultaneously to give meaning to their work by implementing their ideas to produce impactful digital innovations.

Digital intrapreneurs must possess the skills to identify new digital-technology-enabled business opportunities and bring them to fruition, either as a new concept altogether or as an existing, but transformed, business system (World Bank Group 2016). Even though many companies seemingly focus on using innovation to drive commercial growth, what many of them miss is a corporate culture of innovation and a safe and supportive environment for their digital intrapreneurs. Creating that environment requires supportive managers to protect and coach one or several intrapreneurs that they personally trust and want to empower. Many such managers produce many empowered intrapreneurs. The collaboration between intrapreneurs and sponsors can be facilitated by a culture that permits them to act. Together these factors can lead to great levels of digital innovation.

3   Digital Intrapreneurship Model

Based on our review of the relevant literature, as well as our practical experience, we offer the following conceptual model that enables established organisations to surface, identify, and empower digital intrapreneurs to drive digital innovation. Finding, retaining, and supporting digital intrapreneurs, including millennials and GenX digital natives, is a core competency in our times.

Every organisation has control systems that create barriers that slow down intrapreneurs or stop them entirely. How, then, does innovation take place? In every organisation we studied, the key to innovation has taken the form of courageous managers who guide, protect, and clear the way and get resources for one or several intrapreneurs with whom they have close and trusting relationships. In effect, to those who put up barriers that block intrapreneurs, they say, 'I have checked this team out, and they are on the right track. They are acting responsibly. Let them pass'. We call these courageous managers 'sponsors'.

Nowadays, organisations cannot flourish without an organisational knowledge of digital technologies. Some of this knowledge is provided by digitally competent employees. The large issue of how an organisation can learn to act using the knowledge of digital technologies is unpacked below (Fig. 1).

Next, we shall elaborate on each component of the model.

3.1   Sponsors: The Key Factor for Supporting Digital Intrapreneurs

The first factor positively affecting digital innovation is a sufficient number of good sponsors. Often, when business leaders call for more digital innovation, it does not happen. When it works, how does the intent of the leaders to support digital intrapreneurship go through the 'clay layer' of middle managers who are usually driven so hard to achieve short-term goals in established systems that they have no time for new ideas?

In practice, we have found that the answer lies in a special class of managers who, because of their own intrinsic motivation and their relationship with intrapreneurs

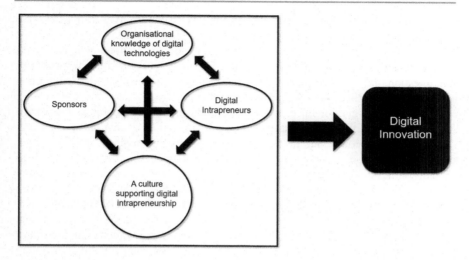

Fig. 1 Digital intrapreneurship model—the corporate solution to a rapid digitalisation

and their teams, choose to go out of their way to help the intrapreneurs. They spend their political capital to support the intrapreneurs even though it is not their 'day job'. As mentioned above, these altruistic managers are called 'sponsors'. Sometimes, they are called champions, but that term is a bit ambiguous because it is often applied not only to the sponsors, who champion the intrapreneurs, but also to the intrapreneurs themselves, who champion their ideas. Thus, the term 'sponsor' is clearer.

Sponsors spend time with intrapreneurs and coach them on both the commercial and the political issues and strategies. They stand up for the intrapreneurs when they are not present and help them access any necessary resources. If an innovative solution works in a given company, it is almost always due to a close and trusting relationship between a self-motivated team of intrapreneurs and their management sponsors. That combination is what moves innovation forward through the inevitable resistance of any corporate system.

Organisations can facilitate sponsorship in several ways. First, companies can train managers to be effective sponsors. This training includes both a description of what a sponsor must look for in an intrapreneur and some dos and don'ts for managing them.

Second, organisations can promote sponsorship by authorising lower-level managers to serve as effective mentors. Companies can provide managers with discretionary budgets to fund the early stages of innovation. These budgets do not have to be large to have a positive effect. Often a rapid prototype and a little travel money can be enough for testing an idea and gathering enough data to make a strong case for pursuing it further.

Third, companies can hold managers accountable for sponsoring innovation. They can feature sponsoring intrapreneurs as a responsibility on the list of the managers' key performance indicators (KPIs). Human resources can assess the sponsors' performance are by asking successful intrapreneurs: 'In your darkest hour, among your management, who supported you and helped you deal with whatever barriers were in your way?' The individuals mentioned in the answer to that question are the true sponsors. Then, counter-intuitively, when the good sponsors are identified, they should not be celebrated.

Great sponsors give credit to everyone around them, so celebrating them publicly will annoy all the others who ended up getting credit for what the sponsor did. This will create jealousy and limit the sponsor's future effectiveness. It is important to value what good sponsors do, but this can be done by congratulating them privately and, like succession planning, by keeping a secret list of good sponsors and promoting them whenever possible. As they rise, the true sponsors can be even more effective in supporting intrapreneurs and the culture that makes them effective.

Fourth, companies can measure their innovation outputs. At 3M, division leaders were held accountable for the number and quality of the innovations coming out of their division. The innovations were graded by the company's innovation rating team from minor improvements to those innovations that could create disruptive products for years to come. The leaders were not prompted to be innovative themselves. To get a good innovation score, a division needed to foster a corporate culture where intrapreneurs could thrive; this was measured using the innovation output of each division. This made having high-quality intrapreneurs and sponsors in their divisions valuable to general managers, who therefore created conditions conducive to intrapreneuring.

The best sponsors are motivated intrinsically, rather than extrinsically. They support intrapreneurs because they buy into the intrapreneurs' ideas and passions. Helping the intrapreneurs gives them meaning and provides them with valued professional relationships. The most effective sponsors are not driven by their ego. In extreme cases, they might have already reached the highest level they could expect to achieve in their career, so now they are giving back to younger innovators who remind them of their previous selves.

Many processes aimed at innovation fail. Idea contests bring out lots of ideas but rarely lead to successful implementation. The result is that they give hope to numerous employees only to crush them eventually. Rather than increasing employee engagement, they cause a short-lived increase in it followed by a long-term decline.

Formal processes like Stage-Gate, which at least intends to provide a pathway to commercialisation, should work better. However, much too often, due to delays between review cycles and an excessive focus on secondary information rather than on the testing of quick prototypes and intrapreneur assessment, they tend to slow down and halt innovation instead of accelerating it. They often become a process that creates more ways to say no and kill an idea rather than building a system for supporting intrapreneurs.

Significant decisions are made by committees, but no one has the ability to dig deep enough to understand the most difficult ideas. Committees may eliminate bad ideas, but they also tend to reject highly innovative and disruptive suggestions because they are hard to understand. What tends to survive are mediocre copycat ideas.

What works for selecting and supporting innovations is not a process, but rather a large set of close relationships between intrapreneurs and their sponsors who have some clout and influence and who trust, spend time with, and give extraordinary support to specific intrapreneurs. These sponsors get to know their intrapreneurs, their team, and their ideas very well. They are in a good position to evaluate the intrapreneurs and their proposed innovations. Their judgement on what the company should invest in is better than that of the committee; additionally, they can help the intrapreneurs to improve their ideas using well-informed questions and coaching.

Successful intrapreneurs, digital or not, often have several committed sponsors occupying different positions at different levels of the organisation. Creating and managing a coalition of sponsors is thus a core intrapreneuring skill.

Consider these facts together:

1. Each intrapreneur usually requires several collaborating sponsors to support and protect their interests and ideas.
2. Many intrapreneurs are needed to deal with the threats and opportunities rapidly generated by exponential digital technologies.
3. Sponsoring is an intimate relationship, which makes it time-consuming; that means that each sponsor can only protect one or few intrapreneurs.

These facts imply that each company needs a great number of sponsors to support the many intrapreneurs necessary to face the era of rapid digital innovation.

Senior leaders cannot possibly provide the volume of sponsorship sufficient to address the opportunities and threats created by exponential technology. Their role is to create the systems and a culture that empower middle managers and even first-line supervisors to serve as effective sponsors. Any intrapreneurship programmes that necessitate the blessing of senior leadership for individual innovations will fail for simple numerical reasons. In the age of digital innovation, authority to give the green light to innovation must be delegated.

3.2 Organisational Knowledge of Digital Technologies

The second factor driving digital innovation is the organisational knowledge of digital technologies. What does this mean? It means that an organisation, as an entity, makes decisions and takes actions as if it understands and is gracefully creative with its use of digital technology. It is not just about how many people with digital skills are employed by a given company; rather, what matters is how an organisation responds to digital opportunities and threats. That is what matters. There are two main elements of the organisational knowledge of digital technology:

1. The presence of a sufficient number of members of an organisation who understand digital technology and can create and implement all the innovations necessary to drive the digital transformations needed by that organisation
2. The way an organisation makes decisions and takes necessary actions to exhibit a fluid knowledge of digital technology.

Some organisations succeed in both aspects. Smart digital thinking pervades every aspect of their corporate functioning. As for the rest of modern organisations, it is unlikely that their largest barrier to digital innovation is a lack of people with the knowledge of digital technologies.

Companies today hire many digital natives. However, if digital innovation does not take place, the issue is more likely that a company is blocking the intrapreneurial spirit of its digitally competent employees, while those with significant digital talent are leaving the organisation or are disengaged and demotivated. See Case 2 below for more on this situation.

The major problem preventing most organisations from acting from a place of understanding of digital technology lies in their management. If management has neither the sufficient understanding of nor the familiarity with digital technology, how can it rapidly foster the organisational knowledge of digital technology?

1. Certainly, widespread education about digital technology is one part of the answer; however, it will probably take time to help the senior management reach the required level of understanding of and familiarity with digital technology where it would be able to properly assess any proposed digital innovations. There are faster approaches to the issue in question.
2. If more senior-level managers put their trust in selecting mid-level managers as sponsors, the growth of digital organisational competence within a company would significantly increase without the need for substituting any senior managers. A cultural transformation aimed towards increasing professional trust is necessary to empower intrapreneurs, and it can also increase the company's organisational intelligence in digital matters much faster than if the company tried to foster a profound digital competence among its senior executives. However, the senior members are still needed to provide wise advice about the core of the business that takes years to develop.
3. If a company learns to give more weight to the character, competence, and track record of its intrapreneurs, with slightly less focus on the initial quality of their ideas, then their sponsors will be able to make better decisions even without a detailed knowledge of digital technologies. In this scenario, the sponsors may augment their understanding of technology by knowing how to recognise and relate to true intrapreneurs.
4. Senior executives and middle managers can build a small set of digitally competent advisors to help them understand and assess proposals related to digital transformation. These advisors may not be highly ranked and may

function best in a formal role as coaches on digital technology, with any advice they offer on more strategic matters being done informally so as not to disrupt the sensibilities of the chain of command.

5. As demonstrated in Case 2 below, a company can acquire digital talent through acquisition; however, if it does not learn how to create an appropriate working environment for its intrapreneurs and the emerging creative work of the twenty-first century, they will soon be gone. A company must not impose its culture on any acquired entities; instead, it must learn from the acquired businesses about how they can better manage their own operations in this new digitally transforming world.

6. If a company has already developed a good organisational capacity to understand what digital transformations it should take on, then it can hire or partner with external organisations to complete the most technical aspects of its digital innovation plans. This requires a culture that knows how to deal with external entrepreneurs and intrapreneurs in vendor organisations.

Big companies in this era often need to partner with smaller digital innovators. To utilise the potential arising from the know-how of external digital entrepreneurs, big firms need to operate and make decisions at or close to the speed of their entrepreneurial partners. Otherwise, the entrepreneurs—or even the digital intrapreneurs within the larger partners—might become frustrated with partnering with a slow-moving firm or, worse even, take advantage of it.

The only way to achieve the necessary operating speed is to delegate the responsibility for managing relationships with external partners to a team of intrapreneurs, who are driving the part of the innovation being done by the larger firm, and let them make decisions with their external partners without constantly waiting to get their permission to make the next move.

3.3 Managing Digital Intrapreneurs: A Core Competency for Digital Innovation

The third method for supporting digital innovation lies in high-quality management of digital intrapreneurs. Motivating intrapreneurs is not necessary; instead, it is sufficient to merely not demotivate them by preventing them from taking their ideas further. A business leader can and should ask complex open-ended questions with the goal of helping them avoid trouble, but, whenever possible, trust them to come up with the right answer by themselves. A leader should also let them make non-fatal mistakes if these questions do not help them see the faultiness of their plan. After all, their plan might be smarter than expected.

A business leader should also be a good friend, who is concerned about the well-being of their innovations. By asking questions about the possible weaknesses in their plans while still letting them come up with the answers, a leader can support their intrinsic motivation. If he or she tells them what to do, their motivation will shift towards getting the permission of the manager (an external motivation), and the spirit of intrapreneurship will be lost. One must let them be the driving force, support them, and clear the path in front of them.

Intrapreneurs require an unusual level of freedom to be effective. This means managers have to trust them to rapidly make decisions about the development of their innovations without having to wait for permission or review. But one cannot trust everyone equally; thus, determining which digital intrapreneurs are worthy of trust and thus which ones to fund is critical to cost-effective digital intrapreneurship.

According to Pinchot (1987), 'Venture Capitalists say, "I'd rather have a class A entrepreneur with a class B idea than a class A idea with a class B entrepreneur"' (Pinchot 1985, pp. 15–16). The same logic applies to choosing the right intrapreneurs and innovations to invest in.

Pinchot (1987) continues:

> 'Picking the people with a passion, attitudes and talent for making the idea work is more important than picking the right plan. ... Corporations can greatly increase their return on innovation efforts by moving the emphasis in their innovation management efforts from selecting the right plan to selecting the right team to trust' (Pinchot 1987, p. 14).

The reason why people are more important than ideas is because almost no innovative idea will work in its original state. No one is that smart and foresighted. Investors need to have an appropriate team that can learn from its setbacks, experiments, and surprises and use that information to develop a functioning plan. For this reason, when deciding which digital innovation to invest in, the intrapreneur and their team serve as two most important factors.

A core part of that task involves seeing the difference between the real intrapreneurs and the individuals that venture capitalists call 'promoters'. Promoters are posers who talk a lot but lack the grit, persistence, courage, and intrinsic motivation to push through all the barriers, setbacks, and changes that will inevitably arise when they will try implementing an innovative idea. Promoters are driven by their ego and a desire for status rather than a genuine commitment to a transformational idea. When things go wrong, they will try to gloss over the problems instead of digging deeper to nip them in the bud. They will try to embellish their ideas instead of acknowledging the need for change. They will redirect supervisory attention to how great it will all be at the end of the journey instead of trying to dig the problem out.

Real intrapreneurs, conversely, are very interested in the pathway leading to the implementation of their ideas. If a supervisor suggests anything that might get in the way of implementing their ideas, they will take it seriously. They will, if necessary, ask questions to understand any related concerns. Alternatively, since they have probably already thought about the potential problems, they will be happy to tell about the ways of mitigating or circumventing the obstacle in question. Moreover, they will be interested in their supervisor's thoughts about the issue.

Following are some things to look for when deciding whether to back a proposal for a digital innovation (Table 1).

Table 1 Ten criteria for approving an intrapreneur's proposal for digital innovation

Criteria	Characteristics
Collaboration	Digital innovations usually span many functions and business units. Thus, collaboration with other business functions, even if they initially occupy hostile silos, is a core intrapreneurial requirement *Does the intrapreneur collaborate effectively?*
Deep involvement with the steps leading implementation	Real intrapreneurs are capable of envisioning the pathway to success as well as the final outcome of the innovation *Is the intrapreneur thinking clearly and in detail about how to implement their idea?*
Honesty	Honesty is a core character trait of successful intrapreneurs. Intrapreneurs may bend the rules or even break them to get something done, but they will always be open and honest with their potential sponsor. Moreover, they will not lie to others, even though at times they may hold their cards close to their chest. If they are not honest and open with their sponsors, they are probably not honest with themselves, which means that they will ignore data that does not support their desired expectations. The result of such an approach will almost certainly be a failure *Are they honest with you?*
Long- and short-term goal setting	Intrapreneurs set goals and assess their progress against them. If they are missing their targets, they want to know why. This helps them stay focussed, experimental, and realistic *Are they interested in assessing their own performance?*
Moderate risk-taking	Successful intrapreneurs take on challenging initiatives but do everything in their power (e.g. early tests of rapid prototypes) to reduce the accompanying risks. They are not gamblers; however, security is not their prime motivator either. The intrapreneurs' sense of security comes believing that they and their team have the ability to handle whatever problems that might arise *Are they good at managing risks?*
Motivation	Real intrapreneurs are intrinsically motivated—motivated from the inside by their values, vision, and purpose. Even though, like anyone else, they like to be paid well, money is not the reason for their new ideas. They innovate because they think their innovation matters above and beyond money. Money is a way of keeping score on how well they are doing in pursuing their vision, but it is not the reason for pursuing the innovation in the first place. This does not mean that they do not need to be paid well. They (particularly the talented intrapreneurs born after 1980) will leave if they find themselves paid substantially less than their peers who are just climbing up the conventional managerial ladder at a leisurely pace *Is their motivation deeper than money or promotions?*

(continued)

Table 1 (continued)

Criteria	Characteristics
Optimistic, inspirational leadership	Intrapreneurs do not have the resources to materialise their vision. Hence, they must inspire others to volunteer and help them construct their dream. Eventually, when they face a big setback (which is almost inevitable in every innovation), they may not claim that they know the solution but rather express their genuine belief that their team will find a way around the issue. If they cannot maintain that optimism, they will lose their followers *Do they attract proactive and inspired followers?*
Persistence	A predominant characteristic of both intrapreneurs and entrepreneurs is a deep persistence. If a senior executive puts a stop to their idea, a promoter will simply switch to another idea to get back in the executives' good graces. Real intrapreneurs are not interested in pleasing executives, so they do not give up. Instead, they find support elsewhere or build a plan to change the executives' mind *Treat persistence as a positive indicator*
Team building	Intrapreneurship, particularly digital intrapreneurship, is not a solo sport. Most innovations require a team. For instance, most digital innovations require a team that contains at least a system architect and a coding manager. Most teams also need a sales and marketing person, and that is just the beginning *Can the intrapreneur attract a team and run it effectively?*
Technical capabilities	A digital intrapreneur does not have to be a star technical talent. In fact, many intrapreneurs will have balanced skills and will usually be comfortable with new technologies and capable of understanding and working with those who excel in detailed tasks *Does the team have the necessary technical skill set?*

Of course, the idea that the intrapreneur wants to pursue is also part of the evaluation process; however, a good idea without a good intrapreneurial team to implement it is of very little value. Too often, in corporate decision-making, the quality of an intrapreneurial team and their commitment to an idea take a back seat to the analysis of the idea. Even worse, sometimes, passionate intrapreneurs are replaced with bureaucrats who lack both the passion for the idea and the intrapreneurial mindset necessary for innovative success.

3.4 A Culture Supporting Digital Intrapreneurship

The fourth factor contributing to effective digital innovation, in addition to intrapreneurs, sponsors, and organisational competence in digital technologies, is a supportive culture. Creating and nurturing a culture where digital intrapreneurs can thrive in the organisation is a core capability for facing the world of exponential digital innovation. Building such culture is not about creating intrapreneurs, since they already exist, often concealed, within established organisations. It is, however, about discovering them, showing them that manifesting intrapreneurial behaviour is safe, and supporting and empowering them. Instead of engaging in an academic discussion of corporate culture, let us display a number of practical activities that can be undertaken to facilitate a digital intrapreneurial culture within an established organisation and give hints on how one can succeed using those activities: applies to the entire chart (see Table 2).

Table 2 Activities within established organisations supporting digital intrapreneurs

Activity	Implementation suggestions
A vision of the organisation's overall destination and goals	Create and communicate a vision that inspires digital intrapreneurs, let them know about any challenges faced by the company, and invite them to come up with digital solutions to those challenges. (Also, keep the door opened for divergent ideas with small budgets, as these may find their application in future.)
Active involvement of management and senior leaders	Keep talking about digital intrapreneurship. Watch for and celebrate successes. Reward managers when their people innovate, so that they do not steal their subordinates' ideas. The H in Help looks like II in the pdf. Help intrapreneurs develop the leadership skills they need. Build a culture that supports intrapreneurship
Support of digital intrapreneurs	Intrapreneurs are as essential to corporate innovation as entrepreneurs are to start-ups. Cherish your intrapreneurs. Build a culture that supports them. Build an intrapreneurial career path. Support implementation by digital intrapreneurs, not just idea inventors and early development specialists. Allow employees time to think and test their ideas
Support of cross-functional teams	Digital innovations often involve changes in the way things are done in the non-digital parts of the organisation. Support cross-functional teams by assigning team members from non-digital sectors of the firm. Give the teams time and the ability to make decisions together. Support the team's decisions instead of letting the decisions propel into turf battles between the functional seniors
Creating a sponsorship culture	Management sponsors who select, coach, protect, and allocate resources to intrapreneurs are the primary support for intrapreneurship. Innovation is more about this relationship than any other process Train and expect managers to sponsor one or more intrapreneurs whose character and innovations they trust

(continued)

Table 2 (continued)

Activity	Implementation suggestions
	Make sponsoring innovations a central part of the corporate culture and every manager's job. Include sponsoring success into management KPIs
Widespread intrapreneurial training	Deliver a short course for everyone to know what intrapreneurs are, what they do, how they act, and the ways they can be effective. Let managers know about the support that intrapreneurs require and how the managers can provide it. Managers, executives, and individual contributors can all attend the same two-hour online training lesson, so they all get to see how the intrapreneurial system works
Idea exposition	Organise both the online and the in-person idea expositions that help intrapreneurs to share their ideas and attract others to join their intrapreneurial teams. Management can also tour the expositions and look for intrapreneurs to support. Expositions can result in the creation of teams that attend innovation accelerators
Use of digital innovation accelerators	Accelerators are action-learning workshops that help teams of intrapreneurs develop their ideas, increase the quality of their teamwork, and bring out their intrapreneurial spirit. They can be full time or part time; however, part time is more common in the corporate world. The workshops usually range from six weeks to six months or longer
Delegation of discretionary time and resources to the lower levels	Today, computers can monitor every minute of an employee's time and document their use of resources. This hinders the casual experimentation, daydreaming, and 'fooling around' that often serve as the source of innovative breakthroughs
	Allocate discretionary budget and time to the lower levels: to individual contributors, their supervisors, and lower-middle management. Offer employees the option of spending some of their time and modest supplies on side projects of their own choice. Let supervisors and lower-level managers sponsor the early stages of innovation from their own discretionary budgets
'Sandbox' or 'seed' fund allocation	Seed funds are pools of discretionary finances reserved for early-stage innovations. Create small local seed funds distributed throughout the company. Seed funds create a route circumventing the bosses who block employees' early-stage ideas. It is not just a monetary grant; it is an implied permission to work on an idea
	Let any employee apply and, if they succeed, give them some time off to pursue the idea. Seed funds generally only award small grants for a rapid prototype test or similar purposes

(continued)

Table 2 (continued)

Activity	Implementation suggestions
Boundary crossing	Since digital innovation tends to cross boundaries, digital intrapreneurs need permission to cross these boundaries and be encouraged when they ask for help. This cultural attribute of generosity can serve as a powerful booster of digital intrapreneurship. Reward cross-boundary generousity. Ask intrapreneurs, 'Who helped you in the early days?'
Anticipation and failure acceptance	Do not punish intrapreneurs for any original mistakes committed in pursuit of an innovation. The best pathway to success involves making your mistakes faster and cheaper and then quickly learning and adapting. Have meaningful 'good try' recognitions and rewards. Make sure these rewards are viewed to be positive by the recipients. Venture capitalists like to invest in entrepreneurs who have experienced both failure and success
Articulation of a digital culture	Establish your company's digital vision. Talk about the kinds of things you hope that digital innovation can do for the company. Say that you need help to make those things happen
Small beginnings	Corporate strategists often discount the value of small innovations, sometimes saying that they are of no significance. However, small beginnings often pave the way for the arrival of major opportunities and serve as places from which to explore and learn about a new possibility. The lean start-up model prescribes a rapid testing of 'minimal viable products'. Value small beginnings and intrapreneurial investigations of new possibilities using small budgets. Then, if particular ideas start to work, spend more on scaling up what already shows signs of success
Assessing the innovation output	Assess the innovation output of each business unit. Create a scale of how impactful an innovation is with many points allocated for disruptive innovations. Give units overall innovation scores, and hold them accountable accordingly Let multiple units get credit for the same innovation if they all made substantial contributions. This promotes cross-organisational cooperation
Developing new ways of organising work	Keep a backbone of hierarchical control, but release innovative structures from it. Create a convenient platform for a network of self-organising and self-directing intrapreneurial teams that function in the chain of command. Let empowered intrapreneurs select their team members from those who wish to join. Let the teams stay together and take on projects cooperatively. When possible, let intrapreneurs be responsible for the execution of their own initiatives

(continued)

Table 2 (continued)

Activity	Implementation suggestions
Giving rewards	Build an intrapreneurial career path that provides successful intrapreneurs with good salaries, sufficient time, and budget to innovate again. Freedom to work on their next ideas is the most effective reward for intrapreneurial success. Reward the whole team, not just the leader. Do not rank people within innovation teams; an 'all boats rise and fall together' reward system promotes teamwork

4   Examples from Practice/Case Studies

The case studies below describe the practical ways of increasing digital intrapreneurship.

Case study 1: Finding, surfacing, and empowering digital intrapreneurs at Deutsche Bahn

The Deutsche Bahn (DB) Group is one of the world's leading mobility and logistics companies. DB employs some 331,600 people around the globe, including roughly 205,000 in Germany (Deutsche Bahn 2019). The company trusts in the innovative potential of its employees and believes in unleashing their potential to develop corporate start-ups. Its programme motivates the employees to work on solutions for problems that they have identified. The programme enables teams of employees and external team members to test and develop their ideas, potentially creating an internal business unit or even and external company. Within the structured programme, desirability, feasibility, and viability are considered to be the focal points.

The corporate entrepreneurship department with its intrapreneurship programme, 'DB Intrapreneurs', is part of the Chief Digital Officer unit of the DB Group. Launched in March 2017, DB Intrapreneurs is a fundamental part of DB's digital and cultural transformation strategy across all its divisions. As internal incubator, the purpose of the programme is to offer all employees the possibility to develop their own digital business models and products in an empowering environment. Moreover, participants gain entrepreneurial mindset and skills.

DB designs and operates the transportation networks of the future. Through the integrated operation of the traffic and railway infrastructures as well as the economically and ecologically beneficial connection of all modes of transport, the company focusses on the transportation of both people and goods. In 2017, it held a market share of 67%. DB's target is to increase punctuality, quality, and reliability of its transport. Its efforts are primarily focussed on improving the travelling experience of its customers, significantly enhancing punctuality, and providing more reliable information to the customers throughout their travels. DB aims to bring more traffic to its environmentally friendly rail network, particularly its freight transport.

Digital transformation and new technologies are changing DB's core business. The company uses digital technologies and methods to offer attractive new products and strengthen those that it already has. Whether on the train, at a station, or on the railway, digital functioning enables it to enhance or simplify its services. In doing so, it increases its capacity and remains environmentally friendly. A 20% increase in the capacity of its rail networks has been achieved through the use of a standardised digital system. DB's aim here is to achieve improved performance, better service quality, greater efficiency, and more growth on the rail network. A part of DB's corporate strategy, the 'digital railway' also promotes the reputation of Germany as an industrially developed country.

DB Intrapreneurs is open to all employees (intrapreneurship track) and business units (called 'co-creation') from all parts of the organisation, from maintenance and engineering to sales. This means that employees can either apply to participate in teams and independently of their own business unit to solve validation problems and create new or improved products and services. Work in teams is always required. Operating independently of their own business unit means that teams pursue their intrapreneurial endeavours in addition to their regular jobs—with the exception of 4 workshop days which they attend within their working hours.

In both cases, DB Intrapreneurs has developed, tested, and iterated a clearly structured innovation process across four stages that see employees first become intrapreneurs and then entrepreneurs:

1. Engagement Phase: Prior to joining a batch, participants can attend several workshop and community events to generate ideas and prepare themselves before joining a batch of teams. A batch includes several teams entering the design phase together to test their problems and solutions. Every employee (and, in some cases, everyone) can participate in these events or get feedback about their ideas. The goal of this pre-batch phase is to encourage potential intrapreneurs and generate new ideas as well as lower the entrance barriers and enable a soft entry into the programme.

2. Design Phase: Across three workshops, intrapreneurs identify and validate a problem as well as develop an initial concept of a solution. During this phase, the participants must pass several gates and, if necessary, restructure and change their team to proceed. The highlight of the design phase is the Pitch Day at the end, where teams pitch before entering the build phase, which is the section where they receive funding and intensive coaching. During this phase, each team is supported by a dedicated method coach.

3. Build Phase: Over the course of three or four months, intrapreneurship teams assess how their products will behave on the market. This includes user research, service design, requirement engineering, development of first low-fidelity prototypes, business case modelling, and the drafting of a go-to-market strategy.

4. Grow Phase: If teams are able to achieve a proof of concept at the end of the build phase, they can develop their own corporate start-up. This encompasses everything, from ramping up of the organisational structures to developing and selling goods, although the process is highly unique and features the evolution of the team outside of the programme.

Workshops during the engage and design phases mostly take place in Frankfurt (Main), with some located in Berlin. Both the build and the grow phases take place in Berlin, in the Digital Base of DB. Within intrapreneurial projects, where teams of employees are allowed to work on their own ideas, such groups are supported by a venture architect. The intrapreneurial team members act as facilitators, project managers, and challengers, giving the group an overall direction. They encourage employees to set up their own corporate start-ups. Coaching includes design thinking, lean start-up, scrum, value proposition design, business modelling, and product management models.

In co-creation projects, where participants co-create together with a business unit, their role transforms. Instead of coaching employees, the members themselves serve as the co-project leads of the ventures and therefore accept partial responsibility for the success or failure of their ideas. Responsibilities are shared with the project lead of the business unit(s). The major asset of the intrapreneurial programme lies in its ability to cultivate specific capabilities of the employees and grant access to both intra- and extra-organisational networks.

There are four different exit options for intrapreneurial ventures:

1. Scaling-up of the corporate start-up inside a newly established business unit
2. Founding of a new subsidiary company wholly owned by DB where the intrapreneurs get chief experience officer positions (e.g. Chief Executive Officer or Chief Operations Officer)
3. Incorporating their business within a given business unit
4. Founding of a new start-up by the intrapreneurs (upon which they leave DB).

There is also another exit—the positive failure. The value of failing is promoted early in the innovation process. For example, if teams find out that there is no problem–solution fit, it is still a valuable and positive experience and a valuable learning tool for both the employees and DB itself. Intrapreneurs learn a large amount in a very short time, which is unprecedented among corporate training opportunities.

A number of teams have been coached and worked on a large variety of ideas. When it comes to idea generation, DB Intrapreneurs encourages participants to think globally. DB believes that ideas should be globally scalable. Thus, successful teams continue to work hand-in-hand with all business units across several silos, since DB considers that interdisciplinarity and co-creation are keys to successful innovation taking place within a corporation.

Like so many other units and companies, DB's business units are facing digital transformation. DB Intrapreneurs believes in using and empowering the innovation potential of its employees to create the digital future of DB. Therefore, DB Intrapreneurs strives to achieve three important goals:

1. Inspire employees and business units to drive innovation by understanding digital transformation.
2. Equip employees with entrepreneurial competencies and skills to foster an innovative and entrepreneurial mindset among them.
3. Support employees as a business unit to validate and build corporate start-ups.

The following case has been prepared in cooperation with DB. We would like to thank Florian Messner-Schmitt, Head of DB Intrapreneurs, and his team for their useful insights.

Case study 2: Obtaining digital talent through acquisition

Many companies, knowing that their current culture can make hiring or developing digital talent that they need difficult, have switched their talent acquisition strategy to buying digitally competent companies, not so much for their operations but rather for their talent.

When one of us was an angel capitalist, we made a disappointing investment wherein the entrepreneur we had invested in had a great engineering team and a good idea that was just too big for the funds and the time that were allocated for it. This entrepreneur was destined to fail. When we invested, we imagined that we could get him to begin earning revenue with a lesser product that moved in the direction of the grand dream before his funds ran out.

Unfortunately, the CEO was unwilling to work on anything other than the full version of his original dream with all its features. Once we learned that he would never change his plan, we wrote the investment off as a failure. However, we then received an offer to sell this company; this gave us a twofold return on our total investment in the firm. The buyer had no interest in the CEO's vision or the CEO himself: the purchasing company was just buying his engineering team. Acquisition is one way to get the talent you need, and considering the team and the company that bought out the firm, I suspect it worked out well for them.

Nevertheless, simply acquiring the digital talent you need is not sufficient since you also have to keep it. In another example, one of us was running a small internet security company with a strong intrapreneurial culture and superstar engineers. To give an example of what it took to keep such talent, consider the following scenario. One of my engineers insisted on this arrangement: even though I was his boss, I could only talk to him when he arrived in the morning or left at night; under no circumstances was I allowed to interrupt his thinking between those two times. Anything I had to say to him could wait until the end of the day. He did not need or want to be managed. Once he agreed to take on a project—which was a matter of persuasion rather than command—he would take it from there.

Subsequently, we were acquired by a publicly traded company at a price of several million dollars per employee. One of the reasons we received such a high price per engineer (and a ridiculous multiplication of revenue) was that, within a week, my non-communicative engineer solved a problem the acquiring company had been working on for six months without any results. Our superstar engineer delivered a working code that got the firm's algorithm to operate to a critical In ternet security standard. Getting engineers with that level of talent can be very valuable, and we were lucky to have had several of them.

As mentioned above, acquiring talent is not enough; you must then keep it. The acquiring company had a very different management style from ours. Their command-and-control style assumed that top management knew what was best. Two years later, none of our former employees were still working for the company that acquired us.

I heard about some of what happened when they tried their hierarchical management style on our self-motivated talent. It was difficult to get my former employees to stay long enough to cash in their stock options.

Not knowing how to nurture and support talented digital intrapreneurs makes the strategy of acquiring them useless. The same principle applies to home-grown talent. Jobs of routine processing are gradually disappearing, either becoming taken over by smart machines or getting shipped to low-wage countries. Increasingly, the jobs that remain require creativity and care—things at which people are still better than machines.

Creativity and care must come from the inside. You cannot force someone to care for their customers, since the motivation to care about them must come from the inside. As Daniel Pink points out, the same applies to creativity (TED 2009). Even rewards reduce creativity by shifting the mind from what psychologists call intrinsic forms of motivation to the extrinsic ones. The emerging kinds of work in the twenty-first century is similar to intrapreneuring and is thus in need of managers who behave more like sponsors than conventional supervisors.

This is particularly true of digital employees. Coders, for example, must make instantaneous decisions on how to structure their code and what path to take to achieve the desired result. To do that well, they must focus entirely on their intrinsic motivation and enter a state of flow. They need to be motivated by their own values instead of worrying about what their boss might think. That is why my superstar engineer asked me not to talk to him during the day. He wanted to be motivated by caring about what he was doing, by his own sense of what was right and elegant, and not by the opinion of his boss who did not really understand his code. That is a lesson for anyone who must manage digital talent. If you have hired the right people, they know more about what they are doing than you do. If you respect that, they might stay.

Case study 3: The School for Intrapreneurs™

This case is about an online action-learning programme at a global company, which, in one year, produced a ten-to-one return and provided a proof of concept that digital intrapreneurship could yield rapid profitable results. Quick wins and the proof of a digital intrapreneurship concept is an important early step in building a culture suitable for digital intrapreneurs. Our client's goals for the programme were as follows:

1. To increase profitable innovation in the IT sector
2. To bring out and implement bottom-up ideas
3. To develop business acumen in IT
4. To build teamwork skills in IT.

The digital intrapreneurship programme was entirely online. The design brief stipulated that no person in the programme could be required to meet with any other participant in person, which was good, since the intrapreneurial teams formed in the programme were often intercontinental, with, for example, one member based in Brazil, another one in the USA, another one in Germany, and another one in Singapore. The School for Intrapreneurs™ included four major parts:

1. *The Doorway to Intrapreneuring,* a three-hour online course covering the basics of intrapreneurship. All of the 1100 IT professionals of the company, including the head of IT, were required to complete it.

   a. For managers, the course showed how to recognise and manage intrapreneurs, with case studies illustrating the role of managers as sponsors.
   b. For intrapreneurs, the course inspired participants to bring out their intrapreneurial spirit and declare their desire to implement their ideas. It taught them more effective ways to move their ideas forward within a bureaucratic organisation.
   c. For the company, the course located potential intrapreneurs, so that management could support the development of their ideas.

   The Doorway was run entirely by software. The company placed the software on a server and gave the participants a login. From that point on, the workshop ran without any faculty involvement. Still, the course had a 95% approval rating from graduates, which is unusually high for a required course. This illustrates the power of software and digital innovation to reduce the marginal cost of training an additional participant to almost nothing. It also illustrates more generally how digital innovation can greatly reduce operating costs.

2. *The Idea Expo* was an online forum where participants could post their ideas and get feedback from the other participants and managers. It served as an online meeting ground for forming teams around some of the ideas.

   The next step for intrapreneurs after the Expo was to move their ideas forward and attend an accelerator that would help them build a business plan for their ideas, teach them about being an intrapreneur, and build high-performance teams. At the end, it gave them an opportunity to present their ideas to senior management.

To get into the accelerator, the participants had to form teams of three or more members, who would all be committed to the same idea. This was done to encourage team leaders to assemble their groups and form ideas that were good enough to attract at least two more members. Twelve teams progressed to the accelerator.

3. *The Pathway to Intrapreneuring* was a quick six-week online accelerator for the innovation projects coming out of the Idea Expo. Each week, there were brief lectures and readings on an aspect of intrapreneuring and building a business plan. The teams received weekly assignments and were required to write reports about how their group would address certain strategic issues.

   The assignment types included elevator pitches, building and testing rapid prototypes, managing the organisational immune system, designing and testing a business model, checking up on teamwork, developing marketing and sales plans, fostering the intrapreneurial spirit, making financial projections, and so on. At the end of each week, the teams presented their work online to two other teams, who then gave them feedback using structured forms. At the end of the accelerator, teams presented their results to a panel of executives. Six teams were funded to continue working on their innovations.

4. *The Journey to Intrapreneuring* was a twelve-week implementation workshop for the teams that were funded to develop their ideas.

As mentioned above, within the first year after the participants graduated from the *Journey to Intrapreneuring*, the programme had already produced a ten-to-one return on all the resources invested in it. Because of word of mouth, thirty more teams applied for the next round of the accelerator.

What was learned from this experiment?

1. There is a vast reservoir of creative talent and intrapreneurial spirit buried in IT departments.
2. If you demonstrate that there is a safe pathway to bring one's ideas to management and get support for them, many digital intrapreneurs will appear. There are far potential digital intrapreneurs buried in most organisations than their management suspects.
3. The means for releasing digital innovations can itself be a digital innovation. The first two courses were delivered almost entirely as pieces of software running on a server.
4. Training intrapreneurial employees who had already been developing their innovative ideas in their own time, rather than starting with generating ideas, produced much faster and better results. This was achieved by selecting teams that had already chosen their ideas. There are generally more than enough good ideas distributed among the employee population at all times.
5. Implementation, and not idea generation, is the rate-limiting step in the innovation process. Many successful ideas had been around for quite some time but had previously lacked a pathway to implementation.

6. A process with several short cycles of rapid prototyping and business model testing and a weekly cycle of presentations caused the plans to evolve rapidly and produced better results than could have been achieved through a series of functional tests that only put it all together at the very end.
7. Implementation support after management had funded the projects was seen as quite helpful.
8. Future versions of this programme should involve more training for the management sponsors of intrapreneurial projects, perhaps as a feature of an existing high-potential leadership development programme.

5 Conclusion and Implications

Intrapreneurship remains an important way to capture the creativity, excitement, and energy of entrepreneurship within a larger firm. It can let employees pursue their ideas with more resources and less personal risk than they would have if they had gone out on their own. For companies, resilient responses to a rapidly changing world require the input of a large number of intrapreneurs. The digital transformation of our society is creating challenges for existing firms and many opportunities for both entrepreneurs and intrapreneurs.

As the COVID-19 pandemic has shown, the world does not always progress smoothly. Occasionally, we face startling discontinuities. These sudden changes favour resilient firms. A firm's capacity for responding to big changes resiliently resides in the intrapreneurs who are empowered to make all the innovations necessary for the company to adapt and create a culture to support them. However, this capacity cannot be developed overnight. It requires changing managerial attitudes and building employee trust in the fact that passionately standing up for an idea is not career-threatening (Hughes et al. 2018; Mustafa et al. 2018). Fortunately, even though building that intrapreneurial muscle is very helpful in the times of sudden change, it is also profitable in the more regular periods of the twenty-first century where rapid changes and disruption, per Moore's law, are normal. Preparation for what Nassim Taleb calls 'black swans', like the coronavirus outbreak, requires many of the same steps and cultural attributes that are necessary for giving a financially informed and beneficial response to these disruptive times.

The contemporary digital world requires the development of habits of intrapreneurial innovation. It requires complete managerial acceptance of the fact that digital transformation is inevitable and that one has the choice of either being the disruptor or being disrupted.

This is not a time to cut back on innovative capacity, but rather, it is a time to expand it so that organisations can thrive in a rapidly changing world. This can be done to generate extra profits in the short term and develop the appropriate organisational systems and culture changes to face the unknown shocks that the future will surely bring.

The benefits of digital intrapreneurship are not just in the new products, but also in the better ways for delivering existing goods and services, often with fast results. Digital intrapreneurship creates opportunities for more intrapreneurs than the traditional applications of intrapreneurship. There are many more high-ROI opportunities to improve the way things are done with digital technology today than there were opportunities to develop new products and services in the industrial era.

This chapter has identified several ways in which companies can surface, choose, and empower digital intrapreneurs. It has shown how the exploitation of new business opportunities can be speeded up. It has also identified more effective ways of operating digitally in the non-digital business areas. Moreover, it has displayed that digital intrapreneurship is needed to reduce the risk of being disrupted by entrepreneurial competition.

We have shown several ways in which companies can bring out and support potential digital intrapreneurs. We have provided the means for distinguishing true digital intrapreneurs who can be trusted from the 'promoters' who are talented speakers that lack the character to persistently work hard and persevere through the difficult times until the eventual implementation of their ideas.

Creating systems and a corporate culture for supporting digital intrapreneurs is a core competency for the times of rapid digital transformation. Some ways of doing that include a clear organisational vision for digitalisation, valuing, training, and supporting intrapreneurs, more managers serving as effective sponsors, empowered cross-functional teams, high risk tolerance, failure analysis, increased cross-organisational generosity, acceptance of small beginnings, discretionary resources allocated to lower levels, and less reliance on command-and-control managerial styles and more on inspiration, coaching, and vision.

Acknowledgements With much appreciation, we acknowledge the many constructive contributions of Ivaylo Tenev, a Hanze International Business student, to this chapter. You have repeatedly pointed out what was not working and what could have worked better. Thank you for your great input, commitment, and passion that have improved the quality of this work. We wish you all the best in your future and are looking forward to seeing your own intrapreneurial spirit in action.

References

Corbett, A. (2018). The myth of the intrapreneur. *Harvard Business Review*. https://hbr.org//06/the-myth-of-the-intrapreneur.

Covin, J. G., Rigtering, J. P. C., Hughes, M., Kraus, S., Cheng, C. F., & Bouncken, R. (2020). Individual and team entrepreneurial orientation: Scale development and configurations for success. *Journal of Business Research* (in press).

Day, D. (1994). Raising radicals: Different processes for championing innovative corporate ventures. *Organization Science, 5*(2), 148–172. www.jstor.org/stable/2635012.

Deloitte Digital. (2015). *Five insights into intrapreneurship*. Deloitte. https://www2.deloitte.com/content/dam/Deloitte/de/Documents/technology/Intrapreneurship_Whitepaper_English.pdf.

Deprez, J. (2019). *Stimulating intrapreneurship—A transnational exploration*. European Social Fund. https://ec.europa.eu/esf/transnationality/TPI-83.

Deutsche Bahn. (2019). *Integrated report*. https://ibir.deutschebahn.com/2019/en/home.

Forbes Technology Council. (2019, September 11). 15 smart ways machine learning helps businesses and entrepreneurs. *Forbes*. https://www.forbes.com/sites/forbestechcouncil//09/11/15-smart-ways-machine-learning-helps-businesses-and-entrepreneurs/#61e54cbd7f67.

Garud, R., & Van De Ven, A. H. (1992). An empirical evaluation of the internal corporate venturing process. *Strategic Management Journal, 13*(S1), 93–109. https://doi.org/10.1002/smj.4250131008.

Gawke, J. C., Gorgievski, M. J., & Bakker, A. B. (2017). Employee intrapreneurship and work engagement: A latent change score approach. *Journal of Vocational Behaviour, 100*, 88–100.

Hayton, J. C., & Kelley, D. J. (2006). A competency-based framework for promoting corporate entrepreneurship. *Human Resource Management, 45*(3), 407–427.

Hughes, M., Rigtering, J. P. C., Covin, J. G., Bouncken, R. B., & Kraus, S. (2018). Innovative behaviour, trust and perceived workplace performance. *British Journal of Management, 29*(4), 750–768.

Kraus, S., Breier, M., Jones, P., & Hughes, M. (2019). Individual entrepreneurial orientation and intrapreneurship in the public sector. *International Entrepreneurship and Management Journal, 15*, 1247–1268.

Lewis-Kraus, G. (2016, December 14). The great A.I. awakening. *New York Times*. https://www.nytimes.com/2016/12/14/magazine/the-great-ai-awakening.html.

Lumpkin, G. T., Cogliser, C. C., & Schneider, D. R. (2009). Understanding and measuring autonomy: An entrepreneurial orientation perspective. *Entrepreneurship Theory and Practice, 33*(1), 47–69. https://doi.org/10.1111/j.1540-6520.2008.00280.x.

Marvel, M. R., Griffin, A., Hebda, J., & Vojak, B. (2007). Examining the technical corporate entrepreneurs' motivation: Voices from the field. *Entrepreneurship Theory and Practice, 31*(5), 753–768. https://doi.org/10.1111/j.1540-6520.2007.00198.x.

Monsen, E., Patzelt, H., & Saxton, T. (2010). Beyond simple utility: Incentive design and trade-offs for corporate employee-entrepreneurs. *Entrepreneurship Theory and Practice, 34*(1), 105–130. https://doi.org/10.1111/j.1540-6520.2009.00314.x.

Mustafa, M., Gavin, F., & Hughes, M. (2018). Contextual determinants of employee entrepreneurial behavior in support of corporate entrepreneurship: A systematic review and research agenda. *Journal of Enterprising Culture, 26*(3), 285–326.

Newman, D. (2019). 5 ways AI is transforming the customer experience. *Forbes*. https://www.forbes.com/sites/danielnewman/2019/04/16/5-ways-ai-is-transforming-the-customer-experience/#72b43c53465a.

OECD. (n.d.). *Blockchain for SMEs and entrepreneurs*. https://www.oecd.org/cfe/smes/blockchainsmes.htm.

Phaneuf, A. (2020, February 19). Top IoT business opportunities, benefits, and uses in 2020. *Business Insider*. https://www.businessinsider.com/iot-business-opportunities-models?international=true&r=US&IR=T.

Pinchot, G. (1985). *Intrapreneuring: Why you don't have to leave the corporation to become an entrepreneur*. New York: Harper & Row.

Pinchot, G., & Pellman, R. (1999). *Intrapreneuring in action: A handbook for business innovation*. San Francisco, CA: Berrett-Koehler Publishers.

Rachinger, M., Rauter, R., Müller, C., Vorraber, W., & Schirgi, E. (2018). Digitalization and its influence on business model innovation. *Journal of Manufacturing Technology Management*. https://doi.org/10.1108/jmtm-01-2018-0020.

Rauch, A., Wiklund, J., Lumpkin, G., & Frese, M. (2009). Entrepreneurial orientation and business performance: An assessment of past research and suggestions for the future. *Entrepreneurship Theory and Practice, 33*(3), 761–787. https://journals.sagepub.com/doi/abs/10.1111/j.1540-6520.2009.00308.x.

Reibenspiess, V., Drechsler, K., Eckhardt, A., & Wagner, H. (2020). Tapping into the wealth of employees' ideas: Design principles for a digital intrapreneurship platform. *Information & Management*, 103287. https://doi.org/10.1016/j.im.2020.103287.

Rossi, R. (2019, July 3). Understanding millennials' and technology's role in the workforce, part one. *Forbes*. https://www.forbes.com/sites/forbesbusinessdevelopmentcouncil//07/03/understanding-millennials-and-technologys-role-in-the-workforce-part-one/#318e5e820344.

Soltanifar, M. (2016). Corporate entrepreneurship and triple helix. In R. Segers (Ed.), *Multinational management*. Berlin: Springer.

TED. (2009). Pink, D. (2009). *The puzzle of motivation*. Retrieved from https://www.youtube.com/watch?v=rrkrvAUbU9Y.

Van Welsum, D. (2016). Enabling digital entrepreneurs. *World Bank Group*. http://pubdocsworldbank.org/en/354261452529895321/WDR16-BP-Enabling-digial-entrepreneurs-DWELSUM.pdf.

Zahra, S., Neubaum, D., & Hayton, J. (2016). *Handbook of research on corporate entrepreneurship*. Edward Elgar Publishing. https://doi.org/10.4337/9781785368738.

Global Environments and Digital Entrepreneurship

Pursuing International Opportunities in a Digitally Enabled World

Di Song and Aiqi Wu

Abstract

Digitalization has tremendously challenged how international opportunities are created and captured. Inspired by researches in the field of both entrepreneurship and international business, this study provides a comprehensive framework toward the impact of digital technologies (DTs) on opportunity pursuit in foreign markets. We identify two perspectives of DTs, i.e., DTs as 'driving force' and DTs as 'disrupting force,' which characterize DTs as a catalyst of experiential knowledge acquisition, and as a factor altering the relative significance of experiential knowledge to opportunity pursuit, respectively. By bridging these two perspectives with the notion of market-specific knowledge and general knowledge within internationalization process theory, some arguments with regard to what specific influences DTs play on international opportunity pursuit are further introduced. We hope this study can potentially offer some nuances to both practitioners as well as the research in the interaction of digitalization and international opportunity.

1 The Relevance of Digitalization to International Opportunity Pursuit

It is undeniable that an increasing number of firms pursue international opportunities in an era of digitalization. In China, for instance, some leading Internet companies such as Alibaba and Tencent make a profit in the global market. Meanwhile, thousands of manufacturing firms are also dependent upon emerging

D. Song (✉) · A. Wu
Zhejiang University, Hangzhou, China
e-mail: songdi@zju.edu.cn

M. Soltanifar et al. (eds.), *Digital Entrepreneurship*, Future of Business and Finance,
https://doi.org/10.1007/978-3-030-53914-6_13

265

technologies to reach their customers outside the domestic country. Indeed, digitalization has challenged the traditional way of entrepreneurial opportunity pursuit. With the help of new technologies, firms can better access to online communities, incubators, and accelerators (Glavas et al. 2019), connect with foreign experts (Sigfusson and Chetty 2013), involve in international activities without abundant investments (Coviello et al. 2017), and so forth. In essence, thanks to this trend, international opportunities are becoming more available for the firm than the past.

However, as international business scholars have repeatedly underscored, practitioners should consider the unique characteristics of foreign markets while conducting cross-border activities. Despite profound effects made by emerging technologies, some differences between the home country and host countries still exist. Cultural distance between each economy cannot be ignored, and protectionism in trade and finance has been strong in recent years. So, how international opportunities could be created and captured in a digitally enabled world? In this article, we aim at offering a conceptual framework by drawing on the research in entrepreneurship, international business, and digitalization to understand this important issue.

2 Background

In order to systematically examine the impact of digitalization on international opportunity pursuit, we first review some associated arguments in literature of both entrepreneurship and international business.[1]

Opportunity is a central concept for international entrepreneurship research in particular (Reuber et al. 2018; Oviatt and McDougall 2005) and for entrepreneurship research in general (Shane and Venkataraman 2000; Kirzner 1997). Following Eckhardt and Shane (2003: 336), entrepreneurial opportunities can be defined as 'situations in which new goods, services, raw materials, markets and organizing methods can be introduced through the formation of new means, ends, or means-ends relationships.' As such, cross-border opportunities are assumed to objectively exist, and necessary knowledge is needed to pursue them (Foss et al. 2013; Shane 2000). Though indispensable role of opportunities has been underscored, some scholars were skeptical about studying entrepreneurial activities exclusively based on the notion of opportunity (e.g., Davidsson 2015; Alvarez and Barney 2014). Empirical researches indicated that entrepreneurial opportunities cannot be automatically translated into superior performance (Wu et al. 2019; Hmieleski and Baron 2008). To interpret the results, we should be aware that Shane and Venkataraman (2000) have already insightfully proposed that there are

---

[1]We argue that to examine these two streams of literature is reasonable. It should be noted that, while the concept of 'opportunity' is central for international entrepreneurship (Oviatt and McDougall 2005; Mainela et al. 2014), international entrepreneurship was regarded to be the intersection of IB and entrepreneurship (McDougall and Oviatt 2000). Further, the analysis of 'opportunity' is a common theme for these two research areas (Reuber et al. 2018).

opportunity costs to take advantage of an entrepreneurial opportunity. Opportunities are always intertwined with the environment where pursued (Young et al. 2018). Therefore, it is of vital importance to jointly consider opportunities and the context where opportunities are created and captured.

To pursue opportunities in the global context, firms are supposed to decide on where, when, and how to create and capture them (Knight and Liesch 2016). To answer these important but related questions, internationalization process (IP) theory (Johanson and Vahlne 1977) provides us a useful guideline on which the current analysis could potentially rely. Inspired by a series of case studies primarily conducted by researchers of Uppsala University in 1970s, IP theory has become one of the prominent perspectives in mainstream international business literature.[2] As IP theory maintains, firms expand abroad in an incremental way because they should accumulate enough experiential knowledge so as to mitigate perceived risks that prevents them from effectively creating and capturing opportunities in foreign markets (Johanson and Vahlne 1977).

In specific, Eriksson et al. (1997) divided international business knowledge into three conceptually distinctive forms, i.e., foreign business knowledge, foreign institutional knowledge, and internationalization knowledge. The first two types of experiential knowledge, highlighting market-related knowledge (i.e., knowledge about customers, suppliers, and competitors) and non-market-related knowledge (i.e., knowledge about rules, norms, government policy and regulations), respectively, were termed as market-specific, whereas internationalization knowledge, termed as general knowledge, is associated with organizational structures for international operations, and thus characterized as those universal and versatile across different markets. The explanation for different types of knowledge is summarized in Table 1. The accumulation of either type of knowledge can be potentially beneficial for lowering perceived risks in foreign markets (Fletcher and Harris 2012; Hilmersson and Jansson 2012; Zhou 2007; Blomstermo et al. 2004), and thus encourage the firm to create and capture opportunities in the market.

Although IP theory was originally developed to study the internationalization pathway of well-established firms, subsequent researches have observed IP theory is also applied to new ventures (Lopez et al. 2009; Hashai 2011). In theory, new ventures are faced with great difficulties to pursue international opportunities, as they have relatively little experiential knowledge and should invest existing resources to create routines adapting to businesses in foreign markets (Sapienza et al. 2006). As such, their activities are largely constrained by insufficient knowledge introduced by IP theory as well. Therefore, it is theoretically and practically meaningful to investigate how cross-border opportunities can be pursued in a digitally enabled world by focusing on elements of IP theory.

---

[2]Some evidence can support this argument. Johanson and Vahlne (1977), as the founding article for IP theory, have been on the list of 'Most cited articles' of *Journal of International Business Studies* (JIBS) (https://www.palgrave.com/gp/journal/41267/volumes-issues/most-cited-articles). As of Dec 13, 2019, this article has been cited for 14,099 times based on Google Scholar. Furthermore, Johanson and Vahlne (2009), as a revised version of the IP theory, have been awarded JIBS decade award in 2019.

Table 1 A brief description of each dimension of experiential knowledge

	Knowledge type	Definition
Market-specific knowledge	Foreign business knowledge	Experiential knowledge about clients, the market, and competitors
	Foreign institutional knowledge	Experiential knowledge about government, institutional framework, rules, norms, and values
General knowledge	Internationalization knowledge	Experiential knowledge about the firm's capability and resources to engage in international operation

Source Adapted from Eriksson et al. (1997)

3 Conceptual Model: The Influence of Digital Technologies to International Opportunity Pursuit

According to Tilson et al. (2010: 749), digitalization refers to 'a sociotechnical process of applying digitizing techniques to broader social and institutional contexts that render digital technologies infrastructural.' Building on this notion, the understanding of international opportunity pursuit in a digitally enabled world can be enriched by an exploration of how digital technologies (DTs) impact on the way of pursuit previously characterized (Autio et al. 2018). The concept of DTs has been broadly defined, and in line with Nambisan (2017), DTs consist of many elements which could be classified into three groups, i.e., digital artifacts (components and functions of product or service), digital platform (architectures hosting complementary offerings), and digital infrastructure (broad digital tools and systems). These three groups of DTs are intertwined with each other and collectively influence entrepreneurial activities (Nambisan 2017).

As aforementioned arguments indicate, either market-specific knowledge or general knowledge is closely associated with international opportunity pursuit. To investigate the impact of DTs, we are now interested in how DTs affect the original relationship. We propose that DTs could be viewed as either one of the two roles, which were labeled as 'driving force' and 'disrupting force,' respectively. The explanation for these two roles is summarized in Table 2. When DTs are viewed as 'driving force,' it is assumed to be a facilitator for acquiring market-specific knowledge and general knowledge. DTs are positioned as the antecedents of knowledge acquisition. In this sense, DTs can be understood as a 'reformer.' By contrast, when DTs are viewed as 'disrupting force,' we regard DTs as the factor that alters the relative importance of experiential knowledge to international opportunity creation and capture. The effect of market-specific knowledge and general knowledge on opportunity pursuit is moderated by DTs. In this sense, DT can be paraphrased as a 'revolutionary.'

To better facilitate the interpretation of two distinctive roles of DTs, we integrate DTs with the model based on IP theory, which is illustrated in Fig. 1. It is shown that DTs can be either viewed as the antecedent of the experiential knowledge or as the contingent effect of the knowledge–opportunity relationship.

Below, we discuss two perspectives of DTs in detail.

Table 2 Two perspectives of DTs

	DTs as 'driving force'	DTs as 'disrupting force'
Assumption	DTs facilitating experiential knowledge acquisition	DTs changing the relative importance of experiential knowledge
Role	The explanatory variable for knowledge acquisition	The moderating effect for the influence of knowledge
Metaphor	DTs seen as a 'reformer'	DT seen as a 'revolutionary'

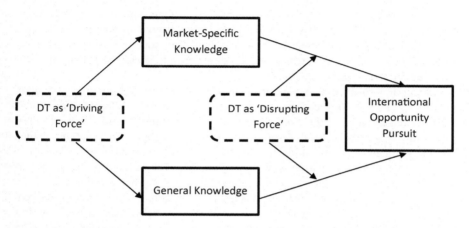

Fig. 1 Influence of Digital technologies (DTs) on international opportunity pursuit

3.1 DTs as 'Driving Force'

The perspective that views DTs as 'disrupting force' underlines the way of experiential knowledge accumulation is influenced by these emerging technologies (Coviello et al. 2017). According to this perspective, both market-specific knowledge and general knowledge could be increasingly accumulated with the help of technologies. Thus, DTs would be indirectly associated with international opportunity pursuit, and the relationship is mediated by experiential knowledge. We discuss how this can happen as follows.

Market-specific knowledge
Enhanced knowledge availability owing to DTs application can directly bring information about the potential market, allowing them to identify which markets are attractive for them (Coviello et al. 2017). Generally speaking, accelerated market-specific knowledge accumulation is gathering an increasing amount of knowledge about other players. By investigating a group of Indian IT firms, Paul and Gupta (2014) claimed psychic distance is largely reduced in recent years, as a consequence of learning from virtual community through online interactions.

Similarly, Pergelova et al. (2019) found that DTs encourage the improvement of international marketing intelligence that would potentially enhance export propensity of SMEs.

In specific, information accessibility about customer's need can be brought by DTs (Autio 2017; Okazaki and Taylor 2013; Yamin and Sinkovics 2006). Many digitally enabled facilities, including e-mails (Prasad et al. 2001), customer databases (Yamin and Sinkovics 2006), and social networks (Alarcón-del-Amo et al. 2018), would encourage international business activities by offering valuable information about customers for the focal firm. In an empirical test concerning internationalization of online apps, Shaheer and Li (2020) observed that between-country distance still has an impact on foreign expansion of these digitalized product providers. However, barriers resulted from distances can be lowered by proactive online user-friendly strategies, including social sharing strategy and virtual community strategy, which encourage the firm to acquire necessary updated information about foreign customers.

Except for customers, experiential knowledge about collaborators and competitors in target market can also be accessed as a result of DTs (Mathews et al. 2016). Gregory et al. (2007) observed from their empirical results that exporters gain knowledge about local distribution channels by using the Internet, which would optimize communication and distribution for these exporters. Overall, a greater amount of information with regard to other players can encourage opportunity creation and capture in specific market by lowering perceived risks.

In particular, compared with established counterparts, we conjecture new venturing firms can benefit more from DTs which help overcome liability of newness (Gabrielsson and Gabrielsson 2011). As novices, new ventures usually deal with the situation where other players are overwhelmingly strangers (Stinchcombe 1965). Such risks would be mitigated through the application of DTs. Glavas et al. (2019) found owners of small firms can utilize digital platforms to collect information about potentially available customers, supporting the notion that DTs might be meaningful for new ventures in this sense.

Foreign market knowledge can not only be accumulated by firm-level business network, but also be derived from entrepreneur's social network through DTs. Especially, social networking platform has transformed the process of information transfer. For instance, by examining how international entrepreneurs accumulate foreign market knowledge on LinkedIn, Sigfusson and Chetty (2013) found some entrepreneurs directly look for reliable foreign partners who possibly provide confidential information.

Furthermore, foreign institutional knowledge, both informal and formal one, can also be acquired with the help of DTs. Knowledge about informal institutions, such as customary habits in a certain market, may be explored and thus fulfilled in a more sophisticated way with the help of DTs (Yamin and Sinkovics 2006; Prasad et al. 2001). The application of DTs allows the reduction of the cost associated with information search beyond the national border. In terms of formal institution, Glavas et al. (2019) found that a more nuanced understanding of regulatory institutions can be encouraged by participating digital platforms, which is achieved via multiple search engines and multimedia resources.

General knowledge

While market-specific knowledge acquisition process can be largely influenced by the application of DTs, it is also true for the acquisition of general knowledge. In particular, the application of DTs may potentially reshape the organizations. Building on a cultural perspective, Mathews et al. (2016) proposed that the emerging technology platforms force the firms to be exposed in a global context, which encourages decision-makers to be more adaptable to and more willing to learn and appreciate about other cultures. This leads to the firm to take a more international identity, and force the firm to know better about how to internationalize. In a similar vein, Autio (2017) underscored that DTs enable a more an adaptable organizational structure for foreign operations, by enhancing the flexibility of the structure to better orchestrate resources and try varied value propositions in foreign markets.

Contingent factor: knowledge acquisition heterogeneity

Although DTs would encourage the firm to accumulate knowledge, it should be highlighted that not all firms can equally benefit (Alarcón-del-Amo et al. 2018; Sigfusson and Chetty 2013; Moen et al. 2008). There are at least three reasons leading to this heterogeneity. Firstly, the amount of knowledge can be accumulated and can be dependent on for what purposes DTs are utilized. To illustrate this notion, it is observed that applying DTs for information search or relationship development can contribute to knowledge accumulation, while using DTs only for sales activity would not bring significantly more knowledge (Moen et al. 2008).

Secondly, knowledge acquisition is also influenced by firm's degree of commitment to technologies. Some past studies support this argument (Glavas et al. 2019; Sigfusson and Chetty 2013). For instance, Alarcón-del-Amo et al. (2018) investigated the role of social media application among export-oriented companies, concluding that only those with high commitment of social media can obtain sufficient market knowledge by communicating better with their customers. In a similar vein, Sigfusson and Chetty (2013) indicated knowledge accumulation could be more effective when proactive activities are taken in the cyberspace.

Thirdly, firm characteristics could also explain the source of this heterogeneity. For example, Moen et al. (2008) argued that firm age could be a significant contextual factor for foreign market acquisition enabled by DTs. To maintain the extant customer relationships, older exporters may be less motivated to use DTs as a way to accumulate new market knowledge. This position is consistent with an organizational learning argument in international entrepreneurship literature which highlights younger organizations are in general more flexible for knowledge acquisition than older ones (Autio et al. 2000; Sapienza et al. 2006). Furthermore, Glavas et al. (2019) observed the internationalization stage and pattern, including the phase of internationalization (i.e., pre, early, later) and the pace of internationalization (i.e., incremental, non-incremental), can also be influential for types of acquired knowledge.

3.2 DTs as 'Disrupting Force'

Another perspective understands DTs as 'disrupting force,' which highlights that functions or affordances of DTs can reshape business activities (Autio et al. 2018; Nambisan 2017; Yoo et al. 2012). The internationalization pattern has fundamentally changed (Coviello et al. 2017; Alcácer et al. 2016; Autio 2017), and the relative significance of experiential knowledge with regard to international opportunity creation and capture is assumed altered, no matter experiential knowledge still plays a role or not. From this perspective, by changing the way of business activities are conducted in the international marketplace, these emerging technologies allow the pursuit of cross-border opportunities less constrained by the amount of knowledge firms possess as suggested by traditional IP theory. Sometimes, DTs also introduce new forms of knowledge and capabilities that firms require in order to pursue international opportunities.

Market-specific knowledge
With regard to market-specific knowledge, there are at least two reasons why it is not equally significant for opportunity pursuit in a digitally enabled world. In the first place, customers get involved in value creation with the help of DTs (e.g., Chandra and Coviello 2010; Amit and Han 2017). Chen et al. (2019) emphasized the relative importance of knowledge for market entry is decreased from the point view of network effects. For app developers, foreign market penetration is sometimes not purposeful since borderless user networks can help to channel to product information to consumers in other countries. Inspired by the research, we conjecture that international opportunity creation and capture is realized largely owing to demand-side network effects rather than purely supply-side knowledge accumulation.

In the second place, alternative governance approach is available enabled by DTs (Coviello et al. 2017; Alcácer et al. 2016). Different from 'prudent' within-firm administrative control documented in early IP theory literature (Johanson and Vahlne 1977), the prevalence of emerging technologies allows the firm to loosely separate each unit of the whole firm in different countries. As such, firms are able to conduct business abroad easily by cooperating with foreign contractors instead of controlling tangible assets. Therefore, enabled by DTs, ownership advantage is not only associated with the proprietary rights over certain resources, but also in connection with the ability to orchestrate resources across the globe (Alcácer et al. 2016). In an empirical investigation of international technology alliances, Lew et al. (2016) observed that fragmentation of product modular permits alliance with the internalization of partner's specialized knowledge, and the relationship between alliance partners is less susceptible to the cultural distance. It demonstrates that comparatively loose collaboration is likely among the international technology alliances setting. Overall, this suggests that with the help of DTs, even if not familiar with the specific market, the firm is also likely to international opportunities.

General knowledge

Digitalization further revolutionizes international business by lowering the relative significance of general knowledge to international opportunity pursuit. Foremost, DTs enable internationalizing firms, especially exporting manufacturers, to sell their products through cross-border electronic commerce channels or platforms by simply clicking the mouse (Tolstoy et al. 2016). This has fundamentally changed the original international business manner since little foreign business knowledge is already adequate for some activities.

At the same time, some other kinds of general knowledge, however, are becoming increasingly indispensable for opportunity pursuit in the international marketplace. For example, Reuber and Fischer (2011) identified three types of online resources, i.e., online reputation, online technological capabilities, and online brand communities, can be instrumental for new venture internationalization. The general knowledge about how to encourage the firm to accumulate these online resources can buffer the risks of doing business abroad (Fischer and Reuber 2014), and facilitate opportunity pursuit. In sum, whereas some part of general knowledge highlighted by traditional IP theory would be less significant for internationalization, successful international opportunity creation and capture requires other additional knowledge.

4 Examples from Practice

EXHIBIT 1: Selling ambers to China with the help of WeChat (DTs as 'driving force')

It is undeniable that China is an attractive market for enterprises around the world. However, it has also been widely acknowledged that doing business in China would not be easy (Ahlstrom et al. 2000), as cultural distance is usually so pronounced and China's institutional development is not as fast as its economic development.

In order to accumulate sufficient knowledge to create and capture opportunities in China, many foreign firms rely on survey reports and business networks. Meanwhile, other entrepreneurs and managers realize that DTs can also play an essential role. For example, WeChat, as one of China's most frequently used social networking platform, has attracted an increasing number of users outside China. Released in 2011, WeChat penetrates into Chinese people's daily life thoroughly and has become a main channel for information exchange of works and social activities in China. It is reported that the number of monthly active users (MAU) has reached 1112 million during the first quarter of year 2019 (Tencent 2019).

Many Chinese tourists find it quite cost-efficient to buy ambers while visiting Poland. In line with the tradition, some Chinese ladies have a habit of wearing the amber necklace to show the elegance. For Polish sellers, accessing to Chinese market means a lot to their amber business. However, without sophisticated knowledge about the market, it seems to be a challenge for Polish businessmen to pursue profitable opportunities in the Far East. The idea of 'beauty' is historically and socially constructed, and the values are sharply different between the East Europe and China. Moreover, as small-sized independent business, Polish sellers have comparatively limited understanding with regard to China's markets and institutions.

To address these shortcomings, a group of amber sellers in Warsaw registered their accounts on WeChat platform after observing a wealth of Chinese clients sent pictures of ambers and sought for advice from their friends through WeChat while visiting the store. By adding WeChat friends with Chinese buyers, these Polish amber sellers repeatedly interact with their customers, delivering ambers through the international express transportation. Some of them even established the WeChat group which allows to introduce new products and simultaneously receive valuable feedbacks from Chinese customers. Because these WeChat groups are generally open for everyone, consumers on occasions invite their friends and relatives who are also interested in Polish amber to the group chat. Through the use of WeChat, amber sellers expand the market scope by accumulating knowledge about the potential customers, which partially overcome the liability of foreignness (Zaheer 1995). Furthermore, these Polish businessmen acquire first-handed knowledge about their customers and competitors in China, as well as significant information regarding values and habits through informal interactions, which allows them to design their products more popular among Chinese customers than before.

EXHIBIT 2: Internationalization at home (DTs as 'disrupting force')

China is one of the major exporters of world's production. Although a growing number of factories have been built in Africa and South Asia over the course of last decade, many companies on the planet still expect for the long-term procurement of a large number of commodities from China. 'Made in China' is perceived to be attractive if price and quality are jointly considered. To explore reliable partners, foreign businessmen used to come to some Chinese cities such as Yiwu[3] and Guangzhou, in order to search for necessary information about the market and the institution. Managers and entrepreneurs in these cities are scarcely trained to speak foreign languages, and therefore, it spends foreign businessmen a lot of efforts to discuss and make the deal. Furthermore, institutional voids in many places of China also discourage foreign companies from collaborating with Chinese counterparts. As a consequence, even though a wide range of valuable opportunities could be possibly explored in China, many foreign companies are blind to them because of possessing insufficient knowledge about China.

In recent years, with the development of digitally enabled trading and payment platforms, there is an alternative approach to do business with suppliers in China. The exchange of commodities is realized through the cross-border e-commerce platforms such as AliExpress (www.aliexpress.com) and DHgate (www.dhgate. com). These digital platforms connect thousands of Chinese small businesses to the

---

[3]Yiwu, a county-level city situated in the center of Zhejiang Province of China, has been widely regarded as 'world's largest wholesale market for daily commodities.' Thousands of village and township enterprises that manufacture various kinds of daily commodities are established in Yiwu.

customers worldwide, and registration on the platform is required for both sellers and buyers before transactions take place. The platform can be accessible for individuals anywhere in the world only if there is an Internet connection. Geographical distance is no longer a big deal.

In DHgate, for example, the platform owner provides the Web page with a number of language versions. Chinese suppliers are allowed to display their products online on a Chinese-language Web page, while foreign buyers could visit the Web site and choose what they expect to order on an English-language Web page. Furthermore, instead of requiring adequate knowledge about Chinese suppliers, foreign businessmen are able to make their decisions by browsing the reviews and the ratings from other buyers. Online payment system endorsed by the platform could also go against the potential opportunistic behaviors, which make the exchange process smooth.

These functions facilitate foreign companies with very limited experiential knowledge about China's institutions and markets to touch the profit opportunities in this market. It illustrates that, with little experiential knowledge, international opportunity creation and capture is also likely when DTs are properly applied.

5 Discussion and Conclusion

5.1 Contribution

By examining how international opportunities are created and captured in a digitally enabled world, the current study would have some implications for both theory and practice. In terms of theory, we provide some nuances to understand the intersection of digitalization and international opportunity pursuit by identifying what roles DTs play in firm internationalization. Drawing on insights from the research in entrepreneurship, IB, and digitalization, we develop a conceptual framework and classify the role of DTs into two distinctive perspectives, namely DTs as 'driving force' and DTs as 'disrupting force.' Whereas DTs as 'driving force' can be interpreted as a catalyst for acquisition of market-specific knowledge and general knowledge, DTs as 'disrupting force' maintain these emerging technologies alter the relative significance of experiential knowledge to international opportunity creation and capture by both lowering the importance for some and putting forward new requirements for the firm. While digitalization and its impact on international opportunity pursuit has been a hot topic (Eduardsen and Ivang 2016), the current study would guide the research in this stream by structuring the role of DTs.

In terms of practical implications, our analysis along with the introduction of the conceptual model might offer some insights for practitioners regarding how DTs have transformed the way that cross-border opportunities are pursued. Primarily, practitioners can learn from this study about the way the accumulation of knowledge conducive for successful opportunity pursuit is facilitated in a digitally enabled world. By demonstrating how firm's stock of both market-specific knowledge and general knowledge can be enriched by using DTs, practitioners are provided some guides with respect to the mitigation of risks associated with international activities.

Secondly, as highlighted by the perspective of DTs as 'disrupting force,' the significance of experiential knowledge may not be as important as how traditional IP theory predicts, because of DTs could disrupt the way how international opportunities are pursued. Thanks to these emerging technologies, new approaches to pursue opportunities are introduced, which allow experiential knowledge less indispensable, but requires some additional knowledge intertwined with the trend of digitalization. By doing this, we offer some insights for practitioners which help to think about their design of business models.

Thirdly, our study also encourages practitioners to scrutinize how to utilize DTs in their activities. Though firms are nowadays extensively exposed to DTs, not all firms can equally benefit from digitalization. In practice, only a portion of firms could successfully take advantage of these technologies and achieve a favorable outcome. Our study emphasizes a few factors that theoretically explain the heterogeneity of the amount of knowledge that firms can accumulate with the help of DTs, which offers some illustrations allowing practitioners to consider how DTs matter for their businesses.

5.2 Future Research

Though some insights are provided by this study, we should acknowledge that we have only done initial works and several avenues can be considered for future researches. Primarily, since we are not ambitious to cover all arguments in this article, some very important insights in the literature may be overlooked. Furthermore, as IP theory, a prevalent approach among international business research, was the basis for developing our conceptual model, readers should be aware that IP theory itself relies on strong assumptions of the firm and the entrepreneur. In general, entrepreneurs are assumed to be basically risk-aversive (Welch et al. 2016), and thus experiential knowledge becomes the cornerstone for international opportunity creation and capture. In this sense, firms largely prefer long-term profits and organic growth. Although some entrepreneurs are quite conservative in practice, other ones are not concern much with international business knowledge (Zahra 2005) and hope to pursue opportunities across the globe as rapidly as possible. Thus, while our conceptual model may be useful, the heterogeneity of both the firm and the entrepreneur is ought to be taken into considerations.

Relatedly, in line with IP theory which fundamentally claims some necessary knowledge should be possessed for effective international activities (Welch et al. 2016; Sapienza et al. 2006), we take a more objective stance which assumes opportunities are 'out there.' However, in entrepreneurship literature, another prevalent stance (i.e., creation perspective) denies this assumption and maintains entrepreneurial opportunities can also be created (Alvarez and Barney 2007). Although a thorough discussion of these two contrasting views is beyond the scope of this study, we should admit that the topic of international opportunity pursuit in a digitally enabled world can possibly be better understood if this creation perspective would be addressed.

A further investigation of DTs as 'driving force' and DTs as 'disrupting force' is another area which can be explored. For instance, scholars can continue to investigate and identify other factors regarding how these emerging technologies facilitate knowledge accumulation and change the relative importance of experiential knowledge. Moreover, as we discuss these two perspectives separately, some efforts can be taken to examine whether and how some specific categories of DTs can play both roles at the same time.

In addition, while our primary focus in this chapter is to explore how to acquire knowledge and how knowledge matters for opportunity pursuit in a digitally enabled world, knowledge perspective studies have also underlined the importance of knowledge application (Alavi and Leidner 2001; Grant 1996). The ability of knowledge application by nature varies across the firms (Wu et al. 2019), and therefore should be considered as the boundary condition for the conceptual framework proposed here.

5.3 Conclusion

There is no doubt that digitalization has challenged the traditional pattern of doing business including opportunity pursuit in foreign markets. Past studies have offered many valuable insights with regard to international opportunity creation and capture in a digitally enabled world, but they are generally scattered and fragmented. Drawing on entrepreneurship literature and IB literature, this study develops a conceptual framework and adds knowledge to the literature by categorizing the role of DTs into two perspectives, that is, DTs as 'driving force' and DTs as 'disrupting force.' We hope this framework is instrumental and could potentially serve as a guide for future researches.

Acknowledgements The authors wish to thank Mat Hughes, Mariusz Soltanifar and Lutz Göcke for their valuable feedback on the early version of the manuscript, and participants at the Colearning seminar for their comments. This work is supported by the National Natural Science Foundation of China (Grant No. 71572174, 71972166) and the National Social Science Foundation of China (Grant No. 17ZDA050).

References

Ahlstrom, D., Bruton, G. D., & Lui, S. S. (2000). Navigating China's changing economy: Strategies for private firms. *Business Horizons, 43*(1), 5–15.

Alarcón-del-Amo, M., Rialp-Criado, A., & Rialp-Criado, J. (2018). Examining the impact of managerial involvement with social media on exporting firm performance. *International Business Review, 27*(2), 355–366.

Alavi, M., & Leidner, D. E. (2001). Knowledge management and knowledge management systems: Conceptual foundations and research issues. *MIS Quarterly, 25*(1), 107–136.

Alcácer, J., Cantwell, J., & Piscitello, L. (2016). Internationalization in the information age: A new era for places, firms, and international business networks? *Journal of International Business Studies, 47*(5), 499–512.

Alvarez, S. A., & Barney, J. B. (2007). Discovery and creation: Alternative theories of entrepreneurial action. *Strategic Entrepreneurship Journal, 1*(1–2), 11–26.

Alvarez, S. A., & Barney, J. B. (2014). Entrepreneurial opportunities and poverty alleviation. *Entrepreneurship Theory and Practice, 38*(1), 159–184.

Amit, R., & Han, X. (2017). Value creation through novel resource configurations in a digitally enabled world. *Strategic Entrepreneurship Journal, 11*(3), 228–242.

Autio, E. (2017). Strategic entrepreneurial internationalization: A normative framework. *Strategic Entrepreneurship Journal, 11*(3), 211–227.

Autio, E., Nambisan, S., Thomas, L. D., & Wright, M. (2018). Digital affordances, spatial affordances, and the genesis of entrepreneurial ecosystems. *Strategic Entrepreneurship Journal, 12*(1), 72–95.

Autio, E., Sapienza, H. J., & Almeida, J. G. (2000). Effects of age at entry, knowledge intensity, and imitability on international growth. *Academy of Management Journal, 43*(5), 909–924.

Blomstermo, A., Eriksson, K., Lindstrand, A., & Sharma, D. D. (2004). The perceived usefulness of network experiential knowledge in the internationalizing firm. *Journal of International Management, 10*(3), 355–373.

Chandra, Y., & Coviello, N. (2010). Broadening the concept of international entrepreneurship: 'Consumers as international entrepreneurs'. *Journal of World Business, 45*(3), 228–236.

Chen, L., Shaheer, N., Yi, J., & Li, S. (2019). The international penetration of ibusiness firms: Network effects, liabilities of outsidership and country clout. *Journal of International Business Studies, 50*(2), 172–192.

Coviello, N., Kano, L., & Liesch, P. W. (2017). Adapting the Uppsala model to a modern world: Macro-context and microfoundations. *Journal of International Business Studies, 48*(9), 1151–1164.

Davidsson, P. (2015). Entrepreneurial opportunities and the entrepreneurship nexus: A re-conceptualization. *Journal of Business Venturing, 30*(5), 674–695.

Eckhardt, J. T., & Shane, S. A. (2003). Opportunities and entrepreneurship. *Journal of Management, 29*(3), 333–349.

Eduardsen, J. S., & Ivang, R. (2016). Internet-enabled internationalisation: A review of the empirical literature and a research agenda. *International Journal of Business Environment, 8*(2), 152–175.

Eriksson, K., Johanson, J., Majkgård, A., & Sharma, D. D. (1997). Experiential knowledge and cost in the internationalization process. *Journal of International Business Studies, 28*(2), 337–360.

Fischer, E., & Reuber, A. R. (2014). Online entrepreneurial communication: Mitigating uncertainty and increasing differentiation via Twitter. *Journal of Business Venturing, 29*(4), 565–583.

Fletcher, M., & Harris, S. (2012). Knowledge acquisition for the internationalization of the smaller firm: Content and sources. *International Business Review, 21*(4), 631–647.

Foss, N. J., Lyngsie, J., & Zahra, S. A. (2013). The role of external knowledge sources and organizational design in the process of opportunity exploitation. *Strategic Management Journal, 34*(12), 1453–1471.

Gabrielsson, M., & Gabrielsson, P. (2011). Internet-based sales channel strategies of born global firms. *International Business Review, 20*(1), 88–99.

Glavas, C., Mathews, S., & Russell-Bennett, R. (2019). Knowledge acquisition via internet-enabled platforms: Examining incrementally and non-incrementally internationalizing SMEs. *International Marketing Review, 36*(1), 74–107.

Grant, R. M. (1996). Toward a knowledge-based theory of the firm. *Strategic Management Journal, 17*(S2), 109–122.

Gregory, G., Karavdic, M., & Zou, S. (2007). The effects of e-commerce drivers on export marketing strategy. *Journal of International Marketing, 15*(2), 30–57.

Hashai, N. (2011). Sequencing the expansion of geographic scope and foreign operations by "born global" firms. *Journal of International Business Studies, 42*(8), 995–1015.

Hilmersson, M., & Jansson, H. (2012). Reducing uncertainty in the emerging market entry process: On the relationship among international experiential knowledge, institutional distance, and uncertainty. *Journal of International Marketing, 20*(4), 96–110.

Hmieleski, K. M., & Baron, R. A. (2008). Regulatory focus and new venture performance: A study of entrepreneurial opportunity exploitation under conditions of risk versus uncertainty. *Strategic Entrepreneurship Journal, 2*(4), 285–299.

Johanson, J., & Vahlne, J. E. (1977). The internationalization process of the firm—A model of knowledge development and increasing foreign market commitments. *Journal of International Business Studies, 8*(1), 23–32.

Johanson, J., & Vahlne, J. E. (2009). The Uppsala internationalization process model revisited: From liability of foreignness to liability of outsidership. *Journal of International Business Studies, 40*(9), 1411–1431.

Kirzner, I. M. (1997). Entrepreneurial discovery and the competitive market process: An Austrian approach. *Journal of Economic Literature, 35*(1), 60–85.

Knight, G. A., & Liesch, P. W. (2016). Internationalization: From incremental to born global. *Journal of World Business, 51*(1), 93–102.

Lew, Y. K., Sinkovics, R. R., Yamin, M., & Khan, Z. (2016). Trans-specialization understanding in international technology alliances: The influence of cultural distance. *Journal of International Business Studies, 47*(5), 577–594.

Lopez, L. E., Kundu, S. K., & Ciravegna, L. (2009). Born global or born regional? Evidence from an exploratory study in the Costa Rican software industry. *Journal of International Business Studies, 40*(7), 1228–1238.

Mainela, T., Puhakka, V., & Servais, P. (2014). The concept of international opportunity in international entrepreneurship: A review and a research agenda. *International Journal of Management Reviews, 16*(1), 105–129.

Mathews, S., Bianchi, C., Perks, K. J., Healy, M., & Wickramasekera, R. (2016). Internet marketing capabilities and international market growth. *International Business Review, 25*(4), 820–830.

McDougall, P. P., & Oviatt, B. M. (2000). International entrepreneurship: The intersection of two research paths. *Academy of Management Journal, 43*(5), 902–906.

Moen, Ø., Madsen, T. K., & Aspelund, A. (2008). The importance of the internet in international business-to-business markets. *International Marketing Review, 25*(5), 487–503.

Nambisan, S. (2017). Digital entrepreneurship: Toward a digital technology perspective of entrepreneurship. *Entrepreneurship Theory and Practice, 41*(6), 1029–1055.

Okazaki, S., & Taylor, C. R. (2013). Social media and international advertising: Theoretical challenges and future directions. *International Marketing Review, 30*(1), 56–71.

Oviatt, B. M., & McDougall, P. P. (2005). Defining international entrepreneurship and modeling the speed of internationalization. *Entrepreneurship Theory and Practice, 29*(5), 537–553.

Paul, J., & Gupta, P. (2014). Process and intensity of internationalization of IT firms—Evidence from India. *International Business Review, 23*(3), 594–603.

Pergelova, A., Manolova, T., Simeonova-Ganeva, R., & Yordanova, D. (2019). Democratizing entrepreneurship? Digital technologies and the internationalization of female-led SMEs. *Journal of Small Business Management, 57*(1), 14–39.

Prasad, V. K., Ramamurthy, K., & Naidu, G. M. (2001). The influence of internet–marketing integration on marketing competencies and export performance. *Journal of International Marketing, 9*(4), 82–110.

Reuber, A. R., & Fischer, E. (2011). International entrepreneurship in internet-enabled markets. *Journal of Business Venturing, 26*(6), 660–679.

Reuber, A. R., Knight, G. A., Liesch, P. W., & Zhou, L. (2018). International entrepreneurship: The pursuit of entrepreneurial opportunities across national borders. *Journal of International Business Studies, 49*(4), 395–406.

Sapienza, H. J., Autio, E., George, G., & Zahra, S. A. (2006). A capabilities perspective on the effects of early internationalization on firm survival and growth. *Academy of Management Review, 31*(4), 914–933.

Shaheer, N. A., & Li, S. (2020). The CAGE around cyberspace? How digital innovations internationalize in a virtual world. *Journal of Business Venturing, 35*(1), 105892.

Shane, S. (2000). Prior knowledge and the discovery of entrepreneurial opportunities. *Organization Science, 11*(4), 448–469.

Shane, S., & Venkataraman, S. (2000). The promise of entrepreneurship as a field of research. *Academy of Management Review, 25*(1), 217–226.

Sigfusson, T., & Chetty, S. (2013). Building international entrepreneurial virtual networks in cyberspace. *Journal of World Business, 48*(2), 260–270.

Stinchcombe, A. L. (1965). Social structure and organizations. In J. G. March (Ed.), *Handbook of organizations* (pp. 142–193). Chicago, IL: Rand McNally.

Tencent. (2019). Tencent announces 2019 first quarter results. https://www.tencent.com/en-us/articles/8003551557911908.pdf. Retrieved July 15, 2019.

Tilson, D., Lyytinen, K., & Sørensen, C. (2010). Digital infrastructures: The missing IS research agenda. *Information Systems Research, 21*(4), 748–759.

Tolstoy, D., Jonsson, A., & Sharma, D. D. (2016). The influence of a retail firm's geographic scope of operations on its international online sales. *International Journal of Electronic Commerce, 20*(3), 293–318.

Welch, C., Nummela, N., & Liesch, P. (2016). The internationalization process model revisited: An agenda for future research. *Management International Review, 56*(6), 783–804.

Wu, A., Song, D., & Yang, Y. (2019). Untangling the effects of entrepreneurial opportunity on the performance of peasant entrepreneurship: The moderating roles of entrepreneurial effort and regional poverty level. *Entrepreneurship and Regional Development.* https://doi.org/10.1080/08985626.2019.1640479.

Yamin, M., & Sinkovics, R. R. (2006). Online internationalisation, psychic distance reduction and the virtuality trap. *International Business Review, 15*(4), 339–360.

Yoo, Y., Boland, R. J., Jr., Lyytinen, K., & Majchrzak, A. (2012). Organizing for innovation in the digitized world. *Organization Science, 23*(5), 1398–1408.

Young, S. L., Welter, C., & Conger, M. (2018). Stability vs. flexibility: The effect of regulatory institutions on opportunity type. *Journal of International Business Studies, 49*(4), 407–441.

Zaheer, S. (1995). Overcoming the liability of foreignness. *Academy of Management Journal, 38*(2), 341–363.

Zahra, S. A. (2005). A theory of international new ventures: A decade of research. *Journal of International Business Studies, 36*(1), 20–28.

Zhou, L. (2007). The effects of entrepreneurial proclivity and foreign market knowledge on early internationalization. *Journal of World Business, 42*(3), 281–293.

Challenges and Opportunities for Digital Entrepreneurship in Developing Countries

Georges Samara and Jessica Terzian

Abstract

This chapter explores the obstacles and opportunities that digital entrepreneurs encounter when they operate in developing countries. Drawing on the varieties of institutional systems framework and on three interviews (two digital entrepreneurs and one consultant), this chapter chalks out the idiosyncratic challenges and opportunities for digital entrepreneurs operating in a developing context. Our findings indicate that digital entrepreneurs face a weak institutional infrastructure and an environment characterized by corruption that obstructs their operations. These weak infrastructures result in the inaccessibility to necessary start-up funds, the lack of policies and regulations that protect and support e-commerce, a weak digital infrastructure, and to a deficiency in digitally competent and experienced labor capital. At the same time, our findings indicate some opportunities stemming from the unique institutional setting in which digital entrepreneurs operate. The opportunities translate into the use of family wealth as a source of start-up financial capital, the use of personal connections as a source of social and human capital, and the rising education on digital entrepreneurship and its benefits. We conclude with some suggestions to improve the current institutional infrastructure for digital entrepreneurs in developing countries.

G. Samara (✉)
University of Sharjah, College of Business Administration, Sharjah, UAE
e-mail: gs50@aub.edu.lb

G. Samara · J. Terzian
American University of Beirut, Olayan School of Business, Beirut, Lebanon

© The Author(s) 2021
M. Soltanifar et al. (eds.), *Digital Entrepreneurship*, Future of Business and Finance,
https://doi.org/10.1007/978-3-030-53914-6_14

1   Introduction

Digital entrepreneurship is defined as the identification and pursuit of entrepreneurial opportunities based on the creation of digital artifacts, platforms, and infrastructures that provide services through technology (Schmidt 2011; Giones and Brem 2017). Digital artifacts consist of applications or any media component that offers a specific function to users (Ekbia 2009; Kallinikos et al. 2013). A digital platform is the collection of a common and shared set of digital artifacts that provide entrepreneurs with a venue for production, marketing, and distribution processes. In the last two decades, digital entrepreneurship has opened new venues for entrepreneurial activities and has transformed the nature of uncertainty inherent to entrepreneurial processes and outcomes (Nambisan 2017).

In a world witnessing continuous and radical innovations, entrepreneurs are developing business ideas that capitalize on the power of technology. Entrepreneurs have the opportunity to offer new products and services to consumers through social media platforms and to use artificial intelligence to measure their impact and reach. Nevertheless, there exists a heterogeneity among digital businesses, where some are entirely tech-dependent (e.g., Web design, e-retail), while others just use digitalization in their marketing and communications operations. In this chapter, we focus on entirely tech-dependent businesses.

Digital start-ups have very low barriers to entry, more porous and fluid boundaries, and do not require costly equipment (Nambisan 2017).They are characterized by flexibility of products or services such that there is no fixed product or service whose features remain constant; rather, product offerings, features, and scope continuously evolve and expand. Furthermore, digital entrepreneurship is no longer restricted to privileged capitalists. Digital entrepreneurs gain access to funding and resources through venture capitalists, crowdfunding, and bank loans (Lingelbach et al. 2005). Crowdsourcing and crowdfunding systems allow the engagement of collective stakeholders in the venture creation process, where entrepreneurs interact with customers, who provide ideas, and with investors that provide capital.

Despite the many opportunities that digital entrepreneurship brings, it has also been linked with high risks of failure given the continuous and radical technological innovations and since the role of employees in a digital business is ambiguous and undefined. Thus, the absence of a mechanic or solid structure makes it more difficult for entrepreneurs to decide and plan a clear operations process that assigns each employee to its corresponding tasks (Brem et al. 2016). The previously mentioned challenges and opportunities for digital entrepreneurship are well documented in the literature, which was mostly conducted in developed countries. However, knowledge about the obstacles and opportunities for digital entrepreneurship in developing countries remains scant.

While the above-mentioned challenges and opportunities to digital entrepreneurship can persist when entrepreneurs operate in developing countries, the embeddedness of a country in a developing context adds additional complexities that may create new challenges and opportunities not usually encountered in developed countries. Indeed, developing contexts are hurdled by the presence of institutional voids, with the state having low law enforcement capacity, and low generalized trust within society (Fainshmidt et al. 2018). Nonetheless, these countries are also characterized by supportive family capital (Samara and Arenas 2017) and sometimes by a high level of knowledge capital, both of which can create opportunities for digital entrepreneurship.

In the following, we first draw on institutional theory and the varieties of institutional systems to describe how the developing context can affect the obstacles and opportunities for digital entrepreneurs. Then, we present two case studies coupled with one expert opinion, to have a closer look on whether the theorized obstacles and opportunities fit with the reality that digital entrepreneurs encounter when they operate in a developing country. While the empirical setting is contextualized in Lebanon; we argue that the findings can be extrapolated to other developing contexts that are subject to similar institutional pressures.

2 Institutional Theory and Varieties of Institutional Systems: Digital Entrepreneurship in a Developing Country Context

Institutional theory emphasizes the role of the social context in determining the behavior of individuals and organizations (Meyer and Rowan 1977). According to institutional theory, individuals are embedded within a social context that has distinct formal and informal rules and regulations that determine the cognitive process through which individuals and organizations behave (Fainshmidt et al. 2018).

In this context, the Varieties of Institutional Systems (VIS) framework has been advanced to discuss how institutions in developing countries may have a distinct impact on individuals and organizations. According to the VIS, there are five institutional dimensions affecting organizational behavior in developing countries: The role of the state, the role of financial markets, the role of corporate governance institutions, the role of human capital, and the role of social capital (Fainshmidt et al. 2018).

In developing countries, institutional voids, which are defined as weak or non-functioning market mechanisms (Jamali et al. 2017), are prevalent. While these voids may lead to challenges for digital entrepreneurs, they may also open new opportunities. Using the VIS framework, we are able to classify institutional voids into internal factors, which are part of the microenvironment, and external factors, which are part of the macroenvironment. Internal institutional voids of a business include human capital, along with their exposure to Information and Communications Technology (ICT) skills, their level of technological awareness, skill-based resources, financial status, and perceptions and attitudes toward society and technology. The external institutional voids include the government, market e-readiness, level of trust in society, the financial market, and supporting industries e-readiness. Despite the fact that successful online venturing is associated with the preceding institutional elements, material and cultural aspects are essential to account for when discussing the success or failure of digital entrepreneurial ventures.

The State can influence the economy through its direct and indirect interventions in the market and through the diverse forms that it can take. There can be four types of states: Welfare State, Developmental State, Predatory State, and Regulatory State, the latter being the state that sets and enforces rules, thus, directly impacting economic activity (Rosecrance 1996). A Welfare State protects and promotes the economic and social well-being of its citizens, mainly through the redistribution of wealth by the government. A Developmental State is concerned with engaging in advancement of business sectors through industrial policy. Within a Developmental State, governments strategically monitor and facilitate business activities, transactions, and e-commerce initiatives. If present, developmental states can develop the needed infrastructure for the reinforcement of new digital infrastructure, hence allowing the necessary ground for entrepreneurs to share and edit their ideas in the process of opportunity formation. Unfortunately, development states are scarcely found in developing countries, where, more often than not, Predatory States dominate. Predatory States are known for being elites who monopolize power through the absence of market competition, discreet decision-making processes, and weak institutional supportive capacity, which translates into the state withdrawing from any activity that can assist, organize, and protect digital entrepreneurs (Carney and Witt 2012).

Financial markets are the core element of institutional systems as they acquire and distribute capital (Davis and Marquis 2005). Developing economies tend to substitute financial markets with internal capital markets, usually based on accumulated family wealth (Steier 2009); thus, limiting in part the growth of businesses as family capital is considered as a finite source. Financial resources play a critical role in digital entrepreneurship. Although online ventures require lower entry cost than that of a bricks-and-mortar business, the lack of financial resources present significant challenges, specifically to those belonging to lower socioeconomic social class.

Corporate governance relates to how companies are managed and controlled. In developing countries, ownership of companies is concentrated within family hands (Khanna and Palepu 1997; La Porta et al. 2000). Therefore, ownership concentration affects how owners, labor, and management interact with each other. The existence of wealthy families is well noted in the Middle East, Latin America, Northern Africa, and Asia. This leads to family firms being the predominant organizational, and the latter are not only concerned with financial returns, but also with nonfinancial benefits such as the family's identity and preserving family influence in the business (Samara and Paul 2019). In the context of digital entrepreneurship, corporate governance levels refer to the extent to which top management leads and organizes a business through incorporating technology and e-commerce ideas and projects. Creating a family supportive environment in which corporate digital entrepreneurship can thrive therefore becomes a double-edged sword. On one hand, digital entrepreneurs may have easy access to family wealth to pursue their entrepreneurial endeavors, but on the other hand they may be faced with family seniors that are reluctant to fund such unknown and uncertain entrepreneurial paths.

The fourth aspect of the VIS taxonomy includes the formation of knowledge and skill within an institutional context and how labor is organized. Labor relations are essential to optimizing human capital and predict whether or not employees in organizations will have the necessary knowledge and skills to engage in strategic activities. More fragmented labor markets result in higher employee turnover rate and flexibility, thus making labor less efficient and effective and shifting the organizing principle to political and/or family connection-based foundations (Aguilera and Jackson 2014). Furthermore, technical knowledge is considered as human capital resource. Particularly in the developing context, acquiring knowledge on digital selling tools and technologies is necessary in developing an online presence and effective communication with Web site developers, industry professionals, and tech-support providers. The level of technical knowledge and resources acquired can be contingent on the availability of a qualified workforce capable of providing digital businesses with the required human capital support. Furthermore, the level of knowledge capital within a nation determines how productively organizations engage with employees. For instance, the availability of knowledge capital in companies allows organizations to invest in firm-specific skills (Jackson and Deeg 2008), while scarcity in knowledge capital may reduce incentives to invest in specific sectors or competencies. In this context, the scarcity of certified and highly skilled ICT specialists might be attributed to the high cost of recruiting and retaining them. Subsequently, the availability of employees with adequate experience and exposure to ICT skills required to successfully undertake e-commerce projects indicates the formation of entrepreneurial prospects. This means that entrepreneurs in developing countries might have to incur the additional cost of recruiting expert-level employees. The low level of ICT awareness among staff members refers to the low level of awareness of e-commerce potential, which could be due to the lack of long-term strategic planning. Moreover, small businesses may not benefit from ICTs due to their lack of knowledge, skills, and resources necessary to excel in the world of digital entrepreneurship. The adequacy of ICT skills such as the number of local content creators and communication and software engineers is an important factor in the level of adoption of technology in entrepreneurship. Furthermore, the adequacy of technical support also plays a role in determining the level of technological incorporation.

From a cultural perspective, in developing countries, societal perspectives on gender play an important role in the credibility and validation of women's resources, which create disadvantages to their entrepreneurial success. Even in the digital workspace and in terms of professional qualification, women face sexism and hostility. There is a disadvantaged stereotype about femininity and beliefs about technological competence (Kelan 2009). Other views on race and social class demonstrate how in advanced Western countries, white elite and upper middle-class males dominate positions of power; so, whiteness and masculinity form the "ideal" entrepreneurial type and consider to be intangible resources to entrepreneurial legitimacy (Ahl 2006).

The role of social capital refers to the degree to which members of society trust other members, also known as the level of generalized trust (Inglehart 1999; Putnam 1993). Prior studies have shown that trust plays an important role in a country's economic activity (Knack and Keefer 1997). The lack of generalized trust implies that individuals and organizations depend on informal networks that are centered on more specific trust, such as family ties. When applied to digital entrepreneurship, market e-readiness refers to the company's, customers' and suppliers' willingness to conduct business electronically. Supporting industries e-readiness consists of the assessment of the development level and cost of support-giving institutions such as IT, telecommunications, and financial ones, whose activities might influence e-commerce adoption and initiatives in developing countries. Hence, trusting a business partner through an e-platform may be a significant factor affecting digital entrepreneurship in developing countries. For example, given that the level of corruption in developing countries is high, people often question whether a business is reliable, safe to deal with, or will accomplish the task given at hand. Trust is built upon "long-term experience of social organization, anchored in historical and cultural experiences." (Rothstein and Stolle 2008, p. 311). This especially applies to developing economies, where corruption is prevalent and has consequences on the trust of the government, in business, and in society. Prior studies have found discrepancies in the level of trust and corruption in developing economies. From the digital entrepreneurship perspective, instead of being a neutral space where all stereotypes differences, or labels are eradicated, the online environment shows to be reflecting social inequalities among aspiring entrepreneurs. Therefore, citizens might find it difficult to trust the validity and fairness of systems in society. Additionally, the importance of social and human capital gathered in previous higher status employment challenges the idea that just about "anyone" can start a credible online business with minimal investment.

3   Cases and Expert Opinion

Below, we present two cases and an expert opinion, which exemplify how embeddedness in a developing context affects the obstacles and opportunities encountered by digital entrepreneurs. The expert opinion provides a wider perspective as our expert has more than ten years of experience working with digital entrepreneurs across the Middle East. Furthermore, the two cases, that we purposefully choose, exhibit the situation of a large business as well as a small business. This allows to show a holistic perspective on the various challenges and opportunities that digital entrepreneurs can face when operating in developing contexts.

3.1 Expert Opinion

We interviewed Dr. Diala Kabbara, a Lebanese emigrant who works in Italy as a consultant for some local and Middle-Eastern companies and is a professor of Entrepreneurship in University of Pavia, Italy. Dr. Kabbara shared her insight and expert opinion via Skype, during the course of an hour-long interview.

According to Dr. Diala., a primary driver to opening any online store is creating a high-value proposition that is customer-oriented targets to solve problems that customers face and eases their pain points.

1. Role of the "3F"s:

Dr. Diala highlights the opportunities that digital entrepreneurs have through capitalizing on the "3F"s: family, friends, and funds. Family and friends are considered as social and/or human capital, and funding includes raising money through crowdfunding, which is exposing one's innovative idea to the public and getting supported financially. Another way to get funded is through creating relationships with accelerators and incubators.

It is crucial for digital entrepreneurs to have capital for their start-ups. Dr. Diala speaks about the importance of financial markets in digital entrepreneurship and introduces the term financial "bootstrapping," which refers to, "launching new ventures with modest personal funds" (Winborg and Landström 2001, p. 235), and satisfying the need for resources without depending on debt or external finances (Smith 2009). Financial bootstrapping techniques are essential for business start-ups, particularly tech-based ones, and include making deals with customers, borrowing from suppliers, low-cost labor, and creating special relationships with individuals and organizations (Smith 2009).

A challenge of digital entrepreneurship in developing countries is funding. In developed countries, you may have a lot of grants to fund businesses. Here, we can refer to the role of the state. The state can either be a barrier to digital entrepreneurship by imposing heavy regulations and bureaucracy, or a supporter, by providing financial support. The government could financially support a specific age or gender group. For instance, in developed countries, the state can hold events and competitions for a specific age or gender group (e.g., female entrepreneurs under the age of 30), where a selected applicant gets funded by the government.

2. Customer Expectations:

Customers in developing countries are accustomed to purchasing items in physical stores, having the experience of trying things on, and using their senses. Virtual purchasing is still a somewhat foreign concept, contrary to that prevalent in developed countries. This could be due to cultural differences nested therein. Developed countries tend to value "the hustle and the grind" and can't afford to waste time or effort. So, it's easier and quicker for them to purchase things online, whereas in less individualistic countries or developing counties, people don't mind and might even be excited to do things the "physical way."

Internet issues pose challenges to digital entrepreneurship in developing countries. For example, Internet fees in Lebanon are very high compared to that in other developed countries. Dr. Diala says, "in Italy, Wi-Fi is even sometimes free in parks, whereas in Lebanon, Internet is expensive and very slow."

Cultural differences among target audiences can play a role in expanding an online company to other regions. As our interviewee mentions, "you can't just scale your online business to another country in the Middle East. Maybe an app in Lebanon may not be accepted in the gulf area."

In addition to these challenges, in developed countries, the types of industries are wide and diversified, whereas in developing counties, industries are narrower and more limited to specific sectors.

3. Network Opportunities:

A network can have two dimensions: personal and professional. Personal links such as family and friends can spread awareness and share one's business through media. Professional connections are crucial, especially in digital entrepreneurship, for they can also provide mutual benefit for both parties. As Dr. Diala mentions, "personal connections are important for creating partnerships with other companies in the future, such as alliances or collaborations." Dr. Diala mentions, "personal connections determine the quantity of people in a network, and social capital determines the quality and variety of your connections." Personal connections can also count as human capital and/or a source of knowledge. Dr. Diala says, "if some of your personal connections have had experience in digital entrepreneurship, then they can give you valuable and useful insight, and share their experiences with you."

The family plays a role in digital entrepreneurship, for it provides financial support, as well as moral support like trust. Families can tolerate and support the trials of their next of kin despite the risk. The family could help in idea generation and may provide consultation in various matters. Dr. Diala mentions, "the family could play an even more important role if a member in the family has had experience in the field of digital entrepreneurship." Families can also pave the way for various networking opportunities.

Increasing one's social capital, being the number of network relationships among people who live and work in society, is crucial for the success of a digital company. That means it is preferable to diversify one's networks, for instance, by making personal connections in different professional fields to gather a variety of suggestions and ideas. Dr. Diala says, "the more networks you have, the more the possibility to get funded."

4. Rise of Tech Devices:

Dr. Diala pointed out an opportunity in the digital industry, being the rise in the number of tech-device (smartphones, computers, etc.) users. Students are being educated on the use of technology, and it is observable that the younger generations avidly use their smart devices.

5. Syndicate and Lack of Human Capital as Challenges:

Dr. Diala discusses the role of syndicates by suggesting that syndicates are not as necessary for freelance jobs such as digital entrepreneurship as it is for other fields. She says, "for digital entrepreneurship, syndicates would mainly be used to share risk, or to provide funds for digital entrepreneurs, and for security or insurance."

Another challenge might be the lack of competent, digitally skilled, and experienced labor capital. According to Dr. Diala, employees should have a set of specific digital skills, competencies and knowledge, such as skills in SEM (search engine marketing), content marketing, social media marketing, and social selling. As Dr. Diala says, "if you don't have these skills, you may not be the right person to go into *digital* entrepreneurship." For recruitment, it is preferable to recruit technologically competent people, rather than only entrepreneurially competent or "business-minded" people. Thus, education is crucial for this matter. The sources of education could be the information and skills acquired during higher degree education, such as courses on data analysis, artificial intelligence (AI), e-computing, digital entrepreneurship, or through paying for online learning, tutorials, and software.

3.2 Case Studies

3.2.1 LebMall Start-up

We interviewed the founder of a start-up called LebMall.com, John (the name of the company and the interviewee has been changed to ensure anonymity). LebMall.com is an e-commerce, multi-vendor Web site that offers brands a platform to sell their items and make commission off of sales. LebMall company has twelve employees that can support up to 1000 orders per day. In addition, LebMall.com offers shipping of its products. In the founder's terms, it's like the "mini-Amazon" of Lebanon. LebMall.com management is currently focusing on the growth of two departments, which are those of electronics and apparel.

1. John's Vision:

The main driver behind starting this digital enterprise was the founder's and his family's search to start a new project that would satisfy the market demands and gaps in the market. John says, "it all started when I witnessed the crisis of brick-and-mortar clothing stores in Jounieh," the city where John was raised, where shops were shutting down. "It is true that there is an economic crisis in Lebanon, in real estate and in big companies, but this crisis can't be applied on clothes since the demand for apparel is a constant." He adds, "stores in malls are also closing, not because people stopped buying clothes, but because people are purchasing them through online platforms such as Aliexpress.com." John elaborates by saying, "one day, my family and I had gathered for a family meeting, where we concluded that the Lebanese economic situation had been declining, negatively impacting our real estate business." Thus, leaving their real estate business on hold, John and his family decided to come up with a new business venture. John suggested e-commerce, and the family board agreed.

2. Personal Connections/Family as Opportunities:

Personal connections can be considered as part of social capital and can serve digital entrepreneurs during their journey. John ardently emphasizes the role of his personal connections in the process of setting up his business. He says, "had it not been for my personal connections, I wouldn't have the number of vendors that my business has, nor would I have been able to equip relatively fast Wi-Fi to LebMall as quickly as I did, through the help of my connections. It would've taken me a year." His family's reputation played an essential role in building those connections and on capitalizing on old connections. Therefore, John's privileged position provided him with sufficient preceding social and financial resources that overcome knowledge limitations to develop his entrepreneurial ideas.

Family can be regarded as a source of both social and financial capital. The level of trust among family members, as well as their moral and financial support, benefits digital entrepreneurs. Family wealth provides advantages in the launch of any type of business. For instance, John attributes the launch of LebMall.com to his family's tremendous support with financial resources. John mentions that the basis of his family profession is real estate. His family enterprise provided the necessary capital to launch LebMall.com; hence, he did not need to search for funding. He says, "if it weren't for my family's enterprise, LebMall would've shut down by the end of the first day."

3. Weak Institutional Infrastructure as a Challenge:

John emphasized the weak institutional infrastructure of Lebanon, which leaves the digital entrepreneur unprotected. In Lebanon, there isn't a law or database that protects e-commerce. John says, "for example, if I lose my password, there is no backup." Nobody can complain about the mishaps or errors that occur in the online world in Lebanon. Additionally, there is a lack of protection for consumers in e-commerce. He says, "if you receive a broken or malfunctioning product, there is nothing you can do about it." As a result of the absence of law for digital entrepreneurship, there isn't a syndicate for e-commerce in Lebanon. This absence indicates that there are no forces that can instill pressure on the government for the declaration of the rights of digital entrepreneurs, such as protection laws or services.

The founder was not hesitant to express the challenges he had faced along his process of launching LebMall. He states that these challenges range from cultural differences to a lack of an online payment system and the deficiency in digital infrastructures for online business transactions. John says, "in developed countries such as the U.S., vendors communicate and sign contracts with the e-commerce platforms via email, whereas in Lebanon, I have to prepare a hard copy version of the contract with a customer. This consists of a lengthy process of going to lawyers, making the contract official, and giving them commission; thus, increasing the probability of customers backing out of their online purchase." He continues by saying, "the stock in Lebanon is not electronic and it's not easy for someone to prepare a feasibility study for investors to invest in or fund online businesses."

John states that the Lebanese bank has prohibited PayPal (the most popular online payment and monetary transaction system), and that the only payment system available in Lebanon is "Ariba," which takes 3% commission on each transaction, when it should only be taking 0.5%, again hinting at corruption disrupting business affairs.

Another difference that John states is that the concept of "e-signature" is not acknowledged in Lebanon: "we send contracts by PDF and ask our vendors to print it out and send it to us by Aramex. So, whereas others do this in a minute, this process takes us two weeks." John adds, "in other countries, it is very simple and easy for anyone to upload a product they want to sell online, whereas, in Lebanon this process is more complicated and time-consuming." In addition, John pays $2000 per month for Wi-Fi, whereas in developed countries, the price of even faster Wi-Fi is $50 per month.

Despite all the disadvantages that digital entrepreneurs face in Lebanon, the founder still wants to make a business footprint in his country: "to begin with, Lebanon is my home. Secondly, in developed countries such as the USA, there exists a lot of monopoly and competitors in e-commerce, like Amazon.com. So, launching LebMall.com in Lebanon gave me an advantage of being a first mover."

John elaborates by saying, "Lebanese citizens consider the price of their online shopping items expensive since they aren't accustomed to paying a large amount of money online; however, little do they know that they already spend its equivalent sum in daily activities or expenditures such as fuel and groceries." He states that Lebanese citizens aren't well informed about e-commerce and digital entrepreneurship isn't well integrated in the Lebanese culture.

The founder also states that LebMall.com has been facing challenges in the apparel department. LebMall.com imports clothes for women in containers from Turkey. During the importing process, they pay shipping taxes on these containers from Turkey to Lebanon, as opposed to people who bring clothes from Turkey in vans or suitcases without paying taxes.

4. Competition as a Challenge:

John expresses that the biggest problem that e-commerce, specifically his company, faces is the competition that imposter stores set by selling knock-off products and fooling customers.

LebMall.com wouldn't be settled in Lebanon if it's not registered in the ministry of economy. John says, "every picture owned by the business has to be registered for copyright; regardless, these pictures are being "stolen" and copied by other stores."

John brought and installed Internet servers from abroad called "Cloudflare" into LebMall.com, which costed him $2000 per month since he realized that with Lebanon's relatively slow internet, customers won't wait more than twenty seconds to press a button and place an order online. Additionally, the financial sector in Lebanon poses a threat to John's online business through imposing high bank interest rates.

Due to weak institutional structures and the prevalence of corruption, people in Lebanon are often not propelled/compelled to properly follow procedures. So, to get things done as efficiently as possible, John likes to keep people motivated by engaging in gift-giving to those who assist him. This can be considered as an additional cost to the business.

5. Human Capital as an Asset:

With respect to the role of human capital, the founder emphasizes on the efforts he and his team have been making to study the Lebanese market and grow the business. For example, they conducted feasibility studies regarding the success of LebMall.com prior to its launch.

This is an indication of his individual drive that led him to train himself. He says, "I know how to develop Web sites through my personal education and curiosity." The founder demonstrated signs of passion for entrepreneurship, determination, will to succeed, and a strive for knowledge and growth during his interview. John, as well as other entrepreneurs operating in developing countries must be willing to take risks, be able to bounce back from failure, and have thorough knowledge of the market and its demands. They must step out of their comfort zones and push themselves to improve their skill-set to attract their customers' attention and engagement. John stated that he's eager to learn, and as a compensation for the low levels of knowledge capital, he and his team are ready to go out of their way to learn further and excel in this endeavor.

Digital entrepreneurs have different approaches and intentions for each of their businesses. For instance, John expanded his company within several industries (electronics, apparel, etc.) with LebMall.com, since he had the capital to do so, whereas below entails how Lynn, the founder of WIB.com (WIB stands for "Women in Business"), targeted a specific industry (beauty industry), having a more limited capital. In addition, John communicated with his costumers solely in the digital space, whereas Lynn, other than using social media and online tools to advertise, adopted a technique dependent on human contact and face-to-face interaction with her customers.

3.2.2 WIB Start-up

We interviewed the founder of WIB.com (WIB stands for "Women In Business") Lynn (the name of the company and the interviewee have been changed to ensure anonymity). WIB.com is an online beauty and health shop. Lynn is a young entrepreneur, who started by selling and managing a single makeup brand, which was the official provider of an original makeup brand in Lebanon. She later decided on incorporating a variety of beauty and skin care brands, and health and fitness items, expanding it into WIB.com.

1. Lynn's Vision:

Lynn's vision was selling good-quality makeup at very fair and reasonable prices compared to other makeup brands. She says that she's been working on the main beauty brand in WIB.com for two years. She spent this time positioning and advertising the brand, in addition to testing the waters with her overseas supplier to make sure she could trust them. Therefore, WIB.com started as a small-scale business at first, but after gathering feedback from customers regarding the quality and the packaging of the products, Lynn has been rapidly growing her business. The founder points out that she associated her drive for starting and succeeding at her venture with the concept of self-actualization, which is "end-goal" in Maslow's Hierarchy of Needs. Self-actualization includes personal development and satisfying one's inner needs of achievement. She says, "as a woman in the Middle East, I am achieving something and contributing to society."

2. Role of Education:

With respect to her education, Lynn has a bachelor's degree in marketing and is currently finishing up her master's degree in finance. The university she received her higher education from did not offer any courses on digital entrepreneurship. Lynn, not having a business background, was motivated to start her online shop by being influenced by her friend who is an entrepreneur and also hadn't studied business. Hence, Lynn participated in workshops and received certificates on online marketing (e.g., the tools to use to promote a brand on social media). Lynn's marketing degree helped in marketing the brand and her store. Additionally, Lynn taught herself some necessary entrepreneurial and technical skills by watching videos and tutorials on online shopping and trend marketing.

3. Role of Social Capital:

Lynn's family was very supportive of her decision to start a business: "my family has always supported me in everything I do that they deem feasible."

In addition to her family's moral support, Lynn's family ties provided her with an opportunity to expose her business to the public. At a dancing event organized and hosted by her brother, where most of her dance students and friends had attended, Lynn found and used the opportunity to promote and sell her brand.

During the event, Lynn sold makeup products at a stand near the entrance, where everyone who walked in was introduced to the what WIB has to offer, along with its quality level and price ranges.

Lynn states that, "personal connections really help in Lebanon; that's just how the way things work here. If you need something, you refer to someone." She gives the example of the time when she needed and was in search for a delivery agency for her business. One of her acquaintances had worked with a particular delivery agency and recommended them to her; so, she didn't face any hesitation in choosing, trusting, and working with this agency.

Moreover, Lynn's close friends supported her and offered various ideas and suggestions regarding her business.

Our interview with Lynn hinted at an important link between social and human capital. The social capital, including personal connections, can serve to form a company's human capital. This is the case with Lynn, as her friends and herself make up WIB's team. When asked about her employees, the founder states that she doesn't refer to them as employees, but rather as members of a team comprised of herself, an editor who is responsible for graphic design and Photoshop, an entrepreneur who also has a cinematography (photography and videography) background, a person responsible for customer support, and another for answering messages on social media. This small team built her Web site and keeps track of inventory. All members of the team constantly work on developing and expanding their skill-set.

In addition to Lynn's personal connections contributing to the company's human capital, they ended up being a big part of the clientele and supporters of her online shop. Lynn says, "in Lebanon, everything is based on Public Relations." When Lynn first introduced WIB to her friends, family, students, and other acquaintances, they weren't reluctant to purchase its products, for they trusted that she wouldn't sell and promote an arbitrary brand of bad quality; thus, they weren't dubious of it being a rip-off due to her good relationships with students and friends and assumed the brand to be of good quality.

Thus, Lynn's asset was her social capital and the trust that comes with it. She gained a lot of customers through her friends, students, and other personal connections. Due to their trust in Lynn and her assessment of quality and standards, many ended up purchasing products to try them out. As she says, "because they know me and trust me, they trusted the brand." So, upon hearing Lynn being associated with the brand, more people were inclined to try out the brand, but this really only goes so far as a "first impression."

Hence, according to Lynn, the key to creating long-lasting customer relationships, maintaining customers' trust, and having loyal customers is not only to consistently deliver of-value products and show them their quality level, design, and packaging, but also to provide them with after-sale services such as customer support and delivery.

The founder points out that for her, "it's also a matter of self-satisfaction or self-esteem." If people were to be dissatisfied with the products and started giving bad reviews or feedback, not only would people lose trust in the brand but also in her judgment. She tries to avoid disappointing people's expectations of anything she promotes and sells for this would affect her self-esteem as an entrepreneur. She says, "that's why I took the time to really work on this brand."

During the process of building customer-brand trust, a crucial step is to be able to experience a product "hands on"; thus, customers use their senses to assess quality. Lynn says, "in the online world, and especially in the makeup business, customers want to see, smell, and touch the product for themselves." Another challenge for Lynn has been the willingness of customers to pay delivery fees. She expresses that due to Lebanon's unemployment crisis, weak economy, and corruption, citizens tend to find delivery charges inconvenient (She charges $5 for delivery and free delivery if a purchase exceeds $75). Lynn mentions that a challenge she faced at the start was her lack of contacts and know-how to go about things.

4. Role of Weak Digital Infrastructure and Risk:

According to Lynn, the payment process has caused her some hurdles: "in Lebanon, it's very difficult to have online money transactions like PayPal; so, I'm using a cash-on delivery system, which slows the process."

Lynn also expresses that as some parts of her entrepreneurial journey got easier, such as getting accustomed to the process of it all (logistics, new-item negotiation, delivery, relationship with supplier, etc.), other areas like customer satisfaction got more challenging, for she had to perform analysis on customer demand.

When it comes to risk management, Lynn says that at first, the risks facing the success of her business were high, but they decreased since she started selling in small quantities, which come with low cost of loss. Moreover, Lebanon has a weak infrastructure and is continuously hurdled with uncertainty and disruption. All of these are obstacles to Lebanese citizens' creativity because they are too preoccupied with such problems that restrict them from devoting their mental energy to innovate ideas and from tackling their creative sides. As Lynn further explains, "an observation for this could be that that Lebanese citizens who immigrate to another country end up being entrepreneurs or innovators and excel in their fields." Moreover, there aren't any bank-loan offers for entrepreneurs to start their business and borrow money from banks as their initial capital. Lynn says, "banks don't support entrepreneurs or digital entrepreneurs. And even if some do, they have really high interest rates. So, it's basically just advertising. Nothing more."

Despite the mentioned impedances, Lynn states that an online business is portable: "the advantage of having an online business is that it can be run from anywhere around the world; so, when I travel, I can take the Web site and online shop with me and simply change my target market and/or language."

5. Role of Financial Capital:

Lynn said that she saved up a bit to gather the necessary financial capital. Furthermore, she states that she didn't need a lot of money as investment for she found that with her digital business, the majority of her costs weren't monetary, rather, they were the time and effort she devoted to grow her store. The founder says that it's much cheaper for one to open an online shop than a brick-and-mortar store, to save oneself from the additional costs it incurs, such as rent and electricity bills.

6. Social Issues:

The terms "young" and "female" are certainly not the standard and typical notions that come to Lebanese citizens' minds when they think of entrepreneurship. Lynn finds it puzzling that the Lebanese don't find being accomplished at a relatively young age usual or normal.

Moreover, gender discrimination is an issue that forms a barrier to women's success in digital entrepreneurship. Lebanon, though can be regarded as a modern country, is still part of the Middle East, where traditional male-dominating mindsets and societies are prevalent. People view women's work as an "attempt," rather than legitimate, added value to society, and this could be demotivating for female entrepreneurs. Lynn says, "in some aspect, I can still sense that because I'm a woman, since whatever I do, people will still think my job is less competent than that of men's. Nevertheless, I'm glad that my team and I are still achieving something." Furthermore, Lynn says, "obviously, I feel a sense of achievement, being a 24-year-old entrepreneur, but people often get shocked when I tell them about my career and academic path, considering my young age."

4   Discussion and Conclusion

We started this chapter by highlighting that we know little about the obstacles and opportunities encountered by digital entrepreneurs embedded in developing countries. Through our study, we unpack these obstacles and opportunities and we present a comprehensive framework highlighting them (see Table 1).

As shown in Table 1, digital entrepreneurs encounter a variety of challenges when operating in developing countries. These challenges include a deficit in funding, lack of policies and regulations that protect and support e-commerce and digital entrepreneurs, deficiency in digitally competent and experienced labor capital, lack of adequate online payment systems, and cultural differences among target audiences. Digital entrepreneurs in developing countries face the challenge of inaccessibility to the necessary funds, due to the scarcity of venture capital markets and "business angels." The state hasn't established laws that provide security for digital entrepreneurs. Syndicates organizing the work of digital entrepreneurs are absent and digital entrepreneurs are left to gather financial resources through crowdfunding, investors, or through family supported funds. The main obstacles for the success of digital entrepreneurship in developing countries are the lack of digital competence, the lack of adequate skills of the workforce, and the lack of information about appropriate laws and regulations. Therefore, recruiting the right human capital with the right skill-set, background and education (self-teaching or

Table 1 Challenges and opportunities for digital entrepreneurship in developing countries

Challenges	Opportunities	Suggestions for improvement
Inaccessibility to the necessary funds, due to the scarcity of venture capital markets and "business angels"	Family as a source of social, human, and financial capital	Encourage funding through both the public sphere and private channels
Lack of policies and regulations that protect and support e-commerce and digital entrepreneurs	Personal connections as a source of social and human capital	State reforms aimed at mandating more protective laws for digital entrepreneurs
Weak digital infrastructure	Rise in the number of technology users	Improving the digital infrastructure, such as providing 5G Internet infrastructure, and introducing and legalizing the "e-signature"
Deficiency in digitally competent and experienced labor capital	Education on digital entrepreneurship (technical skills, online marketing, etc.)	Filling the digital skills gap through educational programs in universities and schools
Lack of online payment systems	Selling niche products	Introducing online payment systems
Cultural differences among target audiences in developing countries	N-A	Producing relevant content and market offerings
Weak institutional structures and corruption	N-A	Taking measures that fight corruption and ensure equal opportunity and legitimate competition

university courses) is essential. Another challenge is the absence of online payment systems, which causes issues during delivery of products. Cultural differences among areas of consumer behavior and societal norms are obstacles to the growth and expansion of digital companies in various developing countries. Lebanon's weak digital infrastructure, slow Internet, and limited industry are all barriers to digital entrepreneurship. Another challenge is the absence of online payment systems, which causes issues during delivery of products for the success of an online business. Therefore, recruiting the right human capital with the right skill-set, background and education (self-teaching or university courses) is essential. Cultural differences among areas are obstacles to the growth and expansion of digital companies in various developing countries. Lebanon's weak digital infrastructure, slow Internet, and limited industry are all barriers to digital entrepreneurship. In addition, as seen in the first case study, high tax rates on importing goods create resistance among digital entrepreneurs to import and in turn to sell their products.

The opportunities of digital entrepreneurship in developing countries include family and personal connections as a source of social, human, and financial capital. Other prospects include an increase in the users of digital devices and excelling in digital entrepreneurship in Lebanon through selling niche products via online stores, for they are high in demand. Furthermore, starting up a digital business in developing countries, where online businesses are scarce provides digital entrepreneurs with the first-mover advantage, as opposed to in developed countries, where there exists a lot of monopoly and high competition in the e-commerce industry (such as Amazon.com).

The two case studies and expert opinion indicate that digital entrepreneurship is a relatively novel concept in developing countries such as Lebanon and requires further development. Digital entrepreneurship requires a variety of competencies and skills, ranging from technical, financial, and managerial to risk-taking, and having an entrepreneurial and innovative culture. Therefore, we suggest that the state needs to mandate more protective laws to digital entrepreneurs and fill the digital skills gap, through education on digital entrepreneurship (technical skills, online marketing, etc.)

To overcome the digital infrastructure through, digital entrepreneurs could spot areas where the Internet is relatively faster and base their businesses around those areas, or pay an additional amount for instilling faster Internet, such as 5G Internet infrastructure. Another challenge is the lack of an adequate legal infrastructure that allows, for example, for an "e-signature," where entrepreneurs have to deal with a time-consuming process of printing, scanning, and faxing. In addition, digital entrepreneurs would benefit from getting funded through both public and private sectors to finance risky, early-stage ventures, and ensure persistence and continuity of funding to these technological projects (Fig. 1).

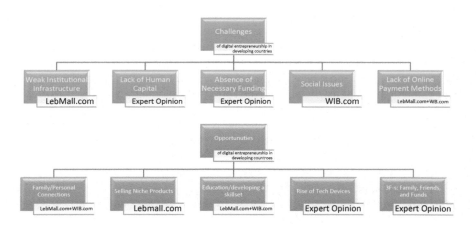

Fig. 1 Challenges and opportunities of digital entrepreneurship based on the case studies

References

Aguilera, R. V., & Jackson, G. (2003). The cross-national diversity of corporate governance: Dimensions and determinants. *Academy of Management Review, 28*(3), 447–465.

Ahl, H. (2006). Why research on women entrepreneurs needs new directions. *Entrepreneurship Theory and Practice, 30*(5), 595–621.

Brem, A., Maier, M., & Wimschneider, C. (2016). Competitive advantage through innovation: the case of Nespresso. *European Journal of Innovation Management, 19*(1), 133–148.

Davis, G. F., & Marquis, C. (2005). Prospects for organization theory in the early twenty-first century: Institutional fields and mechanisms. *Organization Science, 16*(4), 332–343.

Ekbia, H. R. (2009). Digital artifacts as quasi-objects: Qualification, mediation, and materiality. *Journal of the American Society for Information Science and Technology, 60*(12), 2554–2566.

Fainshmidt, S., Judge, W. Q., Aguilera, R. V., & Smith, A. (2018). Varieties of institutional systems: A contextual taxonomy of understudied countries. *Journal of World Business, 53*(3), 307–322.

Giones, F., & Brem, A. (2017). Digital technology entrepreneurship: A definition and research agenda.

Inglehart, R. (1999). Trust, Well-being and Democracy. In M. E. Warren (Ed.), *Democracy and Trust* (pp. 88–120). Cambridge: Cambridge University Press.

Jackson, G., & Deeg, R. (2008). Comparing capitalisms: Understanding institutional diversity and its implications for international business. *Journal of International Business Studies, 39*(4), 540–561.

Jamali, D., Karam, C., Yin, J., & Soundararajan, V. (2017). CSR logics in developing countries: Translation, adaptation and stalled development. *Journal of World Business, 52*(3), 343–359.

Kallinikos, J., Aaltonen, A., & Marton, A. (2013). The ambivalent ontology of digital artifacts. *Mis Quarterly,* 357–370.

Kelan, E. (2009). *Performing gender at work.* Houndmills: Palgrave-MacMillan.

Khanna, T., & Palepu, K. (1997). Why focused strategies may be wrong for emerging markets. *Harvard Business Review, 75,* 41–54.

Knack, S., & Keefer, P. (1997). Does social capital have an economic payoff? A cross-country investigation. *The Quarterly Journal of Economics, 112*(4), 1251–1288.

La Porta, R., Lopez-de-Silanes, F., Shleifer, A., & Vishny, R. (2000). Investor protection and corporate governance. *Journal of Financial Economics, 58*(1–2), 3–27.

Lingelbach, D. C., De La Vina, L., & Asel, P. (2005). *What's distinctive about growth-oriented entrepreneurship in developing countries?* UTSA College of Business Center for Global Entrepreneurship Working Paper (1).

Meyer, J. W., & Rowan, B. (1977). Institutionalized organizations: Formal structure as myth and ceremony. *American journal of sociology, 83*(2), 340–363.

Nambisan, S. (2017). Digital entrepreneurship: Toward a digital technology perspective of entrepreneurship. *Entrepreneurship Theory and Practice, 41*(6), 1029–1055.

Putnam, R. D. (1993). The prosperous community: Social capi- tal and public life. *American Prospect, 13,* 35–42.

Rosecrance, R. (1996). The rise of virtual state. *Foreign Affairs, 47*(1), 45–46.

Rothstein, B., & Stolle, D. (2008). The state and social capital: An institutional theory of generalized trust. *Comparative politics, 40*(4), 441–459.

Samara, G., & Arenas, D. (2017). Practicing fairness in the family business workplace. *Business Horizons, 60*(5), 647–655.

Samara, G., & Paul, K. (2019). Justice versus fairness in the family business workplace: A socioemotional wealth approach. *Business Ethics: A European Review, 28*(2), 175–184.

Schmidt, E. (2011, May 16). The internet is the path to Britain's prosperity. *The Daily Telegraph.*

Smith, D. (2009). Financial bootstrapping and social capital: How technology-based start-ups fund innovation. *International Journal of Entrepreneurship and Innovation Management, 10*(2).

Steier, L. (2009). Where do new firms come from? Households, family capital, ethnicity, and the
    welfare mix. *Family Business Review*, *22*(3), 273–278.
Winborg, J., & Landström, H. (2001). Financial bootstrapping in small businesses: Examining
    small business managers' resource acquisition behaviors. *Journal of Business Venturing*, *16*(3),
    235–254.
Wu, B. (2015, August 21). A moment that changed me—Gamergate. *The Guardian*.

Digital Entrepreneurship for the "Decade of Action"

How Entrepreneurs Can Impact Our Race Towards the Sustainable Development Goals

Manouchehr Shamsrizi, Adalbert Pakura, Jens Wiechers, Stefanie Pakura, and Dominique V. Dauster

Abstract

In 2020, the UN launched the "Decade of Action" to achieve the *Sustainable Development Goals* (SDGs) by the year 2030. As the SDGs are interdependent, intersectional and interdisciplinary, so must be their solutions. This chapter argues that the best way to identify, develop, and scale solutions of such quality is (digital) entrepreneurship, building on the principles of open innovation, cutting-edge technologies, and social business. The COVID-19 pandemic in early 2020 in particular serves as a stark reminder of the interconnected nature of the SDGs and the challenges we face in achieving them. In this article, we explore the third SDG (SDG-3), "Good health and well-being". We show the potential for digital entrepreneurship to foster the rise of new forms of digital health care and to accelerate the digitalization of the healthcare sector. Due to both perceived and real issues of regulatory compliance, user experience, and long investment/ equipment use cycles, SDG-3 has been one of the slowest to adopt innovative solutions by far. We discuss specific areas, such as blended reality or quantum computing, for emerging and future digital health applications. In this chapter, we

M. Shamsrizi (✉)
gamelab.berlin of Humboldt-Universität and RetroBrain R&D GmbH, Hamburg, Germany
e-mail: manouchehr.shamsrizi@leuphana.de

A. Pakura
RetroBrain R&D GmbH, Hamburg, Germany

J. Wiechers
Mensa International, Riskful Thinking Ventures LLC, Cologne, Germany

S. Pakura
University of Hamburg, Hamburg, Germany

D. V. Dauster
Yunus + You - the YY Foundation, Wiesbaden, Germany

© The Author(s) 2021   303
M. Soltanifar et al. (eds.), *Digital Entrepreneurship*, Future of Business and Finance,
https://doi.org/10.1007/978-3-030-53914-6_15

provide: the "memoreBox" of social start-up RetroBrain R&D, a special edition of gamelab.berlin's app "Singleton", and D-Wave's free access to its cloud quantum computing services. All these examples of digital entrepreneurship utilize in whole or in part a combination of *open innovation, future and emerging technologies*, and *social business*, thus supporting our rationale. The article closes with recommendations for different stakeholders of entrepreneurial ecosystems, demonstrating both the necessity and the potential of digital entrepreneurship for the SDGs and the "Decade of Action".

1 Introduction

We have a choice—either we go back on the old tracks, or we build new tracks to take us to a new civilization. We are now in position to build new tracks. We missed our chance in 2008 in building those after the global financial crash. Let us not miss the chance this time. Muhammad Yunus[1]

The 17 Sustainable Development Goals (SDGs) initiated and adopted by all United Nations Member States in 2015 have been a driving force behind numerous initiatives and projects around the world. They constitute an *agenda for sustainable development* that "provides a shared blueprint for peace and prosperity for people and the planet, now and into the future" (United Nations Department of Public Information 2015, p. 1) while also serving as calls to action for a better future. At their core, SDGs are interdisciplinary, intersectional, and interdependent and address a variety of areas that are of critical importance for both humanity and the planet: environmental protection, ending hunger, and reducing inequality are closely linked to, e.g. sustainable consumption and management of natural resources, improving education and providing elementary health care and sanitation for all. Still, five years into the programme timeframe, many initiatives and projects still fail to address this fundamental interconnectedness. These risks fall short of not only their potential, but also interference and competition for already scarce resources. In consequence, the UN declared the 2020s to be the "Decade of Action" (Guterres 2020, p. 1) and has since then appealed to states, corporations, non-governmental organizations, and other stakeholders to more consistently and deliberately combine forces in order to deliver on the goals set out in 2015 (United Nations 2020).

The global COVID-19 pandemic that began to unfold in late 2019, severely shuttering the global economy starting from February 2020 and expected to cause the worst global recession in almost a century (BBC 2020), serves as an additional stark warning of just how necessary an alignment of forces is. At the time of this writing (end of May, 2020), despite rapid and extensive public health measures being taken in many countries, there are more than 5.4 million confirmed cases and

---

[1]Corona Pandemic: Time Is Running Out Fast, A Letter from Prof. Muhammad Yunus (2020).

over 345.000 deaths (WHO 2020). The outbreak of COVID-19 not only sent whole countries into lockdown, but also demonstrated how relatively ill-prepared the world is for a global health crisis, even one that has long been anticipated: Corona viruses, like influenza viruses, have been the cause of previous pandemics and have been actively studied as likely candidates for future pandemics. Despite drawing on lessons learned from recent pandemics caused by CoV, e.g. SARS, MERS, the global response has been mixed (Park et al. 2020; Malik et al. 2016; Hayward et al. 2014), partly because of inadequate databases, comparable to other global public health challenges like antibiotic-resistant infections (Shamsrizi et al. 2020). In many cases, the responses to the crisis from governments, healthcare professionals, and the public demonstrate a significant gap between the claimed commitment to the ideals of SDG-3, i.e. "Good health and well-being", and actual reality in the face of a crisis. This is of particular relevance as health (SDG-3) serves as a foundation for many of the other SDGs (Rosling et al. 2018). Considering the current situation, the slow adoption of digital health in general and digital therapeutics in particular— partly because of plausible reasons (including issues of trust, data protection and reimbursement)—over the past couple of years seems alarming. Still, *digital health* and especially *digital therapeutics* are expected to have a tremendous and positive impact on society if they are adopted by more and more patients, doctors, and other healthcare professionals (Deloitte 2019). One way to foster digitalization in the healthcare sector and to bring better care to more people is through digital entrepreneurship. Technological developments and advances in infrastructure create various opportunities for entrepreneurs (Kraus et al. 2018). However, research on digital entrepreneurship is still in its infancy (Kraus et al. 2018).

In this chapter, we apply a holistic perspective and see entrepreneurship as more than just starting up a new business. Following Hsieh and Wu (2018), we understand entrepreneurship as "the process of designing, launching, and running new business" with its distinct characteristic of "new value creation" (Hull et al. 2007). However, entrepreneurial activity arises from the interplay of stakeholders, institutions, and entrepreneurs themselves (Palmer et al. 2018). Referring to Kraus et al. (2018), providing a state-of-the-art literature review of "Digital Entrepreneurship", we understand digital entrepreneurship "as a "subcategory of entrepreneurship in which some or all of what would be physical in a traditional organization has been digitized" (Hull et al. 2007, p. 293) and is thus defined as "the sale of digital products or services across electronic networks" (Guthrie 2014, p. 115). To summarize, due to the numerous opportunities for entrepreneurial activity, created through digitalization (cf., Hull et al. 2007) and its ability to develop interdisciplinary and intersectoral solutions for complex problems (Breidenbach et al. 2020), digital entrepreneurship offers an impactful instrument for the advancement of sustainable innovations (Kraus et al. 2018), thus the SDGs in general.

2 Digital Entrepreneurship as a Game Changer for Sustainable Development Goals (SDGs)

Every new tech-generation makes our societies more inclusive, healthy, and democratic and leads to our institutions having greater transparency and accountability (Pinker 2018). Through digital transformation, which can generally be understood as the "disruptive implications of digital technologies" (Nambisan et al. 2019, p. 1), many new business and science areas have spawned—and numerous implications for culture and society will most likely be enormous (Hausberg et al. 2019). Murphy et al. argue that it is *entrepreneurship* which has been the main driver for the increase in (western) per capita income over the past 200–300 years (Murphy et al. 2006). Entrepreneurship can transform whole industries and scale solutions in a quicker and more agile way than other economic approaches. It is not only one of the "transversal key competences applicable by individuals and groups", (Bacigalupo et al. 2016, p. 10) as defined by the European Commission, but also a key driver for economic growth "at the heart of national advantage", as Porter (1990, p. 125) noted. Digital transformation has had an enormous impact on most aspects of daily life and has also changed the way organizations and whole industries operate (OECD 2019), facilitating new types of work and self-employment—and paving the way for digital entrepreneurship: "the enterprising human action in pursuit of the generation of value, through the creation or expansion of economic activity, by identifying and exploiting new ICT [Information and Communications Technology] or ICT-enabled products, processes and corresponding markets" (Bogdanowicz 2015, p. 4). The pervasive accessibility of Internet services has lowered the barriers to start a project, organize, and interact online; this fosters ever-new forms of digital entrepreneurship, especially by allowing even those who could not or would not have formed a company traditionally to find an audience and a market (Allen 2018). At the same time, the current state of accessibility and inclusiveness should not be overstated: it is still the privileged elite that utilizes and benefits from digital entrepreneurship opportunities the most (OECD/European Union 2019). When the United Nations Millennium Development Goals (MDGs) were formulated in the year 2000, digital technology had already become a major part of everyday life, but few foresaw the degree to which it would permeate our lives only fifteen years later. In consequence, where the MDGs were mostly formulated in a technology-agnostic manner, the SDGs embrace the central role digital interconnectedness and technology generally have to play in improving the state of the world (Noville-Ortiz et al. 2018).

New ventures can and, more importantly, have a strong incentive, to catalyze structural changes in sectors currently held by large incumbents, whose incentives usually lie with maintaining the status quo (Apostolopoulos and Liargovas 2018; Hockerts and Wüstenhagen 2010). While it is by no means a given that entrepreneurs will be intrinsically motivated towards founding ventures which particularly take into account the SDGs, recent data from countries such as Germany is encouraging. It shows a trend towards more new ventures directed at solving social challenges, expanding renewable energy or improving health (Bundesverband Deutsche Startups 2018). Start-ups are able to challenge established companies by disrupting "existing conventional production methods, products, market structures and consumption patterns, and replace them with superior environmental and social products and services" (Schaltegger and Wagner 2011, p. 223). If this trend is to be harnessed and further encouraged, it is crucial to understand (a) what motivates these entrepreneurs, (b) whether their ventures actually end up providing a sustained and positive impact towards the transition to a "sustainable and resilient path" as laid out by the United Nations (General Assembly of the United Nations 2015; Apostolopoulos and Liargovas 2018), and (c), if not, what can be done to assist or direct them towards providing such benefit. At present, research into these questions remains scarce (Moon 2018). To conclude, we contend that digital entrepreneurship might have the biggest impact on the SDGs, if it is successful to utilize three concepts: *open innovation, future and emerging technologies,* and *social entrepreneurship.* To show how these concepts can help digital entrepreneurs achieve their goals, we will explain each of the three concepts and present examples as case studies of impactful implementations. While every single concept in itself can help elevate digital entrepreneurship in a meaningful way, we argue that a combination of all three may have the biggest impact on the challenges linked with the SDGs, which shall be elaborated using SDG-3.

2.1 Open Innovation as a Key Driver for Digital Entrepreneurship to Enhance SDGs

Open innovation provides a central element in speeding up the digitalization in the healthcare sector through the development and implementation of innovative technologies. As the United Nations Conference on Trade and Development stated (2017), we need "digitally enabled open and collaborative innovation: Fostering open, digital collaborations. Such innovation approaches draw on and recombine multiple sources and forms of knowledge, especially through digitally enabled open collaboration". However, as von Geibler et al. (2019, p. 20) argue, "this early innovation stage proves to be a challenge for corporate practitioners and innovators, largely due to the concept's intangible, qualitative nature and the lack of data".

Open Innovation evolved into an approach that many incumbent firms use regularly. They do not rely solely on knowledge generated within the company, but also facilitate knowledge outside their company to innovate (Bogers and West 2012). Chesbrough (2003) argues that the border between firms and their immediate intellectual environment is not impermeable and therefore enables companies to acquire new knowledge. Sources of valuable knowledge for innovation can be customers, suppliers, and universities (Dahlander and Gann 2010; Brunswicker and Vanhaverbeke 2015). Start-ups face different challenges than incumbent firms, but can just as well facilitate open innovation to succeed. They often lack intangible (e.g. technological expertise) and financial resources (Baum et al. 2000) and are seldom able to form strong strategic alliances (Freeman and Engel 2007). By opening up to external partners (outside in), start-ups are able to compensate for their resource constraints which can positively affect overall firm survival (Eftekhari and Bogers 2015). As Pakura (2020) points out, open innovation acts "as a driver for new organizations", which is especially true at three levels of impact: *firm development, technology development*, and *technology commercialization*. The findings show that start-ups can use different types of relationships with a variety of network partners in order to drive the development and commercialization of innovations. Such relationships can range from loose and informal networking ties to close and formal partnerships, e.g. R&D collaborations with universities and incumbent firms. Although all types of relationships can forward innovation processes of start-ups, Pakura (2019) concludes that "synergetic partnerships, such as R&D collaborations with universities and incumbent firms, create opportunities at all three levels" and that innovation benefits the most from those partnerships. Recent findings suggest that increased links to and knowledge flows from various external partners, particularly in uncertain environments, lead to improved innovation outcomes (West and Bogers 2011). Especially towards the end of the twentieth century, the shift from closed innovation approaches to open innovation models was fuelled by the emergence of digitalization processes (Bogers and West 2012). While the world became more and more digitized, open innovation became a key driver for entrepreneurship and allowed for reducing research costs, spreading risks, and commercializing innovations faster and on a global scale. In recent years, open innovation has been successfully applied in many industry contexts, for example, health care and IT, as well as in academic entrepreneurship (Siegel and Wright 2015), government innovation (Gascó 2017), and social innovation businesses (Nambisan et al. 2019). Chesbrough (2020, p. 3) pointed out how "[o]pening up will speed up [the firms] internal innovation process, and allow you to take advantage of the knowledge of others in your business (outside in), even as you allow others to exploit your knowledge in their business (inside out)". Opening up has the power to create even more experiments, generate more knowledge, and explore more ways to apply that knowledge for challenges (Chesbrough 2020). It can help solving a variety of challenges, but those with a higher level of complexity profit the most from this interconnected approach. The more complex a challenge seems, the more a firm must engage in extensive knowledge sharing to get closer to a solution. Furthermore, opening saves time, which is critical in the healthcare sector, especially when facing a pandemic (Chesbrough 2020). In a global pandemic, where time is of the essence, openness and open innovation can even save lives (Chesbrough 2020). To conclude, digital entrepreneurs that engage with large-scale problems, and/or want to impact complex ecosystems (like the healthcare sector), must consider open innovation approaches.

2.2 Future and Emerging Technologies as Enablers of Digital Entrepreneurship Towards SDGs

While the future is arguably uncertain and many believe that we are living in an "Age of Paradox" (Handy 1995), there are several future and emerging technologies that entrepreneurs can exploit today or where entrepreneurship can profitably contribute to the development or implementation of future technologies. Thinking ahead and implementing future technologies can give entrepreneurs a competitive edge or even enable them to create entirely new markets. So-called future and emerging technologies (FETs) are also part of the "Horizon 2020" programme by the European Union with the goal to "create a fertile ground for responsible and dynamic multidisciplinary collaborations on future technologies and for kick-starting new European research and innovation ecosystems" (Horizon 2020, 2018, p. 4). Future and emerging technologies are self-evidently complex and not widely known and implemented. Implementing them requires a strong strategic focus and the ability to innovate by means of tools that are currently not available in the mass market. Moreover, deeper factors are necessary to obtain economic and social value from technology. Generating technology alone is insufficient and must also be broadly disseminated, and then absorbed and put to work before its full value could be realized, as Chesbrough (2019) argues. To get a short overview of presumably impactful FETs, the World Economic Forum (2020) created an overview that we adopted (Table 1) and that shows not only how FETs like artificial intelligence and quantum technologies will potentially shape our future, but also how they will affect the different SDGs.

While we cannot go into detail regarding the different technologies and their respective effects on society, we will focus on two major technological concepts that we assume will have tremendous impact on achieving the SDGs and which we will take up and reflect in our case studies (see Chap. 4): *Quantum Computing* and *Blended Reality*.

Although it might sound puzzling, quantum technologies are already widespread: "computers, data networks and the majority of medical imaging techniques could not have been achieved without quantum effects. This is because components such as transistors, diodes and lasers all make use of principles of quantum physics" (Federal Ministry of Education and Research 2018, p. 6). These are examples of first-generation quantum technologies that started as scientific endeavours which were then implemented in a myriad of ICTs and everyday devices that we use today. Almost a century after the field of quantum physics was created in Central Europe, an increased understanding of those quantum technologies is now creating new opportunities. As Krutzik and Shamsrizi (2020) outline, the "second quantum revolution" will massively impact the twenty-first century, and is widely seen as "[that which] comes *after* the digital transformation". The manifold areas in which this impact can be seen include "measuring devices with much higher precision, vastly enhanced data communication security, and [...] higher-performance satellites and computers" (Federal Ministry of Education and Research 2018, p. 6). Quantum technologies and their specific applications are based on quantum principles that, in turn, exploit the unique physical principles of the quantum world.

The second example of a potentially impactful FET is the concept of so-called blended reality: Many Health and Exergames use virtual or augmented reality to promote active living and exercise despite the still widely held preconception of gaming being an "unhealthy" (or at least not health-positive) activity. The popular

Table 1 Examples of future technologies

Technology	Impact on the following SDGs	Technology	Impact on the following SDGs
Quantum computing determined optimal carbon capture material	SDG-7, SDG-13	Ultra-high speed, zero-emissions long haul transport, including underground, surface, aviation, shipping and drones	SDG-7, SDG-9, SDG-11, SDG-13
4IR-enabled deployable nuclear fusion using AI to predict disruptions that halt feasibility	SDG-7, SDG-13	Zero-waste advanced materials for clean energy and advanced waste heat capture and conversion	SDG-7, SDG-9, SDG-11, SDG-12, SDG-13
Advanced materials for generation of low-cost and zero-emissions gaseous fuels, incl. ammonia and hydrogen	SDG-7, SDG-13, SDG-14	Quantum-enabled extreme efficiency data centres and supercomputers	SDG-7, SDG-9, SDG-12, SDG-13
Genetic rescue and genome modification for endangered and extinct species and resilience	SDG-14, SDG-15	4IR-enabled internet connectivity for all (drones, satellites)	SDG-1, SDG-4, SDG-5, SDG-8, SDG-9, SDG-10, SDG-11
Attracting and removing micropollutants (synthetic biology)	SDG-6, SDG-11, SDG-13, SDG-14, SDG-15	Quantum cryptography for the prevention of cyberattacks on AI/quantum computers	SDG-9, SDG-16
Low-zero emissions and ultralow-cost desalination technology using advanced materials	SDG-3, SDG-6, SDG-13	AI-enabled privacy-protected, public good digital health platform collating healthcare data, sensors, wearables and genomic data	SDG-3, SDG-16
End-to-end automated, connected and optimized food and fibre system, incl. elimination of spoilage, loss and waste	SDG-2, SDG-12, SDG-13, SDG-15	AI-enabled development of new antibiotics to address microbial resistance to current antibiotics	SDG-3, SDG-10
Low-cost, low-GHG emissions synthetic proteins (AI and synthetic biology)	SDG-11, SDG-12, SDG-13, SDG-15	4IR-enabled "access to care" digital technologies, distribution and delivery systems	SDG-3, SDG-10
Advanced materials for durability of energy-intensive products and materials	SDG-2, SDG-9, SDG-12, SDG-13	Decoding well-being and longevity using AI and sensors for personalized health maps and sequenced genomes and phenotypic data	SDG-3, SDG-10

(continued)

Table 1 (continued)

Technology	Impact on the following SDGs	Technology	Impact on the following SDGs
Zero-emissions chemicals, steel, aluminium, cement using advanced materials and/or biotech (e.g. biocement)	SDG-11, SDG-12, SDG-13	Gene editing (e.g. CRISPR) to tackle human diseases driven by gene mutation	SDG-3

Source Adopted from: World Economic Forum (2020)

VR rhythm-game *Beat Saber,* for example, is "widely considered a good option for exercise in VR" and uses the technology to reach people at home and motivate them to move and stay healthy (Fingas 2020). In a study on the potential health impact of Pokémon Go, Duke University's School of Medicine was able to show that "increases in physical activity were highest among individuals who stood most to benefit from additional activity, such as individuals who are overweight or obese, or who get little regular exercise to begin with" (Will Will 2017). Another illustrative example is provided by blended reality exercise equipment or applications, such as those provided by Peloton (onepeloton.com). Their smart exercise equipment enables its users to sign up for training regimes overseen by remote trainers, to exercise and receive instruction "together" via integrated video conferencing. Other offerings such as *Supernatural* even allow for exercise in full virtual reality (Oculus 2020). Many of these technologies are actively used today, but big technological leaps will make true "Blended Realities" a part of our everyday life. Steincke defines blended reality as the seamless transition between the fully physical and fully virtual, described as a continuum between these two poles. Steinicke (2016) anticipates that in about 30 years, virtual and "real" reality will not only be blended, but even merged, and humans will not be able to perceive any difference The consequences of such a situation have been described as potentially even turning "real" reality into a "homeopathicum" (Sedláček and Shamsrizi 2017) (Fig. 1).

2.3 Social Business as an Essential Element Towards SDGs

As we are entering the second decade of the new millennium, one can observe rather unexpected changes even among thought-leaders of both theory and practice in economy and business: Michael Porter wants his students to create *Shared Value* (Porter and Kramer 2011), BlackRock is "making sustainability integral to portfolio construction and risk management" (Fink 2020) and lets its portfolio companies know that "purpose is the engine of long-term profitability", and the founder of the World Economic Forum, Klaus Schwab, opened this year's WEF Annual Meeting by pointing out that while "'stakeholder capitalism' has been around for a half-century, it has only recently begun to gain traction against the prevailing

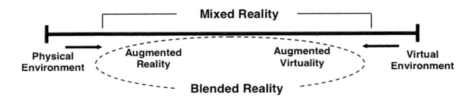

Fig. 1 Blended reality in relation to the physical-virtual environment continuum. *Source* adapted from Milgram and Kishino (1994), in Bower et al. (2010)

shareholder-primacy model of profit maximization" (Schwab 2019). Consistently, the "Ethics in Action"-initiative of the UN Sustainable Development Solutions Network pointed out that "the challenges of sustainable development are primarily ethical in nature"; thus, "the Sustainable Development Goals require 'moral capacity' as much as financial or technical capacity" (Annett et al. 2017). At the core of this SDG-driven transformation is the idea of a "new capitalism", in which both traditional for-profit (blue, cf., Fig. 2) and not-for-profit (red, cf. Fig. 2) organizations are complemented by social entrepreneurial actors in all of their varieties (green, cf. Fig. 2), including the supporting impact investing ecosystem surrounding them:

While "debates about the definition of social business versus social entrepreneurship keep coming up at conferences", the scientific community is "getting closer to clearer definitions" (Grove, as cited in YY Foundation 2019, p. 22). Independently of the definition, it seems that social entrepreneurs may play a

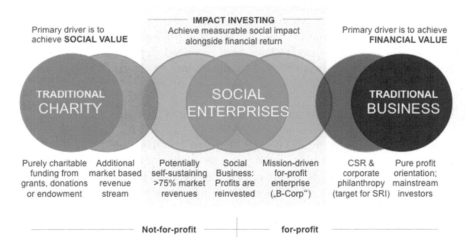

Fig. 2 Continuum of varieties of organisations in the "new capitalism". *Source* Ryder and Vogeley (2018)

major role in creating more inclusive societies (European Commission 2015) and solving the most pressing issues of our time. In particular, social businesses "work in many different areas where they often have a direct impact, such as health, education and infrastructure", as Gass sums up (Gass, as cited in YY Foundation 2019, p. 30). Regarding the definition of social business, the OECD (2014, p. 188), for example, follows a twofold definition of Muhammad Yunus: Type 1) a "'non-loss, non-dividend company' that creates social benefits through the nature of its products, services and/or operating systems", and Type 2) a "profit-maximizing company owned by its poor or otherwise disadvantaged target beneficiaries, or by a dedicated trust". As such, the concept of social businesses is notably distinct from any form of charity. In this sense, combining digital entrepreneurship and social business, we assume that stakeholders are enabled to create scalable solutions— especially in the light of the "Decade of Action". Furthermore, it has also been argued that large corporations/multinational enterprises (MNEs) "[need] a change of course to achieve the UN's Sustainable Development Goals by 2030" (Bruysten et al. 2020). This transformation is strongly driven by "a breed of entrepreneurs who work as employees within companies to develop business solutions for social or environmental problems:" social intrapreneurs. The OECD anticipates that "social businesses can create new sources of income, raise productivity, reduce 'aid' dependency and provide low-income consumers with access to products and services for their basic needs" (OECD 2014, p. 187). With the pressing issues in front of us and the COVID-19 pandemic as a huge "call to immediate action", solutions that tackle a SDG like "Good health and well-being" should and can facilitate both of these worlds, as "Social businesses will have a direct impact on whichever SDGs they engage in" (Gass, as cited in YY Foundation 2019, p. 30).

3 A Conceptual Framework and Canvas of Digital Entrepreneurship for a "Decade of Action"

We see digital entrepreneurship as a necessary component in achieving many, if not all, of the SDGs. A variety of conceptual models, policy frameworks and measurement instruments have been developed to study the driving and impending factors influencing digital entrepreneurship as well as the factors influencing organizational decision-making which furthers sustainable and more generally SDG-oriented business practices. Many of these frameworks, however, adopt a macro-perspective with a focus on the incentives and obstacles faced by multinational enterprises, or organizations that are designed to quickly scale to a global level (George and Bock 2011; George et al. 2016). Yet the vast majority of all enterprises in both highly industrialized and less developed countries are actually small- and medium-sized enterprises (SMEs) (Ayyagari et al. 2017; European Union 2018; Small Business Profile 2018). While the disproportionate impact of MNEs on the overall sustainability should not be understated, SDG-oriented Digital Entrepreneurship, presenting the right overall conditions, potentially may rapidly develop and adapt to niche opportunities. This is due to the domain expertise of its founders and significantly lower regulatory, organizational, and structural constraints with the SDGs being nevertheless supported through socially/environmentally responsible practices. At the same time, it seems unlikely that any single framework could adequately quantify and qualify the wide variety of factors that influence the entrepreneurial activities of SMEs. Following the argument put forward by Kuratko et al. (2015), we agree that only a synthesis of multiple frameworks has any potential to adequately represent Digital Entrepreneurship, especially social digital entrepreneurship. All economic systems are complex networks that are interconnected and interdependent (Bair and Palpacuer 2015; Rasche et al. 2013), and the formation of networks among entrepreneurs, the start-ups they create, and the SMEs they become have been found to be crucial to success (Austin et al. 2006; Dacin et al. 2011). Based on these underlying considerations, we explored the possibilities to help potential digital entrepreneurs to successfully support the SDGs thus positively impacting the "Decade of Action" through the structured application of open innovation, social digital business approaches, and future and emerging technologies. To use these concepts effectively, we developed a special variant of Osterwalder's Business Model Canvas (BMC) (Osterwalder and Pigneur 2010). Our *"Digital Entrepreneurship for the Decade of Action"*—Canvas (short: "Decade of Action"-Canvas) adds multiple layers to the well-known version by Osterwalder to let digital entrepreneurs better engage with the SDGs.

The canvas implements three major new aspects, which we derive from our theoretical triad of open innovation, future and emerging technologies and social (digital) business. These new aspects will directly help future digital entrepreneurs to evaluate how their solutions benefit the SDGs. First, in this canvas, not only the "usual" value propositions are to be explored, but, referring to the definition of social business, also the proposed value to the SDGs. This means that the potential project and its value proposition needs to relate to the SDGs and to explain how it supports achieving them. Second, we refer to the concept of open innovation and the importance of multiple and different types of relationships with a variety of network partners in order to drive the development and commercialization of innovations. We delimited key environmental actors and influencers from key partners. By answering the question "Who is mostly impacting your field of impact/SDGs in the next ten years?" potential entrepreneurs learn that it is often the network to regulatory authorities or other societal or economic multipliers that can bring a competitive advantage. Working on your network and keeping key actors that affect your field of impact can pay off early on. Third, Beneficiaries are of utmost importance to consider: in contrast to customer segments, thinking about beneficiaries enables digital entrepreneurs to embrace the "triple bottom line", where environmental, social, and governmental actors benefit. This sensitization is supported by referencing concepts like Ashoka's Theory of Change, or the social business approach (Drayton 2003). Fourth, referring to future and emerging technologies, "Key Activities" and "Key Resources" force the digital entrepreneurs to

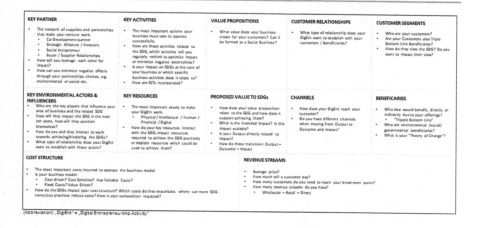

Fig. 3 "Decade of action"—Canvas. *Source* Own table (adapted from Osterwalder and Pigneur 2010)

re-evaluate their solutions with regards to other, more emerging technologies, which might have the potential to improve the impact and/or efficacy of their approach.

To summarize, we developed the "Decade of Action"-Canvas with these four specific adjustments, whereas the other fields of Osterwalder's BMC remain mostly unchanged (Fig. 3).

The most current version can always be found at http://www.doacanvas.org/.

4   Case Studies

4.1   RetroBrain R&D GmbH: MemoreBox

Germany's Federal Ministry of Health's Health Innovation Hub responded, among others, to the COVID-19 pandemic by compiling a list of recommendable "Digital Tools", which either mitigate COVID-19 directly or help address its wider societal impact (Health Innovation Hub 2020). One of the companies mentioned on this list is **digital-therapeutics** company RetroBrain R&D, a spin-off of Humboldt-Universität's Cluster of Excellence. RetroBrain R&D develops a fully gesture-controlled video game console named "memoreBox", which has been called "a benchmark in the therapeutic gamification industry" (LIFT Basel 2015). The overall goal of RetroBrain's solution is to extend the quality of life of the elderly by developing state-of-the-art, evidence-based therapeutic video games. The video game system—classified as a class 1 medical device—supports the prevention of typical age-related diseases and accompanies the therapy of diseases such as dementia or Parkinson's disease.

In a pilot project under the patronage of among others Germany's Minister of State for Digitalization, which studied the health-promoting effects regular gaming has on the social, physical, and cognitive resources of senior citizens, the findings were clear: Compared to non-gamers, gamers showed significant improvements in cognitive performance, gait stability, motor skills, stamina, and coordination. There are also moderate improvements as it pertains to the health-related quality of life, the extent of which is practically significant. There were also positive trends in the subjective experience of pain, which was reduced by regular gaming. As a result of this study, "BARMER [one of Germany's largest health insurance funds] is convinced of RetroBrain's memoreBox", as Dr. med. Mani Rafii, member of the board, comments: "The concept combines movement with enjoyment and games and makes it possible for elderly people to remain mentally and physically fit and to actively participate in society. Since we had positive experiences with the concept within the framework of a pilot phase, we are now rolling it out nationwide, so we can give even more elderly people the opportunity to take part in the preventive and health-promoting capabilities of this video game platform" (Rafii, M., as cited by Jakob-Pannier 2019, p. 1). In 2019, Germany's National Association of Statutory Health Insurance Funds commissioned the Institute for Innovation and Technology of VDI/VDE-IT to conduct a study on the potential impact of digital tools in care and nursing. According to this study, the memoreBox "proves, how people in need of care profit from the use of a digital tool in different fields including their cognitive abilities, social interaction and conclusion, as well as gait quality", and furthermore even the nursing staff benefits" (GKV-Spitzenverband 2019, p. 151). What opened memoreBox the door to the Healthcare Market was the German Act to Strengthen Health Promotion and Preventive Health Care, which has been in effect since the summer of 2015. The need for this law shows how diametrically opposed the two poles of "having fun" and "getting/being healthy" were at that time. The legislator created this law to motivate the health insurance industry to invest more money in prevention. Given that it generally takes fewer resources and is more promising to keep people healthy—instead of trying to heal them after they have taken ill, which takes much more effort and has far lower chances of success,—the legislator created the Prevention Act obligating health insurance companies to allocate sufficient funds to promote meaningful prevention. Like many social business start-ups making use of digital technology, RetroBrain R&D operates in an ecosystem of cross-sectoral quality; besides the "PEP Program" of Ashoka, one may particularly mention the "Impact Factory".[2] Thus, RetroBrain R&D can be studied as an exemplary case for aspects like "key partner", "key environmental actors and influencers", and "beneficiaries" of our "Decade of Action"—Canvas.

---

[2]A joint initiative of a diverse group of founding partners including German family equity company Franz Haniel & Cie. GmbH, Beisheim Foundation, KfW foundation (of the KfW, the German government-owned development bank), and Anthropia gGmbH, a social business itself.

4.2   gamelab.Berlin: Singleton and the #WeVsVirus-Hackathon

Suggesting that "we as a society [can] work together to master the challenges that arise in the wake of the Corona (COVID-19) crisis with new solutions", the Federal Government of Germany had invited people to take part in a virtual "#WeVsVirus" hackathon (https://wirvsvirushackathon.org). Under the patronage of the head of the Federal Chancellery and supported by the Federal Government's "Digital Council", more than 40,000 participants developed digital solutions to problems related to the COVID-19 pandemic. These participants spent 48 h working on altogether 1500 ideas, of which many can be classified as digital entrepreneurship and/or social businesses. Overall, "the model for this attempt to find digital solutions in the global fight against the coronavirus pandemic was a similar event in Estonia" (Hänel 2020, p. 1) and was considered as an exceptional and sophisticated approach of open innovation by a public administration (Gegenhuber et al. 2020). The issues dealt with were mostly the following: 1. Spread of Sars-CoV-2, 2. Provision of Medical Care, 3. Politics Administration, 4. Economy, 5. Solidarity (including Education), 6. Living in (Self-)Isolation; evidently, these issues span all SDGs. As we focus on SDG-3 in this article, we will exemplarily describe the project "Singleton #WirBleibenZuhause", which was chosen to be included in the "Solution Enabler Program"—by which the German government wants to implement the most promising solutions of the hackathon—and which is an especially promising digital solution for mental health in (Self-)Isolation. Originally a research project at gamelab.berlin, Singleton is now offered by the social business spin-off Homo Ludens GmbH, making this case a prototypical example of digital entrepreneurship as a vehicle for social impact.

Singleton is a card game that gamifies time management while encouraging mindfulness in order to help those who traditionally struggle to adhere to to-do lists and tasking. It was initially designed as a physical game and played by the inventor and his fellow researchers at gamelab.berlin (Lilge and Stein 2018). A digital version for Android and iOS was eventually created and open sourced, making it available to a wide community of developers. 60 Singleton cards with entertaining and socially activating challenges were created, which together formed a game that was highly adapted to the organizations needs. Singleton began to be used in all kinds of organizations and companies as a new way to deal with change. In the course of focusing on organizations, the scientists of gamelab.berlin spun out of the university and created a company with the goal of bringing the cultural technology of the game to areas of society that are typically not interested in games. The aim of the spin-off was to design systemic and individual learning processes in such a way that the most natural of all forms of learning motivation could be activated: the joy of discovering something new. In the context of university research, it had already become clear that games can do much more than just entertain. Based on the principles of open innovation, Gamelab developed games for data collection in research, political education, school education on climate change, and neurosurgical training and even created a game for people suffering from lethal diseases. It turned out that game mechanics and forms of motivation have an effect far beyond what we are used to calling games—into the most serious areas of society. The ideas still come from research and the connection with their scientific work remains, but being a social business allows them to have faster development cycles and opportunities for practical applications, which have a concrete impact on the SDGs through Digital Entrepreneurship. The new version of the game enables people to play it for themselves and at home, learning to be more mindful and improve their well-being and health, thus directly helping achieve SDG-3. In this case, expanding the development of Singleton in the course of the #WeVsVirus hackathon is a useful example of how to align the aspects "proposed value to SDGs", "key partner", "customer relationships"/"customer segments", and "beneficiaries" of our "Decade of Action"—Canvas.

4.3 D-Wave Systems: Access to Quantum Computer Processing for Projects Addressing COVID-19

As we have indicated above, quantum computing will certainly have wide-ranging implications and a substantive impact on all aspects of life in the future. This obviously includes the SDGs. Witold W. Kowalczyk of Harvard-spinoff Zapata Computing (2020), a quantum computing software company, identifies five SDGs in particular that will be impacted by the novel computing resources quantum computing provides:

- Zero hunger (SDG-2) via new algorithms for crucial soil composition analysis, nitrogen fixation, etc.
- Good health and well-being (SDG-3) via increased velocity of drug discovery and simulation.
- Clean water and sanitization (SDG-6) via optimized water distribution, new catalyst discovery/development
- Affordable/Clean energy (SDG-7) via advances in materials science leading to, e.g. better batteries
- Climate action (SDG-13) through improved meteorological modelling and analysis.

One company that has stepped up in the wake of the COVID-19 outbreak is the Canadian quantum computing company D-Wave, one of the earliest (Lardinois 2019, p. 1) of the latest generation of quantum computing start-ups. They announced that they would support anyone "focusing on new drugs", but also that they are "open to any research or team working on any aspect of how to solve the current [COVID-19-]crisis, be that logistics, modelling the spread of the virus or working on novel diagnostics". In addition, their partners[3] will provide "engineering expertise to teams that are using Leap 2 for developing solutions"

---

[3]i.a. Volkswagen, DENSO, Jülich Supercomputing Centre.

(Lardinois 2019, p. 1). Founded in 1999, D-Wave is a privately held company. Quantum technologies are believed to be "driving forward a technological revolution" and to become "the engine of innovations in science, economics and society in the twenty-first century", as experimental physicist Prof. Dr. Rainer Blatt sums up the results of the 2016 Lindau Nobel Laureate Meeting on the "second quantum revolution" (von der Stein 2016, p. 1). Regarding the COVID-19 crisis as well as the issues targeted by SDG-3 in general, particularly quantum computing is at the core of D-Wave's impact. According to one of D-Wave's partners, Prof. Dr. Kristel Michielsen from the Jülich Supercomputing Centre, it is promising "to accelerate the solution of complex problems in pharmacology and epidemiology, such as those that have arisen in the unprecedented COVID-19 crisis, by means of hybrid workflows from quantum-classical computer simulations" (Forschungszentrum Jülich 2020). As Analytics Insight sums up, "The company's hybrid quantum-classical cloud service could conceivably help researchers simulate molecular interactions between coronavirus and its target cells, or simulate the spread of the COVID-19 disease in complex settings. It could also help planners optimize supply chains and hospital logistics" (Srivastava 2020) In an interview with IEEE Spectrum, gathering the first week's worth of submissions from coronavirus researchers applying for D-Wave time, the CEO of D-Wave claimed that the initial response to their offer came from teams tackling a range of coronavirus-related problems: "We've seen problems being explored in the following areas: (1) the modelling and simulation of the spread of the virus, (2) the scheduling of nurses and other hospital resources, (3) assessing the rate of virus mutation, and (4) the assessment of existing drugs as potential treatments" (Anderson 2020). Opening up access to their resources also allows other companies in the space which are already committed to the SDGs such as ZAPATA, to work with D-Wave and interested parties to leverage domain, quantum-software and hardware expertise, thus showing the potential of the simultaneous consideration of the aspects "proposed value to SDGs", "key partner", "beneficiaries", and "key activities" (notably its sub-aspect "How are FETs incorporated?") of our "Decade of Action"—Canvas.

5 Conclusion and Implications: Making Open Innovation, Social Business, and Future and Emerging Technologies Work for Digital Entrepreneurship and the "Decade of Action"

The current COVID-19 pandemic shows how important the fight for the Sustainable Development Goals really is and how COVID-19 has prompted a wide variety of open, collaborative responses (Chesbrough 2020). While all SDGs are impacted by the pandemic—especially the neglected issues in SDG-3 (good health and well-being) become apparent—and the need for more and better digital health applications became obvious. Digital entrepreneurs now have to step up and build the next wave of impactful start-ups, notably social (digital) businesses, for the

Decade of Action. Based on our literature review and practical case studies, we developed the following six primary recommendations for action which target all stakeholder of the digital entrepreneurial ecosystem. In doing so, we provide a holistic lens combining the findings of open innovation, social business, and future technologies:

1. Foster knowledge and technology transfer via open innovation from the scientific community beyond businesses towards all actors working on the SDGs, particularly taking into account the necessary access to finance
2. Foster entrepreneurship education, and expand its scope towards continuing education also focusing on senior and mid-career executives
3. Introduce and support social business (and/or social intrapreneurship) in the potentially impactful organizations working on the SDGs
4. Harness the potential of diversity, notably female entrepreneurship (Halberstadt et al. 2018), migrant entrepreneurship (Council of Europe 2019), introverts (Castrillon 2019), entrepreneurs of colour (Kauffman Foundation 2016), and other forms of minority entrepreneurship (Bates 2012)
5. Include founders and entrepreneurial ecosystems as part of the regulatory and economic policy framework to cope with COVID-19
6. To obtain economic and social value from emerging technologies it is not enough generating technology. Moreover, it is necessary that the technology will be disseminated, absorbed and put to action before its full value can be derived (Chesbrough 2019).

Furthermore, our findings culminated in an easy-to-use canvas. We took Osterwalder's "Business Model Canvas" and redesigned it to help digital entrepreneurs effectively tackle the SDGs: *open innovation* for complex problems, *future and emerging technologies* for future proof solutions and *social business thinking* to keep societal issues in mind. The relevance of digital health and therapeutics for achieving the SDGs is rising and an event severely restricting access to healthcare professionals and doctors due to capacity overload or isolation, such as the COVID-19 pandemic, serves as a stark reminder of just how fragile many of our achievements towards particularly SDG-3 can be in the face of global calamity. Fostering an entrepreneurial spirit among young people, but especially those who are not traditional founders such as women, the elderly, people with disabilities, refugees, and others while also encouraging open innovation and cooperation within sectors will help build a more inclusive and resilient economy and health sector.

But how can one use the "Digital Entrepreneurship for the 'Decade of Action'— Canvas" best? Innovative teaching and learning formats at universities and other forms of higher learning—notably those engaged in lifelong learning—have increased, ever since the first formal entrepreneurship education formats were created in the early 2000s. However, many entrepreneurship education curricula continue to disregard the idea of fully Digital Entrepreneurship, not to mention how little is on offer addressing health challenges in particular. As "really big opportunities arise only when brilliant innovation meets overwhelming market needs at just the right time" (von Windheim 2014, p. 35). There are unique opportunities for entrepreneurship education to help shape the digital landscape in Germany and beyond, fostering connections between all stakeholders, which is why —in the spirit of our "Digital Entrepreneurship for the 'Decade of Action'—Canvas"—universities need to bring together all stakeholder and players potentially involved in founding new ventures (von Windheim 2014). Teaching about the SDGs in the same manner as we more generally teach about business ethics and philosophy, must become the backdrop of our entrepreneurship education if we want to achieve the still ambitious agenda set out by the United Nations and transform our society for the better.

Acknowledgements and Contributors The authors would like to thank Alexandra Christiansen, a professional foreign language assistant at the University of Hamburg who provided language support. The authors would like to thank Dr. Christian Stein and Thomas Lilge of Humboldt-Universität zu Berlin's Cluster of Excellence for thematic input and valuable feedback. The authors would like to thank Annalena Feldmüller (University of Hamburg) and Étienne Prinage (Leuphana Universität Lüneburg) for their support as student assistants.

References

Allen, J. P. (2018). Digital entrepreneurship: A path to a more inclusive digital future. In *Americas Conference on Information Systems*, o.S.

Anderson, M. (2020). *Can Quantum Computers Help Us Respond to the Coronavirus?* Available at: https://spectrum.ieee.org/tech-talk/computing/hardware/can-quantum-computing-help-us-respond-to-the-coronavirus Accessed 24 April 2020.

Annett, A., Sachs, J., Sanchez Sorondo, M., & Vendley, W. (2017). *A multi-religious consensus on the ethics of sustainable development: Reflections of the ethics in action initiative.* Economics Discussion Papers, No 2017-56, Kiel Institute for the World Economy. https://web.archive.org/web/20200502233232/http://www.economics-ejournal.org/economics/discussionpapers/2017-56/file.

Apostolopoulos, N., & Liargovas, P. (2018). Unlock local forces and improve legitimacy: A decision making scheme in the European Union towards environmental change. *European Policy Analysis, 4*(1), 146–165.

Austin, J., Stevenson, H., & Wei-Skillern, J. (2006). Social and commercial entrepreneurship: Same, different or both? *Entrepreneurship Theory and Practice, 30*(1), 1–22.

Ayyagari, M., Demirgüç-Kunt, A., & Maksimovic, V. (2017). *SME finance.* World Bank Policy Research Working Paper No. 8241. Available at SSRN: https://ssrn.com/abstract=3070705.

Bacigalupo, M., Kampylis, P., Punie, Y., & Van den Brande, G. (2016). *EntreComp: The entrepreneurship competence framework.* Luxembourg: Publication Office of the European Union.

Bair, J., & Palpacuer, F. (2015). *CSR beyond the corporation: Contested governance in global value chains. Global Networks 15*, supplemental issue (pp. 1–19).

Bates, T. (2012). Minority entrepreneurship. *Foundations and Trends in Entrepreneurship, 7*(3–4), 151–311.

Baum, J., Calabrese, T., & Silverman, B. (2000). Don't go it alone: Alliance networks and startups' performance in Canadian biotechnology. *Strategic Management Journal, 21*(3), 267–294.

BBC (2020). *Coronavirus: Worst economic crisis since 1930s depression, IMF says.* Archived at: https://web.archive.org/web/20200502193359/https://www.bbc.com/news/business-52236936. Accessed 02 May 2020.

Bogdanowicz, M. (2015). *Digital entrepreneurship barriers and drivers, JRC Technical Reports, European Commission Joint Research Centre.* Archived at: https://web.archive.org/web/20200502193539/https://publications.jrc.ec.europa.eu/repository/bitstream/JRC96465/jrc96465_%20digital%20entrepreneurship%20barriers%20and%20drivers%20-%20the%20need%20for%20a%20specific%20measurement%20framework.pdf. Accessed 02 May 2020.

Bogers, M., & West, J. (2012). Managing distributed innovation: Strategic utilization of open and user innovation. *Creativity and Innovation Management, 21*(1), 61–75.

Bower, M., Cram, A., & Groom, D. (2010). Blended reality: Issues and potentials in combining virtual worlds and face-to-face classes. In C. H. Steel, M. J. Keppell, P. Gerbic, & S. Housego (Eds), Proceedings of the 27th ASCILITE Conference (pp. 129–140). Brisbane: The University of Queensland.

Brunswicker, S., & Vanhaverbeke, W. (2015). Open innovation in small and medium-sized enterprises (SMEs): External knowledge sourcing strategies and internal organizational facilitators. *Journal of Small Business Management, 53*(4), 1241–1263.

Bruysten, S., López Ramos, S., & Nowack, D. (2020). *Business as unusual. Making the case for social intrapreneurship.* Available at: https://www.yunussb.com/business-as-unusual. Accessed 24 April 2020.

Bundesverband Deutsche Startups e.V. (2018). Deutscher startup monitor 2018. Available at: https://web.archive.org/web/20200502220520/https://deutscherstartupmonitor.de/fileadmin/dsm/dsm-18/files/Deutscher%20Startup%20Monitor%202018.pdf. Accessed 02 May 2020.

Castrillon, C. (2019). *How introverts can thrive as entrepreneurs.* Available at: https://web.archive.org/web/20200502193648/https://www.forbes.com/sites/carolinecastrillon/2019/01/23/how-introverts-can-thrive-as-entrepreneurs/. Accessed 24 April 2020.

Chesbrough, H. (2003). *Open innovation: The new imperative for creating and profiting from technology.* Boston: Harvard Business School Press.

Chesbrough, H. (2019). *Open innovation results: Going beyond the hype and getting down to business.* Oxford: Oxford University Press.

Chesbrough, H. (2020). To recover faster from COVID-19, open up: Managerial implications from an open innovation perspective. *Industrial Marketing Management.* https://doi.org/10.1016/j.indmarman.2020.04.010.

Council of Europe Portal. (2019). *Intercultural Cities Newsroom: The importance of migrant entrepreneurship to local development.* Available at: https://web.archive.org/web/20200502194003/https://www.coe.int/en/web/interculturalcities/-/the-importance-of-migrant-entrepreneurship-to-local-development. Accessed 02 May 2020.

Dacin, M. T., Dacin, P. A., & Tracey, P. (2011). Social entrepreneurship: A critique and future directions. *Organization Science, 22*(5), 1121–1367.

Deloitte. (2019). *2020 global health care outlook. Laying a foundation for the future.* Available at: https://web.archive.org/web/20200502194143/https://www2.deloitte.com/content/dam/insights/us/articles/GLOB22843-Global-HC-Outlook/DI-Global-HC-Outlook-Report.pdf. Accessed 02 May 2020.

Drayton, B. (2003). Ashoka's theory of change. *SSRN Electronic Journal,* o.S.

Eftekhari, N., & Bogers, M. (2015). Open for entrepreneurship: How open innovation can foster new venture creation. *Creativity and Innovation Management, 24*(4), 574–584.

European Commission. (2015). *The Social Business Initiative.* Available at: https://web.archive.org/web/20200502194245/http://ethmar.social/wp-content/uploads/2017/08/10-sbi-brochure-web_en.pdf. Accessed 02 May 2020.

European Union. (2018). Small and medium-sized enterprises: An overview. Annual Report on European SMEs 2017/2018.

Federal Ministry of Education and Research. (2018). *Quantum technologies—From basic research to market.* Available at: https://web.archive.org/web/20200502194313/https://www.bmbf.de/upload_filestore/pub/Quantum_technologies.pdf. Accessed 02 May 2020.

Fingas, J. (2020). *"Beat Saber" now has an official song designed to keep you fit.* Available at: https://web.archive.org/web/20200502194348/https://www.engadget.com/beat-saber-fitbeat-024917974.html. Accessed 02 May 2020.

Fink, L. (2020). *A fundamental reshaping of finance.* Available at: https://web.archive.org/web/20200502220709/https://www.blackrock.com/us/individual/larry-fink-ceo-letter. Accessed 02 May 2020.

Forschungszentrum Jülich. (2020). Overcoming the corona crisis together. Press Release. Available at: https://www.fz-juelich.de/portal/EN/Press/PressReleases/2020/2020-03-23-corona-fzj-en/_node.html.

Freeman, J., & Engel, J. (2007). Models of innovations: Startups and mature cooperations. *California Management Review, 50*(1), 94–119.

Gascó, M. (2017). Living labs: Implementing open innovation in the public sector. *Government Information Quarterly, 34*(1), 90–98.

Gegenhuber, T., Lührsen, R., Thäter, L., & Scheve, C. (2020). *Wenn sich die Zivilgesellschaft organisiert, um gesellschaftliche Probleme zu lösen.* Available at: https://netzpolitik.org/2020/wenn-sich-die-zivilgesellschaft-organisiert-um-gesellschaftliche-probleme-zu-loesen/. Accessed 27 May 2020.

General Assembly of the United Nations. (2015). Resolution 70/1: Transforming our world: the 2030 Agenda for.

George, G., & Bock, A. J. (2011). The business model in practice and its implications for entrepreneurship research. *Entrepreneurship Theory and Practice, 35*(1), 83–111.

George, G., Howard-Grenville, J., Joshi, A., & Tihanyi, L. (2016). Understanding and tackling societal grand challenges through management research. *Academy of Management Journal, 59*(6), 1880–1895.

GKV-Spitzenverband. (2019). *Digitalisierung und Pflegebedürftigkeit - Nutzen und Potenziale von Assistenz Technologien.* Hürth: CW Haarfeld.

Gomes, R. (2018). *Nobel laureate Yunus on "a world of three zeroes".* Available at: https://www.vaticannews.va/en/world/news/2018-05/yunus-nobel-poverty-unemployment-carbon-emission.html. Accessed 22 April 2020. Archived: https://web.archive.org/web/20200502191953/https://www.vaticannews.va/en/world/news/2018-05/yunus-nobel-poverty-unemployment-carbon-emission.html.

Guterres, A. (2020) *UN plans to launch a "decade of action" to deliver development goals by 2030.* Available at: https://web.archive.org/web/20200502192306http://www.ipsnews.net/2020/01/un-plans-launch-decade-action-deliver-development-goals-2030/Accessed 20 April 2020.

Guthrie, C. (2014). The digital factory: A hands-on learning project digital entrepreneurship. *Journal of Entrepreneurship Education, 17*(1), 115–133.

Halberstadt, J., Spiegler, A., & Pakura, A. (2018). Welche Rolle spielt Unternehmerinnentum für Studierende?: Eine explorative Studie zum (Miss-) Verständnis von Female Entrepreneurship. In C. Onnen & S. Rode-Breymann (Eds.), *Zum Selbstverständnis der Gender Studies II: Technik – Raum – Bildung* (pp. 249–276). Opladen; Berlin; Toronto: Verlag Barbara Budrich. https://doi.org/10.2307/j.ctvddzfp0.18.

Handy, C. (1995). *The age of paradox.* Brighton: Harvard Business Press.

Hänel, L. (2020). *German government hosts coronavirus pandemic hackathon.* Available at: https://www.dw.com/en/german-government-hosts-coronavirus-pandemic-hackathon/a-53080512. Accessed 27 April 2020.

Hausberg, P., Liere-Netheler, K., Packmohr, S., Pakura, S., & Vogelsang, K. (2019). Research streams on digital transformation from a holistic business perspective: A systematic literature review and citation network analysis. *Journal of Business Economics, 89,* 931–963.

Hayward, A., Fragaszy, E., Bermingham, A., Wang, L., Copas, A., Edmunds, W., et al. (2014). Comparative community burden and severity of seasonal and pandemic influenza: Results of the flu watch cohort study. *The Lancet. Respiratory Medicine, 2*(6), 445–454.

Health Innovation Hub. (2020). *(Undigitales) DANKESCHÖN an alle Putzkräfte in Gesundheitseinrichtungen.* Available at: https://eu.eventscloud.com/emarketing/view.php?id=e276a19655 d6870acdd144b49d1a241b7f07f5e4a81b2672e5677d60fc86635555f5f96a3927dd95d07c06af 34a20af0-MjAyMC0wNCM1ZTk0ZGJiOTE3NzQ4. Accessed 26 April 2020.

Hockerts, K., & Wüstenhagen, R. (2010). Greening Goliaths versus emerging Davids—Theorizing about the role of incumbents and new entrants in sustainable entrepreneurship. *Journal of Business Venturing, 25*(5), 481–492.

Hsieh, Y.-J., & Wu, Y. (2018). Entrepreneurship through the platform strategy the digital era: Insights and research opportunities. *Computers in Human Behavior,* 1–9.

Hull, C. E., Hung, Y.-T. C., Hair, N., Perotti, V., & DeMartino, R. (2007). Taking advantage of digital opportunities: A typology of digital entrepreneurship. *International Journal of Networking and Virtual Organizations, 4*(3), 290–303.

Jakob-Pannier, A. (2019). *Pflegebedürftig und aktiv sein - mit der memoreBox geistige und körperliche Fähigkeiten fördern.* Available at: https://www.barmer.de/gesundheit-verstehen/ praevention-und-vorsorge/memorebox-pflegebeduerftig-und-aktiv-sein-25746. Accessed 24 April 2020.

Kauffman Foundation. (2016). *Kauffman compilation: Research on race and entrepreneurship.* Available at: https://www.kauffman.org/wp-content/uploads/2019/12/kauffman_compilation_ race_entrepreneurship.pdf. Accessed 24 April 2020.

Kowalczyk, W. W. (2020). *Let's make quantum computing about sustainability.* Available at: https://www.zapatacomputing.com/lets-make-quantum-computing-about-sustainability/. Accessed 03 May 2020.

Kraus, S., Palmer, C., Kailer, N., Kallinger, F. L., & Spitzer, J. (2018). Digital entrepreneurship: A research agenda on new business models for the twenty-first century. *International Journal of Entrepreneurial Behavior and Research, 25*(2), 353–375.

Kuratko, D. F., Morris, M. H., & Schindehutte, M. (2015). Understanding the dynamics of entrepreneurship through framework approaches. *Small Business Economics, 45,* 1–13.

Lardinois, F. (2019). *D-wave launches its quantum hybrid platform.* Available at: https://techcrunch. com/2019/06/26/d-wave-launches-its-quantum-hybrid-platform/?guccounter=1. Accessed 24 April 2020.

LIFT Basel. (2015). Available: https://www.liftglobal.org/lift-basel-15/speakers/4429. Accessed 02 May 2020.

Lilge, T., & Stein, C. (2018). *Spielwissen und Wissensspiele. Wissenschaft und Gamesbranche im Dialog über die Kulturtechnik des Spiels.* Bielefeld: transcript.

Malik, M., Elkholy, A. A., Khan, W., Hassounah, S., Abubakar, Tran Minh, N., & Mala, P. (2016). Middle East respiratory syndrome coronavirus: Current knowledge and future considerations. *EMHJ-Eastern Mediterranean Health Journal, 22*(7), 533–542.

Moon, C. J. (2018). Contributions to the SDGs through social and eco entrepreneurship: New mindsets for sustainable solutions. Entrepreneurship and the sustainable development goals. *Contemporary Issues in Entrepreneurship Research, 8,* 47–68.

Murphy, P. J., Liao, J., & Welsch, H. P. (2006). A conceptual history of entrepreneurial thought. *Journal of Management History, 12*(1), 12–35.

Nambisan, S., Wright, M., & Feldman, M. (2019). The digital transformation of innovation and entrepreneurship: Progress, challenges and key themes. *Research Policy, 48,* 103773.

Noville-Ortiz, D., De Fatima Marin, H., & Saigi-Rubio, F. (2018). The role of digital health in supporting the achievement of the sustainable development goals (SDGs). *International Journal of Medical Informatics, 114,* 106–107.

Oculus. (2020). *Introducing "Supernatural", a fun new way to stay fit in VR.* Available at: https:// www.oculus.com/blog/introducing-supernatural-a-fun-new-way-to-stay-fit-in-vr/. Accessed 22 April 2020.

OECD. (2014). Enhancing the contribution of social business to sustainable development. In: *Development co-operation report 2014: Mobilising Resources for Sustainable Development.* OECD Publishing, Paris.

OECD/European Union. (2019). The missing entrepreneurs 2019: Policies for inclusive entrepreneurship. OECD Publishing, Paris. https://doi.org/10.1787/3ed84801-en.

Osterwalder, A., & Pigneur, Y. (2010). *Business model generation: A handbook for visionaries, game changers, and challengers.* New Jersey: Wiley.

Pakura, S. (2020). Open innovation as a driver for new organisations: A qualitative analysis of green-tech start-ups. *International Journal of Entrepreneurial Venturing, 12*(1), 109–142.

Palmer, C., Kraus, S., Oner, H., Kailer, N., & Huber, L. (2018). Entrepreneurial burnout: A systematic review and research map. *International Journal of Entrepreneurship and Small Business.*

Park, M., Thwaites, R. S., & Openshaw, P. J. M. (2020). COVID-19: Lessons from SARS and MERS. *European Journal of Immunology, 50*(3), 308–311.

Pinker, S. (2018). *Enlightenment now: The case for reason, science, humanism, and progress.* New York: Penguin Books Limited/Viking.

Porter, M. E. (1990). *The competitive advantage of nations.* New York: Free Press.

Porter, M. E., & Kramer, M. R. (2011). Creating shared value. *Harvard Business Review, 89,* 62–77.

Rasche, A., de Bakker, F. G. A., & Moon, J. (2013). Complete and partial organizing for corporate social responsibility. *Journal of Business Ethics, 115,* 651–663.

Rosling, H., Rosling Ronnlund, A., & Rosling, O. (2018). *Factfulness: Ten reasons we're wrong about the world—And why things are better than you think.* London: Macmillan.

Ryder, P., & Vogeley, J. (2018). Telling the impact investment story through digital media: An Indonesian case study. *Communication Research and Practice, 4*(4), 375–395.

Schaltegger, S., & Wagner, M. (2011). Sustainable entrepreneurship and sustainability innovation. Categories and interactions. *Business Strategy and the Environment, 20*(4), 222–237.

Schwab, K. (2019). *What kind of capitalism do we want?* Available at: https://www.project-syndicate.org/commentary/stakeholder-capitalism-new-metrics-by-klaus-schwab-2019-11?barrier=accesspaylog. Accessed 22 April 2020.

Sedláček, M., & Shamsrizi, M. (2017). Work as an homeopaticum, or: Will we share the (blessed?) destiny of horses? In *op-ed for the brochure of the 48th St. Gallen Symposium, St. Gallen Foundation for International Studies, 10.*

Breidenbach, Krawietz, & Shamsrizi, M. (2020). Embedded law in digital health innovation. *REthinking: Law, 1,* 17–21.

Krutzik, & Shamsrizi, M. (2020). Die zweite Quantenrevolution, oder: "Was nach der Digitalisierung kommt" - und wie(so) für Medizin und Gesundheitspolitik das größte Potential im Allerkleinsten zu finden ist. In Baas, B. (Hrsg.), *Digitale Gesundheit in Europa.* Berlin: Medizinisch wissenschaftliche Verlagsgesellschaft.

Shamsrizi, P., Gladstone, B. P., Carrara, E., et al. (2020). *Variation of effect estimates in the analysis of mortality and length of hospital stay in patients with infections caused by bacteria-producing extended-spectrum beta-lactamases: A systematic review and meta-analysis.* BMJ Open 2020; Available at: https://bmjopen.bmj.com/content/bmjopen/10/1/e030266.full.pdf.

Siegel, D. S., & Wright, M. (2015). Academic entrepreneurship: Time for a rethink? *British Journal of Management, 26*(4), 582–595. Available at: https://doi.org/10.1111/1467-8551. 12116.

Singh, R., Mathiassen, L., Stachura, M. E., & Astapova, E. V. (2010). Sustainable rural telehealth innovation: A public health case study. *Health Service Research, 45*(4), 985–1004.

Small Business Profile (SBA). (2018). 2018 Small Business Profile. Available at: https://www.sba. gov/sites/default/files/advocacy/2018-Small-Business-Profiles-All.pdf. Accessed 25 May 2020.

Srivastava, S. (2020). *Deploying quantum computers in service to combat coronavirus pandemic.* Available at: https://www.analyticsinsight.net/deploying-quantum-computers-service-combat-coronavirus-pandemic/. Accessed 24 April 2020.

Steinicke, F. (2016). *Being really virtual: Immersive natives and the future of virtual reality.* Springer International Publishing.

Sustainable Development. A/RES/70/1. (2015, September 25). Available at: https://undocs.org/en/ A/RES/70/1.

United Nations. (2020). *Decade of action.* Available at: https://www.un.org/sustainabledevelopment/ decade-of-action/. Accessed 20 April 2020.

United Nations Conference on Trade and Development. (2017). *New innovation approaches to support the implementation of the sustainable development goals.* New York. Available at: https://unctad.org/en/PublicationsLibrary/dtlstict2017d4_en.pdf. Accessed 02 May 2020.

United Nations Department of Public Information. (2015). *Sustainable development goals.* Available at: https://sustainabledevelopment.un.org/?menu=1300. Accessed 20 April 2020.

von der Stein, G. (2016). *Quantum technologies to revolutionise the 21st century—Nobel Laureates discuss at Lindau.* Available at: https://idw-online.de/de/news655419. Accessed 24 April 2020.

von Geibler, J., Piwowar, J., & Greven, A. (2019). The SDG-check: Guiding open innovation towards sustainable development goals. *Technology Innovation Management Review, 9*(3), 20–37.

von Windheim, J. (2014). More push than pull. *Physics World, 27*(11), 35.

Wagner, M. (2012). Ventures for the public good and entrepreneurial intentions: An empirical analysis of sustainability orientation as a determining factor. *Journal of SME and Entrepreneurship, 25*(4), 519–531.

West, J., & Bogers, M. (2011). *Profiting from external innovation: A review of research on open innovation.* Available at: https://papers.ssrn.com/sol3/papers.cfm?abstract_id=1949520. Accessed 24 April 2020.

WHO. (2020). *Coronavirus disease 2019 (COVID-19) pandemic.* Available at: https://www.who. int/emergencies/diseases/novel-coronavirus-2019. Accessed 27 May 2020.

Will, A. (2017). *Pokemon Go boosts physical activity, particularly among those who need it the most.* Available at: https://neurology.duke.edu/about/news/pokemon-go-boosts-physical-activity-particularly-among-those-who-need-it-most. Accessed 22 April 2020.

World Economic Forum. (2020). Unlocking technology for the global goals. As part of Frontier 2030: Fourth Industrial Revolution for Global Goals Platform. Available at: http://www3. weforum.org/docs/Unlocking_Technology_for_the_Global_Goals.pdf.

Yunus, M. (2020). *Corona pandemic: Time is running out fast, a letter from Prof. Muhammad Yunus.* Available at: https://www.yunussb.com/blog/2020/3/26/corona-pandemic-time-is-running-out-fast-a-letter-from-prof-muhammad-yunus. Accessed 25 April 2020.

Yunus + You - The YY Foundation. (2019). *Academia report on social business 2019.* Available at: https://issuu.com/yyfoundation/docs/yyf_academia_report_2019_web. Accessed 26 May 2020.